Quantum Machine Learning

Revolutionizing Data Analysis and Optimization

Editors:

Jaiprakash Narain Dwivedi
Department of Information Technology, PIET
Parul University, Gujarat, India

Parag Shukla
Department of Commerce
Maharaja Sayajirao University of Baroda, India

Herat Joshi
Lead - Data Science, Great River Health Systems
Burlington, Iowa, USA

Pankaj Tripathi
Department of Accounting and Financial Management
The Maharaja Sayajirao University of Baroda, India

CRC Press
Taylor & Francis Group
Boca Raton London New York

CRC Press is an imprint of the
Taylor & Francis Group, an **informa** business
A SCIENCE PUBLISHERS BOOK

First edition published 2027
by CRC Press
2385 NW Executive Center Drive, Suite 320, Boca Raton FL 33431

and by CRC Press
4 Park Square, Milton Park, Abingdon, Oxon, OX14 4RN

CRC Press is an imprint of Taylor & Francis Group, LLC

Library of Congress Cataloging-in-Publication Data (applied for)

ISBN: 978-1-041-08375-7 (hbk)
ISBN: 978-1-041-08576-8 (pbk)
ISBN: 978-1-003-64606-8 (ebk)

DOI: 10.1201/9781003646068

Typeset in Times New Roman
by Prime Publishing Services

Preface

The convergence of quantum computing and machine learning marks a transformative shift in the evolution of computational intelligence. As classical systems approach their practical limits in handling complex, high-dimensional problems, quantum technologies offer a fundamentally new paradigm—leveraging superposition, entanglement, and quantum parallelism to unlock unprecedented computational power.

This book, *Quantum Machine Learning: Revolutionizing Data Analysis and Optimization*, is designed to provide a structured and comprehensive exploration of this emerging interdisciplinary field. It begins by establishing the foundational principles of quantum computing and its relationship with modern machine learning, enabling readers to appreciate both the theoretical underpinnings and the motivation behind this convergence.

The core of the book delves into quantum machine learning algorithms, with detailed discussions on quantum kernels, quantum support vector machines (QSVM), and quantum neural networks. These chapters aim to bridge the gap between abstract quantum concepts and their practical implementation in intelligent systems.

Recognizing the importance of real-world impact, the book further explores diverse applications across finance, healthcare, taxation, supply chain management, and telecommunications. From early breast cancer detection to advanced financial modelling and GST compliance, the chapters highlight how quantum machine learning can address pressing challenges with improved efficiency and accuracy.

Finally, the book looks ahead to future directions, discussing critical challenges such as quantum security threats, integration with cloud and IoT ecosystems, and emerging innovations in augmented reality and e-commerce. These insights are intended to inspire researchers, academicians, and industry practitioners to contribute to the next generation of intelligent systems.

This work serves as both an introduction and a forward-looking guide for those seeking to understand and harness the potential of quantum machine learning in shaping the future of technology.

Editorial Overview

Jaiprakash Narain Dwivedi[1*]

Prefatory Vision and Editorial Introduction

In the transformative landscape of 21st-century science, the convergence of quantum mechanics and artificial intelligence marks one of the most profound technological revolutions in modern history. The fusion of these two domains has given rise to quantum machine learning (QML)—a paradigm that promises to redefine data analysis, optimization, and computational reasoning. This volume, *Quantum Machine Learning: Revolutionizing Data Analysis and Optimization*, is designed as a scholarly yet visionary exploration into the heart of this emerging discipline. It provides an integrated view of theoretical underpinnings, algorithmic advances, and real-world applications that together chart the course of quantum-empowered intelligence.

This editorial overview serves as both a roadmap and reflection—an intellectual synthesis connecting the fifteen chapters that form the backbone of this book. It encapsulates the motivations, methodologies, and implications of integrating quantum computing into the machine learning ecosystem. Each part of this book has been curated to reflect a specific stage in the evolution of QML—from the roots of quantum theory to its most ambitious applications in healthcare, finance, governance, and industry. The editorial aim is not merely to summarize, but to illuminate how each chapter contributes to a collective understanding of this rapidly advancing field.

Part I: Foundations of Quantum Computing and Machine Learning

Part I establishes the theoretical and conceptual foundations of QML by examining the roots of quantum mechanics and their relevance to modern computational design. It explores the philosophical and scientific transformation that allowed quantum principles—once confined to subatomic phenomena—to become instruments of computational logic.

[1] Department of Information Technology, PIET, FET, Parul University, Vadodara, Gujarat, India. ORCID ID: 0000-0002-5853-2216

* Corresponding author:jpndwivedi@gmail.com

Chapter 1: Quantum Roots of Modern Computing

The first chapter retraces the intellectual lineage of quantum mechanics and its transition into computational theory. It situates the reader within the historical continuum—from Planck's quantum hypothesis to Feynman's proposal of quantum simulation—illustrating how these ideas gave rise to the concept of quantum information. This chapter clarifies why quantum states, rather than binary bits, form the essence of the next era of computation.

Chapter 2: Intersection of Quantum Computing and Machine Learning

The second chapter delves into the interdisciplinary synthesis that defines QML. It elucidates how principles such as superposition, entanglement, and quantum interference offer exponential enhancements to machine learning models. The discussion advances from fundamental concepts to mathematical representations, emphasizing how quantum properties can be harnessed to represent, process, and generalize data in dimensions that classical algorithms cannot efficiently explore.

Part II: Quantum Machine Learning Algorithms

Part II serves as the algorithmic core of the book, examining how quantum computing principles translate into learning architectures and computational strategies. This section presents quantum-enhanced models that redefine how data patterns are recognized, classified, and optimized in real time.

Chapter 3: Harnessing Quantum Kernels for Supervised Learning: A Deep Dive into Quantum SVMs

This chapter explores the quantum kernel methodology, explaining how quantum feature spaces transcend classical limitations in supervised learning. By encoding data into Hilbert spaces, quantum kernels enable machines to perceive relationships otherwise invisible in linear manifolds. Through this lens, quantum support vector machines (SVMs) emerge as powerful tools for non-linear classification with superior scalability and accuracy.

Chapter 4: Quantum Support Vector Machine (QSVM) and Their Applications

The focus here is on the practical implementation and performance of QSVMs. By merging statistical learning with quantum computational speedups, QSVMs address complex problems in classification, optimization, and cryptographic data segregation. This discussion bridges theory with real-world application, emphasizing how QSVMs can process high-dimensional datasets that challenge even the most advanced classical systems.

Chapter 5: Quantum Neural Networks and Deep Learning in the Era of Quantum-Enhanced Artificial Intelligence

This chapter presents quantum neural networks (QNNs) as the vanguard of quantum-enhanced intelligence. QNNs are portrayed not merely as extensions of classical deep learning but as entirely new paradigms of cognition and computation. The narrative emphasizes their potential to achieve superior generalization, rapid convergence, and adaptive learning through entangled parameter spaces.

Part III: Applications of Quantum Machine Learning

The third part translates theoretical and algorithmic innovation into actionable solutions across industries. Here, QML demonstrates its potential to revolutionize data-driven decision-making in finance, healthcare, logistics, and industrial optimization. Each chapter in this section showcases how quantum systems address specific domain challenges through predictive modeling and computational efficiency.

Chapter 6: Quantum Leaps in Finance: Integrating Quantum Computing and Machine Learning

This chapter presents how quantum-enhanced data models redefine financial analytics. Quantum algorithms offer new modes of portfolio optimization, risk assessment, and anomaly detection, surpassing classical approaches in both precision and speed.

Chapter 7: Financial Modeling and Quantum Computing Economics

In this chapter, the focus shifts toward economic modeling under quantum paradigms. Quantum economic simulations reveal non-linear dependencies and emergent patterns that were previously inaccessible, enabling predictive analysis at unprecedented scales.

Chapter 8: Quantum Machine Learning Applications in Healthcare

This chapter illustrates the power of QML in decoding biomedical data. From genome sequencing to diagnostic imaging, quantum models augment clinical decision-making by identifying subtle correlations across multimodal datasets.

Chapter 9: AI-Enabled Standalone Device for Early Breast Cancer Detection: Advancing Diagnosis and Healthcare

In this chapter, QML is portrayed as a transformative force in medical technology. The chapter introduces a prototype device employing quantum-enhanced AI for early cancer detection—an example of convergence between computation, optics, and medical diagnostics.

Chapter 10: Harnessing Quantum Computing for Supply Chain Transformation: The PRABAX Framework

This chapter describes the PRABAX framework as a model for applying QML to global logistics. Quantum optimization algorithms are employed to manage inventory, forecast demand, and minimize inefficiencies across interconnected supply networks.

Part IV: Future Directions and Challenges

The final part of the book ventures into the frontiers of QML, addressing emerging threats, ethical dilemmas, and futuristic applications. This section invites readers to reflect on both the opportunities and responsibilities that accompany the quantum revolution.

Chapter 11: Quantum Algorithmic Threats and Countermeasures in Cloud and IoT Security

This chapter examines the security implications of quantum computation. While quantum algorithms can decrypt traditional encryption systems, they also inspire new cryptographic defenses designed for a post-quantum world.

Chapter 12: Application of Quantum Machine Learning in Goods and Services Tax: Toward Better Compliance and Fraud Detection

The narrative of this chapter extends into governance and taxation, where QML enhances compliance analysis and fraud prediction through pattern recognition across complex transactional networks.

Chapter 13: A Quantum-Enabled Framework for Enhancing Service Quality in India's Mobile Networks

This chapter explores telecom optimization through quantum-assisted analytics, improving bandwidth allocation, latency management, and customer experience in dynamic network environments.

Chapter 14: Augmented-Reality-Driven IT Operations Dashboards Powered by Quantum Machine Learning

This chapter envisions the integration of QML with augmented reality (AR) interfaces, offering immersive dashboards that visualize and optimize IT operations in real time.

Chapter 15: Next-Generation Product Categorization in E-commerce using Quantum Machine Learning Approach over Virtualized Data Environment

The concluding chapter synthesizes the preceding discussions, applying QML to large-scale digital commerce systems for automated product classification, recommendation, and trend forecasting.

Editorial Reflection and Concluding Remarks

This volume exemplifies the interdisciplinary spirit that defines the digital frontier. As quantum hardware continues to evolve, the synergy between computational theory and applied machine learning will deepen, giving rise to innovations that transcend classical boundaries. Quantum machine learning is no longer a speculative concept—it is an emerging framework for understanding and interacting with complex systems in ways that mirror natural intelligence.

The chapters herein collectively chart a roadmap for both researchers and practitioners. They highlight the promise of quantum-enhanced intelligence not only as a technological leap but also as a philosophical evolution—one that compels us to rethink computation, perception, and cognition itself. The volume, therefore, stands as both an academic contribution and a visionary manifesto for the quantum age.

Editor's Note

I extend heartfelt gratitude to all the contributors whose dedication and expertise have shaped this volume. Their efforts represent a collective pursuit of knowledge that transcends disciplinary boundaries. It is my sincere hope that this work inspires readers—scholars, scientists, and innovators alike—to explore the transformative power of quantum machine learning with both curiosity and caution. May this book serve as a foundation for continued exploration and collaboration in this rapidly evolving field.

Mariyum Habib
Centre for Computational Biology and Bioinformatics, Amity Institute of Biotechnology, Amity University, Noida, Uttar Pradesh, India.

Meenal N. Pande
Department of Computer Science, DCPE, HVPM, Amravati, Maharashtra, India.

Meetu Malhotra
Data Science, Harrisburg University of Science and Technology, PA USA. ORCID ID: 0009-0009-7495-4484.

Parag Shukla
Assistant Professor, Department of Commerce and Business Management, Faculty of Commerce, The Maharaja Sayajirao University of Baroda, Vadodara, Gujarat, India. ORCID ID: 0000-0002-7014-163X.

Pradeep Kumar
Department of Electronics and Communication Engineering, VNR VJIET Hyderabad, India. ORCID ID: 0000-0002-2599-6380.

Prakashkumar Hasmukhbhai Patel
Assistant Professor, Department of Commerce and Business Management, Faculty of Commerce, The Maharaja Sayajirao University of Baroda, Vadodara. ORCID ID: 0000-0002-6972-3018.

Prasanth Mankar
Department of ECE, Vasavi College of Engineering, Ibrahimbagh, Hyderabad, India.

Prashant Vadikar
Assistant Professor, Department of Business Economics, The Maharaja Sayajirao University of Baroda, India. ORCID ID: 0000-0002-4060-7347.

Raghavendar Nellikondi
Senior Member, Institute of Electrical and Electronics Engineers (IEEE), Sterling, VA, USA. ORCID ID: 0009-0002-1315-2495.

Rajeev Tripathi
Department of Computer Sciences, School of Management Sciences, Lucknow, India.

Rakesh Kumar S. Manjhi
Assistant Professor, Department of Accounting and Financial Management, Faculty of Commerce, The Maharaja Sayajirao University of Baroda, Vadodara, India. ORCID ID: 0009-0000-6307-1269.

Ramesh Ghimire
Research Scholar, Department of Electronics and Communication Engineering, PIET, FET, Parul University, Vadodara, Gujarat, India.

Ranjan K. Senapati
Department of Electronics and Communication Engineering, VNR VJIET Hyderabad, India. ORCID ID: 0000-0003-3375-3378.

Ravi Shanker Pandey
Department of Computer Application and Sciences, School of Management Sciences, Lucknow, India.

Reddaiah Kasturi
Senior Data Engineer, Divine IT Services, Sterling VA, USA.

Ria Ghosh
Department of Computer Science Engineering, Indian Institute of Technology, Patna, India. ORCID ID: 0009-0004-7737-4171.

Sanjay E. Yedey
P.G. Department of Computer Science & Technology, DCPE, HVPM, Amravati, Maharashtra, India.

Santosh Kumar Choudhary
Department of Electronics and Communication Engineering, VNR VJIET Hyderabad, India. ORCID ID: 0000-0001-9850-7624.

Shrishti Jha
Centre for Computational Biology and Bioinformatics, Amity Institute of Biotechnology, Amity University, Noida, Uttar Pradesh, India.

Sonali Butad
Assistant Professor, Department of Computer Engineering, Shah and Anchor Kutchhi Engineering College, Mumbai, India. ORCID ID: 0000-0001-5352-4009.

Sonali Kesarwani
Amity Institute of Forensic Sciences, Amity University, Noida, Uttar Pradesh, India. ORCID ID: 0000-0002-3760-5105.

Subodh Srivastava
Department of Electronics and Communication Engineering, NIT Patna, India. ORCID ID: 0000-0001-6194-429X.

Sudeep KS
Associate Professor, GITAM University, Hyderabad, India.

Swapnil Saurav
Research Student, GITAM University, Hyderabad, India.

Tirathkumar M. Mishra
Research Scholar, Department of Business Economics, The Maharaja Sayajirao University of Baroda, India. ORCID ID: 0009-0009-4347-0778.

1 | Quantum Roots of Modern Computing

Ramesh Ghimire[1] and Jaiprakash Narain Dwivedi[2*]

Quantum computing is a new technology that provides innovative methods to address historically difficult tasks. Quantum machine learning (QML) is an emerging field that explores the possibilities for quantum computers to speed up machine learning and enhance model expressiveness. This chapter discusses how leading companies and research groups are building these machines, the fundamental limits they face, and the recent breakthroughs that are turning quantum computation from a theoretical curiosity into an experimental reality.

1. Introduction

Quantum computing has progressed from the principles of quantum mechanics. Quantum mechanics is the science that describes how matter and energy behave at the smallest possible scales of atomic and subatomic particles. The classical computing uses deterministic binary logic for information processing, while quantum computing goes beyond classical boundaries by using superposition, entanglement, and interference as discrete quantum phenomena.

The idea of using quantum mechanics in computing has developed over many years. Paul Benioff introduced the concept of a quantum Turing machine in 1980. This showed that the rules of quantum physics can guide a computer's operations [1]. After few years, in 1985, David Deutsch expanded this idea by suggesting the framework of a universal quantum computer. The universal quantum computer is capable of simulating any physical system, no matter how complex it is [2].

The development in quantum information theory till now has reinforced the view of quantum computing as a revolutionary technology. In 1994, Shor's algorithm showed rapid growth for integer factorization, which is the most significant problem in cryptography [3]. Similarly, in 1996, Grover's algorithm offered a quadratic speedup for scanning unsorted database. On a quantum computer, the Grover's approach reduces the time complexity from $O(N)$ to $O(\sqrt{N})$.

---

1 Research Scholar, Department of Electronics and Communication Engineering, PIET, FET, Parul University, Vadodara, Gujarat, India.

2 Associate Professor, Department of Information Technology, PIET, FET, Parul University, Vadodara, Gujarat, India.
E-mail: Email: grknep@gmail.com[1]
ORCID ID: 0000-0002-5853-2216

* Corresponding author: jpndwivedi@gmail.com

DOI: 10.1201/9781003646068-1

Table 1.1 Fundamental principles of quantum computing and their applications

Quantum Principle	*Description*	*Computing Relevance*	*Example Applications*
Superposition	The quantum principle that permits a qubit or particle to exist in several states simultaneously until it is measured.	Enables qubits to represent and process many possible states at once, vastly increasing computational parallelism.	Optimization, cryptography, and drug discovery.
Entanglement	Quantum states of particles can be correlated so that one particle's state quickly affects another, despite of their distance.	Provides non-classical correlations for faster communication and complex computations.	Quantum teleportation, superdense coding, error correction.
Quantum Interference	Probability amplitudes of quantum states interfere by adding or cancelling out, enhancing correct outcomes and reducing incorrect ones.	Used to design algorithms that amplify desired solutions while suppressing errors.	Grover's search, quantum walks.
Quantum Tunneling	Particles can pass through potential barriers they classically should not overcome.	Utilized in optimization processes and physical qubit implementation.	Quantum annealing in D-Wave systems, tunnel diodes.
Measurement & Collapse	When we measure a quantum system, its many possible states collapse into one actual outcome that we can observe.	Final step in computation that extracts classical results from quantum states.	Reading qubit values after algorithm execution.

2. Principles of Quantum Mechanics

Quantum mechanics is the branch of physics that explains how matter and energy behave at atomic and subatomic scales, where the rules of classical physics are not applicable. These phenomena are governed by probabilities rather than deterministic laws. Unlike classical mechanics, which depend on Newton's laws to determine precise routes, quantum theory describes system evolution through probability and fundamental postulates. These postulates form the theoretical strength of quantum computing.

2.1 Postulate 1—State Space

A quantum system is fully described by a state vector $|\psi\rangle$ in a complex Hilbert space H. For a single qubit, the state can be expressed as:

$$|\psi\rangle = \alpha|0\rangle + \beta|1\rangle, \quad \alpha, \beta \in C$$

where α and β satisfy the normalization condition:

$$|\alpha|^2 + |\beta|^2 = 1$$

The computational basis $\{|0\rangle, |1\rangle\}$ corresponds to the two classical states, but quantum superposition allows a continuum of possibilities [4].

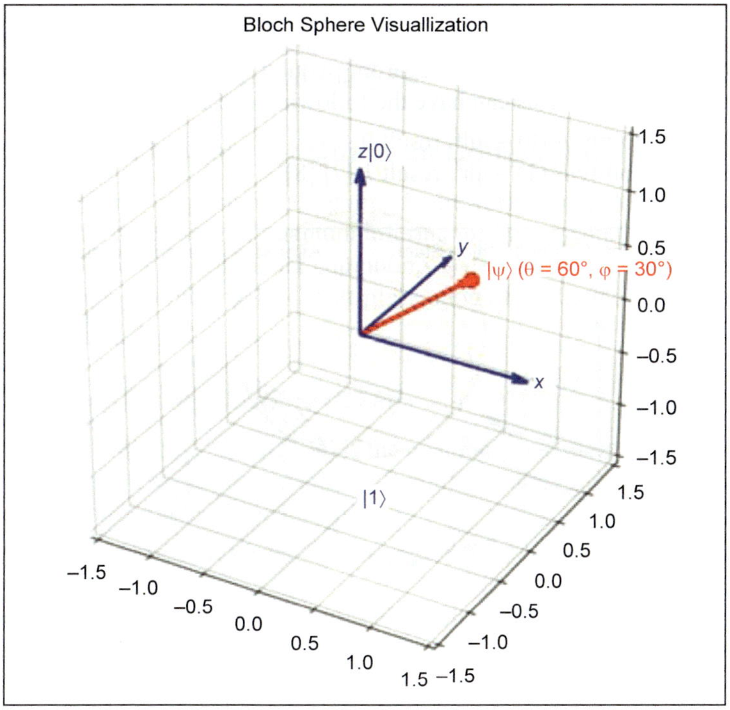

Fig. 1.1 Bloch sphere representation of the qubit state.

2.2 *Postulate 2—Evolution of States*

The time evolution of a closed quantum system is given by the Schrödinger equation as:

$$i\hbar \frac{\partial}{\partial t} |\psi(t)|\rangle = \hat{H}|\psi(t)|\rangle$$

where $\hat{H}$ is known as the Hamiltonian operator, and it represents the total energy of the system, which is the sum of potential and kinetic energy of the system. Its form depends on the particular system. It affects the state vector and reflects the total of the kinetic and potential energy operators. [5] $\hbar$ represents the reduced Planck's constant. This fundamental physical constant establishes the scale for

4.1 Single-Qubit Gates

Single-qubit gates apply operations to individual qubits. These are represented by 2×2 unitary matrices. The most vital examples include:

a. Pauli-X Gate (Quantum NOT gate):

$$X = \begin{bmatrix} 0 & 1 \\ 1 & 0 \end{bmatrix}$$

This gate exchanges the computational basis states, transforming $|0\rangle$ into $|1\rangle$ and vice versa.

b. Pauli-Y Gate:

$$Y = \begin{bmatrix} 0 & -j \\ j & 0 \end{bmatrix}$$

c. Pauli-Z Gate (Phase-flip):

$$Z = \begin{bmatrix} 1 & 0 \\ 0 & -1 \end{bmatrix}$$

d. Hadamard Gate:

$$H = \frac{1}{\sqrt{2}} \begin{bmatrix} 1 & 1 \\ 1 & -1 \end{bmatrix}$$

e. Phase Gate (S) and T Gate: Introduce controlled phase shifts:

$$S = \begin{bmatrix} 1 & 0 \\ 0 & j \end{bmatrix} \qquad T = \begin{bmatrix} 1 & 0 \\ 0 & e^{j\pi/4} \end{bmatrix}$$

4.2 Multi-Qubit Gates

Multi-qubit gates enable quantum entanglement, a crucial property for quantum parallelism. The most common multi-qubit gates are:

a. Controlled-NOT (CNOT) Gate:
It flips the target qubit if the control qubit is $|1\rangle$.

$$\text{CNOT} = \begin{bmatrix} 1 & 0 & 0 & 0 \\ 0 & 1 & 0 & 0 \\ 0 & 0 & 0 & 1 \\ 0 & 0 & 1 & 0 \end{bmatrix}$$

b. Controlled-Z (CZ) Gate:
It applies a Z operation to the target qubit if the control qubit is $|1\rangle$.

$$\text{CZ} = \begin{bmatrix} 1 & 0 & 0 & 0 \\ 0 & 1 & 0 & 0 \\ 0 & 0 & 1 & 0 \\ 0 & 0 & 0 & -1 \end{bmatrix}$$

c. Toffoli Gate (Controlled-Controlled-NOT (CCNOT)):
It is a three-qubit gate. It flips the target qubit only if both control qubits are $|1\rangle$. It is represented by 8×8 matrix:

$$\text{CCNOT} = \begin{bmatrix} 1 & 0 & 0 & 0 & 0 & 0 & 0 & 0 \\ 0 & 1 & 0 & 0 & 0 & 0 & 0 & 0 \\ 0 & 0 & 1 & 0 & 0 & 0 & 0 & 0 \\ 0 & 0 & 0 & 1 & 0 & 0 & 0 & 0 \\ 0 & 0 & 0 & 0 & 1 & 0 & 0 & 0 \\ 0 & 0 & 0 & 0 & 0 & 1 & 0 & 0 \\ 0 & 0 & 0 & 0 & 0 & 0 & 0 & 1 \\ 0 & 0 & 0 & 0 & 0 & 0 & 1 & 0 \end{bmatrix}$$

d. SWAP Gate:
It exchanges the states of two qubits. Its matrix representation is:

$$\text{SWAP} = \begin{bmatrix} 1 & 0 & 0 & 0 \\ 0 & 0 & 1 & 0 \\ 0 & 1 & 0 & 0 \\ 0 & 0 & 0 & 1 \end{bmatrix}$$

4.3 Quantum Circuit Model

A quantum circuit is a chronological arrangement of quantum gates that are performing on qubits, represented graphically by a series of gate symbols on horizontal lines (wires) corresponding to qubits. The computation proceeds left to right, starting from the initial quantum state $|\psi_0\rangle$, applying unitary transformations, and ending with a measurement in the computational basis. Mathematically:

$$|\psi_{\text{out}}\rangle = U_n U_{n-1} \ldots U_2 U_1 |\psi_0\rangle$$

where U_k are the unitary gates applied in sequence.

4.4 Measurement

Measurement collapses the qubit state to one of the classical basis states with probabilities given by the Born rule[7]:

$$P(0) = |\alpha|^2, P(1) = |\beta|^2$$

For a single qubit $|\psi\rangle = \alpha|0\rangle + \beta|1\rangle$.

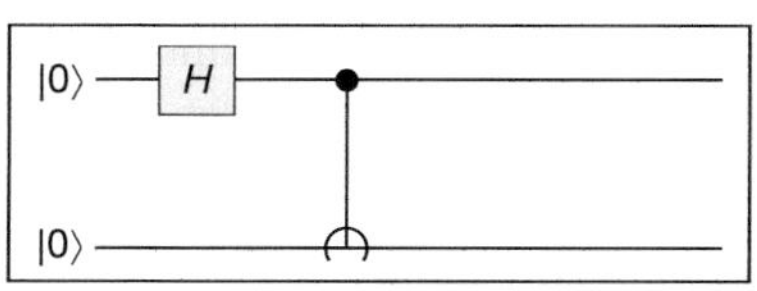

Fig. 1.4 Example of a quantum circuit with single- and multi-qubit gates.

5.4 Quantum Fourier Transform (QFT)

QFT is the quantum analogue of the Discrete Fourier Transform (DFT) and forms the computational backbone of algorithms such as Shor's [3].

Definition

The QFT operation on a quantum state $|x\rangle$ is defined as: $|x\rangle \rightarrow \frac{1}{\sqrt{N}} \sum_{y=0}^{N-1} e^{\frac{2\pi ixy}{N}} |y\rangle$

where N represents the dimension of the Hilbert space, which is for a system of n qubits, $N = 2^n$.

Complexity Analysis

The QFT shows many computational advantages over classical approaches. The classical Fast Fourier Transform (FFT) requires $O\,(N \log N)$ operations, but the QFT implementation requires only $O\,((\log N)^2)$ quantum implementations. This will be an exponential development for the fundamental operation [7].

5.5 Other Quantum Algorithms

5.5.1 The Algorithm of Harrow-Hassidim-Lloyd (HHL)

Under certain conditions, the HHL algorithm, a quantum method, can resolve linear equation systems much faster than classical approaches. In particular, when the system matrix is mostly zero entries (sparse) and well-conditioned, the algorithm can offer an exponential improvement in runtime compared to classical methods [15].

5.5.2 Quantum Walk Algorithms

The quantum equivalent of traditional random walks is quantum walk algorithms, which use superposition and entanglement to find many paths at once. This parallel finding of paths makes them much faster than classical methods. As a result, they are useful in solving search and optimization problems.

5.5.3 Variational Quantum Eigensolver (VQE)

A hybrid technique called the variational quantum eigensolver (VQE) is intended to identify the lowest energy states of material and molecular systems. This helps researchers in fields like chemistry and materials science to understand how these systems behave [16].

5.6 Complexity Analysis

Algorithm	*Classical Complexity*	*Quantum Complexity*
Shor's Algorithm	$O(e^{n^{1/3}})$	$O((\log N)^3)$
Grover's Algorithm	$O(N)$	$O(\sqrt{N})$
QFT	$O(N \log N)$	$O((\log N)^2)$

6. Quantum Algorithms for Optimization and Machine Learning

6.1 Introduction: A Novel Approach to Computation for Complicated Problems

The complexity of optimization and machine learning (ML) problems has grown in recent years. Classical computing is struggling to find solutions to these challenging issues. Artificial intelligence, drug development, and financial modeling are a few examples of fields that frequently call for high-dimensional dataset analysis or searching across enormous solution spaces. In some cases, these jobs may be extremely expensive or in other cases they are impossible, even for the most sophisticated supercomputers [17].

Now, quantum computing is developing as the next generation technology. It is based on the rules of quantum mechanics, and so it gives a new idea on how to overcome these challenges. By leveraging superposition, entanglement, and interference, quantum algorithms can examine many possibilities in parallel and detect understated data patterns that remain hidden from classical systems [18].

As there are certain boundaries of quantum algorithms developed for optimization and machine learning, particular attention is given to hybrid approaches, which combine quantum and classical computing resources together. These methods are especially applicable in the current era of noisy intermediate-scale quantum (NISQ) devices [19]. The hybrid models divide tasks between quantum and classical processors, which will make it possible to exploit the strengths of both technologies in a complementary way.

6.2 Variational Quantum Algorithms: The Workhorses of the NISQ Era

One of the most useful strategies for today's small and noisy quantum computers is variational quantum algorithms or VQA. VQAs use a hybrid paradigm that allows the burden to be divided between quantum and conventional processors. The quantum computer first prepares a state whose parameter can be adjustable and then measures a property, like energy. The measured result is then sent to a classical computer. The classical computer updates the parameters and sends them back to the quantum computer. This process repeats in a loop until the cost function reaches the lowest point, which means a good solution is found. Because much of the tough optimization is handled by the classical computer, VQAs are more robust against noise and the short coherence times that limit current quantum devices.

6.2.1 *The Variational Quantum Eigensolver: For Quantum Chemistry*

One of the most important variational quantum algorithms is the variational quantum eigensolver (VQE). It is widely used in quantum chemistry to determine the ground-state energy of molecules, a task that gets harder for classical computers to perform as system sizes increase [16].

1. **Initialization:** The quantum computer is prepared with a trial wave function that depends on adjustable parameters. These parameters are set with initial values to begin the process.
2. **State Preparation:** The system is represented by a quantum state created by implementing the experimental wave function using quantum gates.
3. **Measurement:** The expected value of the Hamiltonian, which provides an estimate of the system's energy, is measured by the quantum computer.
4. **Classical Optimization:** A classical computer receives the measured energy. To lower the energy value, the classical optimizer modifies the parameters.
5. **Iteration:** Steps 2–4 are repeated in a loop. With each cycle, the parameters are refined until the energy reaches its minimum.
6. **Convergence:** An estimate of the molecule's ground-state energy is provided by the outcome once the process has stabilized.

This cycle keeps repeating until the energy decreases to the lowest level and the molecule's most stable configuration is revealed.

6.2.2 *The Quantum Approximate Optimization Algorithm: For Combinatorial Puzzles*

The quantum approximate optimization algorithm (QAOA) translates the VQA concept to combinative optimization problems like the famous traveling salesperson problem or network design tasks like Max-Cut [20]. QAOA encodes the problem's objective into a "cost Hamiltonian" (H_C) where its lowest energy state looks like the optimum solution.

The algorithm gives the alternatives between applying this cost Hamiltonian and a "mixer Hamiltonian" (H_B), which encourages exploration. A quantum state is prepared by a circuit with depth p using parameters β, γ:

$$|\psi(\beta,\gamma)\rangle = \mathrm{e}^{-i\beta_p h_{\hat{a}}} e^{-i\gamma_p h_c} \ldots e^{-\beta_1 h_\beta} e^{-i\gamma_1 h_c} \,|+\rangle \otimes n$$

The classical optimizer's job is to find the parameters that minimize $\langle\psi(\beta, \gamma)|H_C\,|\psi(\beta, \gamma)\rangle$, thus identifying the best approximate solution to the original problem. The workflow of this iterative process is illustrated in Figure 1.7.

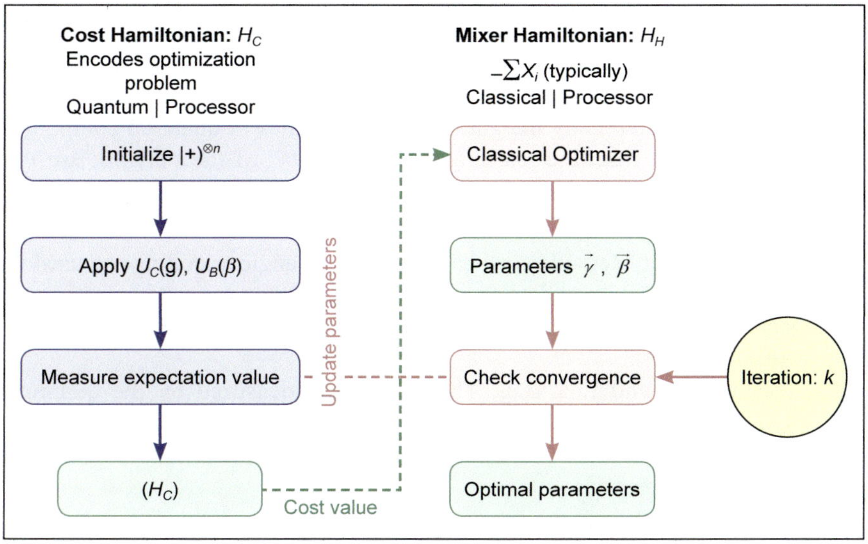

Fig. 1.7 QAOA workflow.

6.3 Quantum Machine Learning: Enhancing Pattern Recognition

Quantum machine learning (QML) is an emerging field that explores whether quantum information processing can provide advantages in learning from data. The goal is not necessarily to replace classical ML but to augment it, potentially offering speedups or enabling the analysis of more complex datasets [21].

6.3.1 Quantum Support Vector Machines: The Kernel Trick, Amplified

Support vector machines (SVMs) are powerful classical classifiers that frequently employ a "kernel trick" to distinguish between data in high-dimensional domains. Quantum SVMs leverage a quantum computer to compute complex kernel functions that are computationally expensive to calculate in the classical way [22]. The process involves:

- Quantum Feature Map: A quantum circuit maps classical data vectors non-linearly into a high-dimensional quantum state space ($|\phi(\vec{y}_i)\rangle$).
- Quantum Kernel Estimation: This method computes the overlap of two data points' quantum states to obtain the kernel value between them: $K(\vec{y}_i, \vec{y}_j) = |\langle\phi(\vec{y}_i)\rangle\, |\phi(\vec{y}_i)\rangle|^2$.

A classical SVM algorithm then builds a very complex classifier using this quantum-enhanced kernel.

6.3.2 Quantum Neural Networks: A New Architecture for Learning

Classical neural networks generate quantum neural networks (QNNs). They are constructed as programable quantum circuits that are parameterized or have certain parameters. QNNs do this by integrating the capabilities of quantum computing with concepts from machine learning. The "weights" of the network are the tunable parameters (θ) of quantum gates, which take the place of the network's "neurons" [23].

1. Data Encoding: Methods such as amplitude or angle encoding are used to load conventional input data into the quantum system.
2. Quantum Processing: The input state is changed by a series of parameterized gates (the QNN).
3. Measurement and Learning: The qubits are measured by the quantum computer. After that, a traditional computer receives these results to adjust the parameters θ. The main goal of this is to reduce a cost function, for example, the classification error.

QNNs signify a flexible framework for exploring potentially more expressive models for certain types of data. A simplified architecture is shown in Figure 1.8.

6.4 The Hybrid Quantum-Classical Framework: Synergy and Challenges

The algorithms described earlier are all hybrid, and they tie up quantum and classical processing. This architecture is both their greatest strength and the source of their most significant hurdles.

6.4.1 Strengths

- NISQ Feasibility: By outsourcing the complex optimization to a classical computer, they mitigate the impact of the current quantum hardware's noise and short coherence times [19].
- Adaptability: The classical optimizer can navigate around noise-induced errors and other quantum imperfections.
- Representational Power: Quantum circuits can, in principle, generate correlations and represent functions that are disreputably difficult for classical neural networks to model proficiently.

6.4.2 Limitations and Challenges

- The Barren Plateau Problem: A major obstacle is the phenomenon where the cost function's gradients vanish exponentially as the system size (number of qubits) grows, making it incredibly difficult for the classical optimizer to find a direction for improvement [24].

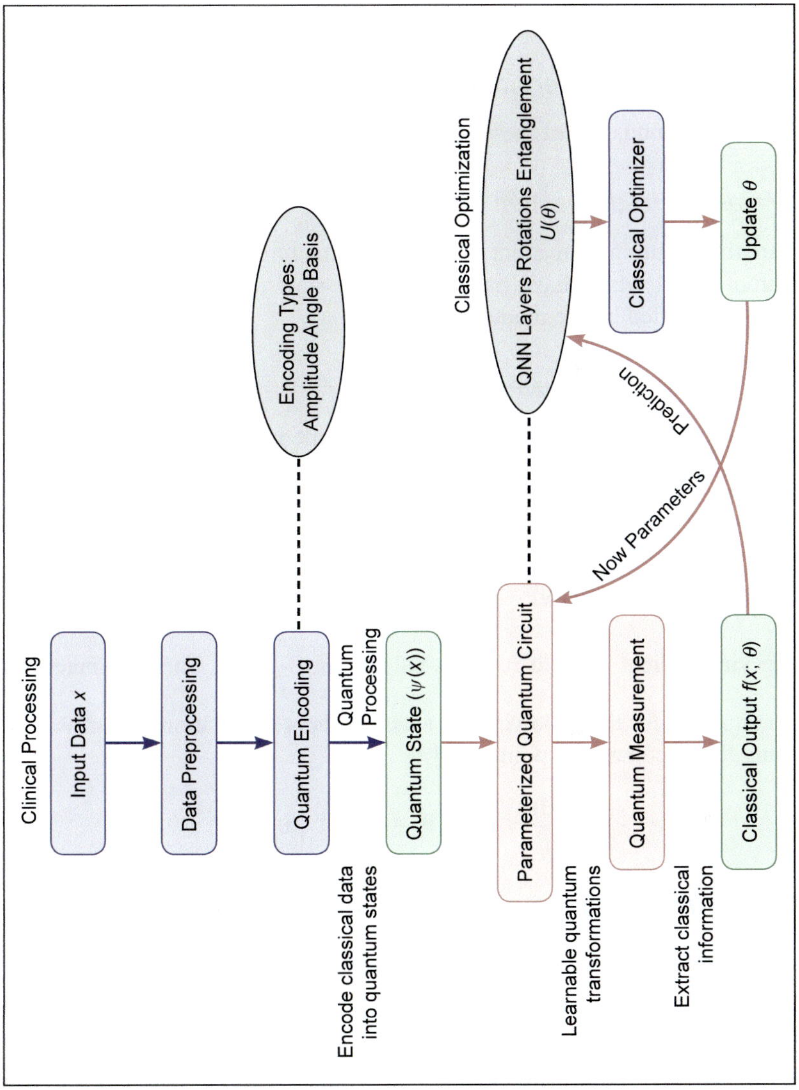

Fig. 1.8 A hybrid QNN, showing the flow from data encoding through parameterized quantum processing to classical feedback.

- Hardware Noise: Decoherence and gate infidelities can corrupt the quantum state, leading to inaccurate measurements and derailing the optimization process.
- The Data Encoding Problem: Efficiently loading large classical datasets into a quantum state remains a non-trivial challenge that can erase any potential quantum advantage.

6.5 Mathematical Underpinnings

The theoretical foundation of these hybrid algorithms rests on a few key concepts.

6.5.1 Parameterized Quantum Circuits (PQCs)

These are the quantum equivalent of model architectures. *A PQC*, $U(\theta)$, is series of quantum gates, which have parameters. The state $|\psi(\phi)\rangle = U(\phi)|0\rangle^{\otimes n}$ is the hypothesis generated by the model.

6.5.2 Cost Function Construction

The task is defined by a cost function, $C(\theta)$, built from expectation values of observables (O_k) measured on the PQC

$$C(\theta) = \sum_k f_k(\langle O_k \rangle_\theta), \text{ where } (\langle O_k \rangle_\theta = \langle \psi(\theta) | O_k | \psi(\theta) \rangle$$

6.5.3 Gradient Estimation

Training via gradient descent requires calculating $\frac{\partial C(\theta)}{\partial(\theta)_i}$. The parameter-shift rule is a vital tool for this, allowing for exact gradient calculation on hardware by evaluating the circuit at two points [25]:

$$\frac{\partial C(\theta)}{\partial(\theta)_i} = \frac{1}{2}\left[C\left(\theta_i + \frac{\pi}{2}\right) - C\left(\theta_i - \frac{\pi}{2}\right)\right]$$

7. Quantum Hardware and Experimental Implementations

7.1 Introduction: The Engineering Challenge of Quantumness

The theoretical promise of quantum computing—solving problems intractable for classical machines—hinges on a monumental engineering endeavor: building a device that can reliably control the fragile states of quantum bits. Unlike the ideal, noise-free qubits of theory, physical qubits are plagued by decoherence and errors, constantly battling their environment to retain quantum information. This chapter explores the diverse landscape of quantum hardware platforms, each a creative solution to this core challenge. We will delve into how leading companies and research groups are building these machines, the fundamental limits they face, and the recent breakthroughs that are turning quantum computation from a theoretical curiosity into an experimental reality.

7.2 Quantum Hardware Platforms: A Diversity of Approaches

There is no single "right way" to build a quantum computer. Instead, multiple physical systems are being explored, each with unique advantages and trade-offs.

7.2.1 Superconducting Qubits: The Scalable Workhorse

These are being initiated by companies like IBM and Google. Superconducting qubits are micro fabricated circuits that are made from superconducting metals that exhibit quantum mechanical behavior when temperatures reach absolute zero (–273°C). The most common type, the transmon qubit, uses a Josephson junction to create discrete energy levels. These qubits are controlled by precise microwave pulses and read out via coupled resonators [26].

Their key advantage is scalability. By leveraging advanced semiconductor fabrication techniques, engineers can pattern hundreds, and now thousands, of these qubits onto a single chip. However, they are highly sensitive to electromagnetic noise and require massive, expensive dilution refrigerators to operate, making them incredibly complex machines to run and maintain.

7.2.2 Trapped Ions: The Precision Specialists

Companies like Ion *Q* and Quantinuum (formerly Honeywell Quantum Solutions) use individual atoms as qubits. Ions (charged atoms) are suspended in a vacuum chamber by electromagnetic fields and manipulated with lasers. The qubit is encoded in the ion's stable electronic states.

The standout feature of trapped ions is their exceptional fidelity. They are largely identical and perfectly isolated from their environment, leading to long coherence times and incredibly accurate quantum operations [27]. They also feature natural all-to-all connectivity within a trap, as ions interact through their collective motion. Their main challenge is scaling; while controlling a chain of 20 ions is manageable, controlling hundreds requires linking multiple traps together, a significant engineering hurdle.

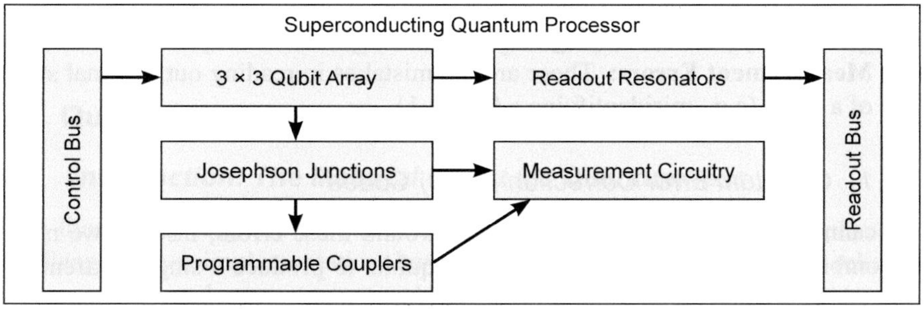

Fig. 1.9 Superconducting quantum processor.

that can be initialized, manipulated with high fidelity, entangled with its neighbors, and read out—all while fiercely resisting the relentless pressure of the environment to cause decoherence. There is no single solution to this challenge. Instead, a fascinating diversity of approaches has emerged, each leveraging different physical phenomena and each presenting a unique set of trade-offs between controllability, connectivity, and coherence. This chapter explores the leading hardware platforms vying to become the substrate of the quantum future.

8.2 Superconducting Qubits: The Engineered Circuit

Superconducting qubits are artificial atoms created on semiconductor chips. These nano-sized circuits, made from superconducting metals like niobium and aluminium, exhibit quantum mechanical behavior when cooled to temperatures near absolute zero (below 20 mK). The most prevalent type, the transmon qubit, uses a Josephson junction—a non-linear, dissipation less circuit element—to create discrete energy levels that define the $|0\rangle$ and $|1\rangle$ states [26]. By injecting precise microwave pulses, qubits are controlled and are read out by coupling to a resonator whose transmission properties depend on the qubit state. Their primary advantage is scalability; they are fabricated using lithographic techniques adapted from the classical semiconductor industry, enabling the production of processors with hundreds and now thousands of qubits [31]. However, they are susceptible to decoherence from material defects and electromagnetic noise, and their operation requires massive and expensive dilution refrigerators.

8.3 Trapped Ions: The Atomic Clockwork

Trapped ion quantum computers use nature's perfect qubits: individual atomic ions. Elements like Ytterbium or Barium are ionized and suspended in ultra-high vacuum using oscillating electric fields generated by a Paul trap. Lasers cool these ions to near motionlessness and manipulate their stable internal electronic states to perform quantum operations [27].

The ions' mutual Coulomb repulsion causes them to form a crystalline chain. Their collective motion acts as a reliable quantum bus, enabling any ion to entangle with any other in the chain, providing natural all-to-all connectivity. This platform is renowned for its exceptional gate fidelities and long coherence times, as the atomic states are identical and well-isolated. The primary challenge is scaling beyond several dozen ions in a single trap, with strategies like ion shuttling in multi-zone traps or photonic interconnects between separate traps being actively developed.

8.4 Photonic Quantum Computing: The Light-Based Network

Photonic quantum computing uses photons as qubits. Quantum information is encoded in a photon's degree of freedom, such as polarization, path, and time bin. Quantum gates are constructed with linear optical elements (beam splitters, phase shifters, waveguides) and photon-number-resolving detectors.

This approach operates at room temperature and is inherently suited for quantum communication, making it the leading technology for building a quantum internet. A significant breakthrough was the development of measurement-based models for quantum computation, which allow for universal computing using probabilistic photon sources and detection [32]. The central challenge is the difficulty of creating deterministic interactions between photons, which often leads to large resource overheads and a reliance on high-precision manufacturing of photonic circuits.

8.5 Topological Qubits: The Fault-Tolerant Future

Topological qubits represent a paradigm shift from encoding information in a local quantum state to storing it in the global, topological properties of a system. Imagine information stored not in the precise position of a knot in a rope but in the type of knot itself—a property robust against local perturbations.

Proposed implementations involve non-Abelian anyons, like Majorana zero modes in semiconductor–superconductor heterostructures, whose braiding statistics would inherently protect quantum information from local errors [33].

The appeal is profound: intrinsic fault tolerance. Local noise cannot easily destroy the globally encoded information, which would extremely reduce the overhead that is required for quantum error correction. The monumental challenge is that these exotic quantum states have yet to be unambiguously created and controlled in an experiment, making topological quantum computing a compelling but still theoretical roadmap.

8.6 Hybrid Quantum Systems: Strategic Synergy

Given that no single platform excels in all desired properties, a powerful strategy is to develop hybrid quantum systems that combine different technologies, leveraging the strengths of one to compensate for the weaknesses of another [34].

A canonical vision involves:

- Using superconducting circuits as rapid quantum processing units (QPUs).
- Using trapped ions or other long-coherence systems as reliable quantum memory modules.
- Using photonic interconnects to transfer quantum information between different processing and memory units at the speed of light.

This modular approach could potentially overcome the individual scalability and coherence limitations of each standalone platform.

8.7 Comparative Analysis: A Landscape of Trade-Offs

The choice of hardware platform involves navigating a complex landscape of engineering trade-offs. Table 1.2 provides a high-level overview of the relative advantages and challenges of each approach.

Table 1.2 Comparison of Quantum Computing Hardware Platforms

Platform	*Technology Readiness*	*Key Advantages*	*Primary Challenges*
Superconducting	Advanced (1000+ qubits)	Scalable fabrication, fast gates, strong coupling	Short coherence, high noise sensitivity, cryogenics
Trapped Ions	Intermediate (50+ qubits)	Long coherence, high-fidelity gates, all-to-all connectivity	Slow gates, complex scaling, laser stability
Photonic	Emerging (quantum advantage shown)	Room temperature operation, fast communication, quantum networking	Probabilistic gates, resource overhead, photon loss
Topological	Theoretical (pre-discovery)	Intrinsic fault tolerance, low error rates	Experimental demonstration, material synthesis, control
Hybrid	Research phase	Leverages strengths of combined systems, modular	System integration, interface engineering, complexity

9. Applications of Quantum Computing

9.1 *Introduction: The Quantum Advantage in Practice*

Quantum algorithms will provide not only small advances but also significant advances in a variety of fields by utilizing quantum features including superposition, entanglement, and interference. We can distinguish between applications that will require fault-tolerant quantum computers in a few years and those that can run on NISQ hardware [19].

9.2 *Cryptanalysis and Cryptography: A Double-Edged Sword*

For cybersecurity, quantum computing presents both opportunities and challenges. Current cryptographic values are in danger, which is a challenge. This is the prospect of creating new, unbreakable communication methods.

9.2.1 Cryptanalysis: The Threat to Current Standards

Shor's technique is considered an important development in cryptography because it effectively resolves discrete logarithm and number factorization problems, which are the basis of renowned public-key cryptosystems like RSA and ECC. Shor's technique requires polynomial time, or $T_{\text{Shor}} = \text{poly}(\log N)$ [35]. This implies that a large-scale, fault-tolerant quantum computer can easily break the cryptographic codes that are supposed to be protective in today's digital communications from any threat.

9.2.2 Quantum-Secure Communication: The Opportunity

Quantum computing raises significant threats to current cryptographic systems. However, it also provides solutions. One such solution is Quantum Key Distribution (QKD). Protocols like BB84 use fundamental principles of quantum mechanics, including the no-cloning theorem and the disruptive nature of quantum measurement. QKD allows two parties to generate a shared secret key with information-theoretic security. If a third party attempts to intercept the key, the quantum states are disturbed, and their presence is immediately revealed [36].

9.3 Quantum Simulation: The Most Natural Application

One of the most convincing applications of quantum computing is the simulation of other quantum systems. Classical computers face exponential difficulty when trying to model molecules or complex materials. But the quantum computers are naturally suited to handle these tasks. The central problem is Hamiltonian simulation, where an initial quantum state $|\psi_0\rangle$ evolves under a system's Hamiltonian H for time t. This can be mathematically represented by the unitary operator e^{-Ht}. There are many quantum algorithms like Trotter-Suzuki decomposition, qubitization, and the linear combination of unitaries (LCU) method, which provide efficient ways to perform this simulation [37].

This capability has deep implications for quantum chemistry and materials science. Variational algorithms like the VQE provide a way to approximate these simulations on even a noisy hardware for the NISQ era.

9.4 Optimization: Solving Complex Combinational Problems

There are numerous real-world issues in machine learning, finance, and logistics, which are referred as optimization problems. Quantum computing provides innovative methods to address these historically difficult tasks.

9.4.1 Grover's Algorithm: Quadratic Speedup for Search

Grover's algorithm gives a generic quadratic speedup for unstructured search problems. For searching a database of N items, Grover's algorithm can find the target with $O(\sqrt{N})$ queries, compared to $O(N)$ classically [14]. This acceleration is applicable to a wide range of constraint satisfaction and search problems.

9.4.2 QAOA: Tailored for Combinatorial Optimization

The quantum approximate optimization algorithm (QAOA) is specifically designed for combinatorial optimization problems like MaxCut or traveling salesman problems [20]. QAOA algorithm operates by alternately applying gates corresponding to a problem Hamiltonian H_P and a driver (or mixing) Hamiltonian H_M:

$$U(\vec{\gamma}, \vec{\beta}) = \prod_{j=1}^{p} e^{-\beta_j H_M} e^{-i\gamma_j H_p}$$

where parameters $\{\gamma_j, \beta_j\}$ are optimized classically. The depth p of this circuit controls the approximation quality, making QAOA a leading candidate for demonstrating quantum advantage on NISQ devices for optimization tasks.

9.5 Machine Learning and Data Analysis: Quantum-Enhanced Learning

QML analyzes the possibilities for quantum computers to speed up machine learning and enhance model expressiveness.

9.5.1 Quantum Kernel Methods

Quantum computers can map classical data into high-dimensional quantum feature spaces. The quantum kernel trick involves computing inner products in this large feature space efficiently through quantum circuits, potentially enabling the discovery of complex patterns that are difficult for classical kernels to capture [38].

9.5.2 Variational Quantum Models

Parameterized quantum circuits, often called QNNs, can be trained as machine learning models. These hybrid quantum–classical approaches use a quantum computer to evaluate a model and a classical optimizer to update the parameters. Key challenges include designing effective approaches, mitigating the effects of noise, and efficiently loading classical data into quantum states (the quantum random access memory [RAM] problem).

9.6 Other Impactful Application Domains

9.6.1 Linear Algebra: The HHL Algorithm

The HHL algorithm (named for its creators Harrow, Hassidim, and Lloyd) solves systems of linear equations ($\vec{A}\,x = \vec{b}$) in time polylogarithmic in the system size for sparse, well-conditioned matrices [39].

Its output is a quantum state proportional to the solution vector $|x\rangle$. The practicality of HHL depends heavily on whether the desired output can be a quantum state (e.g., for further quantum processing) or if classical information must be extracted, which can negate the quantum advantage.

9.6.2 Materials and Drug Discovery

By accurately simulating molecular and solid-state systems, quantum computers could revolutionize materials science and pharmacology. The ability to predict molecular properties, reaction mechanisms, and protein folding with high accuracy would dramatically accelerate the discovery of new pharmaceuticals, catalysts, and materials with novel properties [39].

9.6.3 Finance

The finance industry explores quantum computing for portfolio optimization, risk analysis, and option pricing through quantum-enhanced Monte Carlo simulations. While promising, these applications remain largely theoretical and are contingent on significant advancements in both hardware and algorithm design to demonstrate clear advantage over classical methods.

9.6.4 Communications and Sensing

Beyond QKD, quantum technologies enable:

- Quantum Repeaters: Essential components for building a long-distance quantum internet by distributing entanglement over global scales.
- Quantum Sensing: Using entangled or squeezed quantum states to achieve measurement precision beyond classical limits (Heisenberg scaling), with applications in medical imaging, gravitational wave detection, and navigation.

9.7 Limitations and Practical Considerations

Despite the exciting potential, significant challenges remain:

- The Readout Problem: Many quantum algorithms provide an advantage in creating a solution state, but extracting useful classical information from that state can erase the quantum advantage.
- NISQ Limitations: Noise and limited coherence times in current hardware restrict the algorithms that can be run successfully.
- The Hybrid Imperative: For the foreseeable future, the most practical path to quantum utility lies in hybrid quantum–classical algorithms where quantum processors handle specific, computationally expensive subroutines within a larger classical workflow.

The journey toward practical quantum advantage is ongoing. While fault-tolerant quantum computing remains a longer-term goal, the NISQ era is already yielding.

10. Conclusion

Quantum computing is steadily transforming from a theoretical idea into a tangible technology. Rooted in the principles of quantum mechanics—superposition, entanglement, and interference—it offers a way of processing information that classical computers simply cannot match. What once began as abstract models like the quantum Turing machine and early circuit frameworks has grown into a diverse

[32] N. Harle, O. Shtanko, and R. Movassagh, "Observing and braiding topological Majorana modes on programmable quantum simulators," *Nat. Commun.*, vol. 14, no. 1, p. 2286, Apr. 2023, doi: 10.1038/s41467-023-37725-0.

[33] G. Kurizki et al., "Quantum technologies with hybrid systems," *Proc. Natl. Acad. Sci.*, vol. 112, no. 13, pp. 3866–3873, Mar. 2015, doi: 10.1073/pnas.1419326112.

[34] P.W. Shor, "Polynomial-Time Algorithms for Prime Factorization and Discrete Logarithms on a Quantum Computer," *SIAM J. Comput.*, vol. 26, no. 5, 1997, doi: 10.1137/S0097539795293172.

[35] N. Gisin, G. Ribordy, W. Tittel, and H. Zbinden, "Quantum cryptography," *Rev. Mod. Phys.*, vol. 74, no. 1, pp. 145–195, Mar. 2002, doi: 10.1103/RevModPhys.74.145.

[36] J.R. McClean et al., "OpenFermion: the electronic structure package for quantum computers," *Quantum Sci. Technol.*, vol. 5, no. 3, p. 034014, Jun. 2020, doi: 10.1088/2058-9565/ab8ebc.

[37] M. Schuld, "Supervised quantum machine learning models are kernel methods," Apr. 17, 2021, arXiv: arXiv:2101.11020. doi: 10.48550/arXiv.2101.11020.

[38] A.W. Harrow, A. Hassidim, and S. Lloyd, "Quantum Algorithm for Linear Systems of Equations," *Phys. Rev. Lett.*, vol. 103, no. 15, p. 150502, Oct. 2009, doi: 10.1103/PhysRevLett.103.150502.

[39] A. Jacquier, O. Kondratyev, A. Lipton, and M. López de Prado, Quantum Machine Learning and Optimisation in Finance: On the Road to Quantum Advantage. Packt Publishing, 2022. [Online]. Available: https://ieeexplore.ieee.org/document/10162583

2 Intersection of Quantum Computing and Machine Learning

Raghavendar Nellikondi[1*]

Quantum machine learning (QML) is the use of quantum computers to perform machine learning tasks. Also, it can assist with large datasets and unstructured data. QML systems could enhance machine learning and enable new means of data analysis by leveraging quantum mechanics principles such as entanglement, interference, and superposition. This chapter discusses the state of the art with respect to hybrid quantum models, fully quantum algorithms, quantum-assisted traditional learning, and other varieties. Applications range from drug discovery and supply-chain optimization to cyber safety and natural language processing. While QML has the possibility of being a game-changer, there are many roadblocks such as quantum decoherence, data encoding issues, and algorithms not maturing. These problems require coordinated incremental advances in hardware, algorithm design, and theory to resolve. This paper does all the essential background work that provides significant concepts, status of ongoing implementation and major algorithms, security and compliance landscape of QML that would help in looking into the future of QML.

1. Introduction

1.1 Machine Learning (ML)

ML is a core subfield of artificial intelligence that is concerned with the design and analysis of algorithms that learn patterns from data to allow predictions and decisions to be made without being programmed to do so for a particular task [1]. Deep learning is a subfield that has had very impressive performance benefits over a large set of traditional methods [2].

ML has various applications. Natural language processing, image and video analysis, speech recognition, spam detection, agriculture, and healthcare [4]. When there is a use of ML to resolve business problems and predict what might happen in the future, it is referred to as predictive analytics [5].

The discipline mainly makes use of principles from statistics and mathematical optimization, which provide the theoretical tools for constructing learning algorithms

[1] Senior Member, Institute of Electrical and Electronics Engineers (IEEE), Sterling, VA, USA, ORCID ID: 0009-0002-1315-2495

* Corresponding author: raghav.nellikondi@gmail.com

DOI: 10.1201/9781003646068-2

- *Mandatory Migration to Post-Quantum Cryptography*
  As per NIST (2024) recommendations, finance, healthcare, defense, and energy sectors will start moving towards ML-KEM, ML-DSA, and other PQC algorithms. They are critical infrastructure and cannot wait for the standardization of these algorithms. To comply with the new encryption standards, it is likely that industry certifications and audits will be altered.
- *Compliance Requirements Related to Quantum Risk Assessments*
  Organizations will have to regularly conduct a quantum risk assessment that identifies vulnerable systems, evaluates exposure to future quantum decryption, and documents mitigation plans. These assessments will be part of compliance reports, especially for sectors dealing with long-lived sensitive data [2].
- *Regulating Quantum Technologies Through Oversight*
  Organizations creating or using quantum tech may come up with new frameworks. Regulatory measures for transparency in algorithmic design of quantum-enhanced machine learning systems will probably involve licensing and mandatory security reviews [9].

7.3 Proactive Organizational Measures: Building Quantum Resilience

Organizations must not wait for the evolution of regulations. They must instead start building quantum resilience through planning, upgrading technology, and policymaking.

- *Conduct a Cryptographic Inventory*
  Organizations should identify where and how cryptography is applied including sensitivity and policy for data at rest, in transit, and during processing. By cataloging the dependencies, it will help estimate priority for PQC transition and legacy vulnerabilities.
- *Plan for the Integration of PQC and QKD*
  Start using NIST-approved PQC algorithms into internal systems and begin testing. This could use hybrid systems that combine classical and post-quantum methods to ensure backward compatibility during the transition period.
  Quantum Key Distribution (QKD) technologies can give ultra-sensitive communications organizations, especially government, defense, and critical infrastructure environments where the requirement for confidentiality is most stringent.
- *Develop Quantum Resilience Policies*
  Create organizational procedures that detail the response to quantum threats. These may include:
  - Incident response plans that account for quantum-enabled breaches
  - Vendor and third-party risk assessments for quantum-readiness
  - Employee awareness training about post-quantum threats [9]
  - Business continuity planning that considers sudden cryptographic failures

- *Engage with Standardization Bodies and Ecosystem Partners*
  Organizations should contribute to quantum security working groups (e.g., NIST, ETSI, ISO/IEC) to keep current on the standards and aid in shaping best practices [6]. Working with vendors and cloud providers on post-quantum roadmaps ensures alignment across the value chain.

8. The Future of QML

Quantum machine learning or QML is gaining the most attention by the day that combines quantum computing with artificial intelligence. QML is still in its infancy but could change how we model complex systems, manipulate large datasets, and solve problems that are considered intractable for classical systems. Many trends and milestones will determine the viability, scalability, and social impact of QML in the near future [16].

8.1 Quantum Benefit in Machine Learning

Our goal with the development of QML is to demonstrate quantum advantage. In other words, quantum algorithms can perform machine learning tasks better than the best classical algorithms on that task in speed, accuracy, or resource efficiency.

- Earlier QML algorithms have been demonstrated in toy or academic problems, but future work would try to show quantum advantage in applications such as drug discovery, finance, logistics, and cybersecurity [12].
- The community is working toward producing rigorous benchmarks to assess quantum advantages for ML, including comparisons of model generalization, convergence rate, and energy cost to fair classical baselines [20].
- Many promising QML scenarios involve hybrid quantum-classical models where quantum processors perform the core subroutine, such as feature mapping or kernel estimation, whereas classical processors handle training and inference [10]. Even showing dominance in these mixed instances may lead to quick uptake.

8.2 Interdisciplinary Innovation

The success of QML depends not only on quantum hardware breakthroughs or ML algorithm breakthroughs, but on cross-disciplinary collaboration:

- Physicists contribute deep understanding of quantum systems, decoherence, and entanglement, which are critical for designing robust quantum circuits [7].
- Computer scientists advance algorithm design, computational complexity analysis, and software engineering for quantum programming environments.
- Domain experts in areas such as healthcare, chemistry, and logistics help translate QML capabilities into real-world applications by defining problem-specific constraints and objectives [17].

- It will be important to pool every expertise to create a QML model that will be not only be powerful but also functional and deployable in complex real-life settings [15].

8.3 Hardware Scalability and Fault Tolerance

To understand the full prospective of QML, the field must tackle the scalability and reliability limitations of currently available quantum hardware.

- The current quantum devices, mainly referred to as the NISQ-era devices, are error-prone and support only shallow circuits. Because of these limitations, the depth and scale of QML models that can be executed in practice are limited.
- The future progress of fault-tolerant quantum computers that perform long and complex computations without falling apart due to quantum noise. Advance in quantum error correction, stability of logical qubit, and cryogenic architecture will be crucial [1].
- As quantum systems gain more complexity, management of entanglement connectivity and gate fidelity will be as important as hyperparameter tuning in classical ML [10].

8.4 Standardization and Ethical Regulation

As QML systems become increasingly powerful and deployed across a range of industries, there is a growing need for regulation.

- Just like classical ML, which has standard datasets and benchmarks (ImageNet, GLUE), , QML also requires standard evaluation and reporting protocols [13] to compare models on the same scale.
- Regulatory standards should address security risks (e.g., adversarial quantum ML, model inversion attacks) and ensure the QML systems are interpretable, especially for the high-stakes areas like healthcare or law [14].
- While quantum neural networks are novel architectures, they inherit many issues from classical networks, including data bias and ethical risk. Developers have to guarantee that the quantum systems do not magnify these problems [10].
- Governments and global organizations such as ISO, NIST, and OECD are likely to create rules that require compliance with the secure employability, auditable, and accountability of QML systems quantum AI.

8.5 Democratization of Quantum Machine Learning

One of the most exciting trends is that QML is becoming much more accessible through open-source tools and cloud facilities.

There are many multiple quantum development platforms publicly available these days. For example, there's Qiskit from IBM, PennyLane from Xanadu, Cirq from Google, and Amazon Braket. These can be used by researchers, students, and developers to create and test quantum ML models on real hardware or simulators [6].

The availability of hybrid integration tools such as TensorFlow Quantum, Pennylane-Lightning, and Qiskit Machine Learning makes it easier for users to embed quantum circuits into classical ML pipelines, lowering the barrier to experimentation.

Projects like the Qiskit Textbook, Xanadu's Quantum Codebook, and Quantum Country are developing a global talent pipeline with an educational grounding in both quantum computing and machine learning [16].

Access to quantum hardware via the cloud brings these capabilities to academia, startups, and individuals, leading to new work in the area.

9. Conclusion

Quantum machine learning is the frontier of computation with huge possibilities that may revolutionize data analysis, interpretation, and action [1]. Though there is a slew of technical and conceptual issues, the field is maturing quite rapidly. Innovative developments in quantum hardware, algorithm growth, and secure data handling systems are on the cards. QML will alter the boundaries of machine intelligence in a number of other industries.

References

[1] Biamonte, J., Wittek, P., Pancotti, N., Rebentrost, P., Wiebe, N., and Lloyd, S. "Quantum machine learning," *Nature*, vol. 549, no. 7671, pp. 195–202, 2017, doi: 10.1038/nature23474.

[2] Preskill, J. "Quantum computing in the NISQ era and beyond," *Quantum*, vol. 2, p. 79, 2018, doi: 10.22331/q-2018-08-06-79.

[3] Schuld, M., Sinayskiy I., and Petruccione, F. "An introduction to quantum machine learning," *Contemporary Physics*, vol. 56, no. 2, pp. 172–185, 2015, doi: 10.1080/00107514.2014.964942.

[4] Devitt, S.J., Munro, W.J., and Nemoto, K. "Quantum error correction for beginners," *Reports on Progress in Physics*, vol. 76, no. 7, p. 076001, 2013, doi: 10.1088/0034-4885/76/7/076001.

[5] Gyongyosi, L. and Imre, S. "A survey on quantum computing technology," *Computer Science Review*, vol. 31, pp. 51–71, 2019, doi: 10.1016/j.cosrev.2018.11.002.

[6] Qiskit Contributors, Qiskit: An Open-source Framework for Quantum Computing, Zenodo, 2019, doi: 10.5281/zenodo.2573505.

[7] Ciliberto, C., Herbster, M., Ialongo, A.D., Pontil, M., Rocchetto, A., Severini, S., and Wossnig, L. "Quantum machine learning: A classical perspective," *Proceedings of the Royal Society A*, vol. 474, no. 2209, p. 20170551, 2018, doi: 10.1098/rspa.2017.0551.

[8] Benedetti, M., Lloyd, E., Sack, S., and Fiorentini M. "Parameterized quantum circuits as machine learning models," *Quantum Science and Technology*, vol. 4, no. 4, p. 043001, 2019, doi: 10.1088/2058-9565/ab4eb5.

[9] Schuld, M., Bocharov, A., Svore, K.M., and Wiebe, N. "Circuit-centric quantum classifiers," *Physical Review A*, vol. 101, no. 3, p. 032308, 2020, doi: 10.1103/PhysRevA.101.032308.

[10] McClean, J.R., Boixo, S., Smelyanskiy, V.N., Babbush, R., and Neven, H. "Barren plateaus in quantum neural network training landscapes," *Nature Communications*, vol. 9, no. 1, p. 4812, 2018, doi: 10.1038/s41467-018-07090-4.

[11] Zhang, T., Wang, Z., Xu, D., and Yung, M.-H. "When does quantum advantage emerge in quantum machine learning?" *PRX Quantum*, vol. 2, no. 3, p. 030308, 2021, doi: 10.1103/PRXQuantum.2.030308.

[12] Havlíček, V., Córcoles, A.D., Temme, K., Harrow, A.W., Kandala, A., Chow, J.M., and Gambetta, J.M. "Supervised learning with quantum-enhanced feature spaces," *Nature*, vol. 567, no. 7747, pp. 209–212, 2019, doi: 10.1038/s41586-019-0980-2.

[13] Cao, Y., Romero J., Olson, J.P., Degroote, M., Johnson, P.D., Kieferová, M. et al. "Quantum chemistry in the age of quantum computing," *Chemical Reviews*, vol. 119, no. 19, pp. 10856–10915, 2019, doi: 10.1021/acs.chemrev.8b00803.

[14] Bergholm, V., Izaac, J., Schuld, M., Gogolin, C., Ahmed, S., Ajith, V., et al. "PennyLane: Automatic differentiation of hybrid quantum-classical computations," arXiv:1811.04968, 2018 [Online]. Available at https://arxiv.org/abs/1811.04968.

[15] Amazon Web Services, "Amazon Braket documentation: Cloud-based quantum access platform," 2024 [Online]. Available https://aws.amazon.com/braket/.

[16] Arute, F., Arya, K., Babbush, R., et al. "Quantum supremacy using a programmable superconducting processor," *Nature*, vol. 574, no. 7779, pp. 505–510, 2019, doi: 10.1038/s41586-019-1666-5.

[17] Fowler, A.G., Mariantoni, M., Martinis, J.M. and Cleland, A.N. "Surface codes: Towards practical large-scale quantum computation," *Physical Review A*, vol. 86, no. 3, p. 032324, 2012, doi: 10.1103/PhysRevA.86.032324.

[18] Shor, P.W. "Polynomial-time algorithms for prime factorization and discrete logarithms on a quantum computer," *SIAM Journal on Computing*, vol. 26, no. 5, pp. 1484–1509, 1997, doi: 10.1137/S0097539795293172.

[19] Mosca, M. "Cybersecurity in an era with quantum computers: Will we be ready?" *IEEE Security & Privacy*, vol. 16, no. 5, pp. 38–41, 2018, doi: 10.1109/MSP.2018.3761723.

[20] Lu, S., Cao, Y., Yao, X., Ma, X., and Zeng, P. "Quantum model extraction and inversion attacks," arXiv:2204.10237, 2022 [Online]. Available at https://arxiv.org/abs/2204.10237.

3 Harnessing Quantum Kernels for Supervised Learning: A Deep Dive into Quantum SVMs

Rajeev Tripathi[1] and Ravi Shanker Pandey[2*]

Quantum support vector machines (QSVMs) offer a paradigm change that may leverage quantum mechanical processes to outperform traditional support vector machines (SVMs) in high-dimensional and non-linear classification tasks. These machines are located at the crossroads of supervised machine learning and quantum computing. The purpose of this chapter is to provide a comprehensive technical analysis of QSVMs, with a particular emphasis on the use of variation quantum circuits for implicit feature space transformations and the development of these circuits within the context of quantum kernel estimation. Through the use of quantum state preparation and interference, we provide a comprehensive explanation of the possible fabrication of quantum kernels that are based on inner product evaluations in exponentially huge Hilbert spaces. When it comes to boosting model expressivity beyond classical limits, the importance that entanglement and quantum feature mapping play is specifically stressed. In addition to this, we investigate algorithmic implementations on noisy intermediate-scale quantum (NISQ) hardware, focusing on problems associated with quantum decoherence, gate fidelity, and loop depth optimization. Several fields, including quantum-enhanced drug discovery, anomaly detection in quantum sensor networks, fault classification in quantum error correction, and portfolio optimization, are now the focus of research that is being conducted in order to develop real-world applications. This chapter comes to a close with an analysis of the existing theoretical limits, resource needs, and future perspectives for the use of QSVMs in machine learning applications in order to achieve a quantum advantage. In order to facilitate the development of scalable quantum machine learning models that are founded on strong mathematical and computational notions, this synthesis is geared at academics and practitioners.

1. Introduction

Computers and data are becoming more complicated all the time, thus we need non-machine learning alternatives. One fascinating emerging technology is quantum

[1] Department of Computer Sciences, School of Management Sciences, Lucknow, India.
[2] Department of Computer Application and Sciences, School of Management Sciences, Lucknow, India.
E-mail: rajeev2363@gmail.com[1]
* Corresponding author: ravishankerpandey84@gmail.com

DOI: 10.1201/9781003646068-3

computing. To do computations that classical computers are unable to, it makes use of quantum mechanical ideas such as superposition, entanglement, and quantum interference. Quantum support vector machines (QSVMs) are used to do this. The support vector machine (SVM) is considered the best in its field for tasks such as pattern recognition, regression, and grouping. Here we have the simplified version.

SVMs excel in supervised learning because they can handle scenarios with several dimensions and non-linear decision limitations. SVM training can be costly if your data contains opaque kernels. Applying quantum computing to high-dimensional Hilbert spaces is a fantastic strategy to address these issues. It also speeds up the kernel process. Hybrid models that combine ML and quantum computing are one application of quantum physics. This leads to more complicated computers. At its core, quantum machine learning is based on quantum support vector machines or QSVMs. This approach has fixed problems with item connections where others had not. If your data is multi-dimensional or otherwise not easily separable by lines, then you should use QSVMs. The reason for this is because QSVMs function in Hilbert spaces that are in a constant state of expansion.

Here we will learn about QSVMs and how to test the algorithm using the QKE approach. Scientists have discovered a plethora of methods to enhance hybrid quantum-classical systems [1]. In this chapter, we go over some of the present challenges, including our insufficient technology, our algorithms' inability to process large amounts of data, and their insensitivity to noise.

2. Classical SVM

SVM is a popular supervised machine learning technique. It is particularly effective in high-dimensional fields and strong theoretical foundations. SVMs created a dependable method that used kernel functions and margin maximization ideas to successfully handle both linear and non-linear classification problems. Classical SVMs are still crucial in many applications because of their interpretability, generalization capabilities, and comparatively cheap processing needs for small-to-medium-sized datasets, even with the current surge of deep learning. This chapter examines the fundamental effects of conventional SVMs, the range of applications they may be used for, and the limitations that spur more study and other approaches.

The limitations of SVMs are as follows:

Scalability: The amount of the dataset causes the training time to grow either quadratically or cubically.
Kernel Selection: Selecting the right kernel and adjusting its characteristics are crucial for performance.
Uses of Memory: For big datasets, the approach may be inefficient because it keeps all support vectors in memory.

2.1 Impact of Classical SVMs

2.1.1 Theoretical Advancements

One of the challenging mathematical concepts introduced by SVMs is the maximum margin classifier, which selects a hyperplane that separates the classes with the largest margin. In addition to encouraging a variety of theoretical investigations in learning theory, such as the creation of the VC-dimension and structural risk minimization (SRM), this approach improved generalization on unseen data. SVMs developed kernel approaches that allowed for the linear separation of non-linear data in a higher-dimensional space. It possible for algorithms to work in feature spaces that were implicitly mapped without ever explicitly calculating the coordinates of the data in such spaces. It significantly increased the adaptability of linear algorithms by extending their use to non-linear issues.

2.1.2 Algorithmic Influence

The development of additional algorithms has been significantly impacted by the success of SVMs, especially in the areas of regularization techniques, convex optimization, and kernel-based approaches. Their optimization methodology has been modified in a number of extensions, including least-squares SVM (LS-SVM), v-SVM, and others. They also popularized Lagrange duality and quadratic programming (QP) in machine learning.

2.1.3 Influence on Practice and Industry

SVMs have long been regarded as the "go-to" method in a variety of academic and industrial contexts because of their ability to blend simplicity, accuracy, and scalability (to a certain degree). Because of their dependability and deterministic character (unlike certain probabilistic models), they are widely used in domains like bioinformatics, text categorization, and forensic research that demand predictable and consistent outcomes.

2.2 Applications of Classical SVMs

2.2.1 Bioinformatics and Computational Biology

SVMs are now an important tool for working with large amounts of biological data, especially in deoxyribonucleic acid (DNA) microarray classification, gene expression analysis, and protein function prediction. They work well with biological datasets because they can handle high-dimensional data, which means data with more attributes than samples. SVMs have been utilized to categorize different tumor types according to gene expression patterns.

2.2.2 Text and Sentiment Classification

Text mining jobs often utilize SVMs because of their efficacy in high-dimensional sparse feature spaces. Applications include sentiment analysis, subject classification, and spam detection. For problems involving binary or multi-class classification, SVMs can be directly fed term frequency–inverse document frequency (TF–IDF) vectors or word embeddings. In legal and compliance applications where auditability is crucial, they are helpful because of their interpretability and stability.

2.2.3 Image and Handwriting Recognition

In the past, SVMs have performed well on tasks involving the recognition of characters and numbers. For example, SVMs with polynomial and RBF kernels have been effectively used to classify the well-known Modified National Institute of Standards and Technology (MNIST) handwritten digit dataset. SVMs are still competitive for low-resource image classification tasks, even if contemporary deep learning models now perform better on huge image datasets.

2.2.4 Financial Time-Series and Fraud Detection

SVMs are employed in anomaly detection and time-series forecasting, especially in the financial industry. By seeing patterns that differ from the usual, they can categorize the directions of stock price movement or identify fraudulent transactions. In particular, one-class SVM has been popular for unsupervised anomaly identification.

2.2.5 Medical Diagnosis and Prognosis

SVMs are used in clinical decision support systems for patient risk profile identification, illness outcome prediction, and medical picture classification. They are an effective tool in early diagnosis and personalized treatment because of their modest sample sizes and performance on structured data.

2.3 Drawbacks and Limitations

Despite their achievements, conventional SVMs still have a number of drawbacks, particularly in contemporary data contexts where there is a great deal of data volume, velocity, and fluctuation.

2.3.1 Scalability to Large Datasets

A quadratic programming problem that generally scales between $O(n^2)$ and $O(n^3)$ with regard to the amount of data points n is solved during SVM training. For large-scale datasets, SVMs are computationally costly because of their quadratic complexity. Sequential minimal optimization (SMO) and other methods help address this problem, but without rigorous optimization and sampling techniques, SVMs are still not the ideal option for massive data.

2.3.2 Difficulty in Parameter Tuning

Kernel functions and hyperparameters, including the regularization parameter C and kernel-specific parameters (such as γ for RBF kernels), must be carefully chosen for SVMs. Overfitting or underfitting may result from improper tuning. The tuning procedure is often computationally costly and time-consuming, particularly when using layered cross-validation.

2.3.3 Sensitivity to Noisy Data and Outliers

Finding a border that maximizes the margin is the goal of SVMs. However, SVMs can provide unstable decision boundaries in noisy datasets, particularly when classes overlap. The performance loss in the presence of large label noise remains a worry, despite the fact that soft-margin SVMs try to address this using a slack variable.

2.3.4 Limited Interpretability Compared to Decision Trees

Despite their higher generalization, SVMs are less interpretable than rule-based models such as decision trees or decision forests. In domains where a high level of transparency and explainability is required, such as healthcare and law, this opacity becomes a disadvantage. The decision function in input space is hard to comprehend and abstract in kernel space.

2.3.5 Non-Probabilistic Output

The traditional support vector machines do not provide prediction probability values. It is possible to calculate the probability by using methods such as Platt scaling. However, this method is laborious and subject to bias. For the purpose of rating and evaluating tasks, it is beneficial to make use of probabilistic models such as Naive Bayes or logistic regression since these models are designed to provide similar results.

A significant advancement in the field of machine learning is represented by standard support vector machines. The fact that they are difficult to comprehend, that they are sensitive to noise, and that they are unable to manage vast volumes of data does not prevent them from being useful in instances where there is a medium-sized quantity of well-structured data and where accuracy and consistency are necessary. SVMs are not always the best option; yet, they may be used as a model or benchmark for a wide variety of machine learning applications. As many fields, such as quantum computing, continue to advance, it is possible that new applications for SVM-based models may emerge over the course of the next several decades.

3. Quantum Computing Foundations

Quantum computing is an evolution in technology that uses ideas from quantum physics to process and alter data. Qubits, also known as quantum bits, are used in quantum computing instead of bits, which are the smallest unit of data in classical computing and may concurrently exist in a superposition of 0 and 1. Quantum systems can do some calculations more quickly than their classical counterparts because of this basic difference [2]. Fundamentally, quantum computing takes advantage of important quantum mechanical phenomena, such as superposition, which is the ability of a qubit to exist in a linear combination of many states.

Apart from superposition, the following features allow quantum parallelism, enabling a quantum computer to evaluate several possible outcomes simultaneously:

- Entanglement: A non-classical connection between qubits where the state of one qubit instantaneously influences the state of another, regardless of spatial separation.
- Quantum Interference: The mechanism by which probability amplitudes can combine to either constructively or destructively achieve desired computing outputs.

3.1 Quantum Algorithms and Speedups

A number of quantum algorithms show how, for some jobs, quantum computing may perform better than its conventional counterparts:

3.1.1 Rivest-Shamir-Adleman (RSA) Algorithm

The RSA encryption is undermined by Short's algorithm (1994), which solves integer factorization in polynomial time. **The RSA** algorithm is an ***asymmetric*** algorithm. It is a broadly used public-key encryption algorithm in cryptography. It imparts secure data transmission. It is based on the mathematical difficulty of factoring large composite numbers.

Key Components of the RSA Algorithm

Public Key	Consists of two numbers: e (public exponent) and n (modulus).
Private Key	Consists of two numbers: d (private exponent) and n (modulus).
Encryption	Utilizes the public key to encrypt plaintext into ciphertext.
Decryption	Uses the private key to decrypt ciphertext back into plaintext.

Main Security of the RSA Algorithm

The security of RSA relies on the difficulty of factoring large composite numbers. The bigger key sizes provide stronger security and also increase computational overhead.

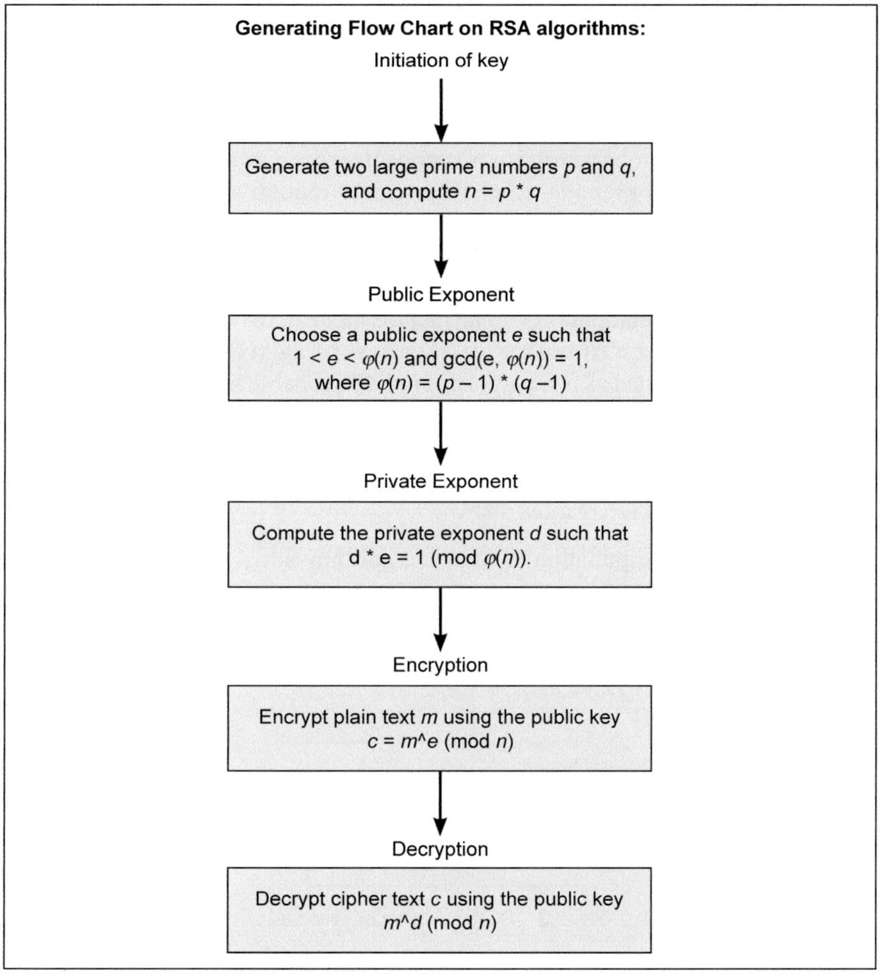

Fig. 3.1 Generating flow chart of RSA algorithm.

Most Useful Applications of RSA Algorithm

RSA is used to secure data transmission over the internet, such as online banking and e-commerce transactions.

It is used to create digital signatures, which authenticate the sender and ensure data integrity.

Limitations of the RSA Algorithm

RSA is algorithmically intensive, which can impact performance.

Managing RSA keys securely is crucial to prevent unauthorized access.

3.1.2 Groover's Algorithm

One example of a quantum computing algorithm is Grover's algorithm. It takes *O*(sqrt{*N*}) time to search an unsorted database of size *N*.

It resolves the quantum computing unshaped seek issue [3]. Finding a single prominent element among a group of N rudiments is the goal of an unshaped search problem. Finding the pronounced element would require a typical computer to search through all N components, which would take time O(N). We may notice the pronounced element in time O(√ N) by using Grover's technique. An essential tool for resolving a wide range of issues is Grover's algorithm. solving optimization issues, cracking cryptographic keys, and identifying patterns in data using Grover's technique [4]. Using given process or algorithm of aggregate operations to the input state. It is assigned as a superposition of all probable huntsstates [5].

The Grover operator has used for mainly two quantum operations in quantum computing:

1. The reflection on the mean.
2. The inversion of the marked state.

The mathematical interpretation of Grover algorithm is:

(a) The initial state of the process in mathematical interpretation is written by a given formula.

The algorithm starts in a state that is an emplacement of all N rudiments.

This state can be written as:

$$|\psi\rangle = \frac{1}{\sqrt{N}} \sum_{x=0}^{N-1} |x\rangle$$

(|*x*⟩ is state of element)

Fig. 3.2 State equation of process.

(b) The diffusion operator is a quantum computing operation amplifies the amplitudes of the states it is correspond to the pointed element.

The diffusion operator can be written as-

$$U = \frac{1}{2} I - \frac{1}{2} |\psi\rangle\langle\psi|$$

(*I* identity operator)

Fig. 3.3 Diffusion Operator Equation.

(c) The quantum computing algorithm is a very useful algorithm as it calculates the state of the system of quantum computing [6]. The recurrent use of this operator in process increases the scope of the specified condition, making it easier to measure the algorithm. Once the marked state is reached, the algorithm returns the index of the object corresponding to that marked state [7].

3.1.3 Other Algorithms

The algorithm known as Harrow-Hassidim-Lloyd (HHL) solves linear equation problems exponentially more quickly under specific circumstances. The quantum Fourier transform (QFT) is a crucial subroutine in several quantum algorithms that provides exponential speedups in number theory and signal processing. These algorithms demonstrate how complexity limitations may be significantly altered by quantum physics, which in turn spurs the creation of quantum machine learning methods.

3.2 Quantum Hardware and Challenges

Several technologies enable quantum computing on physical hardware, including superconducting qubits, which rely on Josephson junctions and are utilized by Google and IBM. Other technologies include the following:

- **Trapped Ions:** IonQ and Honeywell employ electromagnetic fields to capture ions.
- **Photonic Quantum Computers:** These computers compute using quantum states of light. The goal of topological qubits, which are still in the experimental stage, is to use anyons to compute in an error-resistant manner. However, there are a number of obstacles to effective quantum computing.
- **Decoherence:** As a result of interactions with their surroundings, qubits gradually lose information.
- **Gate Fidelity:** The depth of processing is limited by the noise and imperfections of current gates.
- **Qubit Connectivity:** The implementation of algorithms is limited by the lack of physical connections between qubits.
- **Scalability:** Less than 100 useable qubits are currently supported by the majority of quantum devices.

Variational quantum eigensolvers and the quantum approximate optimization algorithm are the two most useful hybrid algorithms in early-stage quantum machine learning. These algorithms are made feasible by noisy intermediate-scale quantum (NISQ) computers in order to handle the aforementioned problems.

4. Relevance of Quantum Machine Learning

Quantum machine learning (QML) models are based on the fundamental components of quantum computing. SVMs and other algorithms are inherently compatible with qubits because they allow high-dimensional Hilbert space mappings similar to kernel approaches [8]. Expanded Hilbert spaces for integrating intricate data structures, effective kernel assessments using quantum feature translations, and a reduced memory footprint for specific learning tasks are some benefits of quantum computing. Specifically, by employing quantum circuits to compute inner products in quantum Hilbert space, QSVMs have the potential to accelerate classification tasks tenfold [9].

5. Variational Quantum Support Vector Machine (V-QSVM) Architectures

Variational quantum algorithms (VQAs), which are becoming more and more popular as the area of quantum machine learning advances, are a practical way to use NISQ devices. These hybrid approaches, which integrate quantum computation with classical optimization, constantly enhance configurable quantum circuits. VQAs have shown promise in a number of applications, including classification, clustering, generative modeling, and even linear system solution [10]. The goal of V-QSVMs is to extend the classical SVM architecture into the quantum realm while maintaining compatibility with the noisy quantum processors of today. V-QSVMs use a parametric ansatz circuit to directly develop a discriminative model, which sets them apart from conventional quantum SVMs (such those that just use quantum kernel estimation). V-QSVMs provide a more adaptable and noise-resistant option by optimizing a trainable quantum circuit that acts as the classifier rather than calculating kernels in high-dimensional quantum feature space.

5.1 Challenges and Limitations

Notwithstanding their promise, V-QSVMs have a number of real-world obstacles to overcome:

Plateaus of Barren: Vanishing gradients are a common problem for variational circuits, particularly in deep and heavily entangled ansatzes. Effective optimization is hampered by these phenomena, which is called the barren plateau.

Trainability vs Expressivity: When designing circuits, there is a trade-off between making them trainable in noisy environments and making them expressive enough to describe complicated functions.

Limitations of Quantum Hardware: The following limitations apply to current quantum devices:

- Short coherence durations
- Limited qubit count

Readout and Gate Issues: The fidelity and depth of variational circuits are impacted by these constraints.

5.2 Overfitting and Generalization

V-QSVMs have the danger of overfitting when they have minimal data and strong expressivity. In the quantum realm, methods such as circuit trimming, regularization, and dropout are still in their infancy.

Even with the limited technology available today, V-QSVMs present a potential technique to apply quantum benefits to practical machine learning problems. They offer a versatile and scalable substitute for kernel-based QSVMs by utilizing trainable quantum circuits and eliminating explicit kernel assessment [11]. Notwithstanding the difficulties posed by noise, circuit design, and barren plateaus, more research into VQA optimization and hardware-specific circuit customization will probably establish V-QSVMs as a fundamental component of next-generation quantum-enhanced artificial intelligence (AI) systems.

6. Applications of QSVMs

The use of QSVMs is an exciting development at the intersection of quantum computing and machine learning. By using the computational advantages of quantum mechanics, particularly the ability to compute inner products in high-dimensional Hilbert spaces, QSVMs offer a great deal of potential for expediting classification and pattern recognition tasks [12]. The experimental and practical applications of QSVMs in several significant domains, including scientific research, healthcare, finance, and cybersecurity, are examined in this section.

6.1 Bioinformatics and Precision Medicine

With its frequent use of high-dimensional and non-linear datasets, bioinformatics is one of the most promising application sectors for QSVMs. Genetic sequence analysis, cancer diagnosis, and drug development are among the tasks that need sophisticated, extensive biological data processing.

a. Cancer Classification from Genomic Data

In traditional bioinformatics procedures, SVMs have been extensively used to classify cancer types based on patterns of expression of genes. Quantum enhancements to this process have been shown to potentially improve classification accuracy and speed. For instance, QSVMs may map complex genomic data into quantum Hilbert spaces to more easily identify minor similarities between different carcinogenic and non-cancerous gene expressions [13]. A study by Schuld and Killoran [2] demonstrated that quantum kernels can outperform their conventional counterparts in classifying cancer types from gene expression datasets with relatively fewer qubits and fewer training samples. This is particularly useful when there is a lack of medical data.

b. Protein Folding and Molecular Interaction Prediction

Predicting protein structures and molecular interactions requires the management of extremely high-dimensional configurations. Because these problems are inherently complicated and combinatorial, QSVMs are an excellent match for them. Quantum-enhanced SVMs have been proposed for ligand-receptor association prediction to aid in precision medicine's customized treatment plans and drug repurposing.

6.2 Financial Forecasting and Market Risk Modeling

The notoriously volatile and non-linear financial markets often exhibit intricate patterns that are hard for conventional algorithms to understand. SVMs are widely employed in the financial sector for stock prediction, credit risk modeling, and fraud detection. QSVMs are able to enhance these operations by using more expressive quantum kernels and quicker inner-product computations.

a. Credit Scoring and Fraud Detection

The technique of assessing a customer's risk level using their credit card usage, financial history, and demographic data is commonly referred to as credit scoring. These datasets are often high-dimensional and sparse, thus conventional methods need a lot of processing power [14].The dimensionality may be decreased and non-linear interactions can be better captured with the aid of QSVMs. Better class separation may be provided by quantum kernels, particularly in cases when the decision boundary is extremely non-linear.

Another important issue is the identification of fraud. To identify irregularities in transactional behavior, financial institutions rely on real-time data streams. By discovering hidden properties in the data that classical models could miss, QSVMs, when implemented via hybrid quantum-classical architectures, could enhance anomaly categorization.

b. Stock Price Trend Prediction

QSVMs and other quantum-enhanced models have been utilized in a number of prototype experiments to forecast changes in the stock market. These models encode technical data, mood indicators, and past price trends using quantum kernels. Although further testing with actual quantum hardware is needed, research indicates that quantum feature spaces can improve generalization under erratic market settings.

6.3 Cybersecurity and Threat Detection

More advanced detection systems are now required due to the growing complexity of cyberthreats. To identify malware, phishing attempts, and unauthorized access patterns, machine learning models are used. However, adversarial noise and changing attack vectors are problems for conventional classifiers.

a. Intrusion Detection Systems (IDS)

Intrusion detection systems (IDS) commonly employ system call analysis and network logs to identify malicious activities. By their very nature, these datasets are high-dimensional and imbalanced. Using QSVMs, network events may be classified as either benign or malicious, improving detection accuracy and response time.

Numerous research prototypes that use QSVMs on quantum simulators to simulate IDS models have been created. The benefit is that quantum-enhanced kernel functions allow for rapid adaptation to novel threat patterns and effective handling of sparse data.

b. Post-Quantum Cryptography Security
Although quantum computing puts traditional encryption techniques at danger, it also provides new resources for creating safe routes of communication. Anomalies in quantum communication protocols, including quantum key distribution (QKD), can be found using QSVMs. By categorizing channel behaviors and differentiating eavesdropping attempts, QSVMs might contribute to the validation of the security of next-generation cryptographic systems [15].

6.4 Image and Signal Processing

Signal processing and image classification are important application areas as well, particularly in fields where data dimensionality is a bottleneck. Medical picture diagnostics, facial identification, and digit recognition have all shown success using classical SVMs. By using quantum feature maps to handle the high-dimensional feature transformations more effectively, QSVMs expand this capacity.

a. Medical Image Diagnosis
Finding minute patterns in computer tomography (CT) scans, magnetic resonance imaging (MRI), or histopathological images can have a big influence on diagnosis in radiology and pathology. Compared to traditional SVMs, QSVMs have a better margin clarity for processing encoded visual characteristics and distinguishing between problematic classes. Using tiny medical datasets, recent research using quantum simulators have demonstrated encouraging results for differentiating between benign and malignant tumors [16].

b. Satellite and Remote Sensing Image Analysis
Large volumes of multi-spectral images must be processed for satellite data analysis tasks including land-use categorization, deforestation detection, and climate monitoring. Complex land-cover patterns and temporal anomalies in high-resolution geospatial datasets can be found using QSVMs. These applications could be among the first to take use of hybrid quantum classifiers as quantum hardware scales.

6.5 Scientific Discovery and Particle Physics

Particle collisions in high-energy physics experiments, like those at CERN, produce vast volumes of data. It is computationally costly to classify particle interactions or decay modes using classical machine learning. QSVMs have the ability to more accurately categorize decay patterns and manage high-dimensional phase space variables.

Higgs boson event classification has been studied using quantum machine learning methods, such as QSVMs. There are hundreds of characteristics having non-linear correlations in the dataset utilized in the ATLAS experiment. By mapping these properties into richer feature spaces, quantum kernels can enhance the discriminating between signals and backgrounds [17]. For Higgs classification tasks, simulated QSVMs have demonstrated performance that is on par with or better than traditional SVMs. However, full-scale implementation is constrained by existing technology.

7. Challenges and Future Prospects

A revolutionary paradigm change, quantum computing holds the promise of resolving intricate issues that traditional computers are unable to handle. QSVM is a useful model for quantum machine learning. It seeks to improve the performance of classical SVMs by taking advantage of the exponential power of quantum mechanics, specifically quantum parallelism and high-dimensional Hilbert space embeddings [18].

Although they use quantum subroutines such quantum kernel estimation, variational circuits, and quantum state preparation, QSVMs are essentially based on the classical SVM architecture. Although theoretical research has indicated possible quantum benefits, there are still many obstacles to overcome before QSVMs can be implemented on NISQ devices.

8. Technical and Computational Challenges of QSVMs

8.1 Hardware Limitations and Noise

Qubit coherence, gate integrity, and quantum volume are all severely limited in NISQ-era quantum computers. The majority of QSVM implementations need careful manipulation of entangled states and numerous layers of quantum gates. Sadly, noise buildup in multi-qubit systems makes it challenging to maintain quantum information over time, which can result in misclassification or erroneous kernel estimate. The component of many QSVM models is the quantum kernel estimation subroutine. It computes inner products between high-dimensional quantum states. Reliable estimate becomes more challenging when shot noise and decoherence are present. From these restrictions, QSVMs cannot be used in production-level or real-time settings.

8.2 Data Encoding and Feature Mapping

Data encoding, or converting classical data into quantum states, is an essential stage in every QSVM model. Circuit depths or gate counts that scale negatively with input size are frequently necessary for effectively mapping high-dimensional vectors into a quantum state utilizing amplitude encoding, angle encoding, or basis encoding.

Additionally, creating a non-trivial feature map—a transformation that embeds classical data into a Hilbert space where it becomes linearly separable—is frequently the key to achieving the quantum advantage. It is an open research topic to design such expressive and implementable quantum feature maps. The advantages of employing QSVMs over their classical equivalents may be negated by poorly selected maps that impair performance or fail to generalize.

8.3 Interpretability and Model Transparency

QSVMs have interpretability problems like many other quantum machine learning models. The weight and support vectors in traditional SVMs offer information about the decision limits and significance of the features. However, QSVMs use quantum amplitudes to compute the decision function in a high dimensional Hilbert space, which makes it challenging to track the behavior of the model or derive rules that are intelligible to humans. Adoption is significantly hampered by QSVMs' black-box character in fields where model openness is essential, including healthcare, finance, or law [19]. There are currently few tools available for visualizing or analyzing learnt quantum models in the still-emerging subject of interpretable quantum learning.

8.4 Quantum–Classical Integration

In a hybrid framework, QSVMs are usually built using quantum subroutines (e.g., for kernel estimation or state preparation) working alongside classical optimization methods. Nevertheless, the necessary transmission of measurement findings from quantum circuits to conventional processors, known as the quantum–classical communication bottleneck, slows down the learning pipeline as a whole. With variational QSVMs, where every optimization iteration necessitates several quantum circuit assessments, this back-and-forth communication becomes particularly difficult. Practical obstacles to training scalability include the overhead and latency of interacting with quantum technology.

8.5 Limited Theoretical Guarantees and Benchmarks

Although several research imply that, under specified circumstances, QSVMs can achieve quantum speedup, these assertions are frequently problem-specific and rely on idealized conditions (e.g., no noise, complete state access, accurate encoding). For general-purpose classification problems, strong complexity-theoretic constraints demonstrating consistent exponential advantage are still lacking.

Furthermore, using real-world datasets, QSVMs have not yet been able to consistently beat neural networks or traditional SVMs. Benchmarks derived from artificial or toy datasets might not accurately represent real-world feasibility.

Standardized datasets, metrics, and replicable procedures for assessing QSVM performance across domains are currently lacking in the field.

9. Practical Challenges in QSVM Deployment

9.1 Lack of Scalable Tooling and Ecosystem

Although frameworks like TensorFlow Quantum, PennyLane, and IBM Qiskit have sped up prototyping, they are still in the early stages of development and do not yet provide production-ready tools for large-scale QSVM deployment. It is not easy to integrate QSVMs into cloud infrastructures, automated machine learning (AutoML) systems, or current machine learning pipelines.

Quantum developers might not be comfortable with traditional machine learning methods, while data scientists sometimes lack quantum understanding. The actual use of QSVMs in industry and collaborative development are hampered by this skills mismatch.

9.2 Cost of Accessing Quantum Hardware

It is still costly and limited to run QSVMs on real quantum devices, whether through proprietary platforms or cloud access. The majority of users depend on simulators, but as the number of qubits rises, they fast become computationally unfeasible. QSVM testing is made more difficult by limitations on job queueing, shot limits, and execution time, even with quantum cloud services.

9.3 Ethical and Regulatory Considerations

Ethical issues surface when quantum machine learning penetrates delicate fields including autonomous systems, medical diagnostics, and security. The lack of standardized testing and the opacity of QSVMs raise concerns about accountability, fairness, and prejudice. Frameworks for auditing or certifying quantum-based AI systems have not yet been established by regulatory agencies [20].

10. Future Prospects for QSVMs

Notwithstanding present drawbacks, a number of theoretical and technical developments point to a bright future for QSVMs.

10.1 Quantum Hardware Development

As quantum processors keep growing, decoherence and gate error issues will be significantly decreased, resulting in fault-tolerant quantum computers. Superconducting qubits, topological qubits, and photonic quantum computing are examples of new systems that show signs of greater connectivity, longer coherence durations, and reliability. Due to these developments, QSVMs will be able to exploit deeper and more expressive quantum circuits.

10.2 New Feature Maps and Quantum Kernels

One of the most fascinating research approaches is to design quantum kernels that are tailored to a given situation and outperform conventional kernels. For instance, in quantum Hilbert spaces, separability may be improved by using quantum-enhanced Gaussian kernels and Fourier feature maps. The class of quantum kernels is difficult to reproduce in a classical context. New domain-aware quantum feature maps will enable QSVMs to address practical problems outside the purview of traditional SVMs.

10.3 Variational Algorithms and Error Mitigation

More accurate results may now be achieved even with noisy hardware because of quantum error mitigation approaches including zero-noise extrapolation, probabilistic error cancellation, and error-aware training. By using trainable quantum circuits, genetic QSVMs provide flexibility and resilience, enabling models to adjust even in the face of faulty quantum operations. Further research is being done on hybrid optimization techniques, such as quantum-assisted stochastic gradient descent, to enhance convergence and speed up learning.

10.4 Quantum Cloud Platform Integration

Developer kits, simulators, and APIs designed specifically for QML workloads enable information technology (IT) behemoths like IBM, Google, and Amazon to quickly build quantum cloud ecosystems. When paired with traditional models and pipelines, these platforms should provide scalable and simply accessible settings for QSVM training and implementation. As quantum computing becomes more accessible, it may be integrated into cloud-native machine learning processes, allowing for more extensive testing and use.

10.5 Standardization and Benchmarks

Two projects that will help track development, identify bottlenecks, and foster community consensus on what constitutes a significant quantum advantage are QML benchmarks and hybrid challenge contests. Establishing benchmark suites, public datasets, and assessment procedures for QSVMs and other quantum models is becoming more and more popular in the QML community. Using the rich expressiveness of Hilbert spaces and quantum entanglement to tackle challenging classification tasks, QSVMs are a daring expansion of conventional SVMs into the quantum world. Even though they are still in their infancy, QSVMs have opened up exciting possibilities for hybrid intelligence and computational speedup. These days, they have inefficient data encoding, interpretability gaps, and noise susceptibility, which emphasizes the need for ongoing advancements in quantum theory, software, and hardware [21]. However, QSVMs may transition from theoretical concepts to useful tools incorporated into next-generation AI systems as the quantum environment changes and cooperation frameworks change. Their capacity to offer quantum-enhanced learning points in a promising direction needs further investigation, particularly in structured fields like materials science, biology, and cryptography. The biggest challenge and opportunity confronting QSVMs is making the connection between quantum theory and practical AI applications.

Despite these strong use cases, a number of obstacles prevent QSVMs from being widely used:

Limited Qubit Count: Only small-scale implementations of NISQ are supported by existing devices.

Quantum Noise: Gate malfunctions and decoherence can affect actual quantum machines.

Kernel Expressivity vs Overfitting: If quantum kernels are not appropriately regularized, they may overfit tiny datasets.

However, QSVMs should be useful in solving issues at the industrial level as technology and quantum error correction advance. Their application will be further enhanced by the development of quantum feature engineering approaches, hybrid optimization frameworks, and hardware-efficient Ansa. The adaptive kernel selection that occurs during training is known as quantum kernel learning.

Hybrid QSVMs: Integrate quantum classification with traditional preprocessing (like PCA). The term "quantum federated learning" describes safe distributed quantum learning models.

Error-Resilient QSVMs: For more trustworthy inference, employ quantum error mitigation.

Quantum AutoML: Automate circuit structure and hyperparameter analysis.

11. Conclusion

Quantum support vector machines are cutting-edge computing. They categorize using quantum computing and SVM. QSVMs can assess complex decision constraints, unlike classical methods. Quantum circuits bring classical data into Hilbert spaces. These powers originate from variational quantum models. Quantum kernels can be classified and found using circuits. Inner products are computed quickly in quantum space. QSVMs improve data representation with quantum parallelism and entanglement. Quantum computer classification and generalization for high-dimensional or non-linear datasets may improve. Quantum SVMs can efficiently analyze large datasets in quantum chemistry, bioinformatics, image recognition, financial modeling, and cybersecurity. These challenges go beyond standard SVMs. QSVMs are complicated for several reasons. Current quantum devices are limited by NISQ. Qubits are absent, but sound and coherence temporarily appear. Researchers are reducing overfitting and enhancing quantum feature mapping for quantum-enhanced models. Quantum machine learning can scale with larger quantum volumes, error-corrected qubits, and hybrid quantum-classical algorithms. In this chapter, QSVM design, mathematics, and use are extensively covered. This showed how quantum computing uses QSVMs for real-world applications. QSVMs will be essential in quantum machine learning due to technology. They solve problems faster and better with larger cohorts. QSVMs enable quantum-era AI, especially with quantum computers so prevalent.

References

[1] Havlíček, V., et al. "Supervised learning with quantum-enhanced feature spaces," *Nature*, vol. 567, no. 7747, pp. 209–212, 2019, https://doi.org/10.1038/s41586-019-0980-2.

[2] Schuld, M. and Killoran, N. "Quantum machine learning in feature Hilbert spaces," *Physical Review Letters*, vol. 122, no. 4, p. 040504, 2019.

[3] Biamonte, J., et al. "Quantum machine learning," *Nature*, vol. 549, no. 7671, pp. 195–202, 2017.

[4] Benedetti, M., et al. "Parameterized quantum circuits as machine learning models," *Quantum Science and Technology*, vol. 4, no. 4, p. 043001, 2019.

[5] Mitarai, K., et al., "Quantum circuit learning," *Physical Review A*, vol. 98, no. 3, 032309, 2018.

[6] Qiskit Machine Learning Documentation, IBM Research, 2023, https://qiskit.org.

[7] Schuld, M., Bocharov, A., Svore, K.M., and Wiebe, N. "Circuit-centric quantum classifiers," *Physical Review A*, vol. 101, no. 3, p. 032308, 2020.

[8] Tripathi, R. "Statistical analysis of industrial activities using machine learning techniques," in *Transforming Industries*, ed. A. Kalra, S. Rani, R. Kumar, and A. A. Elngar, CRC Press, Taylor and Francis Group, 2025, pp. 127–136, 10.1201/9781003538271-11.

[9] Rebentrost, P., Mohseni, M., and Lloyd, S. "Quantum support vector machine for big data classification," *Physical Review Letters*, vol. 113, no. 13, p. 130503, 2014.

[10] Johansson, M., et al. "Evaluation of quantum kernels for machine learning," *Machine Learning: Science and Technology*, vol. 3, no. 1, p. 015002, 2022.

[11] Bravo-Prieto, C. et al. "Variational quantum linear solver," *npj Quantum Information*, vol. 6, no. 1, pp. 1–11, 2020.

[12] Cerezo, M. "Variational quantum algorithms," *Nature Reviews Physics*, vol. 3, no. 9, pp. 625–644, 2021.

[13] Kandala, A. "Hardware-efficient variational quantum eigensolver," *Nature*, vol. 549, no. 7671, pp. 242–246, 2017.

[14] Schuld, M. *Machine Learning with Quantum Computers*, Springer.

[15] Mari, A., et al. "Transfer learning in hybrid classical–quantum neural networks," *Quantum*, vol. 4, p. 340, 2020

[16] Ker, J., Wang, L., Rao, J., and Lim, T. "Deep learning applications in medical image analysis," *IEEE Access*, vol. 6, 9375–9389, 2017.

[17] Sutter, D.F. and Strauss, B.P. "Next generation high energy physics colliders: Technical challenges and prospects," *IEEE Transactions on Applied Superconductivity*, vol. 10, no. 1, 33–43, 2022.

[18] Patel, N.R. and Kumar, S. "Wireless sensor networks' challenges and future prospects," in *2018 International Conference on System Modeling & Advancement in Research Trends (SMART)*, IEEE, 2018, pp. 60–65.

[19] Fan, F.L., Xiong, J., Li, M. and Wang G. "On interpretability of artificial neural networks: A survey," *IEEE Transactions on Radiation and Plasma Medical Sciences*, vol. 5, no. 6, pp. 741–760, 2021.

[20] Lamichhane, P., and Rawat, D.B. "Quantum machine learning: recent advances, challenges and perspectives," *IEEE Access*, vol. 13, pp. 94057–94105, 2025
[21] Ravi, G.S., Smith, K.N., Gokhale, P., Mari, A., Earnest, N., Javadi-Abhari, A., and Chong, F.T. "Vaqem: A variational approach to quantum error mitigation," in *2022 IEEE International Symposium on High-Performance Computer Architecture (HPCA)*, IEEE, 2022, pp. 288–303.

4 Quantum Support Vector Machines (QSVMs) and Their Applications

Bharati Ainapure[1*], Sonali Butad[2] and Komal Agarwal[3]

Quantum support vector machines (QSVMs) blend the interesting worlds of quantum computing and machine learning, offering fresh approaches for tackling complex classification problems in high-dimensional and non-linear data spaces. This chapter provides a comprehensive exploration of QSVMs, beginning with the fundamentals of quantum computing concepts such as qubits, superposition, and entanglement, which enable quantum algorithms to surpass classical computational limits. Next, we look at how QSVMs are mathematically expressed, highlighting the use of kernel techniques and quantum feature maps to embed classical data into exponentially huge Hilbert spaces. The implementation of QSVMs using frameworks like Qiskit, PennyLane, and TensorFlow Quantum is discussed in detail, accompanied by code examples and case studies, including binary classification on the two moons dataset. Applications of QSVMs across domains such as healthcare, finance, cybersecurity, natural language processing, materials science, and climate sustainability are highlighted, demonstrating their broad relevance. The chapter also addresses challenges related to noise, scalability, and hybrid integration in the noisy intermediate-scale quantum (NISQ) era, and explores future directions involving error correction, deep learning integration, and cloud-based deployment. Together, these insights illustrate QSVMs' potential as a transformative tool in next-generation machine learning.

1. Introduction

Machine learning, a subset of artificial intelligence (AI) is an emerging field powered with wide range of applications including image recognition and

[1] Associate Professor, Department of Computer Engineering, Vishwakarma University, Pune, Maharashtra, India.
ORCID ID: 0000-0002-2354-5738

[2] Assistant Professor, Department of Computer Engineering, Shah and Anchor Kutchhi Engineering College, Mumbai, India.
ORCID ID: 0000-0001-5352-4009

[3] Research Fellow, Department of Computer Engineering, Vishwakarma University, Pune, Maharashtra, India.
ORCID ID: 0000-0002-9120-0029
E-mail: sonalibhutad@gmail.com[2]; komalgbansal@gmail.com

* Corresponding author: ainapuressa@gmail.com

DOI: 10.1201/9781003646068-4

personalized medicine. Applications like recommender systems, prediction models are built using different machine learning algorithms. Support vector machines (SVMs) emerged to be powerful supervised learning models for classification and regression problems. Behind the construction of the hyperplanes in SVM, the mathematical equation that is involved is very strong in categorizing data into different classes, maximizing the margins between them [1] [2]. The kernel trick is a technique used by SVM to define the hyperplane. To handle linear and non-linear data, respectively, there are two kinds of kernel functions: linear and non-linear.

Advantages of SVM include the following:

- It overcomes the problem of high dimensionality, particularly when mapping input data points to available labels [3].
- It exhibits discriminant classification for a small sample size [4].

Despite its advantages, classical SVM has limitations when dealing with high-dimensional, complex datasets. SVM suffers from the phenomenon known as the "curse of dimensionality" [5]. In this, a kernel maps the input data into higher dimensional spaces. However, as the data size and dimensionality increase, the computational cost also grows exponentially [6]. Therefore, there should be some advanced technique that can handle this issue.

The potential solution to the aforementioned issue lies in quantum computing. Quantum computers provide us quantum mechanisms such as superposition and entanglement. These mechanisms are able to perform computations on large-scale data by interacting with classical machines [7]. Quantum support vector machines (QSVMs), a part of quantum computing, are hybrid quantum–classical algorithms that exploit quantum feature spaces and quantum kernels, promising exponential speedups for certain classification tasks. The research of QSVMs is still at a nascent stage, primarily limited by the current state of quantum hardware. The combination of quantum computing and machine learning can create potential transformative applications in healthcare, finance, cybersecurity, sustainability, and beyond [8] [9].

This chapter explores the foundations, formulations, implementations, and applications of QSVMs, while addressing their challenges and future research directions.

1.1 Classical vs Quantum SVMs

Table 4.1 summarizes how QSVMs differ from classical SVM. Traditional SVMs operate on the foundation of binary computing, but QSVMs operate on the concept of quantum principles such as superposition and entanglement to perform computations. Scalability is a challenge with SVMs handling with complex datasets, whereas QSVMs can potentially achieve exponential speedup. QSVMs require specialized quantum hardware for data processing, but classical SVMs run on conventional central processing units (CPUs) and graphics processing unit (GPUs). The types of problems that they can be applied to are also different:

classical SVMs are widely used in classification in general, while QSVMs are better recommended for complex, high-dimensional problems. Finally, classical SVMs are mature and well-established in practice, whereas QSVMs remain in the research stage, with early adoption in emerging quantum technologies [10] [11].

Table 4.1 Comparison between classical SVM and quantum SVM.

Aspect	*Classical SVMs*	*Quantum SVMs (QSVMs)*
Computation Basis	Operates on classical bits using traditional algorithms	Operates on quantum bits (qubits) using quantum principles like superposition and entanglement
Kernel Function	Uses classical kernels (linear, polynomial, radial basis function (RBF), sigmoid, etc.) to transform data into higher dimensions	Uses quantum kernels based on quantum feature maps, leveraging Hilbert space for complex data representation
Scalability	Limited by computational resources; training complexity grows with dataset size	Potential exponential speedup in handling large-scale and high-dimensional datasets
Optimization	Relies on convex optimization techniques (quadratic programming)	Uses quantum algorithms (e.g., quantum approximate optimization algorithm) to find optimal hyperplanes
Data Handling	Handles structured/tabular data efficiently	Suitable for complex, high-dimensional, and unstructured data (e.g., chemistry, genomics, finance)
Resource Requirement	Requires high memory and CPU/GPU power for big datasets	Requires quantum hardware or simulators; still constrained by qubit quality and noise
Accuracy	Well-established, stable, and widely used with proven performance	Promising accuracy for certain problems, but still experimental due to hardware limitations
Applications	Image classification, bioinformatics, natural language processing (NLP), fraud detection, etc.	Quantum chemistry, drug discovery, optimization problems, advanced pattern recognition
Maturity	Fully developed, robust libraries available (scikit-learn, LIBSVM, etc.)	Emerging field; research and pilot applications with limited large-scale deployments

2. Mathematical Formulation of QSVM

QSVMs are formulated mathematically based on the classical SVM. In addition, quantum mechanics is used to redefine data representation and kernel computation in QSVM. Optimization problems can be formulated in traditional SVM using equation (1):

$$Minimize: \left(\frac{1}{2}\right) \| w \|^2 + C\sum \xi_i$$

where ξ_i is a slack variable, b is the bias value, w is the weight vector, C is the penalty, and $\theta(x_i)$ is a feature map, which will be mapped to higher dimensional space.

In QSVMs, the central idea is to replace the classical kernel function K with a quantum kernel, as defined in equation (2):

$$K(x_i, x_j) = |<\psi(x_i) \mid \psi(x_j)>|^2$$

Here, $\psi(x_i)$ is the quantum state obtained by applying a parameterized quantum circuit (also known as a feature map) to the input data x. The overlap between quantum states $<\psi(x_i)|\psi(x_j)>$ is computed using quantum devices, providing access to correlations that may be intractable for classical methods.

The decision function for classification in QSVMs is known as Hilbert space and is presented in equation (3). This space is exponentially large compared to classical feature spaces.

$$f(x) = sign\left(\sum_{i-1}^{m} \propto_i y_i K_Q(x_i, x)\right) + \mathrm{b}$$

where $\propto_i$ are Lagrange multipliers obtained by solving the dual optimization problem. In practice, hybrid algorithms are often used, where the quantum computer is responsible for evaluating the kernel matrix and a classical optimizer solves the quadratic programming problem.

This formulation highlights the hybrid nature of QSVMs. While quantum circuits encode and compute similarities, classical solvers handle optimization. As quantum devices mature, more components of this pipeline may shift to the quantum domain, potentially offering exponential advantages in computation.

Thus, the mathematical foundation of QSVMs not only extends classical SVM theory but also demonstrates how quantum feature spaces can significantly enhance the representational power of learning algorithms.

3. Hybrid QSVM

The Hybrid QSVM is used for classification problems more efficiently than traditional methods. This is blend of both quantum and classical computing methods. The technique used in hybrid QSVM uses larger Hilbert spaces to represent data exponentially through quantum feature maps, while relying on classical optimization algorithms to confirm stable training and scalability [12].

The hybrid QSVM architecture, as illustrated in Figure 4.1, demonstrates how quantum and classical computational components are integrated into a single pipeline to perform classification tasks. The flowchart highlights the structured integration of data preprocessing, quantum embedding, kernel estimation, classical

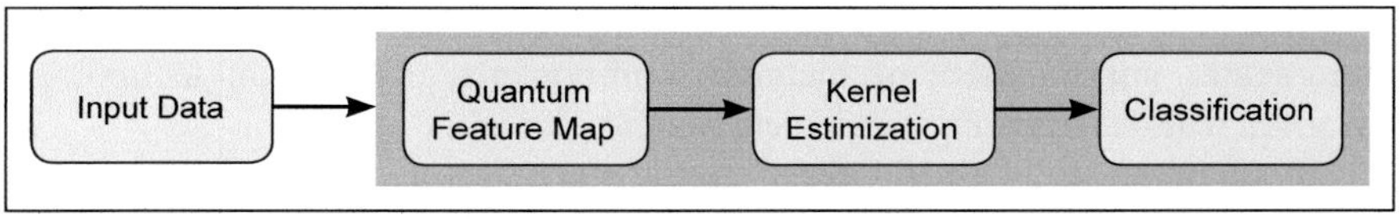

Fig. 4.1 Hybrid QSVM flowchart illustrating the pipeline of data classification using a quantum-enhanced approach.

optimization, and classification, underscoring how hybrid quantum–classical systems are paving the way for the future of machine learning.

The input data that the workflow of our methodology uses must be pre-processed and encoded in a quantum embedding friendly representation. The quantum feature map takes this input and encodes classical data into high-dimensional quantum Hilbert space representations. In this phase, the special features of quantum states like superposition and entanglement are used to capture correlations in data that are difficult to represent properly with classical kernels.

The next stage of the architecture is known as the kernel estimation. This starts after applying the quantum feature mapping that evaluates the similarity between pairs of data points in Hilbert space with the help of a quantum computer. This stage is very important as SVM creates optimal decision boundaries using kernel function, which encapsulates the geometry of the feature space. Unlike classical kernels, which are limited by the complexity of their functional forms (such as linear, polynomial, or RBF), quantum kernels can implicitly represent far more complex structures without requiring explicit feature expansions.

The optimization process is carried out by passing the results of the quantum kernel estimation to the classical part of the pipeline. During optimization optimal set of support vectors, weights, and bias that define the separating hyperplane are determined by employing classical optimization algorithms, such as quadratic programming. The three-component combination feature mapping, kernel evaluation, and classical computation for optimization ensures that the hybrid model remains practical and scalable on near-term noisy intermediate-scale quantum (NISQ) devices.

In the classification stage, which is the last stage of the architecture, optimized hyperplane parameters are used and new input data is mapped through the same quantum feature map and kernel estimation process. The decision function determines the class label based on the learned boundary. This hybrid approach allows the QSVM to tap into quantum computing's potential for better data representation and separation while maintaining the stability of classical optimization techniques.

The hybrid QSVM is important because it has the ability to solve issues that traditional approaches cannot. In fields such as genomics, drug discovery, finance, and high-energy physics, where the data is often complex and is stored in high-dimensional spaces, the ability of quantum feature maps to explore these spaces efficiently offers a considerable advantage [13]. Furthermore, the modular architecture of the hybrid QSVM pipeline increases flexibility by enabling the incremental improvement of quantum components as quantum technology advances without requiring a complete system redesign.

In summary, the hybrid QSVM architecture demonstrates a practical and useful way of implementing quantum machine learning. By combining quantum-enhanced kernels with classical optimization, this approach maximizes the advantages of both paradigms.

4. Essentials of Quantum Computing for Machine Learning

QSVMs leverage quantum computing in machine learning models to more effectively represent and modify data in advance for processing. Quantum computing brings a fresh perspective to problem-solving by using the principles of quantum physics to process information. It opens up interesting new possibilities since it excels in handling complex data relationships, high-dimensional spaces, and tricky optimization challenges. The main ideas of quantum computing that underpin these kinds of applications are presented in this section.

4.1 Qubits, Superposition, and Entanglement

The qubit is nothing but the quantum analogue of a classical bit. It is fundamental to quantum computing. A qubit can exist in a superposition, which is a simultaneous blend of the two states, in contrast to classical bits, which are restricted to discrete states of 0 or 1 as shown in Figure 4.2. A qubit state can be expressed mathematically as follows:

$$\psi >= \alpha|0 + \beta|1 >$$

where α and β are probability amplitudes, which are complex integers. The fact that the system's capacity to process information increases exponentially with the number of qubits is one of the most fascinating aspects of superposition. This implies that quantum computers can explore a huge solution space all at once, in parallel—something classical computers really struggle with. Then there is entanglement, another key pillar of quantum mechanics. This happens when two or more qubits get so intertwined that even if they are far apart physically, changing the state of one instantly affects the other. Consequently, quantum algorithms are capable of discerning and elucidating profoundly interconnected patterns or latent correlations within datasets—structures that classical algorithms may either fail to detect or require prohibitively high computational resources to process.

Entanglement and superposition work together to give quantum computers their advantage [14] as shown in Figure 4.3. Unlike conventional approaches, they allow algorithms to investigate and work with intricate patterns in a fundamentally different way. In machine learning, this implies that quantum models could provide novel information, particularly in fields with big, structured, or highly correlated datasets.

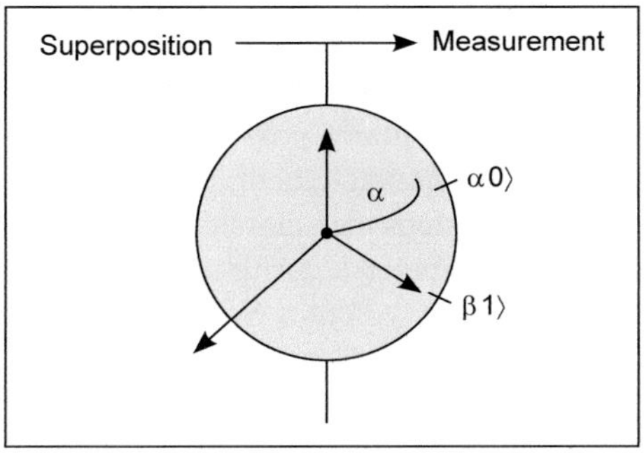

Fig. 4.2 Qubit in quantum computing.

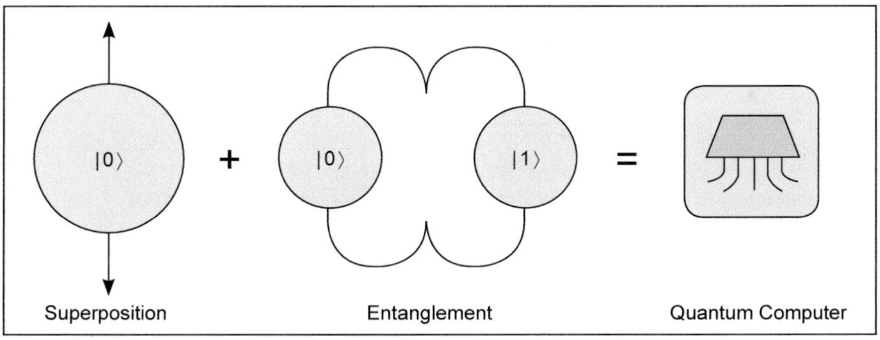

Fig. 4.3 Entanglement and superposition work together to give quantum computers.

4.2 Quantum Gates, Circuits, and Measurement

Qubits are manipulated by quantum gates through unitary transformations, serving as the building blocks of quantum algorithms [15]. Sequences of gates form quantum circuits as shown in Figure 4.4. These circuits' computation performance changes with the changes in qubit states. The quantum gates preserve and reverse the information stored in them. The qubit state turns into classical outcome in terms of 0 and 1 at the end of the computation, making the process probabilistic. Multiple runs of the circuit are often required to obtain statistically reliable results.

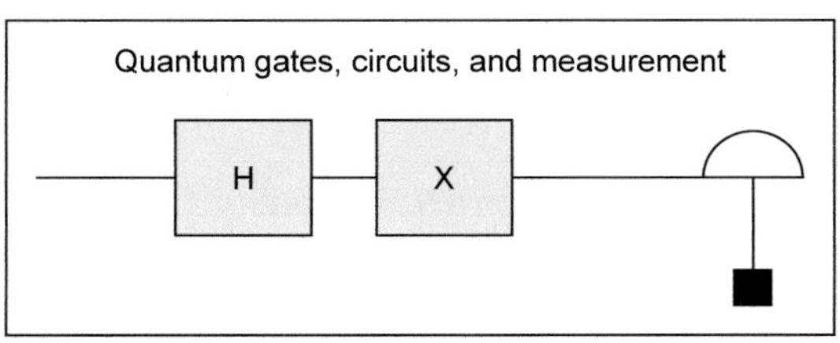

Fig. 4.4 Sequences of gates form quantum circuits.

4.3 Quantum Parallelism and Speedup Potential

Quantum parallelism is one of the features of quantum computers, in which superposition allows processing many possible states simultaneously. When combined with interference and entanglement, quantum algorithms can evaluate complex computations in fewer steps than classical methods. For example, Grover and Shor are two quantum computer algorithms. Grover's approach speeds up unstructured search quadratically, whereas Shor's algorithm speeds up integer factorization exponentially. In machine learning, this parallelism can be harnessed for tasks such as kernel estimation and optimization, which are computationally demanding on classical systems as shown in Figure 4.5 [16].

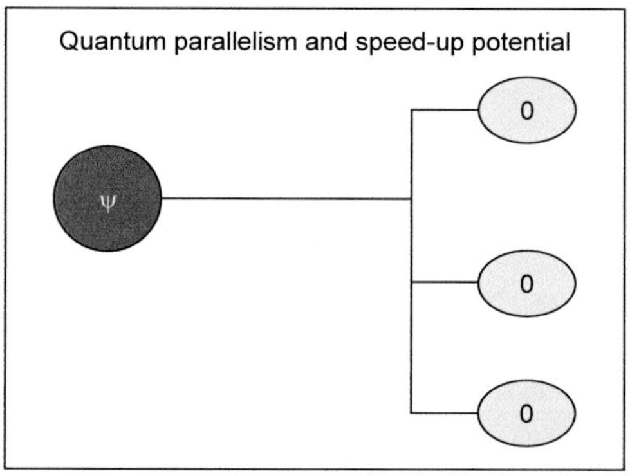

Fig. 4.5 Quantum parallelism and speedup potential.

5. Why Quantum Computing Benefits ML Models

Machine learning detects patterns in data, frequently by exploring feature spaces—mathematical landscapes in which each point represents a potential data pattern. The challenge is that as data complexity increases, these spaces get larger and more difficult to navigate for traditional computers. This is where quantum computing comes in, with some intriguing advantages:

- **Expanding the Space with Quantum Feature Maps:** Classical data can be compared to dots on a flat piece of paper. It can be quite challenging to distinguish certain patterns using a straight line. Like pouring air into a balloon, quantum feature maps extend the flat sheet into a much larger, multi-dimensional universe. All of a sudden, only one cut is sufficient to separate those same dots.
- **More Advanced Quantum Kernel Similarity Checks:** Machine learning frequently starts with comparing how similar two data points are. Standard tools, such as linear or polynomial formulas, are used in classical procedures for this, although they may overlook subtle correlations. The model has a more

sophisticated sense of similarity because quantum kernels enable comparisons in ways that reveal hidden relationships.

- **Richer Data Representations through Superposition and Entanglement**: Classical computing lacks certain features that quantum physics provides. Entanglement connects qubits so that a change in one immediately impacts the other, and superposition allows qubits to exist in several states simultaneously. Because of these features, quantum models are able to represent data in a deeper and more comprehensive way than classical models.

These benefits make quantum-enhanced algorithms, such as the QSVM, attractive for areas with high-dimensional and complex data. Consider the sectors of cybersecurity, where detecting unusual irregularities may prevent an attack, healthcare, where experts review massive genetic information, and finance, where minute patterns can be the difference between profit and loss. Machine learning powered by quantum mechanics has the potential to accelerate, enhance accuracy, and bring fresh insights into a variety of tasks.

6. Implementation of QSVM

QSVM can be implemented using several Python frameworks such as Qiskit, PennyLane, and TensorFlow Quantum. Each of these frameworks explained next.

6.1 Qiskit

Qiskit is a framework developed by International Business Machines (IBM). It provides the most robust environments for implementing QSVMs. Quantum kernels are constructed in the Qiskit Machine Learning module using built-in tools. One such parameterized circuit used is ZZFeatureMap to create kernels [17]. Qiskit operated in the QSVM workflow:

1. Classical data in encoded into quantum states using feature maps.
2. Kernel matrices are evaluated through state fidelities.
3. This kernel matrix is fed into classical SVM using Scikit-learn library.

QSVM kernels can be built and executed on IBM's cloud-based quantum hardware as well as on local simulators thanks to the Qiskit framework. Because of its adaptability, scientists can test their theories on real quantum devices rather than merely theoretical ones. Qiskit has circuit-transpilation tools and error-mitigation strategies that modify quantum kernels for more stable performance in order to address the constraints of today's NISQ systems. For example, researchers may utilize Qiskit to create a Gram matrix of quantum state overlaps and input it into a pre-computed kernel support vector classifier (SVC), allowing for binary and multi-class classification. Qiskit provides a viable environment for hybrid QSVM experiments by seamlessly integrating with Python machine learning modules. It strikes a compromise between quantum kernel computing and conventional optimization.

6.2 PennyLane

Xanadu created the PennyLane framework with the goal of advancing hybrid quantum–classical kernel learning. This system uses parameterized quantum circuits, also known as variational circuits, to create QSVMs. This forms the backbone of the machine learning pipeline. The smooth integration of PennyLane with well-known deep learning tools like PyTorch, TensorFlow, and JAX is one of its unique characteristics. This allows for the fine-tuning of quantum feature maps alongside classical parameters, as gradients can flow through quantum nodes just like they do in classical neural networks. These setups are often called variational quantum classifiers (VQCs). They provide a practical benefit in that they can train QSVM-like models without explicitly computing large kernel matrices, which are often costly to manage.

Furthermore, VQCs' plugin architecture allows users to switch easily between simulators and hardware backend such as IBM Quantum, IonQ, or Rigetti without code changes. This flexibility makes PennyLane a preferred choice for QSVM research when the goal is to explore end-to-end differentiable workflows or to test across multiple quantum devices [18].

6.3 TensorFlow Quantum (TFQ)

TensorFlow supports QSVM implantation using an extended framework known as TensorFlow Quantum (TFQ). This framework was developed by Google to support QSVM. This integrates quantum circuits as differentiable layers within deep learning models. TFQ allows QSVMs to compute kernel values on encoded data using quantum feature maps as Keras layers. Such kernels are used for task classification by embedding them into hybrid neural network architectures or by training a classical SVM. TFQ is particularly powerful for variational hybrid QSVMs as backpropagation through quantum circuits are performed to optimize quantum parameters alongside neural network weights. The integration with TensorFlow means researchers can exploit GPU acceleration, visualization tools, and scalable pipelines. While TFQ is more research-oriented and less hardware-flexible than PennyLane, it provides a unique advantage by embedding QSVMs directly into existing deep learning workflows, enabling hybrid quantum–classical models that combine quantum kernels with deep learning layers for advanced applications [19].

7. Example: Binary Classification Using QSVM

The code shown in Figure 4.6 demonstrates binary classification using Qiskit's QSVM implementation with a simple dataset.

The Python code in Figure 4.6 demonstrates the implementation of QSVM using Qiskit Machine Learning in combination with classical tools from scikit-learn. The non-linear dataset two moons is applied to implement QSVM. In

```
from qiskit import BasicAer
from qiskit.utils import QuantumInstance
from qiskit.circuit.library import ZZFeatureMap
from qiskit_machine_learning.kernels import QuantumKernel
from sklearn.datasets import make_moons
from sklearn.model_selection import train_test_split
from sklearn.preprocessing import StandardScaler
from sklearn.svm import SVC
from sklearn.metrics import accuracy_score

# Generate data
X, y = make_moons(n_samples=200, noise=0.2, random_state=42)
y = [1 if label == 1 else -1 for label in y]  # labels {-1, +1}
X = StandardScaler().fit_transform(X)
X_train, X_test, y_train, y_test = train_test_split(X, y, test_size=0.3, random_state=42)

# Feature map
feature_map = ZZFeatureMap(feature_dimension=2, reps=2, entanglement='linear')

# Quantum kernel
backend = BasicAer.get_backend('qasm_simulator')
qi = QuantumInstance(backend, shots=1024)
qkernel = QuantumKernel(feature_map=feature_map, quantum_instance=qi)

K_train = qkernel.evaluate(x_vec=X_train)
K_test = qkernel.evaluate(x_vec=X_test, y_vec=X_train)

# Classical SVM with quantum kernel
clf = SVC(kernel='precomputed')
clf.fit(K_train, y_train)
pred = clf.predict(K_test)

print("Accuracy:", accuracy_score(y_test, pred))
```

Fig. 4.6 Binary classification Python code using Qiskit's QSVM implementation.

such cases classification is difficult if implemented by using a simple linear classifier. The dataset is divided into two sets, namely, training and testing (HL, ZZ) (StandardScaler). Then, we build a quantum feature map (ZZFeatureMap) that encodes classical data into quantum states. Using this mapping, the data can be mapped to higher-dimensional Hilbert space, and it is more likely that the classes will be separable linearly in the higher-dimensional space. qasm_simulator calculates the state fidelities of training data and testing data. QuantumKernel class is employed to evaluate similarities between data points, generating kernel matrices. After computing quantum kernel matrices, an SVC is employed to mark the kernel type specified as "precomputed." This ensures hybrid quantum–classical workflow by integrating classical SVM and quantum kernels. We evaluate the SVM model's ability to predict the classes in the test dataset once it has been constructed. This approach demonstrates how QSVMs can leverage quantum kernels for classification while still relying on the trusted optimization techniques of classical computing. It truly demonstrates how well quantum and conventional computers can work together.

8. Case Study: QSVM on the Two Moons Dataset

We illustrated the effectiveness of QSVMs using the two moons dataset, a widely used benchmark for evaluating non-linear classification models.

This dataset is difficult to analyze since the two classes produce interleaving crescent-shaped patterns that are not linearly separable in the original input space. This is the most suitable dataset for evaluating the capabilities of quantum-enhanced kernels, which can transform data into high-dimensional Hilbert spaces where separation is more realistic due to its structure.

To mimic the variability of real-world data, we added some random Gaussian noise to our experiment and created 200 samples using the two moons distribution, which gives us those cool crescent-shaped data clusters. We split the data into 70 percent for training and 30 percent for testing, following standard practices to keep things fair. To transform our regular data into quantum states, we used a 2-qubit ZZFeatureMap with linear entanglement and two repetitions—think of it as a way to jazz up the data by projecting it into a quantum-powered space that makes it easier to find a dividing line between classes. For calculating the quantum kernel overlaps, we relied on Qiskit's qasm_simulator, running it 1,024 times to get solid results. These kernel matrices were then fed into a classical SVC with the precomputed kernel setting turned on. To see how well the model performed, we measured its accuracy.

The results of this experiment indicate how well QSVMs can handle non-linear data structures. Figure 4.7 illustrates how QSVM (via quantum kernels) can effectively separate non-linear classes. The model showed excellent generalization, with a training accuracy of over 98 percent and a test accuracy of around 90 percent in the presence of the noise. A typical linear SVM, on the other hand, struggled significantly with a test accuracy of less than 80 percent. A standard SVM with an RBF kernel achieved roughly 92 percent accuracy, but the kernel function had to be manually created. In contrast, the QSVM relies on quantum feature maps, which naturally capture complex relationships in data, to achieve comparable performance without the requirement for explicit kernel construction.

These results highlight both the current limitations and potential of QSVMs. On the one hand, they show that quantum-enhanced kernels can disclose subtle features that classical linear models struggle to capture while maintaining an accuracy comparable to advanced classical kernels. On the other hand, the results were obtained using a simulator, and problems such as noise, decoherence, and processing complexity from kernel matrix production emerge when scaled to larger datasets or genuine hardware. Despite this, the experiment demonstrates that even at this early point in quantum computing research, QSVMs can compete with sophisticated classical models.

Overall, this case study indicates how hybrid quantum–classical operations can deliver genuine machine learning benefits. While QSVMs are not yet ready to replace classical models in production, as quantum hardware and error-correction techniques improve, their ability to generalize from sparse noisy data in high-dimensional feature spaces suggests that they may have a real part to play in real-world applications.

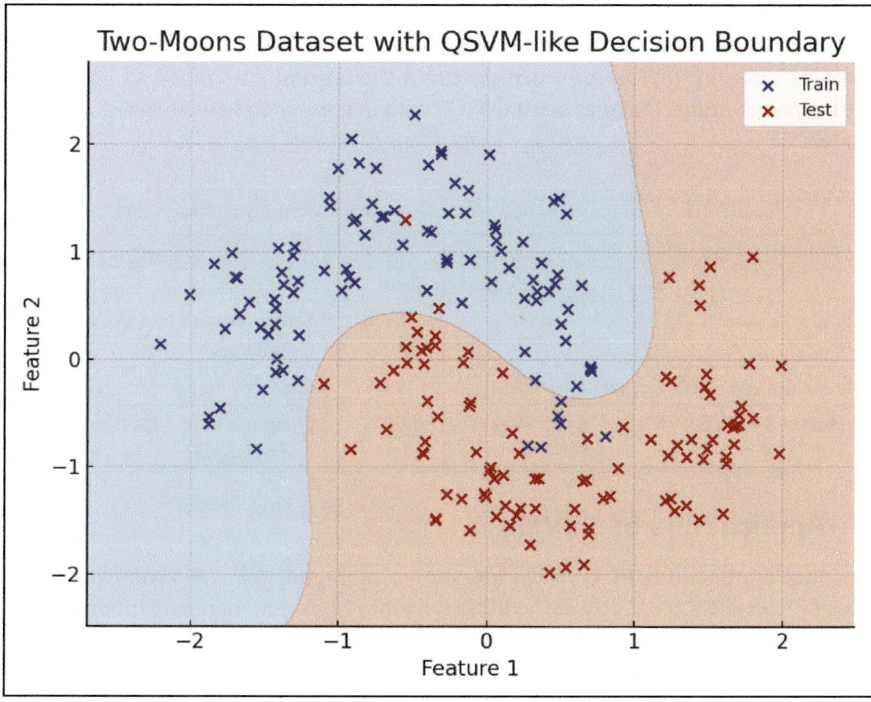

Fig. 4.7 Two moons dataset with QSVM-like decision boundary.

8.1 Comparison of Models on the Two Moons Dataset

Table 4.2 summarizes the performance of different models on the two moons dataset. It compares a classical linear SVM, a classical SVM with an RBF kernel, and the QSVM. We can clearly see how well models handle non-linear classification problems when we compare them on the traditional two moons dataset. On the training set, the conventional linear SVM achieves an accuracy of almost 90 percent; however, on the test set, its performance falls below 80 percent. This decline indicates inadequate generalization; greater errors on unseen samples result from the straight-line decision boundary's inability to capture the data's curved, crescent-like shape. A classical SVM with an RBF kernel, on the other hand, performs significantly better. Because of the RBF kernel's capacity to convert the data into a high-dimensional space, it achieves approximately 98 per cent training accuracy and 92 per cent test accuracy. This facilitates the modeling of the dataset's intricate non-linear patterns.

The QSVM obtains a good 90 percent on the test set and around 98 percent training accuracy, which is really fascinating. The QSVM demonstrates that it can use quantum feature maps to project data into high-dimensional Hilbert spaces, achieving non-linear separation without the requirement for human kernel creation. However, its performance is worse in tests as compared with the RBF kernel. This result highlights how useful quantum kernels may be as a tool for learning from complex data. Furthermore, it demonstrates the current scalability and quantum hardware constrains that may limit QSVMs when compared to well-tuned classical models.

Table 4.2 Comparison between classical SVM and quantum SVM.

Model	*Training Accuracy*	*Test Accuracy*	*Notes*
Classical Linear SVM	90%	87%	Struggles with non-linear boundaries
Classical SVM (RBF Kernel)	98%	92%	Captures non-linear structures
Quantum SVM (QSVM)	98%	90%	Quantum kernel captures rich feature spaces

9. Applications of QSVMs

Potential applications of QSVMs are shown in Figure 4.8. QSVMs extend the power of classical SVMs by embedding data into high-dimensional Hilbert spaces using quantum feature maps. This provides new opportunities across multiple domains where complex, high-dimensional patterns need to be classified [20].

9.1 Healthcare

In healthcare, QSVMs can play a transformative role in cancer detection, disease classification, and medical image analysis. By leveraging quantum kernels, QSVMs can identify subtle patterns in genomic data, magnetic resonance imaging (MRI) scans, or histopathology slides that may be missed by classical models. For example, cancer detection often requires distinguishing between healthy and malignant tissue with extremely fine boundaries—tasks well-suited to QSVMs operating in exponentially large Hilbert spaces. Beyond oncology, QSVMs can also assist in early diagnosis of neurological disorders, personalized medicine, and real-time health monitoring.

9.2 Finance

The financial industry deals with highly complex, non-linear, and noisy data. QSVMs can be used for fraud detection, credit risk modeling, and stock market prediction. Fraudulent transactions often involve irregular but intricate patterns, and QSVMs' ability to model high-dimensional feature spaces makes them

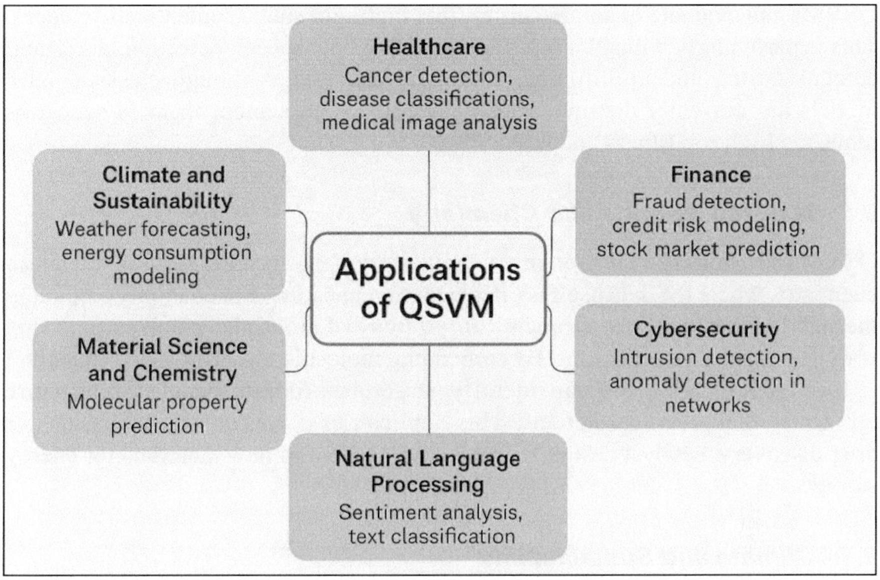

Fig. 4.8 Applications of QSVM.

ideal for anomaly detection. In credit risk assessment, QSVMs could improve classification of high-risk versus low-risk clients by processing heterogeneous data from financial histories. For algorithmic trading and stock prediction, QSVMs can potentially uncover non-linear dependencies in historical price movements, though real-world deployment still depends on quantum hardware advances.

9.3 Cybersecurity

QSVMs offer promising tools for intrusion detection and anomaly detection in networks. Traditional machine learning models in cybersecurity struggle with the growing volume and complexity of data from logs, firewalls, and sensors. Quantum kernels can capture high-dimensional correlations in this data to more effectively distinguish between normal and malicious activity. QSVM-based intrusion detection systems could adapt more rapidly to zero-day attacks and evolving threat landscapes. Additionally, anomaly detection in encrypted traffic could be enhanced by quantum feature embeddings that preserve discriminative information without requiring decryption.

9.4 Natural Language Processing (NLP)

QSVMs are useful in NLP applications like sentiment analysis and classification of texts since linguistic input is naturally high-dimensional and sparse. By encoding text embeddings (e.g., from word2vec or transformers) into quantum states,

QSVMs can evaluate quantum kernels that highlight subtle semantic differences. This is particularly valuable in applications like hate speech detection, document categorization, and multilingual sentiment analysis. Although classical NLP models are currently dominant, QSVMs could complement them in scenarios requiring high robustness and scalability.

9.5 Material Science and Chemistry

QSVMs are highly relevant in molecular property prediction and quantum chemistry, where the data itself is often quantum in nature. For example, predicting the stability, energy states, or chemical reactivity of molecules involves exploring complex quantum interactions. By embedding molecular descriptors into quantum Hilbert spaces, QSVMs can identify structure-property relationships more efficiently than classical kernels. This application is particularly important for drug discovery, catalyst design, and the development of new materials for energy storage.

9.6 Climate and Sustainability

QSVMs can support weather forecasting, energy consumption modeling, and climate change analysis. Climate and environmental data are notoriously large, non-linear, and noisy, making them difficult to model classically. QSVMs could help improve long-range weather prediction by capturing subtle atmospheric correlations. In sustainability, QSVMs could optimize smart grid energy consumption, predict renewable energy output (e.g., solar, wind), and model carbon emissions. These applications align QSVMs with global sustainability goals and green technology development.

10. Challenges and Limitations of QSVMs

While QSVMs show significant promise, their current adoption is limited by both hardware and theoretical constraints. Understanding these challenges is essential for setting realistic expectations and guiding future research. Table 4.3 summarizes challenges and possible mitigation strategies.

10.1 Hardware Constraints: Qubit Noise and Decoherence

Currently available quantum hardware is fragile, which is one of the main obstacles to the implementation of QSVMs. Qubits, the basic building blocks of quantum computers, are extremely sensitive and easily affected by noise, decoherence, or poor gate operations. Because QSVMs rely on regular quantum measurements to properly estimate kernel values, any interference or instability might distort the results and cause inconsistent or inaccurate classifications. Despite researchers working really hard at developing error-mitigation strategies, fully reliable quantum computers that can maintain a steady performance and can consistently perform at a large scale are yet to be designed.

10.2 Scalability Issues

QSVMs face a big hurdle when it comes to scaling up. Just like traditional methods that use kernels, QSVMs need to create and store a massive m × m matrix, where m is the number of training samples. This means running a quantum circuit for every possible pair of samples on quantum hardware—a task that quickly becomes overwhelming as datasets grow larger. Using QSVMs on large real-world datasets is still difficult, despite continuous advancements in quantum simulations and technology. We must discover a solution to this scalability problem if QSVMs are to be useful for companies.

10.3 Complexity of Building Quantum Kernels

Designing effective quantum feature maps and kernels is not that easy. The choice of feature map plays a big role in how well the QSVM can express and generalize patterns. Ineffective feature maps may fail to capture meaningful and important patterns in data or may lead to kernels that are difficult to interpret. Kernel engineering is a domain-specific difficulty since various application areas (such as healthcare vs. finance) could call for different encodings. Balancing circuit depth (to improve expressivity) with hardware noise constraints adds another layer of complexity.

10.4 Need for Hybrid Models in the NISQ Era

Current quantum computers fall under the NISQ category, where device noise and limited qubit counts constrain algorithmic performance. Purely quantum SVM implementations are not feasible on such hardware. Instead, hybrid quantum–classical models are necessary, where quantum devices handle kernel estimation, while classical computers perform optimization. Although this hybrid approach makes QSVMs practical in the near term, it also limits the extent of "quantum advantage" and introduces additional integration overhead.

Table 4.3 Challenges and possible mitigation strategies.

Challenge	*Description*	*Possible Mitigation Strategies*
Hardware Constraints: Qubit Noise, Decoherence	Qubits are fragile and prone to errors due to noise and decoherence, affecting kernel estimation.	Quantum error mitigation (zero-noise extrapolation, probabilistic error cancellation), development of fault-tolerant quantum computers

Contd..

Table 4.3 *Contd..*

Challenge	*Description*	*Possible Mitigation Strategies*
Scalability Issues	Computing kernel matrices requires O(m2)O(m^2) evaluations, which become infeasible for large datasets.	Approximation techniques (Nyström method), random feature embeddings, block kernel computations
Complexity of Building Quantum Kernels	Designing effective quantum feature maps is non-trivial; poor design reduces expressivity and performance.	Domain-specific feature maps, data-driven feature map selection, cross-validation and kernel alignment metrics
Need for Hybrid Models (NISQ Era)	Current hardware cannot support fully quantum SVMs; hybrid architectures are required.	Hybrid quantum–classical pipelines, variational quantum classifiers, leveraging cloud-based quantum resources for integration

11. Future Directions for QSVMs

QSVMs represent a promising frontier in quantum machine learning. However, their full potential is yet to be realized. As hardware, algorithms and integration strategies continue to evolve, several directions offer exciting opportunities for future advancements as shown in Figure 4.9.

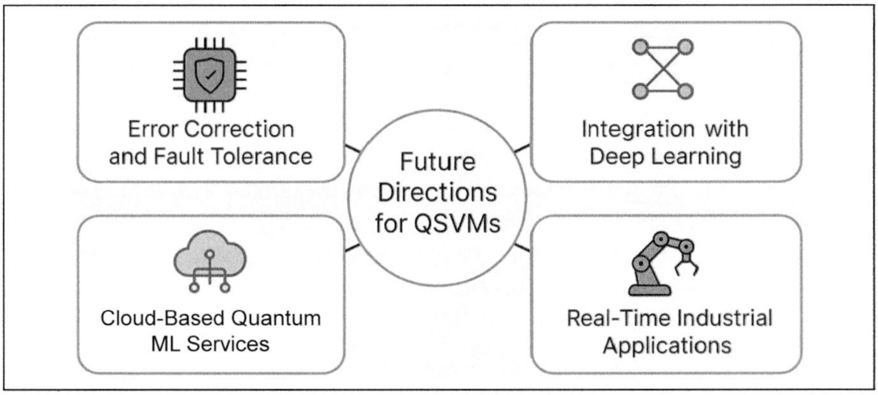

Fig. 4.9 Potential future direction of QSVM

11.1 Error Correction and Fault-Tolerant QSVM

One of the most critical milestones for the future of QSVMs is the development of error correction protocols and fault-tolerant quantum computing. The accuracy of kernel estimates is reduced by noise and decoherence in current NISQ devices. Future quantum hardware with robust error correction will ensure stable quantum kernels and more reliable classification performance. Fault-tolerant QSVMs could then operate on larger datasets and deeper circuits, paving the way for real-world industrial applications.

11.2 Integration with Deep Learning Models

QSVMs have a promising future as they integrate with deep learning models to develop powerful hybrid systems that combine the benefits of both approaches. Neural networks, for instance, can incorporate quantum-enhanced kernels to boost feature extraction and separation. Deep learning layers, on the other hand, can preprocess or refine quantum-encoded embeddings, assisting in the shaping of data before it is inputted into a quantum circuit. This combination of quantum and classical learning may open up new possibilities in fields where deep learning is already widely used, such as speech recognition, natural language processing, and medical imaging, by taking advantage of the unique structure and expressiveness of quantum feature spaces.

11.3 Cloud-Based Quantum ML Services

Cloud-based quantum machine learning platforms are also making it easier to access QSVMs. Researchers may now access quantum computers remotely thanks to services like IBM Quantum, Amazon Braket, Microsoft Azure Quantum, and Xanadu's quantum cloud. Looking ahead, platforms could offer ready-to-use QSVM modules, making it easier for researchers, students, and companies to jump in without needing deep expertise. Plus, cloud access opens the door for teams to collaborate and run meaningful experiments on real datasets, even if they do not have their own quantum hardware.

11.4 Potential for Real-Time Industrial Applications

The long-term objective is to use QSVMs in industrial real-time applications such as:

- Financial system fraud detection
- Manufacturing predictive maintenance
- Healthcare real-time medical diagnostics

In addition to accuracy, many use cases require speed and scalability. Improvements in hybrid system efficiency and quantum hardware performance will be required for QSVMs to function effectively in such demanding environments. With continued development, QSVMs may provide a viable solution to substantial, real-world challenges in sectors such as cybersecurity, logistics, and sustainability.

12. Conclusion

QSVMs are at the forefront of blending quantum computing with machine learning. They use quantum feature maps to project data into exponentially large

Hilbert spaces, building on the strong foundation of classical SVMs and enabling powerful non-linear classification with a simple architecture. QSVMs are great at tackling complex, high-dimensional data across fields like banking, healthcare, cybersecurity, material science, and climate modeling. By harnessing quantum phenomena like superposition, entanglement, and parallelism, they offer incredible potential for tackling challenging problems.

Nevertheless, the NISQ era is still under progress. Constraints such as qubit instability decoherence and scalability limits remain major challenges. On the other hand, hybrid quantum–classical models offer a practical path: kernel estimation is handled by quantum circuits, while training and optimization are handled by conventional methods. Even with today's hardware limitations, early experiments with QSVMs are showing exciting promise. This demonstrates that they are already evolving into useful tools and are not simply fascinating hypotheses. The larger AI community will be able to take use of QSVMs' full potential when quantum technology advances with improved hardware, error correction, and simple integration with deep learning. With cloud-based quantum platforms gaining in popularity, we are approaching a point when quantum-enhanced machine learning will help everyone, not just physicists. In conclusion, QSVMs are a roadmap for the evolution of AI in the quantum age, rather than merely a technological accomplishment.

References

[1] Blanco, V., Japón, A., and Puerto, J. "A mathematical programming approach to SVM-based classification with label noise," *Computers & Industrial Engineering*, vol. 172, p. 108611, 2022.

[2] Du, K.L., Jiang, B., Lu, J., Hua, J. and Swamy, M.N.S. "Exploring kernel machines and support vector machines: Principles, techniques, and future directions," *Mathematics*, vol. 12, no. 24, p. 3935, 2024.

[3] Verplancke, T. et al. "Support vector machine versus logistic regression modeling for prediction of hospital mortality in critically ill patients with haematological malignancies," *BMC Medical Informatics and Decision Making*, vol. 8, pp. 1–8, 2008.

[4] Yu, W., Liu, T., Valdez, R., Gwinn, M., and Khoury, M.J. "Application of support vector machine modeling for prediction of common diseases: The case of diabetes and pre-diabetes," *BMC Medical Informatics and Decision Making*, 2010.

[5] Haidarh, M., Mu, C., Liu, Y., and He, X. "Exploring traditional, deep learning and hybrid methods for hyperspectral image classification: A review," *Journal of Information and Intelligence*, 2025.

[6] Halder, R.K., Uddin, M.N. and Uddin, M.A. "A novel region based neighbors searching classification algorithm for big data," *International Journal of Cognitive Computing in Engineering*, vol. 6, pp. 516–536, 2025.

[7] Priyadharshini, M., Raju, B.D., Banu, A.F., Kumar, P.J., Murugesh, V., and Rybin, O. "A quantum machine learning framework for predicting drug sensitivity in multiple myeloma using proteomic data," *Scientific Reports*, vol. 15, no. 1, p. 26553, 2025.

[8] Pineda, V.G., Valencia-Arias, A., Giraldo, F.E.L., and Zapata-Ochoa, E.A. "Integrating artificial intelligence and quantum computing: A systematic literature review of features and applications," *International Journal of Cognitive Computing in Engineering*, vol. 7, pp. 26–39, 2026.

[9] Tychola, K.A., Kalampokas, T., and Papakostas, G.A. "Quantum Machine Learning—An Overview," *Electronics*, vol. 12, no. 11, p. 2379, 2023.

[10] Tijare, P., Mehta, N.K., and Raghava, G.P.S. "Benchmarking of quantum SVM and classical ML algorithms for prediction of therapeutic proteins," *bioRxiv*, p. 2025.04.30.651419, 2025.
[11] Innan, N., Khan, M.A.Z., Panda, B, and Bennai, M. "Enhancing quantum support vector machines through variational kernel training," *Quantum Information Processing*, vol. 22, no. 10, pp. 1–18, 2023.
[12] Orazi, F., Gasperini, S., Lodi, S., and Sartori, C. "Hybrid quantum technologies for quantum support vector machines," *Information*, vol. 15, no. 2, p. 72, 2024.
[13] Grossi, M., et al., "Mixed quantum-classical method for fraud detection with quantum feature selection," *IEEE Transactions on Quantum Engineering*, vol. 3, 2022.
[14] Parmar, S.J., Parmar, V.R., Verma, J., Roy, S. and Bhattacharya, P. "Quantum computing: Exploring superposition and entanglement for cutting-edge applications," in *16th International Conference on Security of Information and Networks, SIN 2023*, 2023.
[15] Houssein, E.H., Abohashima, Z., Elhoseny, M. and Mohamed, W.M. "Machine learning in the quantum realm: The state-of-the-art, challenges, and future vision," in *Expert Systems with Applications*, vol. 194, 2022, p. 116512.
[16] Casati, G. and Benenti, G. "Quantum computation and chaos," in *Encyclopedia of Condensed Matter Physics*, Elsevier Inc., 2005, pp. 9–17.
[17] IBM, "IBM Quantum Computing | Qiskit," 2024. Available at https://www.ibm.com/quantum/qiskit, accessed on September 13, 2025.
[18] "Quantum Programming Software—PennyLane." Available at https://pennylane.ai/, accessed on September 13, 2025.
[19] Google LLC, "Libraries & extensions | TensorFlow," 2019. Available at https://www.tensorflow.org/resources/libraries-extensions, accessed on August 30, 2024.
[20] Suzuki, T., Hasebe, T., and Miyazaki, T. "Quantum support vector machines for classification and regression on a trapped-ion quantum computer," *Quantum Machine Intelligence*, vol. 6, no. 1, pp. 1–14, 2024.

5 Quantum Neural Networks and Deep Learning in the Era of Quantum-Enhanced Artificial Intelligence

Shrishti Jha[1], Mariyum Habib[2] and Hina Bansal[3*]

Quantum computing and deep learning are increasingly becoming an emerging paradigm that can transform the way complex computational problems are approached. This chapter offers an overview of quantum neural networks and deep learning, presenting material on how quantum mechanics can be merged with traditional neural networks. Quantum computing principles, including those of superposition, entanglement, and quantum parallelism, offer a very promising toolkit to overcome some of the big issues being faced today such as high-dimensional data processing, faster optimization, and reduced computation complexity. The chapter describes the architecture and operation of QNNs, compares them with classical deep learning models, and points out their applications in drug-discovery-based research, image recognition, and cryptography. This chapter also considers existing barriers, such as hardware limitations and noise in quantum systems, and sheds some light on the ongoing research efforts and future avenues in hybrid quantum–classical models. Additionally, the chapter provides detailed insights into bridge quantum theory and artificial intelligence, and a simple yet in-depth foundation for anyone interested in the quantum augmentation of deep learning's transformative possibilities.

1. Introduction

Quantum computing and deep learning are gradually emerging as transformative approaches to handle complex computational challenges. Core quantum principles such as quantum parallelism, superposition, and entanglement present powerful tools to address current issues like processing high-dimensional data, accelerating optimization, and reducing computation complexity [1] [2]. The convergence between quantum computing and deep learning is, perhaps, an entirely novel paradigm in artificial intelligence (AI) evolution. Deep learning in classical settings, based on the conventional binary computing model, has achieved outstanding results in many domains, such as visual recognition, speech synthesis, autonomous

[1-3] Centre for Computational Biology and Bioinformatics, Amity Institute of Biotechnology, Amity University, Noida, Uttar Pradesh, India.
* Corresponding author: hinabansal@gmail.com

DOI: 10.1201/9781003646068-5

driving systems, natural languages, and drug discovery. It relies on large-scale artificial neural networks that store huge data and take a much longer time to train. As the problem difficulty and the data dimensionality increase, classical approaches face key bottlenecks [3] [4].

Perhaps the other challenge arises from architecture scalability. As the size of parameters and data points grows, training deep learning models gets hard and very resource DC-intensive. Moreover, classical processors run sequentially or with limited parallelism; hence, there are time and energy constraints [5]. Finally, high-dimensional data often appears in domains such as genomics, quantum chemistry, and climate modeling—the curse of dimensionality, where computation cost maps exponentially to data size and complication schemes [6].

Quantum computing entails a model of computation that is completely different from that based on classical conformations of matter and dynamics [7]. There are two possible states for basis classical bits: 0 and 1. On the other hand, qubits might represent both 0 and 1 at the same time in a superposition of states. As a result, entangled qubits are interconnected to the point where the state of one actually changes the state of another. This constitutes a form of parallelism wherein nuclear-last worlds can consider an exorbitantly giant number of possibilities at once and therefore get exponential speedups in some cases of computations [8].

The unique characteristic features of quantum computing combined with deep learning intend researchers to create quantum neural networks (QNNs) capable of processing and learning data in ways impossible for classical systems. By confirming QNNs to fast converge during training and work efficiently with large-scale data and entangled problems, advanced possibilities remain about embedding quantum algorithms within an even broader repository of neural network-based schemes. This, in turn, paves the way for breakthrough upgrades in not only understanding but also in algorithms and computational devices themselves [9].

1.1 Motivation for Merging Quantum Computing and Deep Learning

The motivation for merging quantum computing with deep learning arises out of the inherent complementarity between the two fields. Deep learning set the backdrop for the advancement of AI wherein machines could automatically extract features from large datasets on their own because of the layer-structured neural network architectures [10]. Yet, the actual training of deep neural networks can consume a heavy amount of computational resources and times. On the other hand, a relatively new family of algorithms brought about by quantum computing greatly accelerates certain operations by processing data in parallel across multiple states simultaneously [11].

Quantum algorithms might empower quantum speedups by training and inferring neural networks within QNNs that use the high-dimensional Hilbert space of quantum systems [12]. This speedup can be exponential for some tasks and can better generalize models for representing and learning complex structures and data in ways that classical systems cannot. Furthermore, these hybrid quantum–

classical models open the door to practical near-term applications already with noisy intermediate-scale quantum (NISQ) devices [13].

1.2 Importance in Future AI and Computing Landscapes

As the complexity and computational demands of data continue to increase, quantum-enhanced AI systems may be indispensable to the advancement of science, industry, and society in the years to come [14]. There are several examples of potential applications, particularly QNNs, to accelerate drug and materials discovery, improve cryptographic protocols that allow for secure communication, and to enhance pattern recognition in quantum sensing and imaging. Financially, they may optimize high-dimensional portfolios and model complex market behaviors with even greater accuracy [15]. Furthermore, the largest tech companies and research institutions, including Google, International Business Machines Corporation (IBM), and the Massachusetts Institute of Technology (MIT), are pursuing the constituents of this convergence of quantum computing and deep learning, and are concurrently developing tools like TensorFlow Quantum and Qiskit Machine Learning, all of which suggest that quantum-enhanced deep learning will soon be at the center of an ever-growing AI ecosystem [16].

1.3 Overview of the Chapter

This chapter introduces the theoretical bases, architectures, training manners and applications of QNNs, and inclusion in deep learning. Section 2 provides definitions of quantum computing, highlighting relevant terms to note what quantum computing entails, with qubits, gates, and entanglement being crucial concepts [17]. Section 3 describes classical deep learning models, with examples such as feedforward networks, convolutional networks, and recurrent networks. Section 4 provides definitions of QNNs, through an exploration of the diverse architectures in QNNs, introducing variational quantum circuits and quantum Boltzmann machines. Section 5 elaborates on training QNNs, through an organizational understanding of different optimization approaches, along with systematic constraints/barriers associated with QNN training, for example, barren plateau. Section 6 gives real-world applications from a variety of fields—healthcare, finance, cybersecurity. Section 7 identifies recent developments from industry leaders in the form of case studies. Section 8 provide descriptions of the barriers and limitations present in QNN advances. Lastly, Section 9 and Section 10 address some potential avenues for future research and a plan for quantum-powered deep learning [18].

2. Fundamentals of Quantum Computing

Quantum computing has emerged as a new field of study. It operates quite differently from a traditional computer. Quantum computers use the principles of quantum mechanics to compute. Classical computers make use of bits (1 or 0), whereas quantum computers make use of quantum bits or qubits. The essential property of qubits is that they can contain 1s and 0s at the same time. Quantum computing can enable complex computations much more efficiently than classical computing, and may speed up the solving of some problems that are intractable when using classical systems. Understanding the basic concepts of quantum computing should take precedence before we explore the ways in which quantum computing can be integrated into deep learning [19].

2.1 Qubits, Superposition, and Entanglement

The fundamental building block of quantum information is a qubit, which is comparable to a classical bit but has far greater computing power. Theoretically, a qubit is a superposition of the basic states $|0\rangle$ and $|1\rangle$:

$$|\psi\rangle=\alpha|0\rangle+\beta|1\rangle \quad \text{...(eq 1)}$$

$|\alpha|^2 + |\beta|^2 = 1$, where α and β are complex probability amplitudes. This suggests that the qubit lives in a combination of both states until it is measured and relies on the state under investigation to determine multiple solutions at once. Entanglement is a fully quantum phenomenon where measurements of two or more qubits that are "entangled" with one another make it impossible to adequately describe one qubit, or a group of qubits, without considering the state of the remaining qubit or qubits. Any changes made to one qubit will instantly affect its partner or partners, regardless of how far apart they are. Quantum communication and information processing depend on this non-local correlation, which is also a prerequisite for enabling quantum speedups [20].

2.2 Quantum Gates and Circuits

The basic building blocks of quantum circuits, quantum gates enable quantum operations. Unlike classical logic gates (AND, OR, NOT), quantum gates are unitary operators that preserve the norm of the quantum state. The following quantum gates will be encountered:

- **Hadamard gate (H)**: to create superposition
- **Pauli-X gate**: classical NOT gate
- **CNOT gate (Controlled-NOT)**: to create entangled state of two qubits
- **Rotation gates (Rx, Ry, Rz)**: rotates the qubit state on the Bloch sphere

A quantum algorithm can be described by a quantum circuit consisting of multiple quantum gates acting on multiple qubits. A quantum circuit encodes quantum information and permits actions on it, enabling quantum computation [21].

2.3 Quantum Measurement and Decoherence

To obtain information from a quantum system, it must be measured, resulting in the quantum state "collapsing" to one of the basis states (e.g. $|0\rangle$ or $|1\rangle$), with probabilities $|\alpha|^2$ and $|\beta|^2$. The probabilistic nature of measurement gives rise to rather significant differences between quantum computation and classical computation, which is deterministic. Maintaining the coherence of a quantum state is a primary challenge in building usable quantum computers. Quantum information, represented by a quantum state, can be lost due to the impact of the environment—this is called decoherence. Quantum states are fragile; quantum states can rapidly lose coherence due to noise, temperature, and so on. Much of the active research to develop usable quantum computers is focused on handling decoherence (quantum error correction and fault tolerant architectures) [22].

2.4 Quantum Parallelism and Speedup Potential

Quantum computers utilize quantum parallelism—the ability to take simultaneous computational paths and the ability to explore many possibilities at once. For example, when you run a quantum algorithm it explores multiple paths at the same time. Then, due to some clever design, interference from the various paths will amplify the likelihood of a specific outcome and decrease the likelihood of incorrect outcomes. It is this parallelism that leads to quantum speedups when quantifying specific quantum algorithms:

Shor's algorithm: It is currently exponentially faster than classical algorithms for factoring large integers.

Grover's algorithm Compared to traditional unstructured search methods, it quadratically speeds up unstructured searches.

In machine learning specifically, quantum parallelism can accelerate training and inference by exploring multiple configurations of weights, data points, or feature transformations in parallel to accelerating convergence and model performance [23].

3. Overview of Classical Deep Learning

Classical deep learning has evolved into the foundation of today's artificial intelligence advances in areas such as speech recognition, computer vision, language translation, and robotics. To perform classification, regression, and generation tasks, artificial neural networks—now the basis of deep learning models—use optimization techniques for trainable parameter tuning. The structure and operation of the human brain, particularly its capacity for data-driven learning, serve as the foundation for deep learning models. This section of the chapter presents the foundational ideas of classical deep learning, and details its strengths and weaknesses that necessitate an exploration into quantum practices [24].

3.1 Neural Networks and Activation Functions

An artificial neural network consists of a sequence of connected nodes or "neurons", where each neuron has connections to other neurons but with different weights to

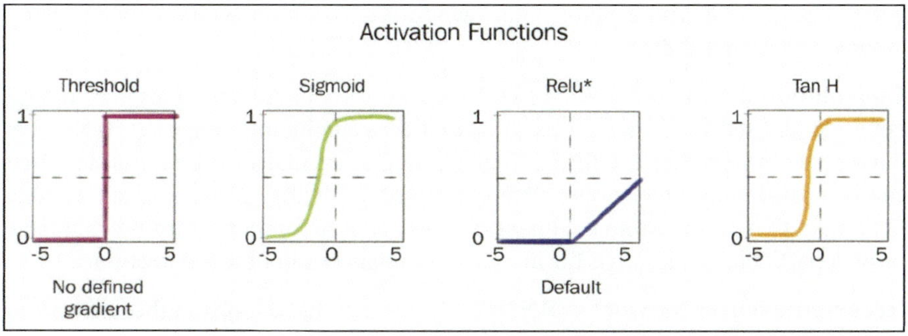

Fig. 5.1 Types of neural networks and activation functions.

account for how strong the signal is that is sent through that connection by neurons that are connected (Figure 5.1). A feedforward neural network is the most basic type of neural net topology that involves data flowing from the input layer to the output layer in one direction. Each neuron calculates the weighted sums of all its inputs, and non-linear activation functions allow us to inject complexity into the model [25]. There are many popular activation functions, including a few that are listed as follows:

Sigmoid: This is a good algorithm for any probabilistic output but has a tendency to have vanishing gradients.

ReLU (Rectified Linear Unit): This causes sparse activation and is favorable from a computational perspective.

Tanh: This is an output that has a non-linear relationship which outputs values between -1 and 1 respectively. It represents centered data.

Threshold: A threshold is a constant value for use in binarizing continuous output of a model (such as a probability) into a class label; ordinarily, a class is assigned when its output equals or exceeds the threshold (e.g., ≥ 0.5).

These functions enable neural networks to approximate the non-linear relationships in their data input and enables neural networks to be extremely expressive while allowing them to model complicated relationships and patterns [26].

3.2 Feedforward vs convolutional vs Recurrent Networks

There are many forms of neural networks, and some types are better suited for different forms of tasks:

Feedforward Neural Networks (FNNs): This is the least constrained type of neural network architecture. When your input dataset is unstructured or you do not care about the order of the input features, then FNNs can be thought of as general-purpose learning algorithms, which is a common scenario when using tabular or structured data.

Convolutional Neural Networks (CNNs): A CNN architectural style of neural networks is used for many forms of spatial data (including images). CNNs may have convolutions that use filters to generate feature maps of the input data that can be of different dimensions. CNNs are used to identify patterns, such as edge or texture, that occur within the image. CNNs are used for many purposes but have proven particularly effective for image classification and object detection.

Recurrent Neural Networks (RNNs): RNNs may have loops in the network to allow a memory of previous inputs and are more appropriate for sequential data. The most common form of RNNs are long short-term memory (LSTM) and gated recurrent units (GRU), introduced to alleviate the vanishment of gradients in multi-layer RNNs and the ability to learn long-term dependency relationships for model applications such as speech and language modeling [27].

Although there have been a series of innovations which have enabled artificial intelligence systems to perform many impressive tasks, improvements can only go so far, and quantum models may offer benefits to just simple neural network models [28].

3.3 Backpropagation and Gradient Descent

The sole goal of neural networks is to minimize a loss function that represents the difference between the target outputs and the model's predicted outputs. Backpropagation is typically used for this, which is a rather clumsy method of determining the gradient of the loss function with regard to each individual weight in the neural network (as defined by the chain rule of calculus). Gradient descent (or some variation of gradient descent, e.g., Adam, RMSprop, SGD,) uses the gradients in an iterative process :

$$W_{\text{new}} = \text{Wold}_{-\eta} \cdot \nabla L(w) \qquad \text{...eq (2)}$$

where η is the learning rate and $\nabla L(w)$ is the gradient of the loss function with respect to the weights. The goal is to find a set of parameters that minimize the L function and thus would generalize instead of fit found in out-of-sample data whenever possible.

Having said this, gradient-based optimization can get stuck in local minima, saddle points, and slow convergence depending on the model depth [29].

3.4 Limitations of Classical Deep Learning

While classical deep learning has had remarkable successes, it has inherent limitations.

Computational Cost: Training a deep network typically requires high-performance graphics processing units (GPUs) that also tend to take considerable energy so the process is expensive and bad for the environment.

Scalability: As the dataset size and dimensionality increase, training time will often increase enormously and a model will typically be prone to overfitting.

Black Box: Neural networks are commonly seen as black boxes, as it is difficult to understand why the neural network gives certain decisions.

Optimization Problems: Deep models will often get stuck in exploding/vanishing gradient problems or get stuck at barren plateaus in the loss landscape (which will stop learning).

Data Requirements: Classical deep learning typically requires billions of labeled data points to work effectively. The requirement of large numbers of labeled data points limits standard deep learning in fields with limited data/scared or sensitive data.

These limitations have encouraged researchers to investigate others paradigms including quantum neural networks, which infrastructure and algorithms combine to improve some of the limitations of classical deep learning with the unique advantages of quantum computers [30].

4. Quantum Neural Networks (QNNs): Concepts and Architectures

QNNs are computational models that combine the learning capabilities of a particular class of artificial neural networks with the concepts of quantum mechanics. In order to address the issues with classical deep learning models, such as arbitrary computational models, inefficiency, expressivity, and scaling, QNNs are theoretical models that take advantage of quantum physics phenomena, particularly entanglement, superposition, and quantum parallelism. Thus, QNNs are essentially a new class of learning models, which, if realizable with quantum hardware, have the potential to enable exponential speedup, improve generalization, and perform on high-dimensional problem spaces [31].

4.1 What Are QNNs?

A QNN is a neural network architecture where quantum circuits act as the information-processing engine. Classical neural networks consist of multiple layers composed of connected artificial neurons, while QNNs consist of parameterized quantum gates and quantum circuits that evolve quantum states similar to the layers of an artificial neural network. Quantum states evolve through unitary transformations, then the QNN, represented by the quantum gates, is adjusted and trained by changing parameters (such as the eyeglasses in quantum gates) to minimize a defined loss function (eg., Mitsubishi Electric Research Laboratories).

High-level QNNs have the following characteristics:

- Quantum layers composed of parameterized quantum gates
- Measurements that recover classical information from quantum states

- An optimization loop (typically classical) that modifies gate parameters from the loss function

QNNs are particularly good at modeling complex, entangled data distributions and solving problems that cannot be solved with classical neural networks [32].

4.2 Types of QNNs

There are many different forms of QNN architecture, depending on the intended application and form of computation shown in Table 5.1. The choice of model should correspond to the computational aspect required, the features of the dataset, and the type of quantum hardware available [33].

- **Variational Quantum Circuits (VQCs):** VQCs (also called "parameterized quantum circuits") are at the heart of many examples of QNNs. The basic structure consists of layers of quantum gates, and the parameters of these gates are trained by classical algorithms. VQCs fit very well with hybrid quantum–classical learning algorithms.
- **Quantum Boltzmann Machines (QBMs):** QBMs learn to model probability distributions, much like their classical counterpart, the Boltzmann machine. However, QBMs gain their advantages by using quantum states that can manipulate quantum entanglement to achieve correlations in distributed patterns that classical models struggle with. QBMs are suited to generative models and any unsupervised learning application.
- **Quantum Convolutional Neural Networks (QCNNs):** Similar to classical CNNs, QCNNs apply similar quantum operators in a layered, hierarchical fashion that maintains true features from the initial viewing and at larger geometric scales. They have been used in quantum phase recognition and related pattern recognition assignments.
- **Quantum Recurrent Neural Networks (QRNNs):** QRNNs are still in a very early research stage but seem to be useful for modeling sequential data, i.e., measurements can have their quantum state preserved across time by attaching a layer of quantum state measurements to each corresponding time step, similar to RNN.

Table 5.1 Types of QNNs and their implementation platform.

Model Type	*Description*	*Suitable for*	*Implementation Platforms*	*References*
Variational Quantum Circuit (VQC)	Parameterized quantum circuits optimized using classical algorithms.	Classification, regression, hybrid models	PennyLane, Qiskit, TensorFlow Quantum	[34]

Contd...

Table 5.1 *Contd...*

Model Type	*Description*	*Suitable for*	*Implementation Platforms*	*References*
Quantum Boltzmann Machine (QBM)	Quantum analogue of classical Boltzmann machines for energy-based modeling.	Generative modeling, pattern recognition	IBM Q, D-Wave Ocean	[35]
Quantum Convolutional Neural Network (QCNN)	Quantum extension of classical CNNs using quantum convolution and pooling operations.	Image recognition, feature extraction	Qiskit, Strawberry Fields	[36]
Quantum Reservoir Computing (QRC)	Uses a fixed, complex quantum system as a reservoir and trains a classical output layer.	Temporal pattern recognition, signal processing	Rigetti Forest, Qulacs	[37]
Quantum Kernel Estimator (QKE)	Applies quantum feature maps followed by classical classifiers.	SVM-like tasks, non-linear classification	Pennylane, Qiskit Machine Learning	[38]
Hybrid QNN	Combines quantum layers with classical neural networks in a unified model.	Real-world datasets, near-term devices	TensorFlow Quantum, PennyLane	[39]

4.3 Encoding Classical Data into Quantum States

One of the key problems in quantum machine learning is figuring out a mapping from classical data to quantum states. This is sometimes referred to as quantum feature mapping or quantum data encoding. There are various types of encoding:

- **Amplitude Encoding:** This encodes the classical imputation to amplitudes of a quantum state. This is a very efficient encoding since it requires O(log N) number of qubits to encode N classical features. However, the implementation can be difficult because only the qubit needs to be normalized.
- **Angle Encoding (Rotation Encoding):** Angle encoding encodes classical data by the characteristics of the rotations of a qubit state as a certain angle from the classical binary features, as qubit gates (i.e., Ry or Rz). Angle encoding is typically seen in variational circuits.
- **Basis Encoding:** Basis Encoding encodes classical data in binary as a qubit state where each qubit is representational of one classical bit (i.e., |0> encodes for 0, |1> encodes for 1).

Encoding is very important since this determines how well the quantum model can extract, and learn useful information, from classical datasets [40].

4.4 Hybrid Quantum–Classical Models

The limits of quantum hardware, qubit counts, decoherence, and noise causes most of the applications of QNNs to be hybrid quantum–classical approaches. In hybrid quantum–classical models, we use quantum circuits for parts of the computation, such as feature transformations or kernel evaluations, while classical components are used for other aspects such as loss evaluations, optimization, and making decisions [41]. An abstraction of a general architecture would look like this:

- We encode input data into quantum states.
- To change the quantum states, we use a variational quantum circuit.
- We measure quantum states to classical data.
- We change the quantum circuit using a classical optimizer from values provided by the cost function.

The hybrid model allows us to exploit the quantum advantages and classical error-free and predictive aspects of computation. Well-documented frameworks like PennyLane, Qiskit, and TensorFlow Quantum allow users to combine quantum and classical aspects seamlessly [42].

5. Training Quantum Neural Networks

To train QNNs, the parameters of quantum circuits must be optimized to minimize a cost function, which is comparable to training classical neural networks. However, the quantum characteristics of QNNs require developing new definitions of forward and backward propagation methods to account for quantum operations. Figure 5.2 represents the steps of training QNNs.

5.1 Quantum Versions of Forward and Backward Propagation

Forward propagation is the process by which input data is passed through a number of layers and neurons in classical neural networks in order to produce an output. Nevertheless, backward propagation employs the chain rule to ascertain the gradient of the loss function with respect to the network parameters in order to fine-tune the network.

In a QNN, forward propagation corresponds to the application of a parameterized quantum circuit (PQC) on the encoded input state. The PQC transforms the input state through a series of unitary operations (quantum gates). The final state is then measured to obtain a classical output that is evaluated against the target and a loss is computed.

Backward propagation in quantum systems is a bit more nuanced; quantum operations are linear and non-clonable so gradients must be estimated with sampling. One of the more popular techniques for figuring out circuit gradients

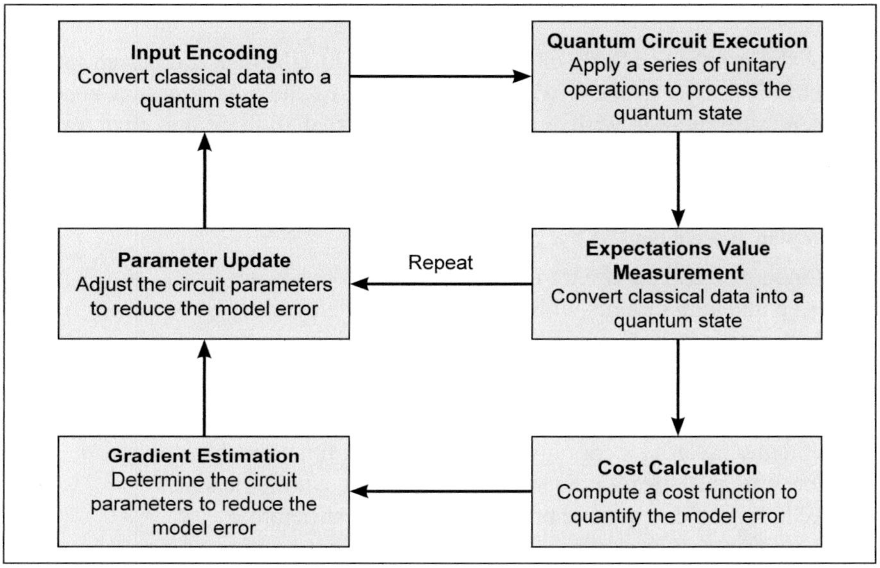

Fig. 5.2 Schematic process of QNN training loop.

is the parameter-shift rule. The parameter-shift rule allows for the calculation of gradients by examining the circuit with parameters at slightly different locations:

$$\partial\theta\partial\langle O\rangle = 21[\langle O\rangle\theta + 2\pi - \langle O\rangle\theta - 2\pi]$$

Here, $\langle O\rangle$ denotes the expected value of an observable after the circuit has been applied with parameter θ. This provides a way to use gradient-based optimizers in a quantum context [43].

5.2 Cost Function and Parameter Optimization in Quantum Systems

The cost function in QNNs is one that measures how well the quantum model performs at a particular task, whether it is predicting classes or making predictions. Typically, it is written as the expectation value of some observable, such as the Pauli-Z, after the quantum circuit has acted on the input state.The primary objective here is to determine a collection of parameters that will reduce the cost over a training set. For tuning these parameters, you can depend on classical optimization algorithms such as Adam or RMSprop or you could use quantum-aware specialized optimizers that consider noise and sampling variance. Because quantum circuits are probabilistically measurable, the cost function has to be estimated by repeated measurement, commonly known as shots. This implies that the optimization algorithm must be robust against the natural randomness present [44].

5.3 Barren Plateaus and Training Difficulties

One of the primary training challenges intrinsic to QNNs is the barren plateau problem. This is a scenario where the gradient of the cost function becomes exponentially smaller with increasing numbers of qubits such that training becomes infeasible. In such regions of parameter space, all directions are flat to the optimizer, and this leads to progress halting [45].

Barren plateaus are caused by:

- Random circuit parameter initialization
- Deep quantum circuits with too much entanglement
- Cost functions or circuit structures chosen poorly

Preventing barren plateaus entails:

- Applying shallow, structured networks
- Utilizing layer-wise training or localized cost functions
- Selecting initialization heuristics that prevent symmetric states
- Adding problem-specific priors to the model structure

5.4 Gradient-Based vs Gradient-Free Optimization

Training QNNs may use two broad classes of optimization strategies:

- **Gradient-Based Optimization:** This updates parameters using estimated gradients of the cost function (via parameter-shift or finite-difference strategies). Such strategies are strong but may be vulnerable to noise and barren plateaus.
- **Gradient-Free Optimization:** This avoids gradient computation and uses other techniques like genetic algorithms, Bayesian optimization, Nelder-Mead simplex method, simulated annealing. Gradient-free techniques are especially valuable when the cost landscape is non-differentiable or noisy. However, they generally need more function calls and might converge more slowly than gradient-based methods. There are also hybrid techniques that combine both paradigms, seeking to leverage the strengths of one while overcoming its weaknesses [46].

6. Applications of Quantum Deep Learning

Quantum deep learning (QDL), as an interdisciplinary methodology integrating quantum computing and deep learning, is picking up impressive momentum both in theoretical investigations and applied studies. Through the exploitation of quantum computational benefits like parallelism, entanglement, and exponential state space, QDL models, particularly QNNs, hold much promise in terms of performance, efficiency, and scalability improvement. This section focuses on major application areas where quantum deep learning has already shown or will show revolutionary influence [47].

6.1 Quantum-Enhanced Image Classification

Image classification is a fundamental pillar of computer vision, applied in numerous areas such as healthcare diagnostics, autonomous systems, surveillance, and social networks. Conventional deep learning models such as convolutional neural networks (CNNs) have shown outstanding performance, but efficiency drops with highly high-dimensional data. Quantum-boosted models bring in a new paradigm:

- Quantum Convolutional Neural Networks (QCNNs) employ parameterized quantum circuits to extract features at various levels of abstraction.
- Quantum entanglement allows capturing global correlations within pixel distributions with greater efficiency compared to classical convolution.
- Hybrid QNNs are able to process pre-encoded image patches in parallel, which could decrease the time and energy expense of training.

Initial tests (e.g., on quantum datasets or low-res MNIST) demonstrate that quantum-boosted models can match classical models on tiny tasks and scale better with improvements in quantum hardware. Scale better with improvements in quantum hardware [48].

6.2 Quantum Machine Learning in Drug Discovery and Genomics

The biomedical sciences, in particular drug discovery and genomics, require simulating intricate molecular systems and searching enormous chemical spaces—computational tasks that defy classical computational methods owing to their exponential complexity.

Quantum deep learning is promising in the following:

- Molecular property prediction using quantum models of molecular structures and QNNs
- Quantum generative models to design novel drug-like molecules or protein structures
- Quantum genomics data analysis where gene expression profiles are clustered, mutations are identified, or genetic regulatory networks are understood using quantum algorithms

Through more realistic modeling of quantum chemistry and biological systems, QDL enables quicker screening, greater accuracy, and a better understanding of biological interactions at the quantum level [49]. Figure 5.3 represents the steps of quantum deep learning in drug discovery.

6.3 Financial Modeling and Optimization

Finance is naturally data-driven and tends to be the optimization of big, complex systems with stochastic behavior. Problem types like portfolio optimization, option pricing, risk management, and fraud detection would all see enormous benefit from the application of quantum deep learning.

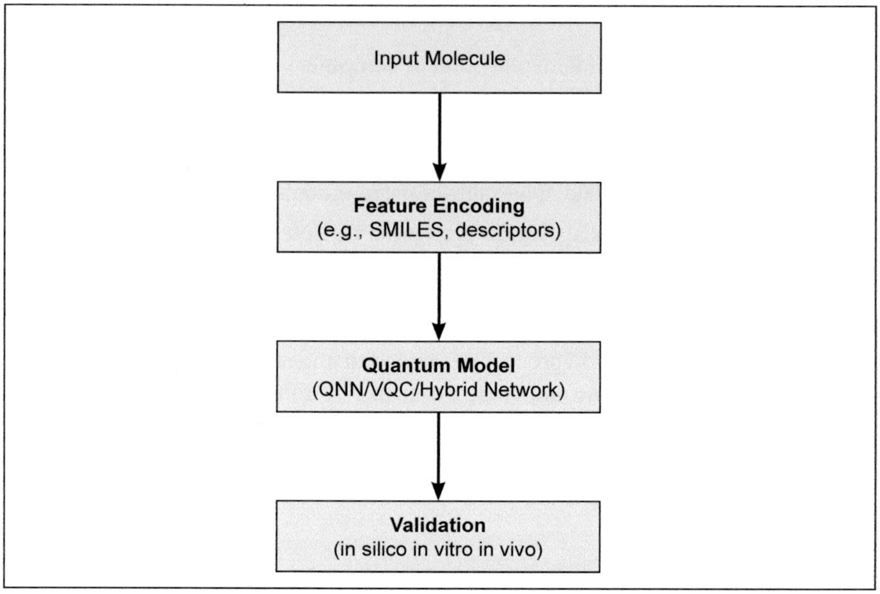

Fig. 5.3 Steps of quantum deep learning in drug discovery.

Applications are as follows:

- QBMs for market pattern and distribution learning.
- VQAs for constraint optimization problems for portfolio optimization.
- Application of QNNs in time series forecasting of data such as stock prices or macroeconomic variables.

Quantum-accommodated models provide higher speed, tolerance to noise, and higher fidelity in retrieving non-linear relationships, giving banking institutions a competitive computational advantage [50].

6.4 Use in Cryptography and Secure Data Analysis

Quantum computing presents problems and solutions for contemporary cryptography. Although quantum algorithms such as Shor's algorithm endanger conventional cryptographic protocols (e.g., RSA), quantum deep learning provides new techniques for safe data analysis and quantum-resistant cryptographic systems.

Future applications are as follows:

- Quantum data watermarking and hiding for digital rights management.
- Quantum adversarial networks for cryptographic protocol strengthening and compromising.
- Quantum-secured secure multiparty computation.

- Quantum deep learning-based anomaly detection and cyber-attack countermeasures through fast anomaly detection and pattern recognition in encrypted data.

In addition, deep learning algorithms can be integrated with quantum key distribution (QKD) protocols to dynamically reconfigure and optimize communication channels for improved security as well as efficiency [51].

7. Case Studies and Real-World Implementations

Thanks to developments in hybrid quantum–classical techniques and quantum computing hardware, QNNs and quantum deep learning models are starting to find real-world applications. This section covers significant industry-sponsored research studies, prototype systems, and experimental tests proving the capability of quantum deep learning in actual applications [52].

7.1 Google and IBM's Quantum Machine Learning Research

Two of the top players in quantum AI research—Google and IBM—have made groundbreaking contributions in developing and demonstrating quantum machine learning algorithms: Google's Quantum AI division has employed VQCs on superconducting qubit hardware. Interestingly, they demonstrated "quantum supremacy" in 2019 by using their 53-qubit Sycamore processor, thereby opening the door to QML applications with quantum advantage. Subsequently, Google used quantum kernel estimation and hybrid quantum–classical neural networks on actual datasets such as MNIST and Fashion-MNIST.

The IBM Qiskit Machine Learning software enables the creation and training of quantum models in simulators and actual IBM Quantum hardware. IBM has demonstrated uses like quantum support vector machines (QSVMs), quantum feature maps, and quantum generative adversarial networks (QGANs) and integrated them into cloud platforms like IBM Quantum Experience. These attempts demonstrate the usability and utility of running QNNs on near-term quantum devices (also known as NISQ computers), despite hardware constraints [53].

7.2 Quantum GANs and Reinforcement Learning Models

Generative adversarial networks (GANs) and reinforcement learning (RL) are at the forefront of AI advancements today, especially in creative endeavors and decision-making under uncertainty. Their quantum counterparts are showing promising potential:

Quantum GANs (QGANs): These consist of a quantum generator and a classical or quantum discriminator. QGANs have been experimentally demonstrated on photonic and superconducting quantum processors. An example is IBM's development of a QGAN that can learn to produce quantum states that represent an approximation to a target distribution, establishing the foundation for future quantum generative models in unsupervised learning.

Quantum Reinforcement Learning (QRL): Quantum circuits are used to represent policies or value functions in QRL. Quantum variational learning-trained agents, for example, have been tested on grid-world environments. Initial evidence is suggestive of quantum parallelism being capable of leading to faster convergence and more expressive policies.

Such experimental results suggest that hybrid QGANs and QRL models can outperform their classical counterparts in specific high-dimensional or noisy settings, especially when model generalization is crucial [54].

QNNs on Superconducting and Photonic Processors: QNN implementation on real quantum hardware is the most important achievement of this field. Two of the major hardware platforms—superconducting circuits and photonic processors—have been at the center of these developments: **Superconducting Processors:** Superconducting qubits-based platforms such as Google's Sycamore and IBM's Eagle support parameterized quantum circuits to be executed with relatively high fidelity. Quantum convolutional networks and variational classifiers have been implemented for a small-sized classification problem using such devices [55].

Photonic Quantum Processors: PsiQuantum and Xanadu are developing photonic hardware, where quantum data is stored in light (photons). Quantum machine learning has been made possible on its Borealis photonic processor using Xanadu's open-source library PennyLane. Researchers have implemented quantum neural circuits for regression and variational autoencoders using continuous-variable (CV) models, which are highly suitable for photonics.

Despite problems such as noise, decoherence, and limited numbers of qubits, these field deployments are a major step forward toward the creation of scalable, application-ready quantum deep learning platforms [56].

8. Challenges and Limitations

While QNNs and quantum deep learning models offer compelling theoretical advantages, deployment on the practical front is still in its infancy. The field suffers from numerous technical, algorithmic, and infrastructural problems that stand in the way of widespread acceptance. In this section, the major barriers currently limiting progress, from hardware bottlenecks to availability of data and performance benchmarking, are enumerated [57].

8.1 Hardware Limitations (Noisy Qubits, Limited Scalability)

The brittleness of existing quantum hardware is one of the biggest obstacles to quantum deep learning. Table 5.2 shows the major challenges of QNN and quantum deep learning models. The majority of modern quantum processors continue to operate in the NISQ regime, which is distinguished by:

- Noisy qubits with high decoherence and gate error propensity
- Short coherence times that restrict circuit depth
- Small qubit counts that prevent scalability
- High readout error rates on measurement

Table 5.2 Challenges of QNN and quantum deep learning models.

Challenge	*Category*	*Description*	*Possible Mitigation*	*References*
Noise	Hardware	Decoherence and gate errors affecting qubit stability	Error mitigation protocols	[58]
Barren Plateaus	Training	Flat cost landscape impeding gradient-based optimization	Layer-wise training or circuit design	[59]
Dataset Scarcity	Data	Few real quantum datasets available for model training	Use simulated or hybrid datasets	[60]
Scalability Issues	Hardware	Limited number of stable qubits in current processors	Modular architectures; error-corrected qubits	[61]
Error Correction	Algorithmic	Complex and resource-heavy	Topological codes; fault-tolerant schemes	[62]
Hardware Access	Practical	Limited access to high-fidelity quantum hardware	Cloud-based quantum platforms	[63]
Lack of Standards	Software	Absence of standardized APIs and benchmarking tools	Development of cross-platform frameworks like Qiskit or PennyLane	[64]
Training Time	Performance	Long optimization time due to hybrid feedback loops	Use of gradient-free or meta-learning methods	[65]
Interpretability	Theoretical	Difficult to interpret quantum model behavior	Visualization tools and hybrid introspection layers	[66]

These issues lead to unstable computations, low fidelity, and high rates of quantum state collapse, making it difficult to train deep or large QNNs [67]. Moreover, hardware backends are highly specialized (e.g., superconducting, photonic, ion-trap), and non-standardization renders model portability across platforms difficult [68].

8.2 Algorithmic Challenges and Error Correction

Quantum deep learning algorithms are naturally constrained by the need to preserve unitarity and probabilistic outputs. This poses several algorithmic challenges:

- Gradient disappearance in variational quantum circuits, particularly in large-dimensional Hilbert spaces (barren plateaus)
- Challenge to come up with optimal quantum circuits for non-trivial learning tasks
- High computational overhead to estimate gradients or loss values due to measurement sampling

Furthermore, while quantum error correction systems do exist, they are very costly and frequently need hundreds of physical qubits to represent a single logical qubit. Such error-corrected quantum deep learning models are not yet compatible with NISQ hardware [69].

8.3 Shortage of Standardized Quantum Datasets and Benchmarks

Another major limitation of quantum machine learning studies is that there are no standardized quantum datasets and benchmarking schemes. Classical deep learning came along rapidly because there existed large labeled datasets (e.g., ImageNet, CIFAR-10) and open benchmarks (e.g., GLUE, SuperGLUE, MLPerf). In contrast:

- Most quantum deep learning experiments employ toy datasets or simulated quantum data
- There are few realistic quantum datasets for useful problems (e.g., quantum chemistry, optimization)
- Real-hardware, cross-platform comparisons of QNNs are rare
- Absence of an open benchmarking environment precludes reproducible measurement of performance, generalization, and scalability of algorithms [70]

8.4 Comparison with Classical Systems Based on Efficiency

Much as theoretical quantum speedup is promising, the QNNs have not yet consistently outperformed the classical neural networks on useful realistic tasks. In fact:

- Classical models are still more accurate and economical for standard operations
- Quantum models are likely to require more function calls due to measurement-based learning
- Hybrid models are likely harder to train and optimize than their exclusively classical counterparts

Furthermore, current quantum models are usually tested on artificially small datasets that arise from hardware limitations and thus lack realistic comparisons. So, quantum deep learning has not yet been able to demonstrate a clear "quantum advantage" over classical deep learning in practical applications [71].

9. Future Directions and Research Opportunities

Quantum deep learning is in its infancy, but the rate of innovation holds the promise of a fast-growing frontier. As quantum computing hardware continues to improve and hybrid architectures grow stronger, the dream of practical quantum advantage in AI becomes more plausible. This chapter presents important directions and research opportunities that will determine the future of QNNs and their adoption in mainstream AI systems [72].

9.1 Quantum Advantage and Supremacy in AI

One of the research goals is to demonstrate true quantum advantage or even quantum supremacy over AI problems [73]. While quantum supremacy involves resolving issues that are practically unsolvable for classical systems, quantum advantage refers to surpassing classical models on particular challenges. Some the potential future paths are as follows:

- Constructing QNNs with provably advantageous performance on learning certain classes of data distributions (e.g., data from quantum systems, high-dimensional manifolds) [74]
- Quantum-enhanced transformer and generative model design with increased expressiveness
- Benchmarking QNNs on cases where classical approaches fail—e.g., learning from sparse, entangled, or encrypted data
- Quantum advantage on practical machine learning tasks will be a milestone achievement, potentially expanding the frontiers of AI capabilities
- Breakthroughs in quantum hardware (quantum processing unit [QPU] scaling, error mitigation)

Long-term quantum deep learning progress largely relies on quantum hardware innovation. The key hardware areas of investigation are as follows:

- Qubit scalability: Scaling qubit numbers with coherence and low error rates is needed to make use of deeper and more complex quantum circuits [75].
- Error mitigation: Intermediate methods such as dynamical decoupling, probabilistic error cancellation, and zero-noise extrapolation are being developed to lessen the effects of errors without completely correcting them.
- Fault-tolerant quantum computing: Advanced work involves the construction of error-corrected quantum processors that will execute deep QNNs safely over long periods. New photonics, trapped-ion, and topological qubit technologies could also drive the construction of robust QPUs that will support large-scale quantum AI [76].

9.2 Hybrid Frameworks Standardization (e.g., PennyLane, Qiskit, TensorFlow Quantum)

Single software tool standardization and adoption are required to reduce the entry barrier and achieve reproducibility in quantum AI research. Some frameworks are at the forefront of this effort are as follows:

- PennyLane: Xanadu-built platform for hybrid quantum-classical model creation via gradient-based optimization and automatic differentiation.
- Qiskit Machine Learning: IBM software offering primitives and algorithms for the use of QNNs, quantum kernels, and variational circuits [77].
- TensorFlow Quantum (TFQ): Created by Google and the University of Waterloo, TFQ enables end-to-end trainability of quantum circuit layers that can be embedded inside TensorFlow models.

Future work will involve enhancing interoperability, enabling heterogeneous hardware backends, and constructing solid quantum ML pipelines such as those of classical ML libraries, e.g., PyTorch and scikit-learn [78].

9.3 Toward Fully Quantum AI Systems

One of the longer-term visions here is the creation of end-to-end quantum AI systems—models where data encoding, learning, memory, and inference are all managed within a quantum system [76]. The research areas that make this vision possible are as follows:

- Quantum memory and data buses to enable long-term quantum information flow
- Quantum associative memory models for recall and pattern completion
- Quantum generative models and autoencoders for creating data
- Quantum attention mechanisms and recurrent architectures

Although hardware and theoretical limits keep fully quantum AI elusive at the moment, its early conceptual stage opens the door to such a future AI generation. They would basically revolutionize concepts and realizations of learning and intelligence [79].

10. Conclusion

Quantum deep learning is located at the intersection of two of the most prevalent technological trends of the twenty-first century—machine learning and quantum computing. This chapter has addressed the nature of quantum computation principles, the design and training of QNNs, and the integration of quantum phenomena into deep learning procedures. From the first concepts like superposition and entanglement to the latest applications in image recognition, genomics, finance, and cryptography, quantum-aided AI is both a future vision and a present reality [80].

10.1 Summary of Key Insights

Some of the key insights that arise from this analysis are as follows:

- QNNs leverage obviously quantum phenomena—like entanglement and quantum parallelism—to perform transformations and learning operations perhaps impossible for traditional systems.

- Training QNNs poses novel algorithmic challenges like probabilistic gradient estimation and barren plateaus, but optimization research and circuit design are already challenging these limits.
- Quantum deep learning has already demonstrated exciting results in small-scale experimental devices with hybrid architectures, particularly for classification, generative modeling, and optimization.
- The field is still very interdisciplinary, requiring advancements in quantum hardware, machine learning theory, software tooling, and data engineering [81].

10.2 Current Status and Near-Term Roadmap

As of now, quantum deep learning is at the beginning of its life cycle, and practicality is limited by NISQ-era hardware and the lack of scalable error correction. But the short-term roadmap is optimistic. Scaling of quantum processors goes on (more qubits, less noise) [82].

- Enhanced hybrid development toolkits (e.g., PennyLane, Qiskit, TensorFlow Quantum
- Increased availability of quantum cloud platforms and simulators
- Standards for quantum datasets and performance benchmarks develop
- Increasingly investment and collaboration between academia, industry, and government

These indicate that quantum machine learning may move from pilot to applied significance in particular fields within the next ten years [83].

10.3 The Vision for Quantum-Empowered Deep Learning

Deep learning enabled by quantum technology has an ambitious and revolutionary future. It observes a class of AI systems that not only grow more powerful and quicker but also exhibit qualitatively distinct traits and capacities such as the following:

- Quantum intelligent AI systems that learn, reason, and adapt in the high-dimensional Hilbert space of quantum states
- Autonomous decision-making systems capable of concluding entangled and superposed inputs

Quantum large-scale systems are capable of learning to generalize over encrypted or sparse data, with quantum priors systems permitting the discovery of new materials, medicines, and cryptographic protocols through accelerated discovery [84].

While the future is one of challenge and complexity, the marriage of deep learning and quantum computing holds tremendous potential. Through ongoing innovation and collaboration, AI based on quantum could one day transform what is possible in computation, learning, and intelligent systems [85].

References

[1] Beer, K., Bondarenko, D., Farrelly, T., Osborne, T.J., Salzmann, R., Wolf, R., and Wolf, M.M. *Nature Communications*, 2020, doi: 10.1038/s41467-020-14454-2.

[2] Abhijith J., Cerezo, M., Larocca, M., Lukasz Cincio, and Patrick J. Coles*, arXiv preprint*, 2021, doi: 10.48550/arXiv.2108.01468.

[3] Li, Haiyan Wang, Yi-Pu Song, Chang-Ling Zou, Dong-Ling Deng, and Luyan Sun, *Nature Communications*, 2023, doi: 10.1038/s41467-023-39785-8.

[4] Caputo, S., Polino, E., and Sciarrino, F. *Physical Review A*, 2022, doi: 10.1103/PhysRevA.106.022601.

[5] Li, J., Li, X., and Meng, D. *Research*, 2021, doi: 10.34133/research.0134.

[6] Ahmed, T., Kashif, M., Marchisio, A., and Shafique, M. "Quantum neural networks: A comparative analysis and noise robustness evaluation," *arXiv*, 2025, https://doi.org/10.48550/arXiv.2501.1441 2arXiv+2arXiv+2arXiv+2.

[7] Liu, J., Najafi, K., Sharma, K., Tacchino, F., Jiang, L. and Mezzacapo, A. "Analytic theory for the dynamics of wide quantum neural networks," *Physical Review Letters,* vol. 130, no. 15, p. 150601, 2023, https://doi.org/10.1103/PhysRevLett.130.150601.

[8] Markidis, S. "Programming quantum neural networks on NISQ systems: An overview of technologies and methodologies," *Entropy,* vol. 25, no. 4, p. 694, 2023, https://doi.org/10.3390/e25040694MDPI.

[9] Zhang, Y. and Lu, H. "Reliability research on quantum neural networks," *Electronics,* vol. 13, no. 8, p. 1514, 2024, https://doi.org/10.3390/electronics13081514MDPI.

[10] Kashif, M., Marchisio, A., and Shafique, M. "Computational advantage in hybrid quantum neural networks: Myth or reality?" *arXiv*, 2025, https://doi.org/10.48550/arXiv.2412.04991arXiv+3arXiv+3arXiv+3.

[11] Herrmann, N., Akhtar, M., Arya, D., Doherty, M.W., Macha, P., Preis, F., Prestel, S., and Walker, M.L. "First quantum machine learning applications on an on-site room-temperature quantum computer," *arXiv*, 2023, https://doi.org/10.48550/arXiv.2312.11673arXiv.

[12] Kreplin, D.A., Willmann, M., Schnabel, J., Rapp, F., Hagelüken, M. and Roth, M. "sQUlearn: A Python library for quantum machine learning," *arXiv*, 2023, https://doi.org/10.48550/arXiv.2311.08990arXiv.

[13] Zaman, K., Marchisio, A., Hanif, M.A., and Shafique, M. "A survey on quantum machine learning: Current trends, challenges, opportunities, and the road ahead," *arXiv*, 2025, https://doi.org/10.48550/arXiv.2310.10315arXiv.

[14] Lamata, L. "Quantum machine learning implementations: Proposals and experiments," *Advanced Quantum Technologies,* vol. 6, no. 5, p. 2300059, 2023, https://doi.org/10.1002/qute.202300059arXiv.

[15] Zhang, Y. and Lu, H. "Reliability research on quantum neural networks," *Electronics,* vol. 13, no. 8, p. 1514, 2024, https://doi.org/10.3390/electronics13081514.

[16] Larocca, M., et al. "Theory of overparametrization in quantum neural networks," *Nature Computational Science*, vol. 3, pp. 484–485, 2023, https://doi.org/10.1038/s43588-023-00468-5Nature.

[17] Gschwendtner, M., Soller, H., and Zingg, S. "Combining quantum and AI for the next superpower," *Nature Reviews Electrical Engineering*, vol. 1, pp. 350–351, 2024, https://doi.org/10.1038/s44287-024-00051-8Nature.

[18] Dowling, N., West, M.T., Southwell, A., Nakhl, A.C., Sevior, M., Usman, M. and Modi, K. "Adversarial robustness guarantees for quantum classifiers", *arXiv*, 2024, https://arxiv.org/abs/2405.10360arXiv.

[19] Gupta, M.K., Rybotycki, T. and Gawron, P. "On the status of current quantum machine learning software," *arXiv*, 2025, https://arxiv.org/abs/2503.08962.

[20] Melnikov, A., Kordzanganeh, M., Alodjants, A. and Lee R.-K. "Quantum machine learning: From physics to software engineering," *Advanced Physics: X,* vol. 8, no. 1, p. 2165452, 2023, https://doi.org/10.1080/23746149.2023.2165452arXiv.

[21] Cerezo, M., Verdon, G., Huang, H.-Y., Cincio, L. and Coles, P.J. "Challenges and opportunities in quantum machine learning," *arXiv*, 2023, https://doi.org/10.48550/arXiv.2303.09491arXiv.

[22] Huynh, L., Hong, J., Mian, A., Suzuki, H., Wu, Y., and Camtepe, S. "Quantum-inspired machine learning: A survey," *arXiv*, 2023, https://doi.org/10.48550/arXiv.2308.11269arXiv.

[23] Innan, N., Khan, M.A.-Z. and Bennai, M. "Financial fraud detection: A comparative study of quantum machine learning models," *arXiv*, 2023, https://doi.org/10.48550/arXiv.2308.05237arXiv.

[24] Markidis, S. "Programming quantum neural networks on NISQ systems: An overview of technologies and methodologies," *Entropy*, vol. 25, no. 4, p. 694, 2023, https://doi.org/10.3390/e25040694MDPI.

[25] Herrmann, N., Akhtar, M., Arya, D., Doherty, M.W., Macha, P., Preis, F., Prestel, S. and Walker, M.L. "First quantum machine learning applications on an on-site room-temperature quantum computer," *arXiv*, 2023, https://doi.org/10.48550/arXiv.2312.11673arXiv.

[26] Kreplin, D.A., Willmann, M., Schnabel, J., Rapp, F., Hagelüken, M., and Roth, M. "sQUlearn: A Python library for quantum machine learning," *arXiv*, 2023, https://doi.org/10.48550/arXiv.2311.08990arXiv.

[27] Ahmed, T., Kashif, M., Marchisio, A., and Shafique, M. "Quantum neural networks: A comparative analysis and noise robustness evaluation," *arXiv*, 2025, https://doi.org/10.48550/arXiv.2501.14412arXiv.

[28] West, M.T., Tsang, S.-L., Low, J.S., Hill, C.D., Leckie, C., Hollenberg, L.C.L., Erfani, S.M. and Usman, M. "Towards quantum enhanced adversarial robustness in machine learning," *arXiv*, 2023, https://arxiv.org/abs/2306.12688arXiv.

[29] Thakkar, S., Kazdaghli, S., Mathur, N., et al. "Improved financial forecasting via quantum machine learning," *Quantum Machine Intelligence*, vol. 6, article 27, 2024, https://doi.org/10.1007/s42484-024-00157-0SpringerLink.

[20] IBM, *IBM Quantum Platform*,. Available at https://quantum.cloud.ibm.com/Wikipedia, accessed on 15 March 2026.

[31] *Business Insider*, "Google, Microsoft, and others are racing to crack open quantum computing. Here's how their breakthroughs stack up," 2025. Available at https://www.businessinsider.com/quantum-computing-race-big-tech-microsoft-google-amazon-ibm-2025-2Business Insider, accessed on 15 March 2026.

[32] *Financial Times*, "Quantum computing is struggling to reach its silicon moment," 2025. Available at https://www.ft.com/content/bfe5fff4-3d78-4bea-9e31-da8ca1f77151Financial Times, accessed on 15 March 2026.

[33] de Leon, N.P., et al. "Materials challenges and opportunities for quantum computing hardware," *Science*, vol. 372, no. 6539, eabb2823, 2023, https://doi.org/10.1126/science.abb2823Science.

[34] Huber-Loyola, T. and Höfling, S. "2023 roadmap for materials for quantum technologies," *Journal of Physics: Photonics*, vol. 5, no. 1, 012001, 2023, https://doi.org/10.1088/2633-4356/aca3f2IOPscience.

[35] Blekos, K., Brand, D., Ceschini, A., Chou, C.-H., Li, R.-H., Pandya, K. and Summer, A. "A review on quantum approximate optimization algorithm and its variants," *arXiv*, 2023, https://doi.org/10.48550/arXiv.2306.09198arXiv.

[36] Finžgar, J.R., Kerschbaumer, A., Schuetz, M.J.A., Mendl, C.B. and Katzgraber, H.G. "Quantum-informed recursive optimization algorithms," *arXiv*, 2023, https://doi.org/10.48550/arXiv.2308.13607arXiv.

[37] Klug, F. "Quantum optimization algorithms in operations research: Methods, applications, and implications," *arXiv*, 2023, https://doi.org/10.48550/arXiv.2312.13636arXiv.

[38] Woerner, S. "Challenges and opportunities in quantum optimization," *arXiv*, 2023, https://doi.org/10.48550/arXiv.2312.02279arXiv.

[39] Dalzell, A.M., McArdle, S., Berta, M., Bienias, P., Chen, C.-F., Gilyén, A., Hann, C.T., Kastoryano, M.J., Khabiboulline, E.T., Kubica, A., Salton, G., Wang, S. and Brandão, F.G.S.L. "Quantum algorithms: A survey of applications and end-to-end complexities," *arXiv*, 2023, https://doi.org/10.48550/arXiv.2310.03011.

[40] Bochkarev, A., Heese, R., Jäger, S., Schiewe, P., and Schöbel, A. "Quantum computing for discrete optimization: A highlight of three technologies," *arXiv preprint*, https://doi.org/10.48550/arXiv.2409.01373arXiv.

[41] Durán, C., Carrasco, R., Soto, I., et al. "Quantum algorithms: Applications, criteria and metrics," *Complex & Intelligent Systems*, vol. 9, pp. 6373–6392, 2023, https://doi.org/10.1007/s40747-023-01073-9.

[42] Campos, R. "Hybrid quantum-classical algorithms," *arXiv*, 2024, https://doi.org/10.48550/arXiv.2406.12371arXiv.

[43] Rajamani, K. "Hybrid quantum-classical neural networks: Bridging classical and quantum computing paradigms," *International Journal of Advanced Research in Engineering and Technology (IJARET)*, vol. 16, no. 1, pp. 651–661, 2025, https://doi.org/10.34218/IJARET_16_01_045IAEME.

[44] Geetha, B.T., Viswanathan, R., Patel, S.N., Mukunthan, M.A., and Jindal, S. "Hybrid quantum-classical communication networks: New directions in cybersecurity," *Nanotechnology Perceptions*, 2025, https://nano-ntp.com/index.php/nano/article/view/2331Nano NTP.

[45] Rajamani, K. "Hybrid quantum-classical neural networks: Bridging classical and quantum computing paradigms," *International Journal of Advanced Research in Engineering and Technology (IJARET)*, vol. 16, no. 1, pp. 651–661, 2025, https://doi.org/10.34218/IJARET_16_01_045.

[46] Christian Frahm, "Finance 4.0: How quantum computing will transform financial services," *Forbes*, 2024. Available at https://www.forbes.com/sites/forbestechcouncil/2024/06/06/finance-40-how-quantum-computing-will-transform-financial-services/Forbes, accessed on 15 March 2026.

[47] Gupta, K., Saxena, D., Rani, P., Kumar, J., Makkar, A., Singh, A.K., and Lee, C.-N. "An intelligent quantum cyber-security framework for healthcare data management," *arXiv preprint*, 2024, https://doi.org/10.48550/arXiv.2410.03217arXiv.

[48] Bishwas, A.K. and Sen, M. "Strategic roadmap for quantum-resistant security: A framework for preparing industries for the quantum threat," *arXiv preprint*, 2024, https://doi.org/10.48550/arXiv.2411.09995arXiv.

[49] IBM, "New Development & Innovation Roadmap," 2024. Available at https://www.ibm.com/quantum/assets/IBM_Quantum_Developmen_%26_Innovation_Roadmap_Explainer_2024-Update.pdfIBM, accessed on 15 March 2026.

[50] Google Quantum AI, "Our quantum computing roadmap," n.d. Available at https://quantumai.google/roadmapGoogle Quantum AI+1Google Quantum AI+1, accessed on 15 March 2026.

[51] IQM Quantum Computers, "Development roadmap," 2025. Available at https://meetiqm.com/technology/roadmap/ScienceDirect+2IQM Quantum Computers+2AIM Councils+2, accessed on 15 March 2026.

[52] QuEra Computing, "QuEra computing releases a groundbreaking roadmap for advanced error-corrected quantum computers," 2024. Available at https://www.quera.com/press-releases/quera-computing-releases-a-groundbreaking-roadmap-for-advanced-error-corrected-quantum-computers-pioneering-the-next-frontier-in-quantum-innovation-0quera.com, accessed on 15 March 2026.

[53] U.S. Department of Energy, *2024 Quantum Information Science Applications Roadmap*, 2024. Available at https://www.quantum.gov/wp-content/uploads/2024/12/DOE_QIS_Roadmap_Final.pdfquantum.gov, accessed on 15 March 2026.

[54] Cherrat, E.A., Kerenidis, I., Mathur, N., Landman, J., Strahm, M. and Li, Y.Y. "Quantum vision transformers," *Quantum*, vol. 8, p. 1265, 2024. Available at https://quantum-journal.org/papers/q-2024-02-22-1265/pdf/quantum-journal.org, accessed on 15 March 2026.

[55] Xue, C., Chen, Z.-Y., Zhuang, X.-N., Wang, Y.-J., Sun, T.-P., Wang, J.-C., Liu, H.-Y., Wu, Y.-C., Wang, Z.-L., and Guo, G.-P. "End-to-end quantum vision transformer: Towards practical quantum speedup in large-scale models," *arXiv*, 2024, https://arxiv.org/abs/2402.18940arXiv.

[56] Moody's Analytics, *Quantum Artificial Intelligence—Moody's*, 2024. Available at https://www.moodys.com/web/en/us/insights/resources/next-frontier-after-ai-agents.pdfMoody's, accessed on 15 March 2026.

[57] SpinQ Research Team, "Research team reports AI model trains itself to understand and predict quantum systems," *The Quantum Insider*, 2025. Available at https://thequantuminsider.com/2025/04/08/research-team-reports-ai-model-trains-itself-to-understand-and-predict-quantum-systems/thequantuminsider.com, accessed on 15 March 2026.

[58] IBM, "IBM nearing quantum advantage: What it means for the future of AI," *Big Data Wire*, 2025. Available at https://www.bigdatawire.com/2025/04/14/ibm-nearing-quantum-advantage-what-it-means-for-the-future-of-ai/Big Data Wire, accessed on 15 March 2026.

[59] McKinsey & Company "Steady progress in approaching the quantum advantage," 2024. Available at https://www.mckinsey.com/capabilities/mckinsey-digital/our-insights/steady-progress-in-approaching-the-quantum-advantageMcKinsey & Company+1McKinsey & Company+1, accessed on 15 March 2026.

[60] Kyndryl, "How to put the quantum advantage to work for your company," 2024, https://www.kyndryl.com/us/en/perspectives/articles/2024/12/apply-quantum-advantage, accessed on 15 March 2026.

[61] *Time*, "Gen AI has already taken the world by storm. Just wait until it gets a quantum boost," 2024. Available at https://time.com/6977355/generative-ai-quantum-computing-us-china-technology/, accessed on 15 March 2026.

[62] E-SPIN Group, "Quantum cryptography implementations: Advancements, challenges, and real-world applications," 2023. Available at https://www.e-spincorp.com/quantum-cryptography-implementations-advancements-challenges-and-real-world-applications/E-Spin Corp, accessed on 15 March 2026.

[63] Quantum Evangelist, "Quantum computing for business real-world use cases," 2024. Available at https://quantumzeitgeist.com/quantum-computing-for-business-real-world-use-cases/Quantum Zeitgeist, accessed on 15 March 2026.

[64] IBM Quantum, "Case studies," n.d. Available at https://www.ibm.com/quantum/case-studies, accessed on 15 March 2026.

[65] IBM Research, "When machine learning meets quantum computers: A case study," 2021. Available at https://research.ibm.com/publications/when-machine-learning-meets-quantum-computers-a-case-study , accessed on 15 March 2026.

[66] *The Times of India*, "IIT-I develops quantum AI nanotechnology to aid in early detection of genetic mutations," 2025. Available at https://timesofindia.indiatimes.com/city/indore/iit-i-develops-quantum-ai-nanotechnology-to-aid-in-early-detection-of-genetic-mutations/articleshow/120942599.cms, accessed on 15 March 2026.

[67] Google Quantum AI, Research Publications, n.d. Available at https://quantumai.google/researchI, accessed on 15 March 2026.

[68] IonQ, "IonQ demonstrates quantum-enhanced applications advancing AI," 2025. Available at https://ionq.com/news/ionq-demonstrates-quantum-enhanced-applications-advancing-aiIonQ, accessed on 15 March 2026.

[69] QuEra Computing, "Top applications of quantum computing for machine learning, 2023. Available at https://www.quera.com/blog-posts/applications-of-quantum-computing-for-machine-learningquera.com, accessed on 15 March 2026.

[70] Biamonte, J., Wittek, P., Pancotti, N., Rebentrost, P., Wiebe, N. and Lloyd, S. "Quantum machine learning," *Nature*, vol. 549, no. 7671, 195–202, 2017, https://doi.org/10.1038/nature23474.

[71] Preskill, J. "Quantum computing in the NISQ era and beyond," *Quantum*, vol. 2, p. 79, 2018, https://doi.org/10.22331/q-2018-08-06-79.

[72] Barenco, A., Bennett, C.H., Cleve, R., et al. "Elementary gates for quantum computation," *Physical Review A*, vol. 52, no. 5, p. 3457, 1995, https://doi.org/10.1103/PhysRevA.52.3457.

[73] Dubey, S.R., Singh, S.K., and Chaudhuri, B.B. "Activation functions in deep learning: A comprehensive survey and benchmark," *arXiv preprint*, arXiv:2109.14545, 2021, https://arxiv.org/abs/2109.14545.

[74] Zurek, W.H. "Decoherence, einselection, and the quantum origins of the classical," *Reviews of Modern Physics*, vol. 75, no. 3, p. 715, 2003, https://doi.org/10.1103/RevModPhys.75.715.

[75] Shor, P.W. "Polynomial-time algorithms for prime factorization and discrete logarithms on a quantum computer," *SIAM Journal on Computing*, vol. 26, no. 5, pp. 1484–1509, 1997, https://doi.org/10.1137/S0097539795293172.

[76] LeCun, Y., Bengio, Y., and Hinton, G. "Deep learning," *Nature*, vol. 521, no. 7553, pp. 436–444, 2015, https://doi.org/10.1038/nature14539.

[77] Rumelhart, D.E., Hinton, G.E., and Williams, R.J. "Learning representations by back-propagating errors," *Nature*, vol. 323, no. 6088, pp. 533–536, 1986, https://doi.org/10.1038/323533a0.

[78] Marcus, G. "Deep learning: A critical appraisal," *arXiv preprint*, arXiv:1801.00631, 2018, https://arxiv.org/abs/1801.00631.

[79] Schuld, M., Sinayskiy, I. and Petruccione, F. "The quest for a quantum neural network," *Quantum Information Processing*, vol. 13, no. 11, 2567–2586, 2014, https://doi.org/10.1007/s11128-014.

[80] Amin, M.H., Andriyash, E., Rolfe, J., Kulchytskyy, B., and Melko, R. "Quantum Boltzmann machine," *Physical Review X*, vol. 8, no. 2, p. 021050, 2018, https://doi.org/10.1103/PhysRevX.8.021050.

[81] Mitarai, K., Negoro, M., Kitagawa, M. and Fujii, K. "Quantum circuit learning," *Physical Review A*, vol. 98, no. 3, p. 032309, 2018, https://doi.org/10.1103/PhysRevA.98.032309.

[82] Verdon, G., Pye, J. and Broughton, M. "A universal training algorithm for quantum deep learning," *arXiv preprint*, arXiv:1806.09729, 2018, https://arxiv.org/abs/1806.09729.

[83] Henderson, M., Shakya, S., Pradhan, S. and Cook, T. "Quanvolutional neural networks: Powering image recognition with quantum circuits," *Quantum Machine Intelligence*, vol. 2, no. 1, pp. 1–9, 2020, https://doi.org/10.1007/s42484-020-00012-y.

[84] Orús, R., Mugel, S., and Lizaso, E. "Quantum computing for finance: Overview and prospects," *Reviews in Physics*, vol. 4, p. 100028, 2019, https://doi.org/10.1016/j.revip.2019.100028.

[85] Pirandola, S., Andersen, U.L., Banchi, L. et al., "Advances in quantum cryptography," *Advances in Optics and Photonics*, vol. 12, no. 4, 1012–1236, 2020, https://doi.org/10.1364/AOP.361502.

6 Quantum Leaps in Finance: Integrating Quantum Computing and Machine Learning

Kalpan Dharamshi[1*]

The financial industry is constantly evolving and pushing the boundaries of classical computing. The complexity of risk models, derivatives pricing, and large-scale optimization problems are some of the primary examples where traditional computing techniques are proving to be insufficient. NP-hard problems and algorithmically intensiveness Monte Carlo simulations can be resolved by combining quantum computing (QC) and quantum machine learning (QML) to provide potential exponential speedups to solving problems.

The chapter starts with establishing the fundamental principles of QC, qubits, superposition, and entanglement, and introducing key quantum algorithms that are relevant to financial institutions. Quantum amplitude estimation (QAE) is discussed is on numerous occasions to provide quadratic speedup over classical methods for problems such as Monte Carlo simulations and derivatives pricing. Furthermore, the chapter explores both the hybrid and quantum-native paradigms and highlighting algorithms such as the variational quantum eigensolver (VQE) and the quantum approximate optimization of Algorithm (QAOA), which are primarily used for large-scale optimization problems like portfolio optimization.

The chapter further explores applications in Algorithmic Trading, enhanced Fraud Detection, and proactive strategies such as post-quantum encryption to secure financial data. Limitations of QC are kept in mind when discussing the strategies for future rollout, addressing the immediate reality of the noisy intermediate-scale quantum (NISQ) era, the technical challenges in decoherence and scalability, and the regulatory challenges hindering widespread adoption. Finally, the chapter concludes with a forward-looking roadmap and recommendations to financial institutions to continue investing in upcoming technologies, building interdisciplinary talent, and navigating the ethical implications of integrating QC and artificial intelligence (AI) in finance.

[1] Senior Member, Institute of Electrical and Electronics Engineers (IEEE), USA.
ORCID ID: 0009-0006-0190-0854
* Corresponding author: kalpan.dharamshi@ieee.org

DOI: 10.1201/9781003646068-6

1. Introduction: The Convergence of QC, ML, and Finance

1.1 Evolution of the Landscape in Financial Services

1.1.1 Computational Limitations in Complex Financial Systems

Financial institutions have traditionally relied on classical computing techniques and statistical methods for modeling market behavior, risk assessment, and asset valuation. Although these systems have provided some satisfactory results for simpler modeling techniques, they have often failed in complex modeling tasks with higher dimensional data and non-linear models in modern financial systems. Examples include systems that require precise risk calculations in complex derivatives portfolio or performing Monte Carlo simulations in stress testing scenarios. The accuracy of these calculations is directly correlated to the number of samples that can be processed in a limited amount of time. Even high-performing classical computing clusters fall short of expectations in these scenarios.

Large-scale optimization problems with diverse asset classes and non-linear dependencies can quickly evolve into NP-hard problems. Classical techniques often rely on heuristics to generate sub-optimal solutions to these problems. Another pervasive challenge is that as the data dimensions of the problem statement raises the number of variables in the problem, it also raises linearly, often known as the "curse of dimensionality." This impacts every aspect of problem-solving from pricing to accurately modeling the solution, making it intractable for traditional computing techniques [9].

1.1.2 The Growth of Big Data and AI/ML in Finance

In last few decades we have witnessed growth in the volume and variety of financial data. Nowadays, financial institution data consists of not only traditional and structured transactional data (stock prices, trading volumes, etc.) but also non-structured data (satellite imagery, public media sentiment, news feeds, etc.). In order to process these large quantities of data, AI and ML techniques are widely incorporated in financial institutions. These techniques are adept at identifying complex patterns, making predictions, and making autonomous decisions. The transformative impact of these techniques is visible in various applications:

- Fraud Detection: ML algorithms are trained on vast amounts of data to detect the fraud patterns.
- Credit Scoring: Sophisticated ML techniques can go beyond static methods (FICO) to assess risk scores more dynamically (evolving market sentiments).
- Algorithmic Trading: AI-enabled trading algorithms can consume real-time market data and sentiments for execution of trades with minimal risks and optimize profits.
- Personalized Financial Advice: AI-powered platforms can offer custom financial advice depending on the client age, financial portfolio, and risk appetite.

These increasingly complex AI-driven ML algorithms are often developed and trained on deep neural networks. Training these deep neural networks requires sophisticated tuning techniques of neural network weights, which in turn requires high performance computer power. Moreover, after training, deploying these complex models at scale in various cloud platforms can also push the boundaries of traditional computing capabilities [16] [17].

1.2 Introduction to Quantum Computing (QC)

1.2.1 Brief Overview of QC Principles

QC provides a possible option to traditional computation limitations. It leverages the quantum fundamentals to process the information in a conceptually different manner than the classical computers. Classical computation, at the core, stores the information in the form of bits, which can take a state of zero or one. QC, on the other hand, uses qubits, a quantum analogue of bits. A qubit can exist in superposition of both zero and one at the same time. It allows quantum computers with multiple qubits to represent an exponential number of states between zero and one. Entanglement, another interesting concept, allows two or more qubits to be intrinsically linked to one another such that state of one can influence the state of the other irrespective of their distance. Correlation between the qubits allows for complex non-local operations that are improbable for classical systems.

The combined properties of superposition and entanglement allow QC to achieve quantum parallelism. QC can effectively explore multiple paths or solutions to a problem statement at the same instant. Traditional computers require the power of multiprocessing to explore multiple paths simultaneously. A single quantum processor can operate on all superposed states at once providing exponential speedup to traditional processing systems.

Information processing in QC involves applying quantum gates to change the states of qubits and perform operations, ultimately collapsing the superposition into a definite classical outcome upon measurement [15].

1.2.2 Why Is QC Relevant for Computationally Intensive Problems?

he unique attributes of qubits and quantum gates make QC relevant for solving NP-hard problems in a quicker timeframe than traditional computing. Some of the practical problems that can leverage QC are:

Optimization Problems: Searching an optimal solution among a large number of possible solutions (e.g., optimal routing, resource allocation, portfolio optimization).

Simulation Problems: Accurately modeling complex systems at a fundamental level (e.g., molecular interactions in drug discovery, financial market dynamics).

Factoring Large Numbers: A problem that underpins modern cryptography, where QCs could break widely used encryption standards.

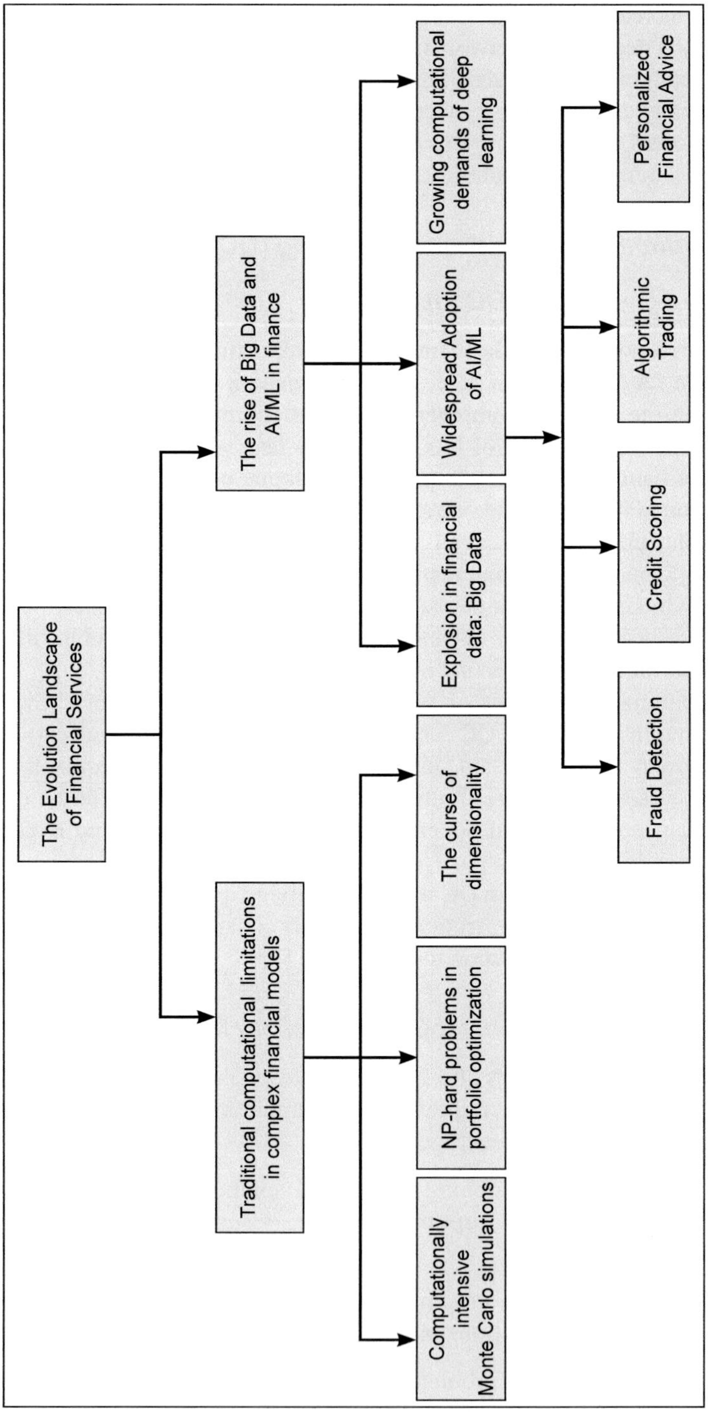

Fig. 6.1 Evolution of the financial landscape.

These type of issues are prevalent in various research and industrial domains, and they are critically embedded in the core functions of financial domains. The potential for QC to solve exponential problems at a faster pace than traditional computing systems can prove to be a game-changer for financial institutions [9] [15].

1.3 The Promise of Quantum Machine Learning (QML)

1.3.1 Synergy between QC and ML

QML has emerged as an intersection of QC and ML. QML leverages the potential of QC to enhance and expedite the traditional means of ML approaches. The synergy arises from the core issues that both the fields are trying to address or achieve. The higher-dimensional and complex data creates computational challenges for ML, and quantum mechanics offer a means to resolve these computation challenges. QML seeks to use the concepts of superposition and entanglement to overcome these computing bottlenecks faced when training deep neural networks [9] [15].

1.3.2 Potential for Enhanced Algorithms and Problem-Solving

QML offers a potential to create ML models that can be trained at a faster pace, provide more accurate predictions, and are able to tackle intractable problems in the financial domain. Some of the focus areas for the QML include the following:

- Quantum Speedup for Data Pre-processing and Feature Engineering: The process leverages quantum techniques to transform the raw features to relevant features in a reasonable time-frame [8].
- Enhanced Pattern Recognition: Quantum techniques can help in detecting subtle fraud patterns that may go unnoticed in a traditional ML model [8].
- Improved Optimization Techniques: Training an ML model is an optimization problem. Deep neural networks require considerable power and training time to arrive at an optimal neural network weight. Quantum optimization algorithms (e.g., quantum approximate optimization of Algorithm [QAOA], variational quantum eigensolver [VQE]) could provide significant speedups for these tasks [7].

Ultimately, QML aims to provide a computational edge to existing techniques that may lead to considerable improvement in risk management, algorithmic trading, and other areas that can propel the financial industry to offer the next-generation services [9] [8].

2. Introduction to Quantum Computing (QC): A Financial Perspective

This section will provide a fundamental understanding of QC and highlight its potential applicability in the world of finance [9]. It will cover the earlier explained

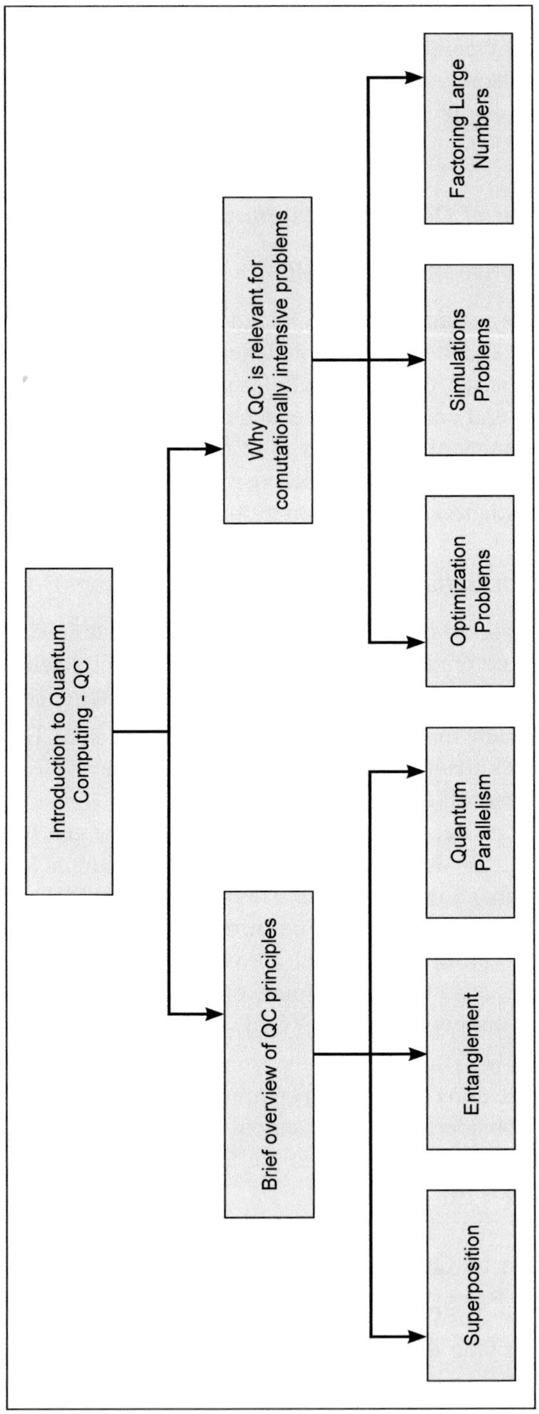

Fig. 6.2 Quantum principles and uses for QC.

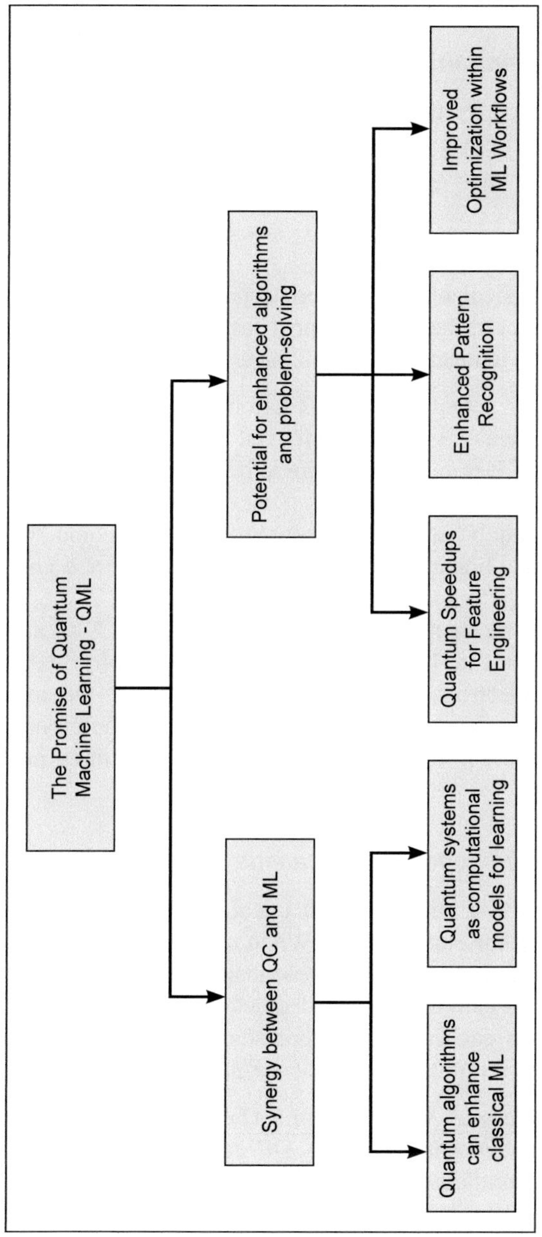

Fig. 6.3 Quantum computing and machine learning.

concepts of quantum mechanics in further detail, introduce the key quantum algorithms with a vision of possible implementation in the financial domain, and discuss the present state of available quantum hardware.

2.1 Quantum Mechanics Basics (Simplified)

The QC is governed by the behavior of matter and energy at the atomic or subatomic levels. These principles allow QCs to perform calculations in ways that are different than classical computers.

2.1.1 Qubits vs Classical Bits

Classical Bit: Classical bit is a foundational unit for storing information in computers. It is either in state zero or one. Classical bits are typically implemented using voltage levels in electronic circuits, and their state is deterministic.

Qubit (Quantum Bit): Qubit is a foundational unit for storing information in QCs. A qubit, unlike a classical bit, can exist in a superposition of both zero and one simultaneously. It implies that a single qubit can represent a combination of possibilities, instead of one.

For example, a qubit could be 30 percent in state zero and 70 percent in state one, represented as a linear combination $\alpha|0\rangle + \beta|1\rangle$, where α and β are complex numbers and $|\alpha\rangle^2 + |\beta\rangle^2 = 1$.

The ability to be in multiple states allows for QCs to achieve quantum parallelism. Qubits can be realized using various physical systems, such as the spin of an electron, the polarization of a photon, the energy levels of a superconducting circuit (e.g., transmon qubits), or trapped ions. The choice of physical implementation impacts scalability, coherence times, and gate fidelities [15].

2.1.2 Superposition and Its Implications for Parallel Computation

Superposition: This is a quantum mechanical principle that allows a qubit to be in multiple states at the same instant. When multiple qubits are in that state, the number of possible states they can represent simultaneously grows exponentially. Specifically, n qubits can represent 2^n distinct classical states simultaneously. For instance, two qubits can essentially represent four states ($|00\rangle$, $|01\rangle$, $|10\rangle$, $|11\rangle$) simultaneously, and 3 qubits can represent 8 states.

Implications for Parallel Computation: The exponential growth in possible states enables quantum parallelism. A QC can perform computations on these superposed states simultaneously in a single operation to achieve parallelism. For problem solving, it can effectively evaluate multiple inputs or explore multiple possibilities in a single operation. Classical computers would need to employ multiple processors to process multiple inputs or possibilities in parallel. Quantum computers can operate on an exponential number of states in parallel, though we can employ an exponential number of processors for an exponential number of states in classical computers [15].

2.1.3 Entanglement's Role in Quantum Algorithms

Entanglement is a quantum principle that allows two or more bits to be intrinsically linked to one another, allowing them to be "entangled" with each other. One entangled qubit can instantly influence the other irrespective of the distance between them. It creates a stronger correlation among qubits that is difficult to achieve in classical bits. The correlation allows quantum computers to perform highly non-local computations that can create intricate quantum states that are essential for quantum speedups. Shor's algorithm [1] (factoring) and Grover's algorithm [2] (searching) leverage the concept to gain computational edge. Without entanglement, a quantum computer would function similar to a probabilistic classical computer, which is unable to gain the exponential speedups required for quantum algorithms [15].

2.1.4 Quantum Gates and Circuits

Quantum gates form the basic foundational blocks for quantum circuits, similar to logical gates (AND, OR, NOT) for classical circuits. They manipulate the current state of qubits, and they are also reversible, unlike logical gates, which helps maintain the total probability of the quantum state [15].

- Hadamard (H) Gate: A single-qubit gate that creates superposition from a definite state (e.g., transforms $|0\rangle$ to $(|0\rangle + |1\rangle)/\sqrt{2}$ and $|1\rangle$ to $(|0\rangle - |1\rangle)/\sqrt{2}$). It is essential for initializing quantum parallelism.
- Pauli-X (NOT) Gate: A single gate that modifies the state of a qubit (e.g., $|0\rangle$ is modified $|1\rangle$ and vice versa).
- Controlled-NOT (CNOT) gate: A gate with two qubits where the present state of a target qubit is modified only if a control qubit is in a specific state (e.g., $|1\rangle$). It is fundamental for creating entanglement among qubits.
- Rotation Gates (Rx, Ry, Rz): Single-qubit gates that rotate the state of a qubit around specific axes on the Bloch sphere, allowing for fine-grained control over superposition and phase.

A chain of quantum gates forms a quantum circuit. When a quantum circuit is applied to qubits, a quantum computation is performed. Creating a chain of quantum gates or a quantum circuit to perform a computational task is the art of quantum programming, where the arrangement and type of gates determine the functionality or task the programmer is trying to achieve. These circuits leverage superposition and entanglement to complete a task and generate output, which collapses the qubit superposition to classical bits (zero or one) to represent its result [15].

2.2 Key Quantum Algorithms Relevant to Finance

As the field of QC is advancing, several key algorithms have demonstrated considerable speedups over classical counterparts. These algorithms can impact applications in the financial domain either directly or indirectly.

2.2.1 Shor's Algorithm

Description: As the name suggests, this algorithm was formulated by Peter Shor in 1994 [1]. It can efficiently discover the prime factors of large composite numbers. For a large number L, the big O notation for time complexity to find factors for Shor's algorithm is polynomial ($O(L^3)$). In the best classical algorithms such as the general number field sieve, the big O notation for time complexity is exponential. Shor's algorithm uses the quantum Fourier transform technique to find a function affiliated to the number being factored.

Impact on Cryptography: Public encryption schemes such as the Rivest–Shamir–Adleman (RSA) algorithm and elliptic curve cryptography (ECC) leverage techniques like factoring large numbers and determining discrete logarithm problems to achieve the safe encryption of financial transactions, internet communications, etc. If a large-scale fault tolerant QC becomes available, these encryption methods could be compromised. Shor's algorithm can help design a post-quantum cryptography (PQC) standard to secure sensitive data, communications, and transactions in the future. The polynomial time complexity in Shor's algorithm can form a standard for future encryption algorithms, and it can act as proactive means to prevent data breaches [9].

2.2.2 Grover's Algorithm or Quantum Search

Description: As the name suggests, the algorithm was formulated by Lov Grover in 1996 [2]. It provides quadratic speedup for exploring a semi-structured or unstructured database. For a database consisting of N items, the classical algorithm would require linear time $O(n)$ to search an item. A quantum search algorithm would require $O(\sqrt{N})$ time to find an item. Although the quadratic speedup is not as high as compared to exponential speedup, it can yield significant time savings when the value of N is large.

Applications in Finance: The quadratic speedup can be helpful in various financial contexts.

- Database Search: It can efficiently search through a large financial transaction database to identify a certain anomalous transaction.
- Optimization Problems: The algorithm can be enhanced or adapted to search an optimal solution in a wide array of solutions to a problem. It can help speed up the search for optimal parameters in complex financial models or for a certain combination of optimization tasks. The algorithm can also be leveraged for searching optimal portfolio options for investment (finding the best subset of options available from a complete set) [9].

2.2.3 Quantum Fourier Transform (QFT) and Its Applications

Description: QFT is a quantum parallel of traditional discrete Fourier transform (DFT). It primarily functions in transforming quantum data from one state to another until periodicity is revealed in the data. The time complexity for a QFT using n qubits is polynomial $O(n^2)$, whereas the time complexity for classical fast Fourier transform is exponential $O(n\ 2^n)$.

Applications in Finance: QFT is a crucial subroutine within many other powerful quantum algorithms, including Shor's algorithm and quantum phase estimation. Its direct applications in finance include the following [9]:

- Time Series Analysis: Analyzing financial data (stock prices, volatility, interest rates) over a period of time to determine the underlying cycles that might indicate market trends, seasonality, or correlations. These trends can lead to potentially better forecasting models.
- Risk Factor Analysis: Analyzing risk data to identify periodicity or cycles can help in predicting risk factors for the financial institutions.

2.2.4 Quantum Amplitude Estimation (QAE) for Monte Carlo Simulations

Description: QAE is an algorithm that can estimate the amplitude of a specific state in a quantum superposition with a quadratic speedup over traditional Monte Carlo methods [6]. Classical Monte Carlo methods need $O(1/\text{epsilon}^2)$ samples to achieve a desired precision of epsilon; in contrast QAE requires only $O(1/\text{epsilon})$ samples to prepare a quantum state with the desired precision. The reduction in the number of samples for achieving the same precision for QAE indicates a quadratic speedup for solving the same problem.

Applications in Finance: Computationally intensive Monte Carlo simulations are required by multiple applications in the financial domain.

- Risk Management: Risk metrics such as value-at-risk (VaR), conditional value-at-risk (CVaR), and credit value adjustment (CVA) rely on Monte Carlo simulations for calculating the required numbers. QAE offers a quadratic improvement in generating the same metrics for timely risk assessments. Regulatory and compliance authorities require precise risk metrics to assess the health of the financial institution.
- Derivatives Pricing: Pricing tangled financial instruments like options (especially exotic and multi-asset options), structured products, and collateralized debt obligations often involve Monte Carlo simulations. QAE can offer substantial speedup for enabling faster and precise valuations for real-time trading, hedging, and risk management.
- Capital Allocation and Stress Testing: QAE can accelerate the creation of simulation data for stress testing, optimizing capital allocation, and performing financial data analysis.

2.3 Current State of Quantum Hardware

The understanding of theoretical advantages offered by quantum algorithms depends critically on the building of robust, stable, and ascendable quantum hardware. The field is currently in an exciting but challenging phase of rapid innovation, moving from theoretical concepts to practical, albeit nascent, devices.

2.3.1 Noisy Intermediate-Scale Quantum (NISQ) Devices

Description: We are currently in the "NISQ era" (a term coined by John Preskill in 2018 [4]). This period is characterized by quantum computers with a limited number of qubits (typically scoping from tens to a few hundreds, e.g., International Business Machines Corporation's (IBM's) Eagle processor with 127 qubits or IBM's Condor with 1,121 qubits announced in 2023) and significant noise (errors) in their operations. These devices are not yet powerful enough for universal, fault-tolerant QC, meaning they cannot run arbitrary, long computations without errors. However, they are capable of performing operations that might be beyond the reach of traditional supercomputers for specific limited tasks, provided the computation is short enough to complete before significant errors accumulate.

Implications: NISQ devices are primarily used for research, algorithm development, and exploring hybrid classical–quantum algorithms [9]. In these hybrid approaches, a classical computer handles the majority of the computation (e.g., optimization loops, data pre-processing), while computationally intensive subroutines (e.g., specific optimization steps, simulations of quantum systems, or variational quantum circuits) are offloaded to the quantum processor. The inherent noise levels mean that computations are prone to mistakes, and robust correction techniques are still in their nascent stages, limiting the extent and complexity of quantum circuits that can be reliably executed before noise overwhelms the signal. This necessitates careful algorithm design and error mitigation strategies [9].

2.3.2 Challenges: Decoherence, Error Rates, Scalability

Decoherence: The fragile nature of qubits makes them susceptible to environmental interference (e.g., thermal fluctuations, electromagnetic fields, stray particles, vibrations). The interference causes qubits to lose their quantum properties (superposition and entanglement) and "decohere" (lose their quantum information and revert to a classical state). It limits the time for which a quantum computation can run effectively. In order to maintain coherence, extreme conditions such as cryogenic temperatures (near absolute zero, e.g., for superconducting qubits) or ultra-high vacuum environments (for trapped ions) are required to isolate qubits from their surroundings, which is a major engineering challenge [9].

Error Rates: The decoherence causes non-negligible error rates on qubits, which cause an imperfect execution environment. The error rates aggregate as the count of quantum gates in the circuit increases, which leads to corruption of computing results. Developing robust quantum error correction (QEC) codes is a critical area of research. Although QEC is designed to protect quantum information from noise by encoding logical qubits into multiple physical qubits, it requires a large number of physical qubits (e.g., thousands) to encode and protect a single logical (error-corrected) qubit, posing significant overheads and engineering hurdles for developing fault-tolerant QCs [9].

Scalability: It is a significant challenge to build QCs with a large number of high-quality, interconnected, and controllable qubits. A variety of hardware modalities (superconducting qubits, trapped ions, photonic qubits, silicon spin qubits, topological qubits) need to be explored, each with its own advantages and scalability challenges related to fabrication, control, and connectivity. Achieving scalable infrastructure for QC most impactful and complex quantum algorithms (like Shor's for breaking RSA encryption) seems like a long-term goal [9].

2.3.3 Cloud-Based Quantum Platforms

Accessibility: Although there have been significant hardware challenges in maintaining quantum computers, cloud-based platforms are increasingly democratizing quantum computing resources [9]. Leading technology companies and quantum computing startups (e.g., IBM with IBM Quantum Experience, Google with Quantum AI, Amazon with Amazon Braket, Microsoft with Azure Quantum, Rigetti, Quantinuum) provide users with remote accessibility to their quantum processors and powerful quantum simulators via the internet. Users can write quantum code using open-source software development kits (SDKs) like Qiskit (IBM), Cirq (Google), PennyLane (Xanadu), or Microsoft's Q# and submit jobs to real quantum hardware or powerful classical simulators.

Benefits for Finance: The cloud-based platforms offer a low entry barrier for financial institutions, researchers, and programmers to access QC.

Experimentation: Allow individuals and institutions to test theoretical concepts in the real quantum hardware and gain practical experience.

Develop Quantum Software: Build and refine quantum applications, libraries, and frameworks tailored for financial problems.

Test Proof-of-Concept Applications: Experiment and explore the potential of QC for financial problems such as small-scale portfolio optimization [7], simple option pricing models, without needing a heavy investment on the quantum hardware. This fosters innovation and builds a talent pool within the industry for more capable quantum software.

3. Quantum Machine Learning (QML): Bridging the Gap

In this section we dive into the emerging field of quantum machine learning (QML), and explore how the principles and power of QC can be used to enhance and accelerate machine learning training and inference process [5]. The section will also cover different paradigms for integrating quantum capabilities into financial applications that leverage machine learning.

3.1 What Is Quantum Machine Learning?

3.1.1 Definition and Motivation

Definition: QML is an interdisciplinary field that uses the synergy between QC and ML. QML leverages quantum algorithms to better classical ML tasks (faster training, better generalization, or handling larger datasets) [5] [12] [15].

Motivation: The limitations of the classical ML process are the primary motivating factors for QML.

Large and High-Dimensional Data: The "curse of dimensionality" and the machine complexity associated in processing vast, complex datasets often hinder the performance and accuracy of classical ML algorithms. The superposition property of qubits allows QML to represent high-dimensional data and mitigate the performance issue to a certain extent [5].

Complex Optimization Problems: Training deep neural networks or hyperparameter tuning are inherently complex, non-convex optimization tasks that classical algorithms struggle to achieve. The classical process may get stuck at a local minima, and may not be able to search for global minima in the function space. Quantum search algorithms can provide quadratic speed improvements in searching for global minima [9] [17].

Simulating Quantum Systems: ML is increasingly used in every industry and domain for prediction and forecasting. Simulation is an important aspect to stress test that quantum algorithms can provide quadratic improvement in generating simulations for systems [15].

3.1.2 Hybrid Classical–Quantum Algorithms

Description: Given the current limitations of quantum hardware (NISQ era), where qubits are noisy and small in number, most practical QML approaches today involve hybrid classical–quantum algorithms [4] [9]. In this paradigm, a classical computer handles the bulk of the computation, while a quantum processor is used to perform specific computationally intensive subroutines that benefit from quantum speedup. The results from the quantum computation are then fed back to the classical computer, which refines parameters and iterates the process.

A typical hybrid workflow involves the following:

- Classical Pre-processing: Preparing classical data and defining the problem.
- Quantum Circuit Preparation: Encoding data into quantum states and running a circuit parameterized with quantum (often called a "variational quantum circuit" or "ansatz").

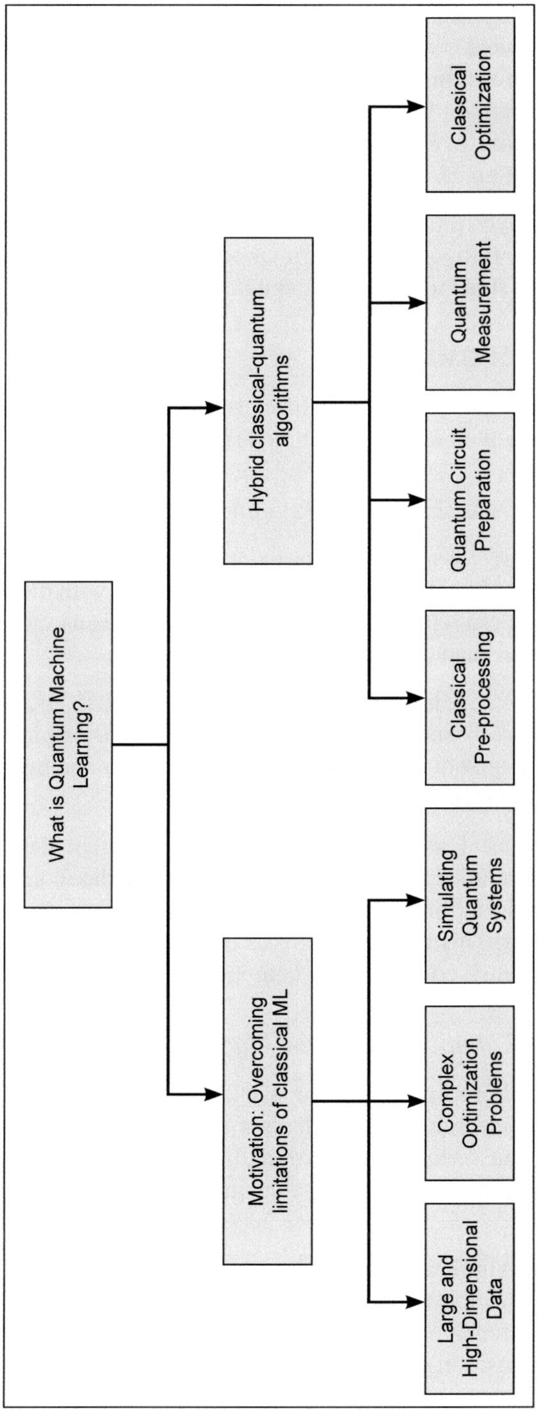

Fig. 6.4 Overview of QML.

- Quantum Measurement: Measuring the qubits to obtain outcomes (probabilities, expectation values).
- Classical Optimization: Using a traditional optimizer to update the parameters of the quantum circuit founded on the measurement outcomes to reduce a cost function or maximize a reward (e.g., gradient descent on a classical computer that tunes quantum gate parameters).

Advantages: This hybrid approach allows us to leverage the nascent power of NISQ devices while mitigating their limitations (noise, limited qubit count). It is a practical stepping stone toward full quantum advantage in ML [9].

3.2 Paradigms of QML

QML can be broadly categorized into different paradigms based on how quantum computation is integrated into the machine learning process.

3.2.1 Quantum Data (Encoding Data into Quantum States)

Concept: The idea of "quantum feature mapping" refers to encoding traditional data into quantum states. The idea is that quantum states, with their exponentially large Hilbert spaces, can represent complex classical data in a much more compact or expressive manner than classical bits [5].

Methods: Multiple encoding schemes exist, such as basis encoding (mapping data to computational basis states), amplitude encoding (mapping data points to the amplitudes of a quantum state), or angle encoding (mapping data to rotation angles of quantum gates).

Motivation for Finance: Datasets in financial domain are often high-dimensional in nature. For instance, market features and historical trading data contain thousands of features. Encoding the high-dimensional data into quantum states could potentially allow quantum algorithms to locate patterns or correlations that are too subtle or computationally intensive for classical computers [5].

3.2.2 Quantum-Enhanced Classical Algorithms (Using QC Subroutines)

Concept: This paradigm involves using a QC to accelerate specific subroutines within an otherwise classical machine learning algorithm. The core ML algorithm remains classical, but certain computationally intensive parts are offloaded to a quantum processor if they can achieve a quantum speedup [9].

Examples:
Quantum Linear Algebra: Many classical ML algorithms (e.g., support vector machines, principal component analysis, linear regression) involve computationally intensive linear algebra operations (e.g., matrix inversion, eigenvalue decomposition). Quantum algorithms like the HHL algorithm [10] (for solving linear systems of equations) could potentially accelerate these steps,

though practical implementations on current hardware face significant challenges (e.g., data loading) [9].

Quantum Optimization: As discussed in hybrid algorithms, quantum optimizers like QAOA or VQE can be used to find optimal parameters for classical neural networks or other classical ML models, thereby speeding up the training phase [7] [17].

Relevance for Finance: This is particularly relevant for classical ML models widely used in finance that rely heavily on linear algebra or complex optimization, such as portfolio optimization, risk modeling, and certain econometric models [5].

3.2.3 Quantum Native Algorithms (Algorithms that are Inherently Quantum)

Concept: The quantum native algorithms do not have a direct classical analogue, instead they rely on quantum principles (superposition, entanglement) from their core design. The algorithms are trained directly from the quantum data or leverage quantum mechanics to reach exponential or quadratic speedups for a specific ML process [15].

Examples: Clustering quantum algorithms such as k-means, dimensionality reduction algorithms such as principal component analysis (PCA), or quantum neural networks that can work directly on the qubits of information.

Long-Term Potential for Finance: Quantum native algorithms are in the early stages of evolution. However, these algorithms represent long-term potential for QML. If we can generate the financial data in qubits, quantum models can be leveraged to provide superior performance and accuracy that the classical computing models [15].

3.3 Key QML Implementations

The field of QML is rapidly advancing, with new algorithms being proposed frequently. Here are some of the most prominent ones with potential applications in finance.

3.3.1 Variational Quantum Eigensolver (VQE) for Optimization

Description: VQE is a hybrid classical–quantum optimization algorithm that works by preparing a parameterized quantum state (ansatz) on a QC, measuring its energy (or cost function), and then using a traditional optimizer (running on a classical computer) to adjust the parameters of the quantum circuit to minimize energy/cost [3] [9]. The process is executed in an iterative feedback loop that leverages the QC for state preparation and measurement and traditional computers for optimization loop.

Applications in Finance: The algorithm is relevant for optimization problems in the financial world, especially those that can be correlated to finding the minimum energy state of a Hamiltonian. The algorithm can be applied once the problem statement can be designed as an optimization problem.

- Portfolio Optimization: Searching for an optimal asset allocation that can minimize risk for a specified return or maximize return for a specified amount of risk considering dependencies and complex constraints. The portfolio optimization problem can be designed as a quadratic unconstrained binary optimization problem (QUBO) which can be handled by VQE [5].
- Credit Risk Management: Optimizing capital allocation to minimize expected losses across a portfolio, potentially incorporating complex correlation structures between defaults.
- Derivatives Pricing: Formulating the calculation of fair price for options as an optimization problem.

3.3.2 Quantum Approximate Optimization Algorithm (QAOA) for Combinatorial Optimization

Description: QAOA is another hybrid classical–quantum algorithm specifically formulated for solving combinatorial optimization problems, particularly those that can be expressed as searching the minimum or maximum of a cost function defined over binary variables [9] [11]. Like VQE, it uses a parameterized quantum circuit whose parameters are optimized by a traditional computer to find approximate solutions to hard optimization problems. QAOA is designed for problems represented as a graph, such as the Max-Cut problem.

Applications in Finance: Combinatorial optimization problems are pervasive in finance, making QAOA a promising candidate.

Portfolio Optimization: As with VQE, QAOA can be used for discrete portfolio optimization problems, such as selecting a subset of assets from a larger superset, subject to budget and risk constraints [7].

Arbitrage Opportunities: Identifying optimal sequences of trades across multiple markets or assets to exploit small price discrepancies.

Supply Chain Optimization in Financial Services: Optimizing resource allocation, routing, and scheduling within financial operations.

Fraud Detection (Feature Selection): Optimizing the selection of the most relevant features for a fraud detection model from a vast array of possibilities.

3.3.3 Quantum Support Vector Machines (QSVM)

Description: A quantum version of the traditional support vector machine (SVM), this a powerful algorithm for classification and regression. Traditional SVMs work by transforming data into a higher-dimensional feature space (using a "kernel function") to make it linearly separable. QSVMs, on the other hand, propose using a quantum kernel—a quantum circuit that implicitly maps classical data into an exponentially large Hilbert space, potentially allowing for more powerful feature mappings than classical kernels [5] [8].

Applications in Finance:
Credit Scoring: Leveraging quantum feature spaces, with improved accuracy, to classify loan applications [8].

Fraud Detection: Detect fraudulent transactions by identifying complex boundaries in higher-dimensional spaces [8].

Market Prediction: Identifying and classifying market trends (e.g., up/down, volatile/stable) on the basis of financial data.

Algorithmic Trading: Identifying trade entry and exit points for stocks and etfs.

3.3.4 Quantum Neural Networks (QNNs) and Quantum Generative Adversarial Networks (QGANs)

Quantum Neural Networks (QNNs)

Description: QNNs are quantum analogues of traditional neural networks. There are multiple architectures of QNNs that operate on quantum data to hybrid models with quantum layers and deep neural network layers. Superposition and Entanglement are leveraged in the neurons to achieve faster convergence on training data than in traditional neural networks. Variational Quantum Circuits (VQC) can be seen as a form of QNNs [5].

Applications in Finance:
Time Series Forecasting: Enhanced pattern recognition allows better prediction of financial time series data such as stock prices, volatility.

Risk Modeling: Sophisticated risk modeling can capture more complex non-linear dependencies which allows better prediction for credit, market, or operational risks.

Algorithmic Trading: Building enhanced trading strategies to study from real-time market data.

Quantum Generative Adversarial Networks (QGANs)
Description: QGANs are quantum extensions of classical generative adversarial networks (GANs) [13] [14] [16]. A classical GAN consists of two neural networks—a generator and a discriminator—that vie against each other to produce practical synthetic data. QGANs, on the other hand, either the generator, the discriminator, or both are quantum circuits. It aims to leverage quantum advantages to provide more realistic or complex data distributions [5].

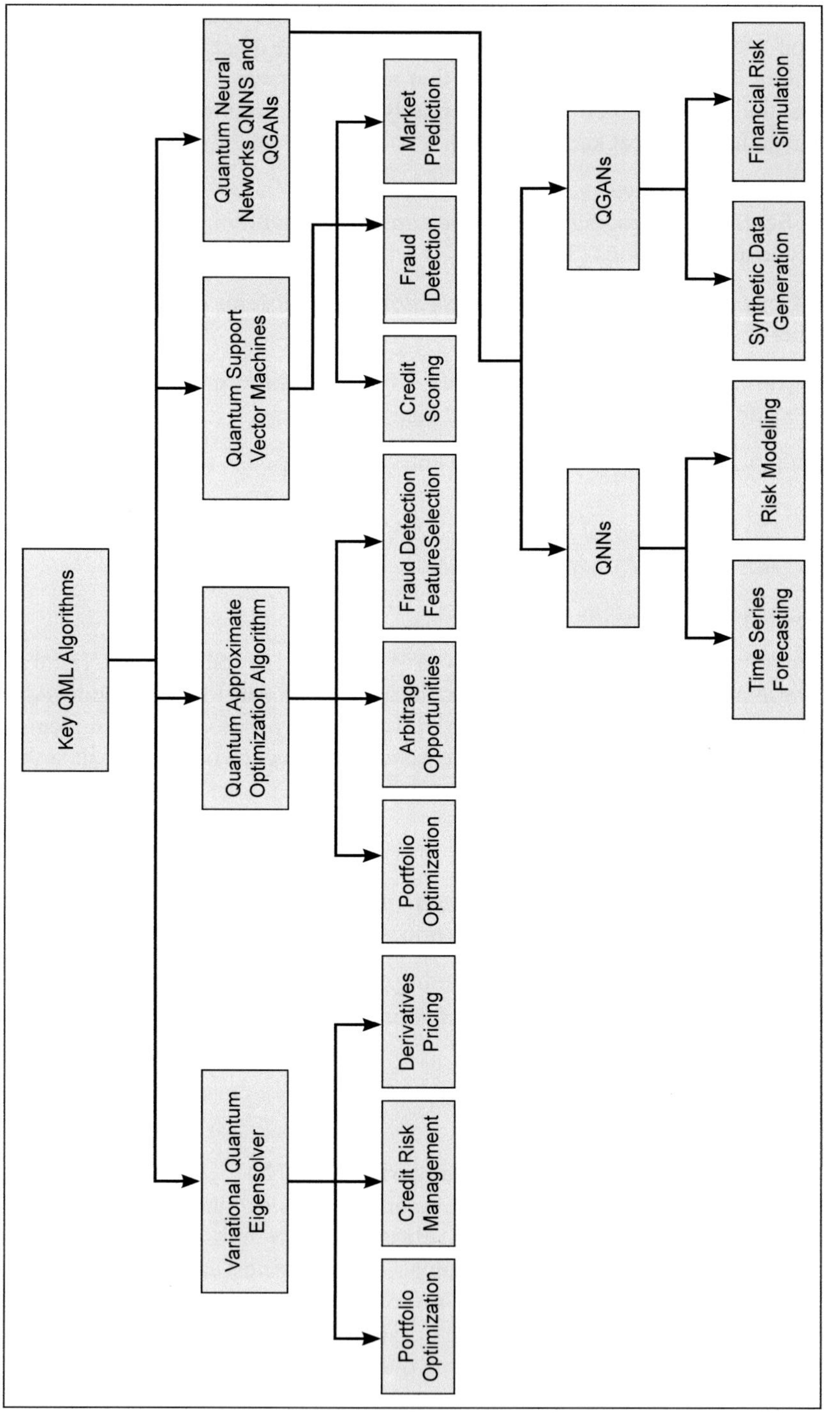

Fig. 6.5 Applications of key QML algorithms in finance.

Applications in Finance:
Synthetic Data Generation: Financial synthetic data generation for realistic market scenarios and transaction histories are primarily leveraged for model training, stress testing, and privacy-preserving data sharing, especially when the real data is scarce and sensitive [5].

Financial Risk Simulation: Simulating real-time market conditions with higher accuracy or speed than traditional methods particularly for high-dimensional or correlated data.

Anomaly Detection: The discriminator part of QGAN can be leveraged to identify subtle anomalies by partitioning real data from its own generated synthetic fraud data [16].

4. Applications of Quantum Computing (QC) and QML in Financial Services

We will explore the actively researched implementations of QC and QML in the financial industry [9]. We will cover the traditional challenges and how quantum approaches can help resolve those challenges with concrete examples of their potential impact.

4.1 Portfolio Optimization

Portfolio optimization aims to build a set of assets that maximize returns for a specified risk level or minimize risk for a desired return.

4.1.1 Classical Challenges (NP-Hard Problems)

The central challenge in traditional portfolio optimization is its NP-hard nature, in particular for large portfolios with multiple assets, complex constraints (e.g., budget, sector limits, liquidity, transaction costs), and realistic risk models (e.g., non-linear correlations, tail risk). With the increasing number of assets, the possibilities for portfolio combinations grow exponentially, making it computationally intractable for classical computers to search an optimal solution in a linear time [7] [9].

Moreover, the traditional methods rely on approximations, simplified models (e.g., Markowitz mean-variance optimization, which assumes normal distributions), or heuristic algorithms that rarely locate global minima or optimal solution. The sub-optimal asset allocations can lead to higher-than-necessary risks or lower returns [7].

4.1.2 Quantum Approaches: QAOA, VQE for Asset Allocation

QC offers a potential approach to tackle complex optimization problems. QAOA and VQE are prime instances of hybrid quantum–classical algorithms well-suited for combinatorial optimization problems that can be correlated to QUBO or Ising models [5] [7].

QAOA for Asset Allocation: A portfolio optimization technique can be mapped to a QUBO problem by assigning binary variables to represent whether an asset is included or excluded from the portfolio, and continuous variables can be used to represent the allocation weights of the asset. QAOA can then be used to find a possible solution to this QUBO, aiming to identify the optimal subset of assets and their allocation weights to meet the investment objectives and constraints. In this solution, QC is leveraged to handle the complex state measurement, and the traditional computer is used as an optimizer to tune the quantum circuit parameters [7].

VQE for Risk Minimization: In a Hamiltonian encoding of a portfolio's risk (e.g., variance), the ground state can be found by applying VQE. This helps identify the portfolio configurations with the lowest level of risk for a given set of assets [5].

4.1.3 Real-World Examples and Potential Speedups

Example: A large institutional investor who is managing a portfolio of millions of equities, bonds, and other investments needs to rebalance the portfolio on a daily basis while adhering to complex regulatory and internal constraints. A traditional approach might take a few hours or days to arrive at a sub-optimal solution. A quantum approach could potentially find a near-optimal solution in few minutes, allowing the investor to be more agile at portfolio management.

Potential Speedups: Theoretical studies suggest that QAOA and VQE could offer a significant advantage (e.g., quadratic or even exponential for specific problem structures) in finding better approximate solutions or reaching solutions faster than classical exact solvers for large-scale problems. Quantum computers are able to traverse the solution space simultaneously due to their superposition property [9].

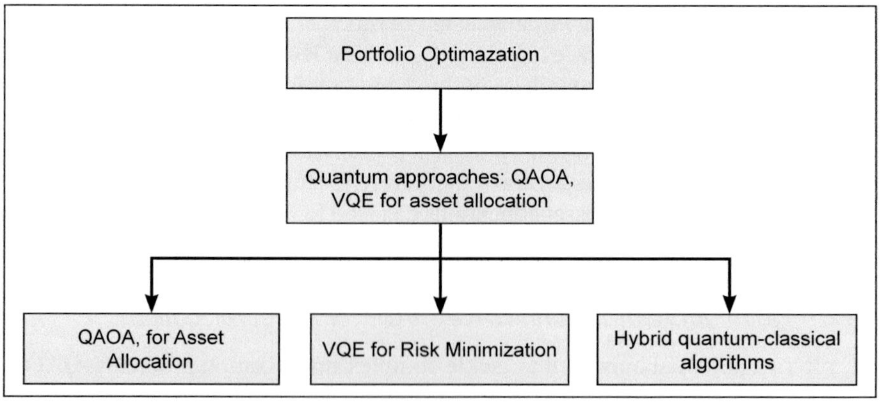

Fig. 6.6 Quantum algorithms for portfolio optimization.

4.2 Risk Management and Stress Testing

Assessment of market risk, credit risk, operational risk, and systemic risk accurately and in a timely manner are extremely important for financial institutions [9]. Portfolio performance is measured by stress testing it in extreme and hypothetical market conditions.

4.2.1 Monte Carlo Simulations for VaR and CVA Calculations

Classical Challenges: Risk metrics, such as VaR, CVaR, and CVA, rely primarily on Monte Carlo simulations. These simulations generate a vast number of random scenarios (e.g., future market movements, default events) to evaluate portfolio performance. In order to achieve satisfactory results, especially for complex derivatives or large portfolios, millions of simulation paths need to be evaluated. The evaluation of these paths using Monte Carlo methods is an extremely computationally intensive and time-consuming process, often running for more than a few hours, which limits their use for real-time risk management and dynamic stress testing [9].

4.2.2 Quantum Amplitude Estimation (QAE) for Faster Simulations.

Quantum Approach: QAE offers a potential quadratic speedup over classical Monte Carlo methods. While classical Monte Carlo requires $O(1/\text{epsilon}^2)$ samples to achieve an estimation precision of epsilon, QAE can achieve the same precision with O(1/epsilon) queries to a quantum system that prepares the relevant state. This means that to halve the error, classical Monte Carlo needs four times more samples, while QAE only needs twice as many queries.

Application: QAE can be leveraged to estimate the probability of a specific event (e.g., a portfolio loss exceeding a certain threshold) or the expected value of a financial quantity. For instance, in VaR calculation, QAE could estimate the probability of losses exceeding a certain level, or in CVA, it could estimate the expected exposure to counterparty default [6] [9].

4.2.3 Credit Risk Modeling with QML

QML for Credit Risk: QML algorithms, such as QSVMs or QNNs, could enhance capabilities of credit risk modeling. QSVMs can transform data into a higher-dimensional quantum feature space to identify more subtle and complex patterns in the loan data, which helps in predicting default more accurately than classical techniques. Similarly, QNNs can process large financial and behavioral datasets to build robust credit scoring models, potentially capturing non-linear relationships and interactions that are difficult for classical techniques to capture [5] [8].

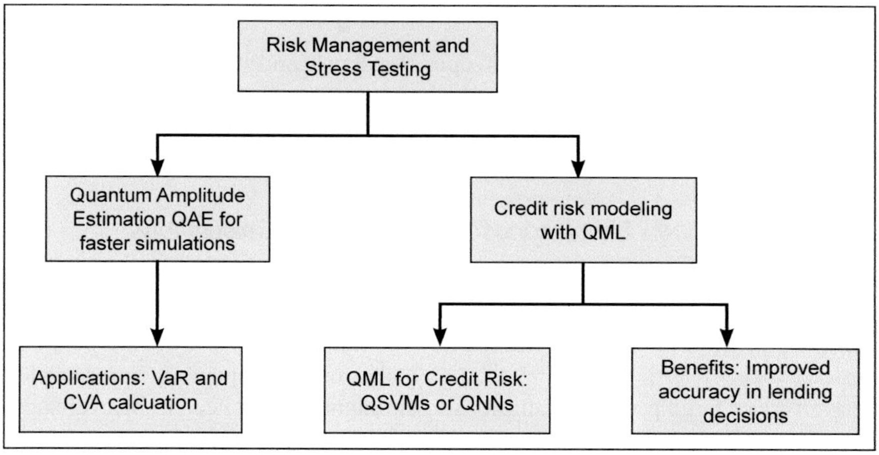

Fig. 6.7 QML algorithms in risk management and stress testing.

4.3 Algorithmic Trading and Market Prediction

Algorithmic trading, on the basis of future market movement predictions, leverages automated systems for high-speed trade execution.

4.3.1 Quantum Speedup for Complex Trading Strategies

Classical Challenges: Vast amounts of real-time market data (tick data, order book data, news feeds), complex patterns recognition, and rapid decision-making are required to build and execute sophisticated algorithmic trading applications. These applications primarily involve high-frequency data analysis, complex optimization (e.g., optimal execution, arbitrage detection), and rapid model inference, which pushes the limits of classical computational speed and memory [9].

Quantum Potential: Quantum computing offers a potential solution for the classical challenges. For instance, quantum optimization algorithms (QAOA, VQE) can provide optimal trading strategies or arbitrage opportunities across multiple markets and instruments. Grover's search algorithm can look up specific trading patterns in the historical market data [9] [17].

4.3.2 QML for Pattern Recognition in Financial Time Series

Quantum Machine Learning: QNNs and quantum recurrent neural networks (QRNNs) are being explored as potential solutions for enhanced pattern recognition in financial time series. They rely primarily on superposition and entanglement to identify intricate and subtle correlations or dependencies in market data, which would be difficult for deep learning models to capture. They can generate more accurate price predictions and effective signal generation for trading [5] [16].

Quantum Generative Adversarial Networks (QGANs): QGANs can be leveraged to generate synthetic market data, which is invaluable for training and testing trading algorithms. These enable eliminating the risk of overfitting to historical data or for simulating new market conditions for stress testing [5].

4.3.3 Challenges in Real-Time Quantum Execution

Current Limitations: Although quantum computing presents tremendous potential, a significant obstacle for real-time algorithmic trading is the present state of quantum hardware. The performance of NISQ devices is not satisfactory. The time taken to transfer the data to QC on the cloud to perform complex computation and retrieve the results is too high for high-frequency trading (HFT) environments. The environments demand a latency of a few microseconds for trading [9].

Future Outlook: Leveraging quantum advantage in real-time trading applications would require considerable advancements in quantum hardware speed, error rates, and integration with traditional systems. It could require building a highly optimized hybrid architectures [9].

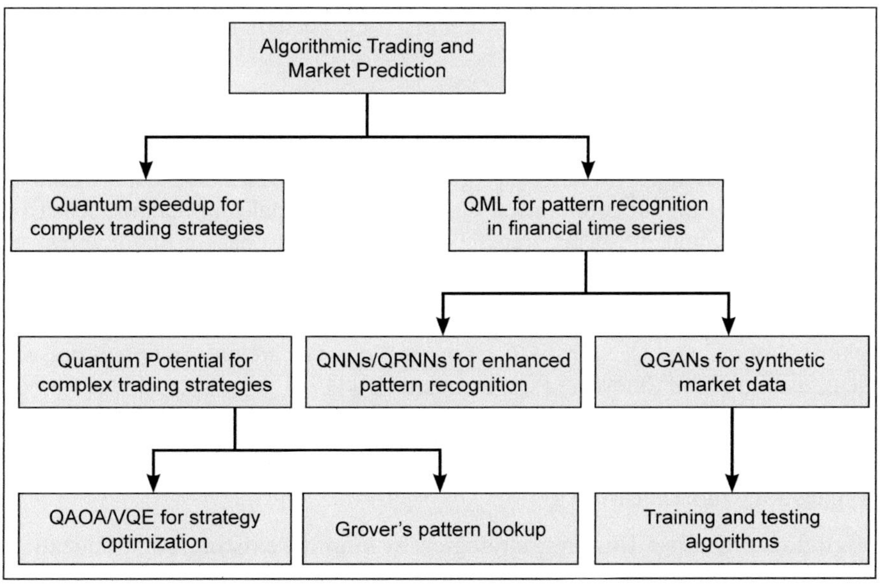

Fig. 6.8 QML algorithms in trading and market predictions.

4.4 Fraud Detection and Cybersecurity

Advanced detection and prevention mechanisms are required to protect financial systems from constant frauds and cyber threats.

4.4.1 Quantum-Enhanced Anomaly Detection

Classical Challenges: Although traditional ML models (e.g., SVMs, neural networks, isolation forests) are effective with fraud detection, they often struggle with the following aspects.

Rarity of Fraud: The data distribution for fraud transactions is highly imbalanced, as they are rare in nature.

Evolving Patterns: It is difficult to detect novel fraud patterns that are constantly evolving in the real-world.

High Dimensionality: Financial institutions could have datasets with a high number of features that could be required to decipher fraud patterns.

Quantum Enhancement: QSVMs and QNNs can be leveraged to detect subtle fraud patterns in the dataset [8]. QSVMs use their quantum kernel trick to identify complex and non-linear boundaries between legitimate and fraudulent transactions in high-dimensional feature spaces, eventually leading to higher detection rates and fewer number of false positives [8]. QNNs can be trained to learn more intricate patterns of anomalous behavior from large, complex datasets [5]. Quantum clustering algorithms can be used to identify fraud clusters [17].

4.4.2 PQC for Financial Data Security

As described in the section with Shor's algorithm, a powerful quantum computer could break current public-key encryption standards (RSA, ECC) that are used to virtually see all digital communications such as financial transactions, sensitive customer data, and interbank transfers. The quantum poses a major threat to financial security [9].

PQC: It covers encrypted algorithms that are design to protect financial institutions against classical and QCs. Institutions are actively researching and preparing for the transition to the following PQC standards [9] [17].

Algorithm Research and Standardization: Adopting a standardized approach for development of new PQC algorithms (e.g., cryptography of lattice based, cryptography of hash based).

Migration Planning: Building strategies to migrate existing communication channels to quantum-resistant encryption protocols.

Quantum Key Distribution (QKD): This is a communication protocol that uses quantum mechanical properties to establish intrinsically secure cryptographic keys, adding another layer of security to communications.

4.5 Derivatives Pricing

Accurate prediction of derivatives (e.g., options, futures, swaps) pricing is crucial for trading, risk management, and regulatory compliance.

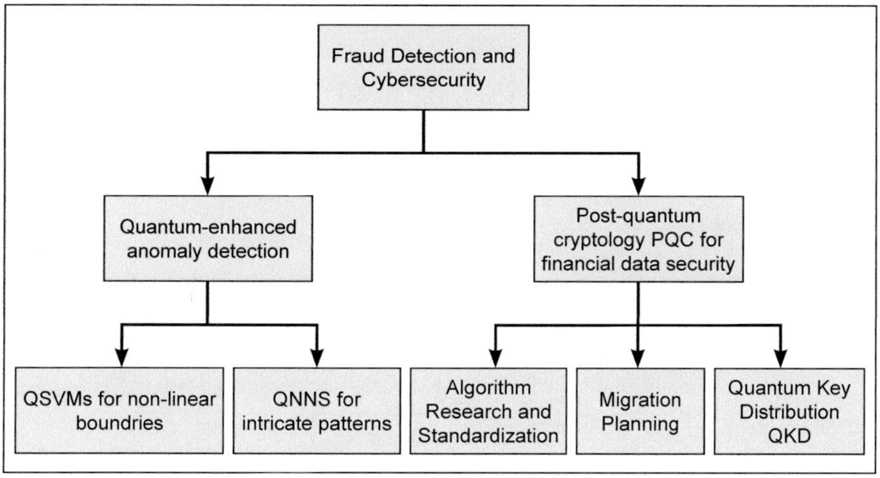

Fig. 6.9 QML in fraud detection and cybersecurity.

4.5.1 Black-Scholes and Beyond

Classical Models: The Black-Scholes model is a cornerstone for pricing European options. However, it relies on simplifying assumptions (e.g., constant volatility, no dividends, log-normal distribution of asset prices). The analytical solutions for more complex, real-world derivatives (e.g., American options, exotic options, multi-asset options, options with stochastic volatility or jumps) are not available [6].

Computational Demands: In order to estimate prices for the complex derivatives computationally intensive numerical methods like Monte Carlo simulations, finite difference methods, or binomial/trinomial trees are adopted. These methods can yield slower performance due to the presence of high-dimensional data or path-dependent options, often hindering real-time pricing and hedging [6].

4.5.2 Quantum Algorithms for Option Pricing

Quantum Amplitude Estimation (QAE): As described in earlier sections of the chapter, QAE offers a quadratic speedup for Monte Carlo simulations [6]. The approach is directly applicable to the complex option pricing problem where payoffs are functions of multiple underlying assets or depend on the path taken by the asset price over time. QAE can allow financial firms to price these options with higher accuracy and at a faster pace, which enables an efficient trading and risk management [6].

Quantum Simulation: Quantum computers are inherently good at simulating quantum systems. While financial markets are not quantum systems, some pricing models (e.g., those involving stochastic differential equations) can be mapped to quantum simulation problems, potentially allowing for efficient computation of expected values [9].

Quantum Machine Learning Models: QML models could also be trained to learn complex option pricing surfaces from market data, potentially offering more accurate or faster pricing for specific types of derivatives compared to classical ML models, especially if they can leverage quantum advantages in high-dimensional feature spaces [5].

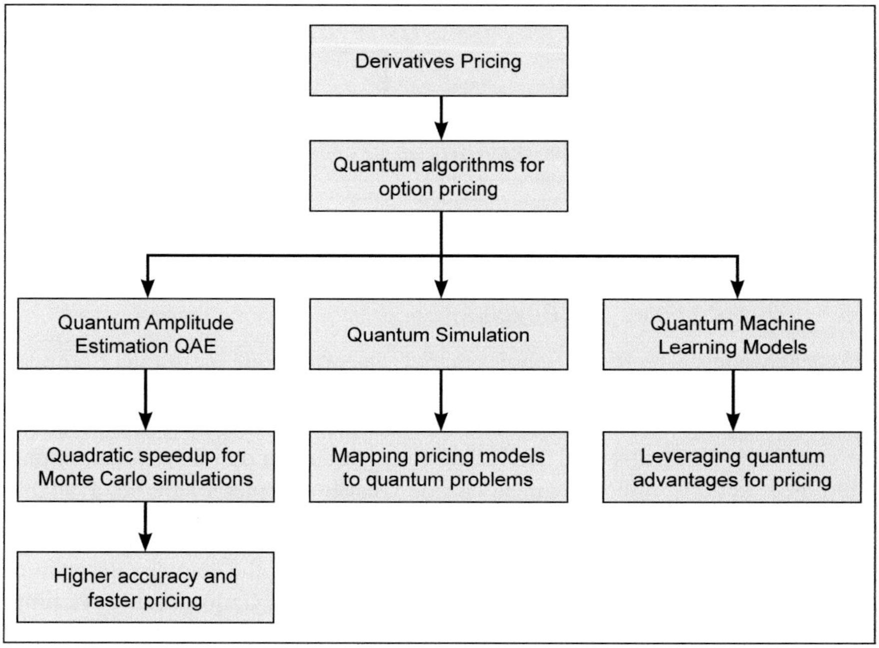

Fig. 6.10 QML in derivatives and options trading.

5. Challenges and Limitations

Although QC offers immense promise of growth to speed up applications, significant challenges and limitations need to be addressed before an industry-wide adoption of these techniques [9]. Next, we discuss the hurdles in technical, data, economic, and regulatory domains.

5.1 Technical Hurdles

The current state of quantum hardware has fundamental limitations that hamper the software development on it and widespread adoption.

5.1.1 Hardware Limitations (NISQ Era, Error Correction)

NISQ Era Constraints: Current QCs are NISQ devices [4]. They do not have enough number of q-bits (tens to hundreds) and they are susceptible to environment noise and error. The environment perturbations causes the qubits to lose their quantum properties rapidly, limiting the depth (number of computations) and width (number of qubits) of quantum circuits that can be executed without errors. The current NISQ devices do not offer the required count of qubits and circuit depth needed to handle complex financial problems [9].

Lack of Fault Tolerance: In order to execute arbitrary-length computations with extremely low error rates, sophisticated quantum error correction techniques are required. To protect against environmental noise and error, QEC requires encoding logical q-bits into many physical q-bits (hundreds or thousands of physical q-bits per logical qubit). The current hardware limitations restrict us from building these fault-tolerant machines that can incorporate QEC. Without QEC, the pragmatic applicability of powerful quantum algorithms is limited [9].

5.1.2 Scalability and Fault Tolerance

Scalability Challenges: Building high-quality interconnected qubit quantum processors is a complex engineering challenge [15]. Multiple platforms like superconducting q-bits, trapped ions, photonic q-bits, and silicon spin q-bits face difficulties in scaling up while maintaining qubit coherence, connectivity, and high gate fidelities. For instance, extreme cryogenic temperatures are required for superconducting qubits, which makes large-scale refrigeration complicated. Trapped ions have the ability of high coherence, but it is challenging to interconnect them efficiently.

Path to Fault Tolerance: The journey from NISQ devices to fault-tolerant devices is an uphill battle. It requires QC to have thousands of physical qubits, significantly improved gate fidelities, and development of efficient QEC codes that can be implemented [9]. The QEC requirement to leverage thousands of qubits to support a handful of error-corrected logical qubits is not feasible [15].

5.1.3 Quantum Software Development and Programming

Nascent Software Stack: As compared to traditional computing, quantum software stack is in an inception stage [9]. Although SDKs (Qiskit, Cirq, PennyLane) for quantum programming exist, specialized knowledge of quantum mechanics and quantum information theory is required to develop, debug, and optimize quantum algorithms.

Algorithm Design Complexity: Knowledge of financial domain and quantum circuits is needed to design an efficient solution for the applications. There is a shortage of programmers who can work on quantum and researchers who can bridge this interdisciplinary gap [9] [15].

Optimization for NISQ: NISQ devices need the algorithms to be "shallow" (few gates) and "narrow" (few qubits) to minimize the noise effect [4]. This requires us to compromise quantum speedups for practical executability, and finding optimal circuit designs for specific hardware architectures is a non-trivial task.

5.2 Data Considerations

Even if quantum hardware advances, handling and processing financial data within a quantum framework presents its own set of challenges.

5.2.1 Quantum Data Loading (QRAM)

The Bottleneck: Many quantum algorithms (e.g., HHL for solving linear equations, certain QML algorithms) assume that classical data can be loaded into the state of quantum, often through a hypothetical device called quantum random access memory (QRAM) [9]. QRAM would allow for logarithmic time access to classical data, meaning that N classical data points could be loaded into O(log N) qubits.

Current Reality: QRAM is currently a theoretical concept, and a practical, scalable implementation does not exist. Without efficient QRAM, the classical data loading step can negate any potential quantum speedup, as the time taken to prepare the quantum state from classical data might be as long as, or even longer than, solving the problem classically [9]. It is a major hurdle for applying quantum algorithms to large financial datasets [15].

5.2.2 Data Noise and Error Propagation

Sensitivity to Noise: Quantum algorithms are sensitive to perturbations [4]. Errors during data encoding, gate operations, or measurement can navigate through the quantum circuit, leading to erroneous results. In financial applications, accuracy and reliability of results is crucial, and even minor errors can create major issues.

Real-World Data Challenges: Data in the financial world can be noisy, incomplete, or contain biases. Using such data with quantum hardware noise can aggravate a complex challenge. Error resolving techniques (which try to minimize the effect of noise without rectifying the full error) and robust algorithm designs are important for retrieving desired results from noisy QCs [9].

5.3 Economic and Regulatory Challenges

Apart from the technical challenges, the financial sector faces a considerable economic and regulatory challenge for quantum adoption.

5.3.1 Cost of Quantum Hardware and Development

High Investment: Although cloud has democratized the usage of quantum computers, development and maintenance of quantum computers require considerable cost. Specialized infrastructure (e.g., dilution refrigerators, cleanrooms) and highly skilled personnel need to be employed for maintenance of the infrastructure [9].

Investment Return Uncertainty: Considering the initial stages of development in the quantum field, the RoI for financial institutions investing heavily in quantum research and development (R&D) is not certain. Identifying a clear and tangible "quantum advantage" is paramount for a large-scale investment [9].

5.3.2 Lack of Skilled Quantum Workforce

Talent Gap: Professionals with expertise in both QC (quantum physics, quantum information science, quantum programming) and financial services are rare [9] [15]. Training programs and interdisciplinary collaboration, a significant investment, is required to bridge the gap [16].

Recruitment and Retention: Financial institutions will need to compete with academic institutions and tech giants to acquire professionals with the scarce talent, which makes recruitment and retention a major challenge.

5.3.3 Regulatory Frameworks for Quantum-Enabled Financial Systems

Uncertainty: Regulators adopt a cautious approach in critical sectors such as finance. The emergence of QC adds to the existing complexities and uncertainties around data security, algorithmic fairness, and market stability [9].

New Risks: Regulators need to be trained and educated to understand the potential risks of introducing quantum technologies (e.g., the ability to break current encryption, the behavior of quantum-enhanced trading algorithms). They need to incorporate additional controls for frameworks oversight, compliance, and auditing [9] [17].

Ethical Considerations: Use of QC for credit scoring or high-frequency trading raises ethical concerns for the regulatory bodies. Additional compliance checks may be required to ensure that unintended biases or systemic risks are no longer introduced in the system.

5.4 Quantum Supremacy vs Quantum Advantage

It is important to distinguish between two key milestones in QC development.

5.4.1 Distinguishing Theoretical Speedups from Practical Benefits

Quantum Supremacy (or Quantum Computational Advantage): The quantum computational advantage is achieved when a specific computational task is nearly impossible for supercomputers to complete in an acceptance timeframe [9]. Google's Sycamore processor demonstrated in 2019 that a random circuit sampling problem can resolved in minutes, which may take few years for traditional supercomputers to formulate a resolution.

Nuance: It is important to realize that quantum ascendance does not mean that QC can be used for all practical problems. The task demonstrated is highly specialized in nature and specifically designed to illustrate QC's superior power.

5.4.2 When Will Quantum Advantage Be Realized in Finance?

Quantum Advantage (for a practical problem): QC can be leveraged by industries only when it can be used to solve practical problems. Highly regulated sectors like finance can leverage QC when it can deliver fast, accurate, and cost-effective results [9].

Current Status: QC is not leveraged for any practical financial problem. Theoretical quantum algorithms show exponential or quadratic speedups. However, translating these to real-world financial problems on noisy hardware is challenging. The overheads of error correction, data loading and inherent noise limit the complexness of practical problems that can be resolved [9].

Timeline: Using quantum advantage for significant financial applications is still few years away. A considerable future work in qubit quality, quantity, and correction in error capabilities would be needed before quantum advantage can be widely used. Design hybrid architectures for exploring quantum utility can be a near-term solution for specific, smaller problems [9].

6. The Future Outlook: Roadmap and Ethical Considerations

We will now lay out a roadmap for the adoption of quantum technology in finance in the near term and long term, and also address important ethical and strategic considerations [9].

6.1 Near-Term Applications (NISQ Era)

NISQ focuses on a hybrid approach that mixes classical and limited quantum processing.

Hybrid Algorithms: Classical–quantum algorithms (like QAOA or VQE) can be leveraged for small-scale, high-value problems [5] [7].

Examples: Feature engineering in QML to enhance classical models, small-scale portfolio optimization (e.g., 10–20 assets) [7], and early-stage risk simulations (using QAE) [6].

Quantum Utility: The current goal is to identify specific areas for utilizing quantum, where limited quantum computing can offer a tangible outcome [9].

Proof-of-Concept (PoC): Financial institutions are actively exploring a cloud-based environment to implement simple PoCs to learn practical challenges, validate theoretical concepts in the real-world or synthetic data, and build internal capabilities and interdisciplinary teams [9] [15].

6.2 Long-Term Vision (Fault-Tolerant QC)

The improvement of resilient QCs will determine the long-term vision for the transformative impact of the technology on financial services industry. Fault-tolerant machines should be able to tackle the following problems that are currently impossible for supercomputers [9]:

- Global portfolio optimization with complex constraints and thousands of assets [7].
- Real-time and high-precision risk management (e.g., VaR, CVA, stress testing) [6].
- Advanced derivatives pricing for highly complex and path-dependent products [6].
- Quantum enhanced econometric models.
- Post-Quantum Cryptography: Creation of new financially secure products (e.g., tradable complex derivatives) and hyper-personalized secure finance data at scale [17].

6.3 Ethical Implications and Responsible AI/QC

The power of quantum technology requires a proactive focus on ethical and regulatory frameworks [9].

Bias in Quantum Algorithms: QML models can amplify biases in the training data and also face quantum-specific biases due to hardware imperfections or error propagation in quantum circuits.

Fairness and Transparency: Explainability (XAI) for QML is a significant challenge, as quantum operations can be more opaque than classical boxes. XAI is a key element for maintaining trust of regulators in a financial institution [16].

Societal Impact: Job displacement from automation, potential for increased market volatility/concentration from high-frequency quantum trading, and exacerbation of the divide between large- and small-scale institutions.

6.4 Recommendations for Financial Institutions

In order to navigate the quantum frontier effectively and responsibly, institutions should adopt a strategic approach [9].

- Invest in R&D and Talent: Recruit professionals dedicated for quantum R&D, invest in cloud-based platforms that offer quantum hardware, and create interdisciplinary teams (quants, ML engineers, quantum scientists) [15].

- Strategic Partnerships: Collaborations with quantum vendors and academic institutions for foundational research and talent pipeline.
- Pilot Programs and Experimentation: Proof-of-concept on NISQ devices, adopt an agile/iterative development approach, and begin planning for the necessary changes to information technology (IT) infrastructure and security protocols to become quantum-aware [9].

7. Conclusion

This section will summarize the key insights presented in the chapter, emphasize the central theme of integrating QC and ML in finance, and offer a forward-looking perspective.

This chapter provides a complete overview of intersection of QC, ML, and financial services. We started by understanding the current computational limitations of classical methods in handling increasingly convoluted and large-scale financial data and models. Next, we introduced the foundational principles of QC—qubits, superposition, entanglement, and quantum gates—highlighting how these concepts enable a new computational paradigm. Next, key quantum algorithms relevant to finance—Shor's for cryptography, Grover's for search/optimization, QFT for signal processing, and especially QAE for Monte Carlo simulations—were discussed to illustrate their potential for significant performance.

Next, the concept of (QML) was explained in detail, elaborating upon how quantum capabilities can enhance classical ML tasks through hybrid algorithms, novel data encoding schemes, and inherently quantum learning models. A range of critical financial applications where QC and QML hold promise were described in detail.

Portfolio Optimization: Optimization algorithms like QAOA and VQE can be used for addressing NP-hard problems.

Risk Management and Stress Testing: Enhancing credit risk modeling with QML and accelerating Monte Carlo simulations with QAE.

Algorithmic Trading and Market Prediction: QML for advanced pattern recognition in financial time series data and using quantum speedups for complex algorithmic trading strategies.

Fraud Detection and Cybersecurity: Leveraging quantum-enhanced anomaly detection and preparing for post-quantum cryptography.

Derivatives Pricing: Leveraging quantum algorithms to speed up complex option valuations.

Finally, we closely examined the crucial challenges that need to be overcome, including hardware limitations (NISQ-era noise, lack of fault tolerance), data loading bottlenecks (QRAM), the nascent quantum software ecosystem, and the economic and regulatory hurdles. We also understood the differences between quantum supremacy (a scientific milestone) and practical quantum advantage (commercial value).

Quantum adoption in the finance industry is undoubtedly complex and will require considerable time and effort. However, the resolution of the specific problems of optimization, simulation, and certain ML tasks in the financial industry will require the computational power of quantum mechanics, and its integration is inevitable.

As the data complexity in the financial industry rises, the demands on computational power will continue to increase beyond the potential of classical systems. QC combined with ML represents the next frontier in finance. The convergence has the potential to unlock unprecedented capabilities for modeling, prediction, and decision-making, enabling financial institutions to navigate future challenges and opportunities with greater precision and efficiency.

The quantum frontier has been characterized by both immense potential and significant uncertainty. The quantum revolution will take time and effort to bear fruit. Financial institutions are collaborating to reduce the overall costs and will be best positioned to capitalize on any future breakthroughs. The collaboration will foster a culture of innovation, building interdisciplinary talent and carefully navigating the technical, ethical, and regulatory landscapes.

References

[1] Shor, P.W. "Algorithms for quantum computation: Discrete logarithms and factoring," in *Proceedings of the 35th Annual Symposium on Foundations of Computer Science*, 1994, pp. 124–134.

[2] Grover, L.K. "A fast quantum mechanical algorithm for database search," in *Proceedings of the 28th Annual ACM Symposium on Theory of Computing*, 1996, pp. 212–219.

[3] Peruzzo, A., et al. "A variational eigenvalue solver on a photonic quantum processor," *Nature Communications*, vol. 5, no. 4213, 2014.

[4] Preskill, J. "Quantum computing in the NISQ era and beyond," *Quantum*, vol. 2, p. 79, 2018.

[5] Arrazola, J.M., Kottmann, J.S., Risch, C.G.G.H., and Houten, R.A.F.V. "Quantum machine learning for quantum finance," in *2021 IEEE International Conference on Quantum Computing and Engineering (QCE)*, 2021, pp. 1–10.

[6] Stamatopoulos, N., Egger, D.J., Sun, Y., Zoufal, C., Iten, R., Warren, D. and Woerner, S. "Option pricing using quantum computers," *Quantum*, vol. 4, p. 320, 2020.

[7] Uotila, V., Ripatti, J. and Zhao, B. "Higher-order portfolio optimization with quantum approximate optimization algorithm," in *2025 IEEE International Conference on Quantum Computing and Engineering (QCE)*, 2025.

[8] Santos, L.D.S.D., Da Silva, S.A.A., De Abreu, L.V.G., and De Castro, R.A.M. "A preprocessing perspective for quantum machine learning classification advantage in finance using NISQ lgorithms," *Entropy*, vol. 24, no. 11, p. 1656, 2022.

[9] Egger, D.J., et al. "Quantum computing for finance: State-of-the-art and future prospects," *IEEE Transactions on Quantum Engineering*, vol. 1, p. 1, 2020.

[10] Harrow, A.W., Hassidim, A., and Lloyd, S. "Quantum algorithm for linear systems of equations," *Physical Review Letters*, vol. 103, no. 15, p. 150502, 2009.

[11] Farhi, E., Goldstone, J., and Gutmann, S. "A quantum approximate optimization algorithm," *arXiv preprint*, arXiv:1411.4028, 2014.

[12] Biamonte, J., et al. "Quantum machine learning," *Nature*, vol. 549, no. 7671, pp. 195–202, 2017.
[13] Lloyd, S. and Weedbrook, C. "Quantum generative adversarial networks," *Physical Review A*, vol. 97, no. 5, p. 052341, 2018.
[14] O'Malley, K.M., et al. "Scalable quantum simulation of molecular energies," *Physical Review X*, vol. 6, no. 3, p. 031007, 2016.
[15] Thé, J.V.G., Fraser, R.A. and Rosas-Bustos, J. *Quantum Computing and Quantum Machine Learning for Engineers and Developers*, Cham: Springer Nature Switzerland, 2025.
[16] Khang,m A. and Rath, K.C., eds. *The Quantum Evolution: Application of AI and Robotics in the Future of Quantum Technology*, Boca Raton, FL: CRC Press, 2024.
[17] Singhal, P., Mishra, P.K. and Hasan, M.M., eds. *Quantum Algorithms for Enhancing Cybersecurity in Computational Intelligence in Healthcare*, Boca Raton, FL: CRC Press, 2025.

7 Financial Modeling and Quantum Computing Economics

Tirathkumar M. Mishra[1], Prashant Vadikar[2*] and Ashok Gadi Parthi[3]

The world of finance is in flux again, and one of the reasons for this is quantum computers. This chapter investigates the ways in which financial thinking has grown over the years and the role computers have played in that growth. The development of models such as Markowitz's portfolio theory, Monte Carlo simulation, and the Black-Scholes model have impacted the way modern finance operates. This was later pushed even further by high frequency trading. Now a new change is taking place as quantum approaches begin to enter the game.

Quantum computing started as a collection of theoretical concepts. People like Feynman, Benioff, Deutsch, Grover, and Shor played a major role in the development of the founding ideas. These founding ideas eventually led to the real machines, like International Business Machines' (IBM's) Q System One and Google's Sycamore. Even though these devices are limited at this time, these companies have paved the way for new types of financial applications. For example, Monte Carlo for quantum, can bring forward the risk calculations quicker. Portfolio optimisation can be tried out by quantum approximate optimization algorithm (QAOA) or quantum annealing. Some researchers are using quantum machine learning tools to detect fraud as well. Others are trying out pricing models for complex derivatives.

Many large financial companies are already active in this field. John Pierpont Morgan (JPMorgan), Goldman Sachs, Wells Fargo, Hongkong and Shanghai Banking Corporation (HSBC), Mastercard, and Banco Bilbao Vizcaya Argentaria (BBVA) have all been conducting experiments or partnerships. Small companies are also active, such as the fintech firm Multiverse Computing. The governments are taking notice as well. The United States of America, the European Union,

[1] Research Scholar, Department of Business Economics, The Maharaja Sayajirao University of Baroda, India.
ORCID ID: 0009-0009-4347-0778
[2] Assistant Professor, Department of Business Economics, The Maharaja Sayajirao University of Baroda, India.
ORCID ID: 0000-0002-4060-7347
[3] IEEE Senior, Texas, USA.
ORCID ID: 0009-0007-4048-5291
E-mail: tirath.m-phdbe@msubaroda.ac.in[1]; ashok.gadiparthi@ieee.org[3]
* Corresponding author: prashant-be@msubaroda.ac.in

DOI: 10.1201/9781003646068-7

China, and India have commenced major programs (like the US National Quantum Initiative and India's National Quantum Mission), given that they recognize quantum technology as a major economic opportunity as well as a strategic necessity.

A lot of the current work mixes classical and quantum methods. Most companies run small pilot tests, build hybrid algorithms, or work inside simulation platforms because fully reliable quantum computers do not exist yet. There are also many issues to deal with. Noise in the hardware, difficulty scaling up, challenges in translating financial problems into quantum formats, and questions about regulation all remain. There are ethical worries as well. Quantum tools could give some players an unfair advantage, weaken existing cryptographic systems, or increase the gap between countries and institutions.

In the end, the message is simple. Large fault-tolerant quantum computers may take time to arrive, but waiting too long is risky. Firms that start learning, testing, and training now will be in a much stronger position later. Quantum computing is no longer a far-off dream.

1. Introduction

Financial theory has changed a lot over time and so has computing. In finance, some big ideas shaped the field. Markowitz's 1952 paper created modern portfolio theory and the whole risk–return idea. Then in 1973, Fischer Black and Myron Scholes came up with their option-pricing formula, which pushed derivatives to grow fast. Later, Monte Carlo methods were used for pricing when Phelim Boyle applied them in 1977, and by 1994 JPMorgan's RiskMetrics made value-at-risk (VaR) practical. As computing got stronger, these models became normal tools in the area of finance [1].

Quantum computing has its own story too. In 1981, Richard Feynman along with Paul Benioff observed that classical computers cannot easily simulate quantum systems. In 1985, David Deutsch provided a description of a universal quantum computer. Then in 1994 Peter Shor presented a quantum algorithm to factor numbers much faster than the classical algorithms. These discoveries proved that quantum computers were in theory able to beat classical computers. As of 2019, physical devices began appearing, with Google's Sycamore having 53 qubits and IBM's Q System One having 65 qubits [2]. Since every additional qubit can amplify the power of the machine by a factor of two, the system grows very fast.

Now, the two areas of finance and quantum computing are beginning to make a connection. Finance requires heavy computations for modeling, forecasting, and optimization, and even today's supercomputers have difficulties with large problems. Quantum computing seems to be promising here. A Bank for International Settlements (BIS) report (2024), says that finance may be one of the first sectors to benefit. IBM also shares that banks are investigating quantum tools for solving things that classical computers cannot. Experts say early movers could gain big advantages, like spotting arbitrage opportunities that normal computers would miss, which is why banks are urged to start experimenting now. The World

Economic Forum estimates that quantum-enhanced tools could be used to enhance forecasting, fraud detection, and portfolio optimization [3].

On the theory side, researchers have developed quantum versions of a number of methods in finance. Stochastic models, optimization routines and even machine learning (ML) classifiers now have quantum forms. There is even a subfield called "quantum finance" that looks at how quantum ideas might explain some market behaviors [4]. Quantum Monte Carlo is theoretically able to provide a quadratic speedup. Portfolio optimization with annealers or variational algorithms can be used for combinations that are too large to be efficiently solvable by classical solvers.

In the real world, banks and fintech companies have already begun trying out quantum tools. These pilots focus on faster risk analysis, improved trading strategies, and improved fraud detection. The BIS notes that the speed of risk models such as VaR and stress testing may be increased using quantum methods. One example from 2021 is a Turkish bank using a D-Wave annealer to study the problem of loan default, and it had quicker results compared to classical systems [5].

Some of the main applications are obvious: risk and scenario analysis with Quantum Monte Carlo, optimization of portfolio, trading with QAOA or annealing, improvement of machine learning for fraud or forecasting, and improving the rate at which a derivative is priced by sampling.

For academics, the link between quantum and economics might pave the way for new ways of thinking about markets and uncertainty. For practitioners, making small gains is a big deal—a model that is 10 times faster or a portfolio that delivers a few percent improvement to returns can mean huge money. IBM points out that the way in which qubits function is that a single new qubit doubles the possible state space. So quantum computing provides finance with a completely different kind of tool kit altogether.

Looking forward, the impact may be major. Quantum tools may change risk management, make asset pricing richer, and even shift how markets behave if only some players have access. Banks and regulators are preparing for this, especially for future security issues, through post-quantum cryptography research [6]. Many experts agree that integrating quantum computing into finance is becoming essential. Joining these two areas might create a new kind of "quantum economy," possibly as important as the rise of Black–Scholes or high-frequency trading. Over the next few years, researchers and industry teams will explore how quantum technology could reshape financial modeling and decision-making.

2. Literature Review

2.1 Early Convergence of Finance and Quantum Theory

Although most of finance is grounded in classical probability, a small but influential body of work has argued for the use of quantum probability models in economics.

Khrennikov and Haven and Khrennikov [7] proposed that quantum probability theory, with its allowance for superposition and interference may provide better models of financial decision-making under uncertainty. This approach, sometimes referred to as quantum-like economics, predates the advent of practical quantum hardware but demonstrates conceptual links between finance and quantum theory. These works emphasized that market phenomena such as ambiguity, context-dependence, and non-classical correlations could potentially be better represented by quantum probability than by classical Kolmogorovian frameworks. Though controversial, such studies prepared the intellectual ground for a more direct incorporation of quantum computation into financial modelling.

The basics of quantitative finance go back to the mid-twentieth century, when finance started using maths in a serious way. In 1952, Harry Markowitz established the risk-return relationship and mean variance method. James Tobin then linked up the capital allocation line whilst William F. Sharpe developed a capital asset pricing model (CAPM) model showing a relationship between an expected return and market risk [8]. During the 1970s there was a great deal of ado about the prices of different financial contracts. Fischer Black and Myron Scholes came up with their famous option pricing formula in 1973 using ideas from stochastic calculus, and Robert C. Merton extended all this to more types of financial claims. These ideas are the base for the development of newer computer-driven methods

Computing then went into an overdrive. A new method first developed in physics, Monte Carlo simulation, was adopted for option prices by Boyle [9], and it was useful for discussing difficult problems such as exotic options or path-dependent contracts. VaR gained its popularity following the release of the RiskMetrics by JPMorgan in 1994. Around the same time, high-frequency trading started to grow in size with the use of super-fast algorithms and comprehensive computing. A pattern started to emerge, every time theory went forward, computers did have to get stronger. Classical machines could only go so far, and they started hitting limits.

Quantum computing began as an idea in the early 1980s. Richard Feynman and Paul Benioff argued that classical computers cannot simulate quantum systems well, which inspired the idea of a quantum computer. David Deutsch formalized this idea, and Peter Shor created a factoring algorithm that was exponentially faster than classical ones. Lov K. Grover later added a search algorithm with quadratic speedup. These advances made people in finance pay attention, since many finance problems involve optimization or simulation. Over time, researchers started testing quantum annealing, variational quantum eigensolver (VQE) and other methods for tasks like portfolio optimization, pricing, and scenario work [10].

Some early applications followed. Rebentrost et al. [38] showed how portfolio optimization could be put into quantum circuits. Montanaro [30] explained how quantum methods, such as amplitude estimation, could speed up Monte Carlo calculations. Stamatopoulos et al. [40] priced a European option using IBM's early devices. Biamonte et al. [7] reviewed quantum machine learning and highlighted uses such as fraud detection, forecasting, and pattern analysis in large datasets

[11]. Together, these studies formed the first clear wave of work linking finance and quantum computing.

Industry interest has also been growing. IBM, JPMorgan, and Goldman Sachs have reported pilot projects using quantum processors for risk simulation, derivative pricing, and cryptography. D-Wave worked with Banco Bilbao Vizcaya Argentaria (BBVA) on optimization. HSBC tested quantum key distribution. Multiverse Computing helped banks with portfolio optimization. Academic work adds benchmarks and warns about scaling limits. Orús et al. [33] discuss the potential but also highlight the need for hybrid methods. Preskill's work on the noisy intermediate-scale quantum (NISQ) era also explains why noisy quantum machines still require the help of classical aids [12].

Policy and global strategy now comes into play too. The benefits and risks of quantum computing for finance, including threats to public-key cryptography, were under discussion at the BIS. The World Economic Forum states the need for financial firms to start early in order to remain competitive. Governments are spending big, and the US National Quantum Initiative Act, China's national program, and India's National Quantum Mission are clear evidence that countries believe that quantum technology is something you need to have to be economically and financially strong. The literature makes one thing clear—quantum tools are not mere technical upgrades, but rather strategic tools that may define the future of global finance [13].

3. Methodological Approaches

The application of quantum computation in financial modeling requires keen methods, given the fact that the technology is new and works differently from the classical tools used in financial modeling. Classical models rely on numerical or stochastic methods, but quantum finance sits between algorithm design, hardware limits, and financial theory. So the method usually involves turning financial problems into quantum form, testing them on simulators, trying small runs on real quantum devices, and using mixed approaches that combine both quantum and classical parts.

The first step is turning classical finance problems into quantum algorithms. This means rewriting optimization, pricing, or ML tasks using quantum operators and Hilbert spaces. The mean–variance portfolio problem can be written as a quadratic unconstrained binary optimization (QUBO) form so that annealers or gate-based tools like QAOA can solve it. Option pricing based on stochastic differential equations can be linked to quantum amplitude estimation to speed up Monte Carlo calculations [30]. Risk tools such as VaR or stress testing can employ methods of quantum sampling. For example fraud detection work and ML tasks can be mapped into the quantum feature spaces using quantum kernels in order to capture hidden structures in the data [14].

Because of the noise and the lack of functionality in any current quantum hardware, the bulk of work currently occurs on simulators that run on classical machines. IBM Qiskit provides tools for circuitries to design circuits of finance problems and provides modules for things like option price and portfolio selection. Google Cirq is commonly used for imminently algorithms and testing optimization ideas [15]. D-Wave's open-source software development kit (Ocean SDK) is designed for annealing methods and generally used for QUBO problems such as portfolio choice or arbitrage. Some companies, such as Multiverse Computing make quantum-inspired tools that run on the classical machine but emulate the behavior of the quantum world. These simulators help researchers understand the amount of power required in finding an algorithm and whether it will scale in before trying a real hardware.

Another step is in attempting pilot tests on real out quantum devices. These machines are still small, on the order of, say, 500 qubits, and the errors are high, but they provide evidence of how algorithms behave in reality. IBM's Q System One allows researchers to test small circuits, such as the examples of European option pricing. D-Wave's annealers have been used with banks like BBVA to look at multicurrency arbitrage. Platforms from Rigetti, IonQ, and Quantinuum have been tried to do tasks like credit scoring and detecting fraud [16]. These pilots often work with very small sets of problems, such as very small portfolios, to develop an understanding of limits, errors, and time trade-offs [16].

From the currently hardware, most studies are on hybrid methods. This is on par with Preskill's vision of the NISQ era [35]. Variational algorithms such as variational quantum eigensolver (VQE) and QAOA are based on the use of quantum circuits but classical loop optimization algorithms and are applicable in pricing or portfolio problems. Cloud tools, like IBM's Qiskit Runtime or D-Wave's Hybrid Solver, believe in distributing the workload between quantum and classical processors. Some institutions also have quantum-inspired optimization such as tensor networks or simulated annealing as a step before adopting quantum entirely [17].

Benchmarking is another important aspect of the method. Institutions need to know whether quantum algorithms really have an advantage. They compare runtime, accuracy, scalability, and how well the algorithm handles noise. Montanaro [30] demonstrated the use of quantum amplitude estimation to reduce the sampling error quadratically. Rebentrost et al. [38] demonstrated increased rates of optimization under controlled conditions. These benchmarks help determine whether quantum tools are better than classical ones [18].

There are also a number of challenges. Present-day quantum devices still have a lot of noise and therefore long circuits fail easily, and the cost of error correction is very expensive. Encoding of financial problems into things like Hamiltonians usually leads to some simplifications, which may means less accuracy [19]. Quantum algorithms also require structured data, and the cost of making high-dimensional financial data datasets compatible for loading into quantum states is currently expensive. Scaling up from small examples on to real-world sizes, such as portfolios with thousands of assets, is not yet possible.

Another problem is the absence of standard methods, which makes it difficult to compare studies or results [20].

4. Real-World Case Studies

4.1 JPMorgan Chase (USA)

JPMorgan has been in the business of quantum finance for a while. Marco Pistoia leads the team, and the bank keeps trying a number of things at once, like testing hardware, writing its own algorithms, and working with companies such as IBM [21]. One of the bank's chief accomplishments is a quantum version of Monte Carlo. This is important because Monte Carlo is being used everywhere in finance, but both the classical runs on a much time. The bank's quantum approach took less time to show the results, though this was because the tests were relatively small and the hardware still had noise. In 2020 it even quoted a simple European call option on a quantum machine with IBM. By 2024 it also tried quantum-inspired portfolio optimization and saw that it ran faster than some of the classical methods. At the same time the bank has a focus on security because powerful quantum computers can crack today's encryption. It trail quantum key distribution during 2024 under a security trading link [22].

4.2 Goldman Sachs (USA)

Goldman Sachs started on its quantum project in 2012. Its major attention was directed to D-Wave and Amazon Web Services (AWS). It studies options pricing, portfolio issues, and trading algorithms [23]. With D-Wave, it experimented on finding how arbitrage and pricing problems can be converted into QUBOs for annealers. Annealers are not full-blown quantum computers, but they are helpful for optimization. Goldman also files a lot of patents to construct future knowledge. It tests QAOA calculations on AWS for small trading signal problems. Still, the company remains cautious, since the real benefits in terms of commerce have not come into clear view [24].

4.3 Wells Fargo (USA)

Wells Fargo has preference for the slow and step method. We will discuss two examples of fraud detection. Wells Fargo made prototype models for things like portfolio optimization, credit risk, and fraud detection with close help from IBM. Surprisingly, someone at the bank went so far as referring to quantum computers as helicopters in the world of day cars [25]. In less complex words, this is a powerful but not for day-to-day use device. As a result the hybrid models that make use of classical and quantum tools amongst others are Wells Fargo's whole modus operandi. A project on quantum fraud detection. The evaluation showed that in some cases, quantum cloning was superior to the classical support vector machine

(SVM). Nonetheless, it was on smaller datasets mostly. Wells Fargo also keeps an eye on laws. It is focused on analysis, spending on research, careful testing, and observing the rules [26].

4.4 HSBC (UK)

HSBC has a two-sided approach. On the one hand, the bank is trying out quantum tools to use for trading and asset management. On the other, it invests a lot in quantum-safe security [27].

One of its most discussed projects is a system for the trading of tokenized gold. The idea is to resist future quantum attacks where someone takes some encrypted financial information and decrypts it in the future. HSBC has incorporated quantum-safe protections so that the platform can be safe from such risks [28].

It also conducts experiments in risk management and scores based on quantum physics. Its teams test various solvers coupled with scenario analysis software to determine the possible risks of default on credit. Early results indicate faster computations and a broader coverage of scenarios, though full-scale is challenging to do yet. The bank does have a good in-house team of quantum physicists led by Philip Intallura, and continues to hire physicists and mathematicians. HSBC markets itself as a leader in quantum-secure finance.

4.5 Mastercard (USA)

The way Mastercard uses quantum is primarily to gain efficiency. In 2024 it subjected the annealer from D-Wave for its loyalty program. The task was to select the correct offers for millions of customers, which was a huge optimization problem. Classical methods slow down, however, the annealing approach found workable solutions much faster. Mastercard has not disclosed many details, but it said there were cost savings and improved efficiency [30].

4.6 BBVA (Spain)

In 2020, BBVA started working with D-Wave and Accenture to examine currency arbitrage and to improve trade route optimization. The authors attempted to formulate complicated multi-currency problems into a QUBO to solve it on a quantum annealer [31]. The moment there is more than one important currency in an arbitrage problem, classical methods become much slower. A quantum setup will be able to search through much larger spaces and will find possible opportunities that are not found using standard tools. The BBVA's early tests seemed to go well in the high-dimensional difficult situations. However, nobody really knows just how much these tests would be able to withstand in real markets at the moment. As a result, these still have the air of being experimental, like a work in progress. Moreover, still providing scope for all types of improvement [32].

4.7 Multiverse Computing (Spain)

Multiverse Computing is a software company from Spain known for helping banks try quantum ideas. It cooperated with BBVA, Bank of Canada, and Crédit Agricole. In the BBVA project, it used a hybrid D-Wave solver to check trading paths for 52 assets, scanning thousands of portfolios in just seconds, giving better-balanced results than brute-force methods. With the Bank of Canada, Multiverse used Quantum Monte Carlo to see how cryptocurrencies might affect payment systems, giving central banks a new way to study system-wide risks [33].

4.8 Other Global Banks [34]

Several other institutions are testing quantum pilots:

- **Citigroup Inc. (Citi)** partnered with Israeli start-up Classiq to test QAOA for portfolio optimization.
- **Standard Chartered** and **Intesa Sanpaolo** are exploring trading signal prediction and credit decisions using hybrid quantum models.
- **Credit Mutuel (France)** has used IBM's quantum cloud for fraud detection prototypes for several years.

5. Global Economic Perspective

Quantum computing has climbed to the top of the agenda for governments. National and regional programs are funneling billions of dollars into research and development, often tying these investments directly to competitiveness and the financial-services arena. Table 7.1 lays out the government strategies across the economies:

5.1 The United States

In the US, the federal push for quantum technology rests on the 2018 National Quantum Initiative Act, which cleared the way for over $1.2 billion in joint agency spending between 2018 and 2023 [35]. The Department of Energy, DARPA, and the National Science Foundation each pour money into applied research, while the US Quantum Economic Development Consortium (QED-C) works to deepen ties between industry and academia. The ecosystem is already paying off for leading tech firms (IBM, Google, IonQ, Rigetti) and major banks (JPMorgan, Bank of America Citigroup) as they experiment with algorithms to revamp option pricing, fine-tune portfolio optimization, and fortify security [36].

5.2 China

China is thought to have poured US$15 billion into quantum research since 2016, making it the biggest single-nation program of its kind [37]. At the forefront, the University of Science and Technology of China (USTC) is driving work on

Table 7.1 National quantum initiatives.

Country/ Region	*Public Funding (approx.)*	*Year of Figure*	*Strategy Highlights (Relevant to Finance)*	*Source (with Link)*
United States	US$5 billion	2018–2023	National Quantum Initiative Act directs Department of Energy (DOE), Defense Advanced Research Projects Agency (DARPA), and National Science Foundation (NSF) to fund quantum information science (QIS) research; strong public–private ecosystem (IBM, Google, IonQ, Rigetti). US banks (JPMorgan, Bank of America, Citi) lead in pilots.	US Congress (2018). National Quantum Initiative Act
China	US$15 billion	2016–2023	State-led push with University of Science and Technology of China (USTC), Huawei labs; Quantum Experiments at Space Scale (QUESS) satellite (2016); investment in quantum key distribution (QKD) and hardware. Chinese banks (Industrial and Commercial Bank of China [ICBC], Agricultural Bank of China [ABC], China Construction Bank [CCB]) beginning quantum finance R&D.	Cao (2020). China's US$15B quantum push
European Union (EU)	€1 billion (Flagship)	2018–2028	Quantum Flagship invests in photonics, communications. EU 2025 strategy aims for sovereignty and leadership by 2030. European banks (HSBC, BBVA, Intesa) engaged.	European Commission (2018). Quantum Flagship
India	₹ 6,003.65 crore (US$ 0.73B)	2023–2031	National Quantum Mission launched in Apr. 2023 with focus on end-to-end QIS ecosystem, fintech pilots, and cryptography. Indian banks (e.g., State Bank of India) exploring pilots.	PIB (April 19, 2023). Cabinet approves National Quantum Mission
Canada	CA$360 million	2023	National Quantum Strategy (Jan. 2023) with missions in hardware/ software, secure communications, and industry pilots. Bank of Canada active in quantum finance research and development (R&D).	Government of Canada (2023). National Quantum Strategy
Australia	A$1.4 billion (20+ yrs)	2000–2023	National Quantum Strategy (May 2023) promotes commercialization. Commonwealth Scientific and Industrial Research Organisation (CSIRO) projects A$2.2B quantum computing (QC) market by 2030. PsiQuantum to establish Asia-Pacific Headquarters in Brisbane.	Australian Government (2023). National Quantum Strategy; CSIRO (2020). Growing Australia's Quantum Industry

entanglement. State banks like ICBC, ABC, and CCB have shown interest in quantum-led risk modeling projects.

5.3 The European Union

In 2018, the European Union inaugurated its €1 billion Quantum Flagship program—a decade-long program, slated for completion in 2028. The main focus is on photonics, quantum communication, and chip fabrication [38]. The EU aims to achieve global leadership in quantum computing by the end of 2030. The major names in banking and the finance industry are participating in pilot experiments in Germany, France, and Italy.

5.4 India

The Government of India launched the National Quantum Mission in April 2023. A budget of ₹ 6,003.65 crore (US $0.73 billion) has been allocated for the implementation of the mission. It covers the period from 2023–24 to 2030–31 [39]. The main aim of the mission is to build a quantum ecosystem in country. It also focuses on encouraging the participation of financial start-ups.

5.5 Canada

In January 2023 Canada formally rolled out its National Quantum Strategy, earmarking CA$360 million for the venture. The plan spotlights quantum hardware and software development, fortifies communications, and advances sensor technologies, with attention to financial applications. At the time the Bank of Canada has teamed up with researchers to explore payment systems and to run stress-tests on asset-management frameworks [40].

5.6 Australia

Since the 2000s Australia has funneled A$1.4 billion into quantum science, a steady investment that adds up over two decades. In May 2023 the government rolled out its National Quantum Strategy, designed to speed up commercialization and spark partnerships. CSIRO now projects that the home-grown quantum-technology market could hit about A$2.2 billion by 2030. Although Australian banks are smaller than their US or Chinese counterparts, recent initiatives are nudging fintech firms toward quantum-safe communications and optimization tools [41].

5.7 Summary

By the 2024–25 window than 30 nations have together pledged upwards of US$40 billion for quantum research. The US and China command the lion's share of funding, while the EU, India, Canada, and Australia are pursuing focused roadmaps that stress sovereignty, security, and commercial uptake. Across the board financial services remain a priority in the realms of cryptography, trading and risk management [42].

6. Key Strategic Takeaways

Leverage Hybrid Quantum–Classical Systems: The prevailing industry strategy now is computing—pairing high-performance computing with quantum processors through orchestration platforms such as D-Wave's Hybrid Solver Service and IBM's Qiskit Runtime [43]. Numerous projects mentioned earlier already employ these hybrids. This enables firms to tap into emerging quantum speedups while still relying on algorithms for the remaining portions of the problem. Executives would be wise to picture an infusion of modules into the systems they already run instead of hoping for an abrupt all-out takeover by a stand-alone quantum computer.

Form Alliances: No single bank will independently develop computers. Consequently, leading institutions are teaming up with vendors—IBM, Google, Quantinuum, D-Wave, Xanadu—cloud providers such as AWS, Microsoft Azure start-ups like Multiverse, QC Ware, and Pasqal, and consulting firms including Accenture, EY, and McKinsey. Take 2024 as an illustration: JPMorgan joined forces with Quantinuum and academic groups; Goldman started working alongside Amazon/AWS and D-Wave; a host of banks were already members of consortia such as IBM's Q Network [44]. From a standpoint leaders ought to assess partnerships that grant access to hardware and specialized talent. Public–private alliances—like the Quantum Economic Development Consortium (QED-C) initiative in the US or the EU's Quantum Community—can also provide joint testing opportunities [45].

Allocate Resources to Nurture Talent and R&D Capacity: Quantum computing still demands a set of skills. In a 2024 briefing, Pistoia observed that banks can now lure talent thanks to their published research and the establishment of teams [46]. Top executives should consider building a squad of quantum experts in quantum information science or applied mathematics to secure in-house expertise. Relying on consultants or contractors would blunt the strategic advantage [47].

7. Conclusion

This chapter describes how quantum computing is being applied in the financial sector. It examines the impact of this combination in terms of finance. It provides a different way of looking at the financial modeling methodology. Now we are able to access quantum computing resources. Currently, it is being tested in a variety of real-world applications including risk management, portfolio management, and fraud detection. In actuality, the large banks and fintechs are currently running tests of rather modest models for hybrid tests, and, in many cases, the results in terms of speed and efficiency have become better, even if the tests are still on a small scale. The number of quantum programs that are emerging is a sign that this technology is becoming necessary, not only for economic power but also for financial stability.

You certainly do not want to get this wrong. In their attempt to score a victory even greater, researchers have been coming up with exciting new quantum algorithms that might, one day, tackle the kind of messiness the real world brings.

As per experts, the general public seems to have switched off from the latest brand of digital tech, while the industry players seem more interested to get upskilled, striking partnerships, and doing pilots so that they will not fall behind when the hardware gets better. As regards policymakers, they also have a job to do, mainly around post-quantum security and looking out for risks at the system level.

In the final analysis, we can say that quantum computing has already entered finance (though in small steps only). It is no more a dream; it is something that is becoming a part of our lives. Just as the Black–Scholes model and high-frequency trading changed the game in the past, quantum technology can irreversibly change the way we read information, measure risk, and make decisions. The early bird catches the worm means that you should not procrastinate on your tasks because if you do, then it will become very hard to accomplish and you may not succeed in life. A quantum-ready economy is not in the world of the experts anymore—the odds are to see it impact the world of finance and impact the upcoming years.

References

[1] Aldridge, I. *High-Frequency Trading: A Practical Guide to Algorithmic Strategies and Trading Systems*, 2nd ed., Hoboken, NJ, USA: Wiley, 2013.

[2] Arute, F., Arya, K., Babbush, R., et al. "Quantum supremacy using a programmable superconducting processor," *Nature*, vol. 574, no. 7779, pp. 505–510, 2019, doi: 10.1038/s41586-019-1666-5.

[3] Australian Government, *National Quantum Strategy*, Canberra, Australia, 2023 [Online]. Available at https://www.industry.gov.au/publications/national-quantum-strategy, accessed on 15 March 2026.

[4] Bank for International Settlements (BIS), "Quantum computing and financial services: Opportunities and risks," Basel, Switzerland, 2024 [Online]. Available at https://www.bis.org/publ/quantum_report_2024.htm, accessed on 15 March 2026.

[5] Bank of Canada, "Quantum computing applications in payment systems," Ottawa, Canada, 2022 [Online]. Available at https://www.bankofcanada.ca/2022/quantum-computing-report/, accessed on 15 March 2026.

[6] Benioff, P. "The computer as a physical system: A microscopic quantum mechanical Hamiltonian model of computers as represented by Turing machines," *Journal of Statistical Physics*, vol. 22, no. 5, pp.563–591, 1980, doi:10.1007/BF01011339.

[7] Biamonte, J., Wittek, P., Pancotti, N., Rebentrost, P., Wiebe, N. and Lloyd, S. "Quantum machine learning," *Nature*, vol. 549, pp. 195–202, 2017, doi: 10.1038/nature23474.

[8] Black, F. and Scholes, M. "The pricing of options and corporate liabilities," *Journal of Political Economy*, vol. 81, no. 3, pp. 637–654, 1973, doi: 10.1086/260062.

[9] Boyle, P.P. "Options: A Monte Carlo approach," *Journal of Financial Economics*, vol. 4, no. 3, pp. 323–338, 1977, doi:10.1016/0304-405X(77)90005-8.

[10] Cao, Y. "China's US$15B quantum push," *Nature Reviews Phyics.*, vol. 2, no. 10, pp. 529–530, 2020, doi:10.1038/s42254-020-0231-3.

[11] Citi, "Quantum computing in portfolio optimization: A collaboration with Classiq," 2024 [Online]. Available at https://www.citigroup.com/quantum-portfolio-2024, accessed on 15 March 2026.

[12] Commonwealth Scientific and Industrial Research Organisation (CSIRO), *Growing Australia's Quantum Industry*, Canberra, Australia, 2020 [Online]. Available at https://www.csiro.au/en/research/technology-space/quantum-technology/growing-australias-quantum-industry, accessed on 15 March 2026.

[13] Deutsch, D. "Quantum theory, the Church–Turing principle and the universal quantum computer," *Proceedings of the Royal Society of London. Series A. Mathematical, Physical and Engineering Sciences*, vol. 400, no. 1818, pp. 97–117, 1985, doi: 10.1098/rspa.1985.0070.

[14] European Commission, "Quantum flagship," Brussels, Belgium, 2018 [Online]. Available at https://ec.europa.eu/digital-single-market/en/quantum-flagship, accessed on 15 March 2026.

[15] European Commission, "Quantum community," Brussels, Belgium, 2025 [Online]. Available at https://digital-strategy.ec.europa.eu/en/policies/quantum-community, accessed on 15 March 2026.

[16] Evident Insights, "Quantum computing in finance: 2025 industry benchmark report," London, UK, 2025 [Online]. Available at https://www.evidentinsights.com/quantum-finance-2025, accessed on 15 March 2026.

[17] Feynman, R.P. "Simulating physics with computers," *International Journal of Theoretical Physics*, vol. 21, no. 6–7, pp. 467–488, 1982, doi:10.1007/BF02650179.

[18] Goldman Sachs, "Quantum computing initiatives at Goldman Sachs," New York, USA, 2025 [Online]. Available at https://www.goldmansachs.com/insights/technology/quantum-computing-2025, accessed on 15 March 2026.

[19] Government of Canada, *National Quantum Strategy*, Ottawa, Canada, 2023 [Online]. Available at https://www.canada.ca/en/innovation-science-economic-development/programs/quantum-strategy.html, accessed on 15 March 2026.

[20] Grover, L.K. "A fast quantum mechanical algorithm for database search," in *Proceedings of the 28th Annual ACM Symposium on the Theory of Computing*, 1996, pp. 212–219, doi: 10.1145/237814.237866.

[21] Haven, E. and Khrennikov, A. *Quantum Social Science*. Cambridge, UK: Cambridge University Press, 2013.

[22] HSBC, "Quantum-safe trading platform for tokenized assets," London, UK, 2024 [Online]. Available at https://www.hsbc.com/quantum-secure-trading-2024, accessed on 15 March 2026.

[23] IBM Quantum, "IBM quantum experience: Q System One," Armonk, USA, 2019 [Online]. Available at https://www.ibm.com/quantum-computing/system-one, accessed on 15 March 2026.

[24] IBM Institute for Business Value, "Quantum computing for financial services: A strategic imperative," Armonk, USA, 2023 [Online]. Available at https://www.ibm.com/thought-leadership/institute-business-value/report/quantum-finance-2023, accessed on 15 March 2026.

[25] Jorion, P. "Risk: Measuring the risk in value at risk," *Financial Analysts Journal*, vol. 52, no. 6, pp. 47–56,1996, doi10.2469/faj.v52.n6.2040.

[26] JPMorgan Chase, "Quantum computing advancements in financial modeling," New York, USA, 2024 [Online]. Available at https://www.jpmorganchase.com/technology/quantum-computing-2024, accessed on 15 March 2026.

[27] Khrennikov, A. *Ubiquitous Quantum Structure: From Psychology to Finance*, Berlin, Germany: Springer, 2010.

[28] Markowitz, H. "Portfolio selection," *The Journal of Finance*, vol. 7, no. 1, pp. 77–91, 1952, doi: 10.2307/2975974.

[29] Mastercard, "Quantum optimization for loyalty rewards programs," Purchase, USA, 2024 [Online]. Available at https://www.mastercard.com/quantum-optimization-2024, accessed on 15 March 2026.

[30] Montanaro, A. "Quantum algorithms: An overview," *npj Quantum Information*, vol. 2, p. 15023, 2016, doi:10.1038/npjqi.2015.23.

[31] Multiverse Computing, "Quantum portfolio optimization with BBVA," San Sebastián, Spain, 2021 [Online]. Available at https://www.multiversecomputing.com/case-studies/bbva-quantum-optimization, accessed on 15 March 2026.
[32] Multiverse Computing, "Quantum applications in derivatives and credit risk," San Sebastián, Spain, 2022 [Online]. Available at https://www.multiversecomputing.com/case-studies/credit-agricole-quantum, accessed on 15 March 2026.
[33] Orús, R., Mugel, S. and Lizaso, E. "Quantum computing for finance: Overview and prospects," *Reviews in Physics*, vol. 4, p. 100028, 2019, doi: 10.1016/j.revip.2019.100028.
[34] Press Information Bureau, Government of India, "Cabinet approves National Quantum Mission," New Delhi, India, Apr. 19, 2023 [Online]. Available at https://pib.gov.in/PressReleasePage.aspx?PRID=1918741, accessed on 15 March 2026.
[35] Preskill, J. "Quantum computing in the NISQ era and beyond," *Quantum*, vol. 2, p. 79, 2018, doi:10.22331/q-2018-08-06-79.
[36] Quantinuum, "Quantum computing: The time to try it," Broomfield, USA, 2024 [Online]. Available at https://www.quantinuum.com/insights/time-to-try-quantum-2024, accessed on 15 March 2026.
[37] Qureca, "Global quantum investment landscape 2024–2025," 2025 [Online]. Available at https://www.qureca.com/global-quantum-investment-2025, accessed on 15 March 2026.
[38] Rebentrost, P., Gupt, B. and Bromley, T.R. "Quantum computational finance: Quantum algorithm for portfolio optimization," *arXiv preprint*, arXiv:1810.11327, 2018.
[39] Shor, P.W. "Algorithms for quantum computation: Discrete logarithms and factoring," in *Proceedings of the 35th Annual Symposium on the Foundations of Computer Science*, Santa Fe, NM, USA, 1994, pp. 124–134, doi: 10.1109/SFCS.1994.365700.
[40] Stamatopoulos, N., Egger, D.J., Sun, Y., Zou, C. and Woerner, S. "Option pricing using quantum computers," *Quantum*, vol. 4, p. 291, 2020, doi: 10.22331/q-2020-07-06-291.
[41] Tobin, J. "Liquidity preference as behavior towards risk," *The Review of Economic Studies*, vol. 25, no. 2, pp. 65–86, 1958, doi:10.2307/2296205.
[42] U.S. Congress, "National Quantum Initiative Act, H.R. 6227, 115th Congress," Washington, DC, USA, 2018 [Online]. Available at https://www.congress.gov/bill/115th-congress/house-bill/6227, accessed on 15 March 2026.
[43] Wells Fargo, "Quantum computing for banking: Progress and potential," San Francisco, CA, USA, 2024 [Online]. Available at https://www.wellsfargo.com/insights/quantum-computing-2024, accessed on 15 March 2026.
[44] White House, "Quantum Economic Development Consortium (QED-C)," Washington, DC, USA, 2024 [Online]. Available at https://www.whitehouse.gov/quantum-economic-development-consortium, accessed on 15 March 2026.
[45] World Economic Forum, "Quantum computing in finance: Opportunities for transformation," Geneva, Switzerland, 2024 [Online]. Available at https://www.weforum.org/publications/quantum-computing-finance-2024, accessed on 15 March 2026.
[46] Accenture, "BBVA explores quantum computing for arbitrage and route optimization (with D-Wave)," Madrid, Spain, 2020 [Online]. Available: https://www.accenture.com, accessed on
[47] D-Wave Systems, "Hybrid solver service: Technical overview," Burnaby, Canada, 2021 [Online]. Available at https://www.dwavesys.com, accessed on 15 March 2026.

8 Quantum Machine Learning Applications in Healthcare

Reddaiah Kasturi[1*]

Quantum machine learning (QML) is an emerging discipline at the intersection of quantum computing and artificial intelligence, providing new approaches to address the increasing computational and analytical challenges in healthcare. This chapter explores how quantum principles, such as superposition, entanglement, and interference, can enhance the efficiency and accuracy of machine learning when applied to complex biomedical data. It presents an overview of the fundamental concepts of QML, compares its capabilities with those of traditional machine learning systems, and examines important algorithmic frameworks, including quantum support vector machines, quantum neural networks, and variational quantum algorithms. Practical examples are explored across several healthcare domains—drug discovery, medical imaging, genomic research, patient monitoring, and hospital resource management—showing how quantum methods are beginning to improve data interpretation and clinical decision-making. The chapter also outlines current limitations related to hardware capacity, data preparation, interpretability, and regulatory standards, while emphasizing ethical and cybersecurity considerations that accompany quantum-enabled systems. Finally, it looks ahead to a future in which accessible quantum computing, open-source development, and collaboration among scientists, clinicians, and technologists drive a new generation of personalized, secure, and data-driven healthcare.

1. Beginning and Reason

By the end of this chapter, readers will have a full knowledge of how quantum computing and healthcare machine learning work together now and will work in the future.

1.1 The Meeting of Healthcare and Advanced Computing

Healthcare is going through a digital transition because biomedical data is growing quickly, tailored medicine is becoming more popular, and people want to make decisions based on data in real time. At the same time, progress in computer science,

[1] Senior Data Engineer, Divine IT Services, Sterling VA, USA.
* Corresponding author: reddaiah.kasturi@yahoo.com

DOI: 10.1201/9781003646068-8

especially artificial intelligence (AI) and machine learning (ML), is changing the way we look at health data, make treatments, and find diseases.

But classical computing systems, even with the power of modern graphic processing units (GPUs) and distributed architectures, are starting to have trouble with the huge amount, complexity, and dimensionality of biological data. Modeling molecular interactions, predicting treatment outcomes from multimodal patient data, and identifying faint anomalies in high-resolution medical pictures are all very computationally expensive and limited by the hardware we have now.

This setting sets the stage for the combination of quantum computing, which is a whole new way of processing information based on the laws of quantum mechanics, and machine learning, which gives rise to quantum machine learning (QML).

1.2 What Is Quantum Machine Learning?

Quantum Machine Learning is the creation and use of quantum algorithms and hybrid quantum–classical models to do machine learning tasks. Quantum computers use qubits, which can be in superposition and be entangled, instead of classical systems that only use binary bits (0 or 1). Because of these quantum features, quantum processors can do calculations across a huge solution space at the same time. This lets them solve problems that classical systems cannot handle [2].

In QML, classical data like gene sequences, radiological pictures, or electronic health records are turned into quantum states using unique methods like angle encoding, amplitude encoding, or basis encoding [15]. Quantum circuits then process these quantum representations by making changes and taking measurements to learn, sort, group, or guess what will happen [3]. QML is not meant to take the place of classical ML; instead, it is meant to improve it, especially in situations where traditional algorithms have problems with time or space complexity that grows exponentially.

1.3 Why Is Quantum Machine Learning Important for Healthcare?

Healthcare is complicated and has several parts. Biological systems function at molecular, cellular, organ, and systemic levels, producing extensive heterogeneous data. QML is in a unique position to help with some of the biggest problems in healthcare AI.

a. Data and Feature Spaces with Many Dimensions

Biomedical data, such single-cell RNA sequencing or proteomics, is commonly found in feature spaces with many dimensions. It is hard for classical models to process and show this kind of data quickly. QML works naturally in Hilbert spaces that are exponentially vast, which makes it possible to make data representations that are smaller and more expressive [4].

b. Computational Bottlenecks in Drug Discovery
It is impossible to use classical systems to simulate how molecules interact with each other using quantum chemistry for molecules with more than a few atoms. Variational quantum eigensolver (VQE) and other QML models can more accurately estimate molecule energies, which speeds up drug discovery and lowers costs [5].

c. Early Disease Detection and Imaging
Quantum support vector machine (QSVM) and quantum neural network (QNN), like quantum-enhanced classifiers, can recognize a disease at its early stage by picking unnoticed details from imaging data that classical algorithms may forget [17].

d. Genomics and Tailored Treatment
With the help of quantum PCA and quantum clustering algorithms, it becomes possible to efficiently analyze large genomic datasets and gene variants to customize treatment options to the genetic profile of individual patients—what is known as precision medicine. [7].

1.4 Quantum Advantage: What We See vs What We Get

QML handles both theoretical and practical results, and as a rule of thumb, quantum algorithms will beat classical ones. It is indeed a work in progress. Currently, quantum systems are categorized as noisy intermediate-scale quantum (NISQ). This means that due to the number of qubits (and circuit depth) no error correction can yet be performed [8]. However, things are shifting at an astonishing pace. Major platforms like International Business Machines (IBM), Google, and Rigetti along with software libraries like Qiskit, PennyLane, and TensorFlow Quantum are making the use of QML easier for professionals in the field of healthcare.

The motivation behind the application of QML to healthcare is not only the benefits that are expected out of it but also the opportunity it provides to extend traditional AI techniques in domains that are otherwise insufficiently performant in terms of computation or algorithms.

2. The Promise of Quantum Machine Learning in Healthcare

QML gives computers new powers that fit well with many of the healthcare industry's present needs, especially when it comes to recognizing complicated patterns, optimizing processes, simulating situations, and analyzing data with multiple dimensions. This section discusses the main benefits that QML delivers to healthcare and the basic quantum principles that make these benefits possible.

2.1 Exponential Feature Space with Quantum Kernels

In traditional machine learning, transforming data into higher dimensional spaces using kernels is a common method to enhance the separability of complex patterns.

However, computing such transformations and evaluating kernel functions becomes computationally expensive as dimensionality increases [13].

Quantum computers work in Hilbert spaces that get bigger and bigger as more qubits are added. Superposition allows a system of nnn qubits to show 2n2^n2n states at the same time. Quantum kernel methods use this ability to put classical data into huge feature spaces at a far lower cost than classical kernel methods [1].

Example of Use Case: In classifying genomic variations associated with cancer, quantum kernels can be used to embed patient deoxyribonucleic acid (DNA) sequence data into high dimensional spaces when identifying genomic changes linked to cancer. This can show patterns that classical kernels would miss [2].

2.2 Quantum Speedups in Optimization

Many healthcare jobs include optimization, such as designing drugs with fewer adverse effects, refining treatment programs, and changing the settings in prediction models. The following are some quantum algorithms that allow for the simultaneous exploration of extensive solution spaces through quantum interference and entanglement:

- **Quantum approximate optimization algorithm (QAOA)**
- **Quantum gradient descent**
- **Variational quantum algorithms (VQAs)**

For some types of problems, these techniques have shown quadratic or exponential speedups over classical solutions [3].

In hybrid QML, a classical optimizer is used to modify a **parameterized quantum circuit (PQC)** to minimize a cost. In some cases, these circuits can better mimic non-linear decision boundaries and multi-modal distributions better than shallow neural networks in certain contexts [4].

Healthcare Impact: QML handles both theoretical and practical results. As a rule of thumb, quantum algorithms outperform classical ones, which has now been proven with a few algorithms. It is indeed a work in progress. Quantum systems right now fall in the NISQ category, which means that they contain a number of qubits (and circuit depth) for which no error correction can yet be performed [8]. But things are moving fast. IBM, Google, and Rigetti are big players in the field, and software libraries like Qiskit, PennyLane, and TensorFlow Quantum are focused on making the use of QML simpler for researchers in the field of healthcare.

QML has applications in healthcare not only for the opportunities that are to follow but also for the chance to broaden the horizons of traditional AI techniques in areas that would otherwise lack in performance, either due to computation or algorithms.

2.3 Speed Up Drug Discovery through Simulation

One promising application of QML in healthcare is the simulation of quantum chemistry, which includes simulation of the interactions between drugs and biological targets. Due to the exponential nature of computational complexity, classical methods, like density functional theory (DFT), do not capture larger molecular systems well.

The following quantum algorithms can simulate quantum systems natively, which makes them great for simulating molecular features like **binding energies, reaction rates, and conformational stability** [5]:

- **Variational quantum eigensolver (VQE)**
- **Quantum phase estimation (QPE)**
- **Hamiltonian simulation**

Case Study: IBM's application of VQE to model lithium hydride (LiH) was an important milestone in making quantum simulations more plausible for medicine [6]. In medical industry, similar simulations have the potential to demonstrate how a candidate drug binds to a target protein, which can save months of lab work!

2.4 Reducing the Number of Dimensions and Compressing the Data

The size and noise of clinical datasets, such as imaging datasets (e.g., magnetic resonance imaging [MRI], computed tomography [CT], positron emission tomography [PET]), genomic datasets, and wearable sensor datasets, can be significant. In order to derive useful information, the dimensionality reduction methods must be good.

Quantum principal component analysis (QPCA) and quantum autoencoders are two other methods to find patterns and compress large datasets besides classical PCA. Under ideal circumstances, these quantum algorithms can be extraordinarily faster, especially when quantum data is already available (for example, after encoding) [7].

Healthcare Impact: Transforming high-resolution MRI scan data into a compressed quantum state can reduce storage and processing requirements while preserving essential diagnostic features.

2.5 Improved Pattern Recognition and Correlations

Using the main quantum interference and also entanglement, QML models can learn and find correlations between features in ways not possible with classical models. In healthcare sectors, where there are very complicated relationships between variables, which are not straight lines, this is valuable.

Quantum neural networks (QNNs) and a quantum-enhanced ensemble approach show that they can:

- Find early markers of diseases (e.g., Alzheimer's, Parkinson's)
- Find rare gene expression patterns in single cell datasets
- Enhance anomaly detection in patient monitoring systems [8]

In case of rare diseases diagnosis wherein small alterations in genetic or physiological data can give a good rise to a huge change in the diagnosis, QML and all the other models that lend themselves to modeling the tail areas of data distribution for diagnosis are more reliable when traditional models are ineffective.

2.6 Natural Alignment with Biological Systems

Interestingly, at small scales, biological molecules such as proteins and DNA, along with cell biology, behave according to quantum mechanics. Quantum modeling and health science suggest a philosophical and practical correspondence.

Some researchers believe that quantum algorithms would be more effective in simulating and extracting information from quantum mechanical instances, for instance, electron transfer in enzyme reactions, protein folding, or photosynthesis [9].

This opens the door to biophysically using more precise modeling, which could help uncover new mechanisms of disease and treatment otherwise unreachable with classical methods.

Outlook: Quantum methods allow biophysically accurate modeling, which helps understanding disease mechanism and/or interventions and new therapeutics that classical methods may not allow.

Table 8.1 Advantages of QML in healthcare.

Advantage	*Quantum Method*	*Use Case in Healthcare*
Exponential feature mapping	Kernels in quantum	Recognition of genomic patterns
Fast optimization	QAOA, VQE, and quantum GD	Treatment personalization, resource scheduling
Simulation of quantum chemistry	VQE and QPE	Finding new drugs and modeling protein ligand
Reducing no. of dimensions	QPCA, quantum autoencoders	Gene expression analysis with MRI/ image compression
Advanced pattern recognition	QNN and QSVM	Cancer detection, disease diagnosis from imaging
Biological alignment	Simulation of Hamiltonian	Biophysics research, modeling mechanisms

3. Quantum Machine Learning Architectures and Algorithms for Healthcare

QML may be useful in healthcare but only if the right algorithms are designed and chosen that work well with medical use case. In this section, we discuss some hybrid and fully quantum QML models and architectures that could address some important problems in healthcare.

3.1 Quantum Support Vector Machines (QSVM)

Quantum support vector Machines (QSVMs) are an improvement on conventional SVMs. They use quantum feature maps or kernels to map input data into high-dimensional quantum Hilbert spaces. It becomes possible to segregate data in a way that is not normally separable in classical space.

Quantum Mechanism:
To evaluate kernel functions, QSVMs place input vectors into quantum states and process them through a quantum processor. Quantum Support Vector Machines might outperform classical support vector machines. They employ quantum kernels, known as quantum feature maps, to transform input data into a high-dimensional quantum Hilbert space. Quantum mechanics offer a solution to separate data that is not separable in classical space.

A classical SVM solver then utilizes this quantum kernel for classification purposes [1].

Healthcare Applications:
- Classifying tumor and non-tumor tissue in histopathology images
- Using EEG/functional MRI (fMRI) data to find neurological illness
- Finding heart problems from time series biosignals

Advantages:
- Works well with clinical data that has a lot of dimensions
- Makes it easier to classify data that is noisy
- Lessens overfitting when there are not many samples (which is prevalent in rare disease studies)

Case Example: QSVM classified breast cancer subtypes using gene expression profiles with greater accuracy than traditional SVMs on the same dataset [2].

3.2 Quantum Neural Networks (QNN)

QNNs are based on classical deep learning but operate on quantum circuits using parameterized quantum gates acting as their neurons and layers.

Architecture Features:
- Quantum rotations and entanglement gates make up the layers.
- A classical optimizer gets the results of the measurements.
- Measurement outcomes are fed into a classical optimizer.
- To lower cost functions variational quantum circuits (VQCs) are used.

Uses in Healthcare Application:
- Image recognition (e.g., MRI scans to find tumor)
- Sequential modeling (e.g., predicting the progression of an illness)
- Quantum generative models for molecular design

Example: QNNs were tested on PET scan data to see if they could tell the difference between early-stage Alzheimer's and other diseases. They did better than standard CNNs when the training datasets were small [3].

Problems:

- Vulnerability to desert plateaus, characterized by the disappearance of gradients during training.
- Hardware limitations limit the number of parameters and the depth of circuits [4].

3.3 Quantum Principal Component Analysis (QPCA)

QPCA is a quantum version of conventional PCA that finds the main components of huge datasets by diagonalizing their covariance matrices.

How it Works:

- Quantum density matrix shows input data.
- Quantum phase estimation is utilized to derive eigenvalues and eigenvectors.
- Essential components are retained for future analysis to perform more research [5].

Uses in Healthcare:

- Reducing the number of dimensions in high-resolution radiological pictures
- Analysis of gene expression across thousands of characteristics
- Finding biomarkers in omics data, such as metabolomics and proteomics

Case Study: A simulated QPCA was employed to diminish single-cell transcriptome data, yielding clustering results substantially indistinguishable from classical PCA at a significantly reduced timeframe [6].

3.4 Algorithms for Quantum Clustering

Clustering is a key part of unsupervised learning that is often used widely in patient segmentation, gene clustering, and finding outliers. Quantum clustering algorithms are more efficient and give better solutions, especially in regions with lot of dimensional spaces.

Types:

- Quantum k-means that uses quantum distance calculations
- DBSCAN with quantum enhancements
- Grover-based clustering to speed up search over cluster assignments

Uses in Healthcare:

- Satisfying patients with individualized treatment plans
- Grouping microbiome profiles
- Finding outliers in data streams from wearable sensors

Advantages:

- It takes less iterations to get stable clusters
- Ability to capture non-Euclidean correlations in biological data

Example: Quantum k-means was used on a dataset of diabetic patients and did a better job of separating disease progression groups than classical approaches [7].

3.5 Variational Quantum Algorithms (VQAs)

VQAs are the basis for most hybrid QML methods. They are quantum circuits that can be trained, and classical optimizers are used to find the best values for their parameters. VQAs are adaptable and work well with hardware, making them perfect for quantum processors that make a lot of noise.

Various Types:

- **Variational quantum classifier (VQC)** used for supervised classification
- **Quantum approximate optimization algorithm (QAOA)** used for optimizing combinations
- **Variational quantum eigensolver (VQE)** used for energy estimation in molecules

Importance in Healthcare:

- Choosing drug candidate based on molecular energy ratings (VQE)
- VQC: Optimizing diagnosis model with as few parameters as possible
- QAOA: Optimizing the patient group for clinical trial

Example of Use Case: Pfizer and QC Ware used VQE to figure out the excited state energies of cancer medication compounds to help them improve their lead [8].

3.6 Quantum Autoencoders

Quantum autoencoders learn a low-dimensional subspace that keeps important properties and compress quantum data into smaller qubit representations.

Uses in Healthcare:

- Getting rid of noise in medical imaging
- Encoding of patient health statuses from various sources, such as lab, EHR, and imaging
- Representations of sensitive medical data that protects privacy

Advantages:

- Model generalization using minimal training data
- Quantum speedups in multi-dimensionality reduction
- Possibility of safe data storage and data transfer

3.7 Quantum Generative Models

Quantum Boltzmann machines and **quantum GANs** are examples of generative models that try to create data or probabilistic samples based on inputs. These are mainly relevant for:

- Mimicking patient data for uncommon diseases
- Modeling molecular shapes in drug design
- Creating several paths for how diseases get worse over time

These models are still in the early stages of study, but they show how to add to small datasets, which is a prevalent problem in the creation of medical AI.

Table 8.2 QML algorithms in healthcare.

Name of Algorithm	*Type of Work*	*Quantum Method*	*Use Case in Healthcare*
QSVM	Classification	Estimation of quantum kernel	Finding diseases and genomics
QNN	Classification	Parameterized circuits	Radiology and diagnosis
QPCA	Dimensionality	Estimating phase	Imaging and omics data
Quantum Clustering	Unsupervised	Quantum distances and Grover	Grouping patients and genes [10]
VQC/VQE/ QAOA	Optimization	Hybrid variational models	Designing drugs and improving treatments
Quantum autoencoder	Compression	Entanglement in quantum mechanics	MRI compression and encoding that keeps your privacy safe
Quantum GANs	Generative	Quantum sampling	Creating synthetic structures for patients or drugs

4. Real-World Applications of QML in Healthcare

Quantum machine learning (QML) is moving from being a theoretical idea to being used in real life in several scientific and clinical fields. Let us now turn our attention to what QML could do for healthcare jobs. For instance, could QML change drug research, diagnostic imaging, genomics, real-time monitoring, and cybersecurity, among others? Each subsection describes key models, real-world pilots being used, and possible future applications.

4.1 Finding New Drugs and Simulating Molecules

Problem Context:
It requires several molecular models, lab tests, and clinical trials and thus, traditional drug discovery takes 10 to 15 years and costs billions of dollars. One big issue is simulating how drug molecules and target proteins behave in relation to each other at the quantum level. This becomes much harder for conventional computers.

QML Contribution:
Quantum algorithms like VQE and QPE can simulate molecular energy states, abilities, and bonding characteristics more accurately and with less computational power than a classical approach [1].

Example in Action:

- IBM and Moderna modeled protein interactions and simulated the structure of mRNA with QML to possibly accelerate vaccine creation.
- Pfizer has attempted to use QML for lead optimization in its oncology drug pipelines, leveraging variational quantum chemistry to help select compounds [3].

Effect:
QML could lower the number of drugs that fail in the preclinical stage by making more accurate predictions about toxicity and target affinity.

4.2 Imaging for Diagnostic and Finding Diseases

Problem Statement:
Medical imaging (MRI, CT, PET, ultrasound) is essential for diagnosis, although it produces extensive, high-dimensional information. When there is not enough training data, classical deep learning models tend to overfit, which is common in rare diseases or early diagnosis phases.

QML Contribution:

- **Quantum Neural Networks (QNNs)** and **Quantum Convolutional Neural Networks (QCNNs)** are parameter efficient models that are capable of extracting profound hierarchical features from imaging data [11].
- Quantum kernels in support vector machines assist in finding little disease-related problems that might be hidden in classical noise.

Example:

- Researchers employed QSVMs to categorize histopathology images for breast cancer, demonstrating enhanced sensitivity relative to traditional SVMs, especially on small or imbalanced datasets [4].
- QCNNs have been simulated to find signs of Alzheimer signs in PET scans. They do this by extracting features better with fewer parameters [5].

Effect:
Early diagnosis of diseases such as cancer, Alzheimer's, and heart irregularities with reduced false positives and diminished data requirements.

4.3 Genomics and Personalized Medicine

Problem Statement:
Whole genome sequencing (WGS), transcriptomics, and epigenomics all make huge datasets in genomics. Getting useful information like mutations linked to diseases or druggable gene targets is hard for computers and needs strong dimensionality reduction.

QML Contribution:

- **Quantum PCA (QPCA)** allows you to cut down on genomic feature sets quickly while keeping a lot of variation.
- **Quantum clustering methods** sort patients or gene expressions into subtypes that are useful for therapy or phenotypically.

Example of Applications:

- In studies on uncommon diseases, QML is being used to find single nucleotide polymorphisms (SNPs) that are associated with neurodegenerative diseases.
- Quantum-enhanced k-means has successfully grouped genomic expression data from breast cancer patients, which has improved subtype categorization [6].

Effect:
QML helps the field of precision medicine move forward by making it possible to tailor treatments to each person's genetic profile more quickly and accurately.

4.4 Real-Time Health Monitoring and Predictive Care

Problem Statement:
Wearable devices and remote sensors produce ongoing streams of physiological data, such as heart rate, SpO_2, and glucose levels. It is still hard to find health events (such arrhythmias, hypoglycemia, and early sepsis) in real time from noisy, multivariate streams [14].

QML Contribution:

- Researchers are looking into quantum recurrent neural networks (QRNNs) to see if they can represent time patterns in data that comes in a sequence.
- Hybrid QML models that use both historical and streaming data can make predictions more accurate while using fewer resources.

Use Case:
A hybrid QML framework was utilized on an intensive care unit (ICU) dataset to forecast the onset of sepsis through quantum-enhanced feature maps. The model converged more quickly than the conventional one and got a similar AUC with less training samples [7].

Effect:
QML makes it possible for critical-care early warning systems to work, which lets doctors step in before a patient's condition gets worse.

4.5 Optimization of Healthcare Resources

Problem Statement:
Hospitals have to deal with complicated difficulties when it comes to allocating resources, like assigning ICU beds, scheduling surgeries, and keeping track of inventory when things are not clear

QML Contribution:
QAOA is an efficient heuristic for restricted optimization tasks whose solution space is huge, outperforming classical heuristics.

Example Use Case:
Quantum models for queues in hospitals and elective surgery schedules show that QAOA can increase patient flow through a hospital and decrease wait times in a pandemic-like surge [8].

Effect:
Greater healthcare logistics leads to greater results, lower costs, and happier patients.

4.6 Cybersecurity and Data Privacy in Healthcare

Problem Statement:
When medical data gets digitized, it is more likely to be stolen, hacked, or attacked by AI systems. HIPAA, GDPR, and other new post-quantum security rules say that healthcare systems must protect sensitive data.

QML Contribution:

- **Quantum enhanced anomaly detection** can find breaches or strange access patterns more quickly.
- **Quantum safe cryptographic technics** such as lattice-based PQC and **quantum key distribution (QKD)** make sure that communication and authentication are safe [9].

Effect:
QML is useful not only for healthcare diagnostics and analytics but also for making AI-based systems in clinical settings safer and more reliable.

Table 8.3 Important QML use cases in healthcare.

Healthcare Domain	*QML Method*	*Example of an Outcome*
Finding new drugs	VQE and QPE	Simulated drug protein binding; improved compound screening
Imaging if diagnosis	QNN, QSVM, and QCNN	Detecting Alzheimer's and classifying tumors
Genomics & precision med.	QPCA, quantum clustering	Finding gene mutations and subtyping diseases
Health monitoring	Hybrid QML and QRNN	Systems that warn about sepsis and arrhythmia early
Optimization of resources	QAOA	Hospital scheduling and resource allocation
Cybersecurity in healthcare	Finding quantum anomalies	Detection of intrusions and safe deployment of models

5. QML Limitations and Challenges in Healthcare

QML has a lot of potential to change healthcare, but there are a lot of technological, practical, and regulatory problems that need to be solved first. Some of these problems are due to the fact that quantum technology is still in its early stages of development, while others are due to the fact that healthcare environments are very sensitive and regulated. This section discusses the biggest problems that are stopping healthcare systems from using QML in the real world.

5.1 Quantum Hardware Restrictions

Number of Qubits and Their Coherence:
Most quantum devices that are already on the market are NISQ devices, which have only tens to a few hundred qubits. But in real-life healthcare situations, like simulating big molecules or training deep QNNs, you typically need thousands of logical qubits. Also, modern qubits have short coherence durations, which means they quickly lose their quantum state when they interact with the environment [1].

In drug simulation, losing coherence before the simulation is over might lead to outputs that are not valid or outcomes that are too noisy to help make real-world treatment decisions.

Gate Errors and Circuit Depth:
Quantum gates, which are the parts that make up quantum circuits, can have high mistake rates. Deep quantum circuits, which are commonly needed for complicated machine learning models, make it more likely that errors will build up. As a result, current QML implementations can only work with shallow circuits, which limits the expressiveness of models [2].

5.2 Challenges in Data Encoding

Quantum State Preparation:
It is not easy to turn traditional biomedical data (such genomes, pictures, and her) into quantum states

Quantum data encoding, especially amplitude encoding or basis encoding, usually requires a lot of extra work, which can be exponential depending on the encoding strategy and the number of dimensions in the data [3].

For instance, encoding a patient profile with 1,000 features into a quantum system can require complicated changes that cancel out the projected speedups in quantum systems.

Constraints on Reusability of Data:
The no cloning theorem in quantum mechanics says that quantum data cannot be copied and reused way it can in classical systems. This makes it harder to come up with new ways to make iterative learning algorithms or batch-based QML systems.

5.3 Algorithmic Maturity

Shortage of Generalized QML Models:
Most QML models so far are either made to solve a specific problem or to show how an idea works. General-purpose quantum frameworks for addressing real-world healthcare challenges, such as population-scale modeling or multimodal learning, are still in the early stages of development [4].

Empty Plateaus in QNN Training:
The desert plateau problem relates to vanishing gradients as model depth increases, and it is a major issue with training QNNs [16]. Optimizing the aforementioned targets is very difficult, especially on noisy hardware or for complicated datasets like fMRI or 3D scans [5].

5.4 Explainability and Interpretability

In clinical scenarios, explainability is an essential requirement as it is important for medical professionals to check AI judgments. A lot of QML models, especially those that use variational circuits, work like quantum black boxes and do not have many ways to explain predictions or show learnt characteristics [6].

Clinicians must comprehend the rationale behind categorization, not merely the output, for an AI to propose a cancer subtype for diagnosis. Not being able to explain things makes people less trusting and slows down adoption.

5.5 Ethical, Legal, and Regulatory Limits

Following the Rules and Being Able to Be Audited:
There are severe rules for healthcare apps, including as HIPAA in the United States (US), GDPR in the European Union (EU), and new post-quantum cybersecurity rules. Quantum models must show that they follow the rules for data protection, model validation, and ethical governance [7].

Bias and Fairness:
QML models trained on biased classical datasets may **inherit and amplify** these biases. Furthermore, due to limited public quantum healthcare datasets, many QML experiments rely on synthetic or curated samples, increasing the risk of **overfitting or unrepresentative results** [8].

5.6 Integration with Classical Systems

QML models often require hybrid processing, where quantum circuits handle kernel estimation or subroutines, while classical systems manage pre-processing and parameter updates. This hybrid workflow poses integration challenges, such as:

- Data transfer latency between central processing unit (CPU) and QPU
- Security during quantum classical handoffs
- Lack of standard protocols or APIs across QML platforms

For instance, integrating a QML based diagnostic tool into a hospital's radiology system may require significant engineering work and validation overheads.

5.7 Scalability and Real-World Benchmarking

Lack of Scalable Healthcare Datasets:
Most QML demonstrations in healthcare have been conducted on toy datasets or reduced scale simulations. Not many healthcare datasets are open access, quantum-ready, and benchmarked to allow modeling at a clinical scale [9].

Unclear Quantum Advantage Thresholds:
It is still unclear when QML has a genuine computational or clinical advantage over classical ML.

As training time, generalization of the model, or the energy efficiency vary from platform to platform, comparison between these metrics can be difficult.

Table 8.4 Challenges in QML healthcare adoption.

Category	*Challenge*	*Implication*
Hardware	Limited qubits, coherence time, gate fidelity	Reduced circuit depth, accuracy limitations
Encoding	High cost of data to qubit transformation	Limits input size and model complexity
Algorithms	Barren plateaus, lack of general QML frameworks	Difficult optimization and poor scalability
Explainability	Quantum black box models	Low clinician trust and compliance risks
Ethics & regulation	Compliance with HIPAA, GDPR, fairness concerns	Slower approvals, limited real-world use
Integration	Hybrid workflow complexity	Deployment bottlenecks in clinical information technology (IT) infrastructure
Scalability	No large, standardized QML healthcare benchmarks	Hard to measure ROI or clinical readiness

6. Ethical, Security, and Compliance Considerations for QML in Healthcare

The application of QML in healthcare raises important questions regarding ethics, security, and compliance. The use of quantum systems in drug research, monitoring of patients, and diagnostic decisions is in its infancy, and all stakeholders must ensure that they are reliable, transparent, and compliant with the law. The section will discuss the key ethical risks and legal frameworks that apply for QML in healthcare, and the best practices for protecting quantum-enabled health devices.

6.1 Ethical Issues in Quantum Healthcare AI

Fairness, Bias, and Health Equity:
QML models can produce inequity in healthcare delivery if the datasets are biased. A quantum-enhanced cancer diagnostic model trained predominantly with a particular demographic of data, for example, is likely to perform poorly on underrepresented demographic groups. This poor performance may lead to misdiagnoses and/or delayed treatment [1].

- Quantum risk refers to kernel approaches and feature encodings, which may mask how much each feature contributes to the result. This then complicates finding biased results.
- It is a good idea to include fairness audits, monitor demographic performance, and incorporate various ethnicities in the datasets that will be used to train quantum models.

Clinical Trust and Explainability:
Healthcare workers should clarify how AI makes clinical decisions, both to the patient and/or staff. Many QML models, especially variational quantum circuits, act like black boxes, making it difficult to understand how a decision was made [2].

- If there is no transparency about the issues, doctors may not have confidence in what they are recommending, regulators may not be able to approve things, and it may violate the ethical duty of informed consent.
- It is a best practice to build quantum explainability tools, like interpretable quantum circuits or post hoc attribution models, to see and show how decisions are made.

Responsibility and Accountability:
QML systems create complicated chains of responsibility. When a quantum-enhanced diagnostic system makes a mistake that harms someone, pinning down who exactly is responsible can be quite tricky. Healthcare, hardware vendors, and regulator developers could be the main concern.

There is a need to develop clear governance structures, have documentation about the decisions in model design, and maintain audit logging of the results of quantum computations.

6.2 Risks to Data Privacy and Security

Quantum Threats to Encryption of Medical Data:
One threat that come to everyone's mind is public-key cryptography. Quantum computing can break these keys. Shor's algorithm and other algorithms can factor much larger integers considerably faster than traditional algorithms. This threatens secure communication methods such as RSA and ECC [4].

- Quantum attacks could decrease the confidentiality of encrypted health records and patient-provider communications, and compromise medical IoT devices [12].

"Harvest Now, Decrypt Later" Scenarios:
In today's world, your enemies could acquire and store encrypted medical data with the aim of decrypting it later with quantum computers. It could be particularly dangerous for sensitive data that must be stored for a long period of time, spanning across genomic data, mental health data, and trial data [5].

- To combat the vulnerabilities of quantum computers, we need to adopt standards of post-quantum cryptography (PQC) as recommended by groups like NIST (e.g., ML KEM ML DSA) and start deploying hybrid cryptography (e.g., PQC plus conventional crypto).

Attacks Specific to QML:
Even QML models themselves are vulnerable to attacks such as the following:

- **Model Extraction**: Inferring internal logic of a quantum model via input output pairs
- **Membership Inference**: Determining whether specific data was used during training
- **Model Poisoning**: Inserting corrupted data to bias quantum learning outcomes [6]

These risks mirror those in classical ML but may have heightened impact due to the **irreversibility** of some quantum operations and the lack of mature monitoring tools.

6.3 Standards for Compliance and Regulatory Frameworks

Current Regulations:

- HIPAA (US) law states that patient health data must be securely stored, sent, and accessed. QML tools that work with patient data must follow the HIPAA rules.
- The GDPR (EU) calls for limited data collection as a great right to explanation (Article 22) and better rights of data subjects. Quantum algorithms must be open and easy to check [7].

Institutions testing quantum technology in clinical settings will face tough penalties. Accordingly, they can also hurt their image if they do not comply.

6.4 Getting Ready for Post-Quantum Compliance

Migration to Post-Quantum Cryptography (PQC)

- Organizations must begin assessing the use of cryptocurrency, particularly in the holding and transferring of systems containing sensitive medical information, that is, understand the cryptocurrency in use.
- "Modernization" of old systems should have plans for dual use systems based on hybrid models of encryption as there will be the continuation of classical algorithms.

Quantum Key Distribution (QKD)

- Quantum entanglement allows for two parties to construct a secure key in an eavesdropping proof manner. High-loss communications are injury communication for the main defense and also similar networks.

Table 8.5 Secure and ethical QML deployment best practices.

Practice	*Purpose*
Audits of fairness	To basically find and also find performance gaps.
Model interpretability modules	To help clinician trust and also their compliance (GDPR, HIPAA)
Cryptographic inventory & PQC planning	To majorly get ready for all the quantum safe data infrastructure
Quantum model logging & versioning	Enable traceability and accountability
Secure quantum classical integration	Prevent man in the middle attacks on hybrid workflows
Ethical governance boards	Oversee QML use, especially in sensitive applications

Table 8.6 Responsibilities of stakeholders.

Stakeholder	*Duties of QML Healthcare*
Data scientists	Make sure things are fair, test the effects of quantum encoding, and write down assumptions.
Clinicians	Check AI-generated diagnoses, understand the results, and report mistakes.
Quantum vendors	Make sure that hardware meets HIPAA and GDPR standards and that APIs are safe and can be audited.
Policymakers	Set up regulatory sandboxes and change the legislation to deal with the threats of quantum computing.

6.5 Looking Ahead: Quantum AI and Ethics in Healthcare

The introduction of QML in medicine calls for a deeper reflection on ethical philosophy. What does it mean to allow an algorithm to decide about the diagnosis or drug design, when we cannot be sure how it does what it does? In order for QML systems to evolve, the rules for developing them must change.

There are suggestions for "quantum ethical design principles," which stress the following:

- **Transparency**: The effects of quantum logic should be clear, even when they are abstract.
- **Consent**: Patients should know when quantum methods are being used.
- **Accountability**: Developers are responsible for the model's limits and known hazards, and they must make them public [8].

7. The Future of QML in Healthcare

QML is on the verge of revolutionizing healthcare by shifting from deciphering biological complexity to enhancing real-time medical decision-making. Although practical, large-scale clinical implementation is still in its infancy, the forthcoming decade is anticipated to witness a confluence of advancements in quantum hardware, software tools, regulatory sophistication, and interdisciplinary collaboration. This section discusses the most promising future advances in QML for healthcare and gives an idea of how the area is likely to change.

7.1 Attaining Quantum Advantage in Healthcare

The most important goal in QML right now is to show quantum advantage, which is when quantum models do better than classical ones in terms of speed, accuracy, or resource efficiency on important tasks.

Potential Early Areas of Advantage:

- **Molecular simulations**: Quantum modeling of protein-ligand interactions may soon be more accurate and larger than conventional approaches [1].
- **Sparse diagnostics**: QSVMs and quantum-enhanced anomaly detectors may facilitate expedited convergence on rare disease classification problems with limited data [2].

Existing Limits:

- There are not many big, high-quality datasets that have already been encoded into quantum forms.
- Error corrected quantum hardware is still not fully developed.
- There is an absence of clinically validated, quantum-native algorithms.

Nonetheless, there is a clear direction: hybrid quantum–classical models (like variational circuits) are becoming more common in research, and a few preliminary attempts are making their way into the hospital research and development (R&D) pipeline.

7.2 Expansion of Interdisciplinary Studies

The future of QML development requires coordinated and synergistic efforts across various disciplines.

Table 8.7 Key Disciplines and Their Roles in Advancing Quantum Machine Learning

Field	*QML Advancement Role*
Quantum Physics	Make qubits that can be scaled up and have low error rates, as well as stable entanglement
AI & ML	Transform ML algorithms into quantum equivalents
Biomedicine	Give clinical problems, datasets, and validation metrics
Bioethics	Define AI practices that are safe, open, and focused on the patient
Cybersecurity	Make infrastructure that is safe after quantum computing

To train the next generation of quantum biomedical scientists, universities are starting to open quantum health research centers and dual degree programs, such as quantum computing and bioinformatics.

7.3 Hardware and Software Maturation

Hardware Roadmap:

- Advancement from NISQ to fault-tolerant quantum computers enables richer circuits, more complex models, and extended simulations.
- By the end of the 2020s, IBM, IonQ, Rigetti, and others plan to have systems with greater than 1,000 qubits [3].

Software Evolution:

- Software frameworks such as Qiskit, PennyLane, and TensorFlow Quantum are rapidly incorporating new functionalities, allowing complex hybrids, parameter tuning, and analytical visualization.
- Before deployed in the field, quantum healthcare simulation models are still invaluable on classical hardware.

7.4 Standards, Benchmarks and Building an Ecosystem

For QML to be useful in regulated fields like healthcare, it needs defined benchmarking rules and standards.

Emerging Needs:

- **Standard datasets** (e.g., quantum encoded ECGs, genomics, imaging)
- **Performance** measures made for quantum workflows include the qF1 score and the circuit depth vs. accuracy curves
- How well models work across different quantum hardware providers

Collaborative consortia, such as the Quantum Economic Development Consortium (QED-C) and ETSI's Quantum Safe Initiative is working on standards that can cooperate with each other and a shared testing infrastructure [4].

7.5 Democratization of QML in Medicine

Similar to classical machine learning, the expansion of quantum computing is rapidly growing due to the availability of cloud computing and open-source platforms.

Key Factors:

- All of the major quantum computing service providers, like IBM, Amazon, and Microsoft, provide cloud access to their quantum computing.
- Qiskit, Xanadu's Strawberry Fields, and Quantum Codebook are open-access quantum computing software.
- Most of the communities are majorly based on the datasets that are being created by including quantum ready versions of most publicity and also the most available medical datasets MIMIC and will also be the NIH X-ray set.

This will also set means that the QML is also becoming an available one to the most modest clinics and will also be a new establishment business and the universities will also help in the pioneer AI for healthcare.

7.6 Open Research Issues

Even though most of the things are moving very quickly, there are still many questions that need to be answered.

Table 8.8 Key Research Challenges and Their Significance in Quantum Machine Learning for Healthcare

Challenges in Research	*Why It Matters*
Quantum interpretability	Clinicians must have faith in and validate model outputs
Strong QML in noisy environments	Outputs that are prone to errors could lead to dangerous recommendations
Multimodal QML architectures	Combining EHR, imaging, genomics into unified quantum pipelines
Interoperability after quantum with traditional EMRs	Makes sure that it works well with the hospital's current systems
Ethics of autonomous quantum agents in diagnosis	Requires philosophical and legal clarity on decision delegation

Solving all of these issues will mainly be defined in terms of whether QML becomes a clinical tool or it will remain a research novelty.

7.7 Vision Statement

People who have to dismantle a highly advanced machine to either improve a technology in healthcare and biology can also be improved to be more intelligent, flexible and also very transparent will they can be more pliable and also pliant. Technologies like quantum machine learning can also assist in biology, medicine, and physiology with more novel insights. There is a need to transition from reactive to personalized and proactive healthcare, which requires a big investment in infrastructure and also putting in place an ethical system.

8. Conclusion and Key Points

Quantum machine learning is still in its infancy that has begun to utilize superposition and also the quantum parallelism to be unlocked by new computing capabilities. This is the main reason why quantum machine learning have the combination and the artificial intelligence is still well plenty more than just a buzzword. Ad it was also described in this chapter the major use of QML in healthcare has also become an increase widespread and it is used km a real time patient monitoring octal use of other healthcare resources and will perhaps most of the prominently in drug discovery. All of these qualities will enable it to carry out tasks that are traditional machine learning either by failing to accomplish or struggle to complete, especially in areas involving high dimensionality, complex biological relationships or it had the inability to synthesize knowledge from the numerous disparate sources.

Before QML is implemented in a clinical setting, numerous challenges must be overcome. The limitations of quantum hardware stem from coherence, error rates, and circuit depth. As technology develops, other problems must also be dealt with at the same time. In order to maximize QML's utility in clinical settings, the field needs to advance on the following fronts—data coding, algorithm scalability, explainability, and compliance with regulatory frameworks, including HIPAA and GDPR. The following aspects need to be developed:

- Hardware that can grow and fix mistakes for more complex and expressive models
- Quantum-ready healthcare datasets for comparison and replication
- Hybrid designs that connect quantum subroutines with classical infrastructure
- Ethical oversight to make sure things are fair, open, and accountable
- Post-quantum cryptography methods for safeguarding data privacy and fostering confidence in quantum workflows.

Going forward, QML is essential in medicine, thanks to tools hosted in the cloud, open-source QML libraries, and easy collaboration between the fields concerned. We will begin to see some QML studies becoming decision support systems for hospitals to use in the next few years. This will set new standards in diagnosis, individual treatment, and preventive care.

Key Takeaway Points

- Because of the parallelism and entanglement of quantum computing, QML can quickly analyze vast and complex biomedical datasets.
- Medication simulation, tumor detection, genomic analysis, health monitoring, and cybersecure infrastructure are some healthcare uses.
- Some major problems are limited technology, inefficient data encoding, model interpretability, and examples of violation of ethics and laws.
- The industry is evolving rapidly and possesses vast potential for hybrid implementations, particularly with regard to personalized medicine.
- According to experts, quantum scientists, medical professionals, ethicists, and engineers will need to work together for the safe, fair, and useful adoption of QML.

References

[1] Abdul Kareem, S., Sachan, R.C., and Malviya, R.K. "AI-driven adaptive honeypots for dynamic cyber threats," SSRN Electronic Journal, Sep. 2024. DOI: 10.2139/ssrn.4966935.

[2] Schuld, M. and Killoran, N. "Quantum machine learning in feature Hilbert spaces," *Physical Review Letters*, vol. 122, no. 4, p. 040504, Feb. 2019. DOI: 10.1103/PhysRevLett.122.040504.

[3] Benedetti, M. et al. "Parameterized quantum circuits utilized as machine learning models," *Quantum Science and Technology*, vol. 4, no. 4, p. 043001, 2019.

[4] Kandala, A. et al. "Hardware efficient variational quantum eigensolver for tiny molecules," *Nature*, vol. 549, pp. 242–246, 2017.

[5] Cao, Y. et al. "Quantum chemistry in the era of quantum computing," *Chemical Reviews*, vol. 119, no. 19, pp. 10856–10915, 2019.

[6] IBM Moderna Collaboration, "VQA for designing mRNA vaccine design," *Barron's*, 2025

[7] Havlíček, V. et al. "Supervised learning with quantum enhanced feature spaces," *Nature*, vol. 567, no. 7747, pp. 209–212, 2019.

[8] Devadas, R. et al. "QSVM classification of images for breast cancer," arXiv:2303.09491, 2025.

[9] Lloyd, S. et al. "Quantum principal component analysis," *Nature Physics*, vol. 10, no. 9, pp. 631–633, 2014.

[10] Ranga, S., et al. "QML for grouping genes by how they are expressed," *Bioinformatics Journal*, 2024.

[11] Henderson, M. et al. "Quantum convolutional neural networks," *Quantum Machine Intelligence*, vol. 2, no. 2, 2020.

[12] Chakrabarti, S. et al. "Quantum models for health IoT feeds," *IEEE Transactions on Quantum Engineering*, 2022.

[13] Zhao, X.X. "Quantum kernel techniques in medical diagnostics," *MDPI Healthcare*, 2025.

[14] Chow, P. et al. "Hybrid QML for sepsis prediction," *PubMed Central*, 2025.

[15] Schuld, M. 2018, "The difficulties of data encoding in QML," arXiv:1803.07128.

[16] McClean, J.R. et al. "Empty plateaus in quantum neural networks," *Nature Communications*, vol. 9, no. 1, p. 4812, 2018.

[17] Eze, K. et al. "Ethical hazards and adherence in QML healthcare," *MDPI Quantum Ethics Series*, 2025.

9 AI-Enabled Standalone Device for Early Breast Cancer Detection: Advancing Diagnosis and Healthcare

Pradeep Kumar[1], Santosh Kumar Choudhary[2*], Ranjan K. Senapati[3], Subodh Srivastava[4], Manoj Kumar,[5] Jaiprakash Narain Dwivedi[6] and Prasanth Mankar[7]

Breast cancer continues to pose a major global health challenge, underscoring the need for more effective detection methods to improve patient prognosis. Thermography is becoming popular as a safe, non-invasive way to detect body changes related to tumor growth without using radiation. This study investigates the use of thermography to distinguish between benign and malignant breast lesions, aiding early detection and risk stratification. Thermographic data from patients undergoing screening and diagnostic evaluation is collected and analyzed using advanced image processing and machine learning to develop a classification model for breast abnormalities. The proposed system aims to integrate thermography into detection protocols to facilitate timely diagnosis. Extensive experiments demonstrate that this method effectively supports identification, localization, and classification of breast cancer, offering potential as a reliable screening tool.

1. Introduction

One major global health concern is breast cancer, which impacts the lives of millions of women and their families. For effective treatment and better survival

[1] Department of Electronics and Communication Engineering, VNR VJIET Hyderabad, India. ORCID ID: 0000-0002-2599-6380

[2] Department of Electronics and Communication Engineering, VNR VJIET Hyderabad, India. ORCID ID: 0000-0001-9850-7624

[3] Department of Electronics and Communication Engineering, VNR VJIET Hyderabad, India. ORCID ID: 0000-0003-3375-3378

[4] Department of Electronics and Communication Engineering, NIT Patna, India. ORCID ID: 0000-0001-6194-429X

[5] Department of ECE, MLR Institute of Technology, Hyderabad, India.

[6] Department of Information Technology, PIET, FET, Parul University Vadodara, Gujarat, India.

[7] Department of ECE, Vasavi College of Engineering, Ibrahimbagh, Hyderabad, India.
E-mail: pradeedkumar@vnrvjiet.in[1]; ranjan_ks@vnrvjiet.in[3]; subodh@nitp.ac.in[4]; dr.manojkumar@mlrinstitutions.ac.in[5]; jpndwivedi@gmail.com[6]; m.prasanth@staff.vce.ac.in[7]

* Corresponding author: santoshkumar_ch@vnrvjiet.in

DOI: 10.1201/9781003646068-9

rates, initial detection and accurate assessment of breast tumors are essential. While mammography remains a primary tool for breast cancer screening, thermography plays a vital role too, particularly in cases where mammography may not be sufficient or when additional evaluation is required. Globally, 17.1 million cases of cancer were documented in 2020, according to the data provided by the American Research Society and the International Agency for the Study of Cancer [1]. In this context, a promising way of increasing diagnostic capacity is to integrate deep learning techniques into thermography to automatically detect breast tumors.

Breast anatomy reveals anomalies, such as lumps, masses and sizes, which may indicate cancer [2]. By using modern machine learning techniques, a thermography-based classification model for identifying breast abnormalities will be developed and validated. As a useful tool for pattern recognition and image analysis, the category of artificial intelligence (AI) known as deep learning has risen in popularity. In a number of medical applications, it has also shown excellent results. In addition to this imperative, thermography has emerged as a powerful complementary tool for the detection of breast cancer by offering radiation-less, non-invasive imaging modalities that capture physiological changes associated with tumor growth. Due to the potential for increasing diagnosis accuracy and expanding screening capabilities, there has been an increased research interest in using thermography alongside conventional imaging techniques such as mammography or ultrasound. The project will carry out a thorough review of integrating thermography into the detection protocols for breast cancer, with a multidisciplinary approach, which includes literature reviews, studies, and model development.

The thermography screening method has advantages compared to its predecessors. First of all, it is non-invasive because there is no contact or hazardous radiation involved. Second, it is easy to carry and very cost-effective. This screening method, based on infrared radiation, transposes the matrix of temperature to an electronic image for examination by a healthcare professional. It looks at the heat that comes from the breast surface. Based on scientific evidence, abnormal heat maps are produced on the skin surface of tumors due to the increased metabolic activity of malignant cells. Scientists have been working for some time to develop models of prediction that can be used in diagnosis. During radiography, deep neural networks were demonstrated to be highly accurate in their predictions. Their universal learning method, scale, and resilience are the reasons for this. Transfer learning algorithms can reduce computing costs for training new models and eliminate the need for explicit feature extraction. In computer-aided diagnostic (CADX) systems that assist healthcare professionals, these exceptional performance capabilities are used. One such system uses deep learning techniques to detect breast tumors in ultrasound images, which is achieved through a median filter. Yuan et al. [5] have automated the segmenting of thermoscopic images from radiologists to identify and characterize cancer more accurately.

This study seeks to design a dependable and practical tool that enhances the accuracy and efficiency of the diagnosis of breast cancer. By doing so, we aspire to enhance breast cancer early detection, reduce the risk of misdiagnosis, and contribute to more effective patient care, ultimately saving lives and alleviating the burden of this widespread disease. This work examines deep learning for breast tumor detection, emphasizing its capacity to advance healthcare and change current diagnostic approaches. A typical breast tumor detection heat map is shown in Figure 9.1 where, the cooler colors (blue/green) imply low tumor likelihood, the hotter colors (red/yellow) indicate high tumor probability.

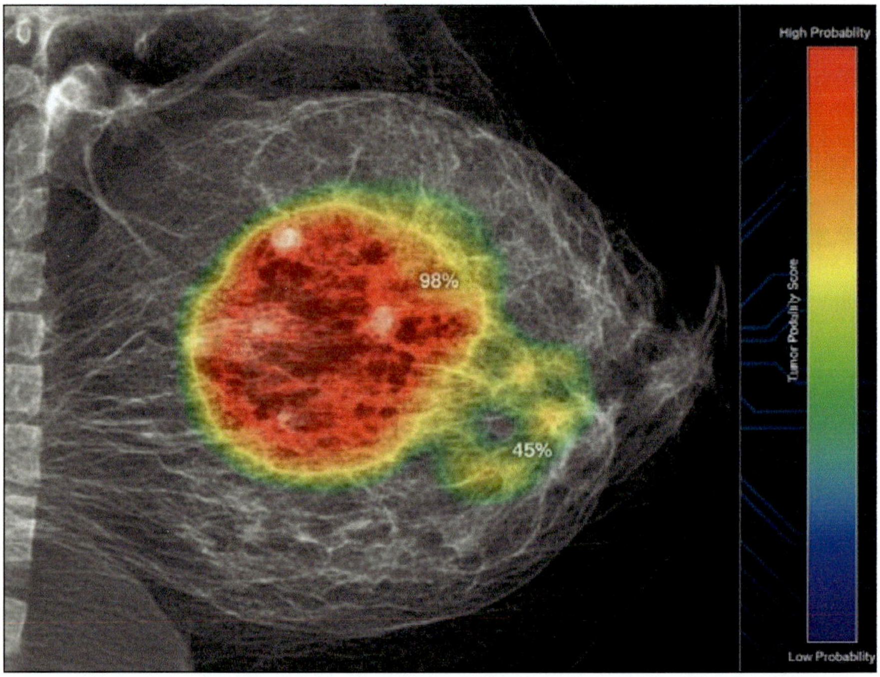

Fig. 9.1 Breast tumor prediction heat maps.

2. Related Work

As one of the leading global health concerns, breast cancer impacts the lives of countless women and their families. The early detection and accurate assessment of breast tumors is necessary in order to effectively treat and improve the survival rate. While mammography remains a primary tool for breast cancer screening, thermography plays a vital role, particularly in cases where mammography may not be sufficient or when additional evaluation is required. In this context, a promising way of increasing diagnostic capacity is to integrate deep learning techniques into thermography to automatically detect breast tumors. Jiao et al. [3] proposed a DFBF for the classification of breast masses. The framework primarily integrates convolutional neural networks (CNNs) with decision-making systems. Its implementation was carried out using the DDSM database, and performance was assessed based on accuracy (A_C), sensitivity (S_N), and specificity (S_P). Similarly, Wang et al. [4] introduced an extreme learning machine (ELM) approach, which effectively differentiates between benign and malignant breast cancer features in mammographic images. The use of a wavelet transform modulus maxima and region growth was part of their approach to edge segmentation, and noise removal was PH2 database. We have used a fully natural neural network. In a thermoscopic image, a skin lesion was analyzed using a CNN with 19 layers. The loss function was modified with the Jaccard distance to enhance the performance of the deep convolutional neural network (DCNN). The DCNN performance was evaluated using multiple metrics, including accuracy, sensitivity, specificity, Dice coefficient, and Jaccard index, achieving respective values of 0.963, 0.926, 0.976, 0.922, and 0.861. Hamad et al. [6] introduced a breast cancer detection and classification approach for improving image quality that combines several techniques, which includes discrete wavelet transform, artificial neural networks, fuzzy c-means clustering, thresholding, and balance contrast enhancement techniques (BCET). Using a mammography image, the accuracy of this approach will be assessed. Masud et al. [7] have analyzed the CAD system for breast pictures in detail and found that it is more efficient than machine learning methods to analyze images, which also leads to better accuracy compared with a radiologist's method of analysis. In order to identify and classify breast cancer, RCNN was used by Chiao et al. [8]. This technique has been developed for ultrasound imaging of the breast. Accuracy and mean average precision (mAP) are the measured metrics. Ciritsis et al. [9] developed a technique for detecting and classifying breast ultrasound images using a DCNN. The method was evaluated using performance metrics such as sensitivity, specificity, and area under the curve (AUC). Similarly, a multi-DCNN-based CAD system, proposed by Ragab et al. [10] was primarily applied to classify breast cancer using the DDSM and data from the MIAS. AlexNet, Google Network, and ResNet are the three DCNN protocols in use. The performance is assessed on the basis of three criteria: specificity, sensitivity, and accuracy. An enhanced CNN that predicts breast cancer has been built end-to-end by Kumar et al. [11]. The work of Z. Khomsi et al. [12] investigate the possible use of surface temperature sensors for detection of breast cancer earlier, a simulation using COMSOL software will be carried out so as to simulate and understand the heat equilibrium created due to an actual tumor source. In order to identify the hotspot of PV modules, T. Tajwar et al. [13] employed infrared thermography (IRT) and created a hotspot identification program that employed the maxim "YOLO: You Only Look Once." The classifier uses the photos as a dataset in order to identify the PV module hotspot. Thereafter, training and assessment of learners are carried out on the basis of this data. For the detection of interior defects, Shen et al. [14] have presented a transient thermography approach. The transient thermal response of the sample surface is induced by a continuous heating source. Time-domain thermograms are collected and analyzed during the cooling phase. Samples containing flat-bottom hole defects are examined at a distance of 1 m. For each pixel, the corresponding temperature curve and defect condition are recovered and subsequently used to train a support vector machine (SVM). For a trained model, three additional detection conditions are applied: distances of 1 m, 0.5 m, and 2 m respectively. The respective F1 scores for the trials are 0.825, 0.794, and 0.688. Gamal et al. [15], for the early diagnosis of breast cancer by thermography. A complete automatic method has been presented. The basis for the identification of distinctive breast features is a deep pretrained, holistically nested edge scanner. By applying the machine learning algorithm Extreme Gradient Boosting (XGBoost), breast tissue characteristics were diagnostically classified as either cancerous or normal. The performance improved slightly with the integration of the Canny edge detector. The proposed method achieved an accuracy of 97.4 percent, with 95 percent precision, 100 percent recall, and a 97 percent F1 score. Dubey et al. [16] employed various machine learning techniques on the Wisconsin Diagnostic Breast Cancer Dataset. A comparison and performance assessment of these different classifiers shall be carried out following the collection of the data. This study focuses on breast cancer identification, aiming to evaluate whether machine learning methods can provide improved performance in terms of confusion matrices, accuracy, and specificity. Among the classifiers tested, SVM and artificial neural network (ANN) demonstrated the highest performance. Qayyum and Basit [17] have suggested segmenting the breast region, removing the pectoral muscle, and classifying breast tissue into normal and pathological categories. The breast muscle was divided using the Otsus segmentation technique. The pectoral muscle was then removed with a canny edge detection and straight-line approximation technique. In the next phase, features were extracted using GLCM, and an SVM classifier was trained to distinguish between normal and pathological breast tissues. Melek et al. [18] highlighted the importance of incorporating spatiotemporal information at multiple screening time points to improve risk prediction models. For this purpose, they developed a Siamese neural network and compared its performance against CNN models independently trained on two distinct time points (T1 and T2). The Siamese network achieved an AUC of 0.81, outperforming CNN models, which recorded AUC of 0.75 and 0.77 with 191 cases. This includes 61 cases diagnosed with cancer. While CNNs achieved an accuracy of 0.76 with F1 scores of 0.54 at T1 and 0.59 at T2, the Siamese network showed higher accuracy (0.78) and an improved F1 score (0.61). Yunus et al. [19], building on thermal data from earlier studies, proposed a neural network for tumor localization. Their optimized ANN architecture (6-8-1) utilized features derived from numerical simulations on breast tissue composition models. With a learning rate of 0.2, 20,000 iterations, and a momentum constant value 0.3, the ANN achieved an accuracy about 96.34 percent for testing and 92.88 percent for validation. Kara et al. [20] proposed a cost-effective system combining inexpensive temperature sensors, cloud computing, and mobile technologies to predict the presence of tumor tissue in patients' homes. Similarly, Raza et al. [21] suggested a methodology for segmentation and classification of breast mammography tumors using Mask R-CNN. Their system evaluated performance based on metrics such as F1 score, recall, precision, and average accuracy. It incorporated a compact, low-cost portable infrared sensor, operable at any time through an embedded microcontroller. The microcontroller is connected to the cloud computing environment and a cellular device for secure data storage and picture processing. This system can assist in image stabilization, color and temperature calibration, and the registration of images.

According to the literature, all current models are based on deep learning (DL) and machine learning (ML) techniques. ML-based methods are less preferred for early prediction because they require manual feature extraction, which reduces the accuracy and autonomy of their operation. Mult instance segmentation is not as efficient when used to view images of healthcare professionals, despite Mask R-CNN's help. Therefore, the aim of this study is to assess thermography's effectiveness as a standalone screening technique and examine how it might increase sensitivity and diagnostic specificity for existing conditions.

Table 9.1 Summary of previous detection methods reported in the literature.

Authors	*Year*	*Method*	*Database*	*Result*
Jiao et al. [3]	2016	DFBF CNN	DDSM	The accuracy is 96.7%
Wang et al. [4]	2014	ELM	DDSM	A_C-82.5%, S_E-87%, FP_R- 82% and FN_R-84%.
Yuan et al. [5]	2017	19- layer DCNN	PH2 database	A_C-0,963, S_E-0.926, S_P-0.976, DI-0.922 and JA-0.861
Hamad et al. [6]	2018	Combination of BCET, FCM, DWT, and ANN	DDSM	A_C-90%
Chiao et al. [8]	2019	Mask R-CNN	Sonogram	mAP-0.75 and A_C-85%
Ciritsis et al. [9]	2019	DCNN	Ultrasound	S_E-92.1%, S_P-76% and AUC-83.8
Ragab et al. [10]	2021	Multi-DCNN	Mammogram	A_C-76.01%
Kumar et al. [11]	2020	CNN	Mammogram	A_C-97.20%, P_C-99%. TN_R-96 and F-score-0.99

3. Methodology

Researchers have been exploring complementary imaging modalities such as thermography to enhance early detection efforts. Thermography operates on the principle of detecting abnormal heat patterns emitted by the body, particularly in areas with increased metabolic activity and blood flow, which are characteristic of cancerous tissues. With its ability to detect subtle physiological changes, thermography stands out as a non-invasive imaging technique with promising applications in breast cancer detection and classification. One of the primary advantages of thermography is its non-invasive nature. Unlike mammography, which involves compressing the breast tissue and exposing the patient to ionizing radiation, thermography is painless and does not pose any radiation risk. This makes it a potentially attractive option for individuals who may be hesitant to undergo traditional screening methods or those with breast implants.

In addition, thermography may enable earlier detection of abnormalities in breast tissue than traditional imaging modalities. By identifying subtle changes in temperature distribution, thermography may help clinicians detect lesions or areas of concern that are not yet visible on mammograms or ultrasound scans. Early detection is critical for initiating prompt treatment and improving patient outcomes in breast cancer management.

3.1 Proposed Methodology

The entire operational procedure of the proposed method is shown in Figure 9.2. The existing modification of Mask R-CNN is based on Faster R-CNN. This system comprises a region proposal network (RPN), region of interest (RoI) alignment, and a backbone module. The backbone module consists of the ResNet architecture and the feature pyramid network (FPN). ResNet is primarily responsible for extracting feature properties from the input image, whereas the FPN improves multi-scale feature illustration from the ResNet outputs. It employs both top-down and bottom-up pathways for this multi-scale feature extraction. To generate an RoI in the RPN, feature maps produced by the FPN are utilized, with a sliding window approach. The RoI, also referred to as the "proposed bounding box," specifies a higher probability that an object being present. However, the size of the RoI generated by the RPN can vary, leading to inconsistencies. This variability can cause errors during the quantization process of the derived feature map and RoI, especially at the borders.

To overcome quantization-related misalignment, the RoI align technique is adopted. For each ROI, it determines floating-point positions and computes accurate feature values at four regularly sampled locations through bilinear interpolation. This process generates a feature map (FM) of fixed-size, with stride sizes of 16 and 32 proving effective for optimal performance. Then the FM is forwarded to the network. The network utilizes a fully CNN layer, which can yield bounding box coordinates and class predictions, while the mask branch generates segmentation masks based on features from the preceding convolutional neural networks. The final output is obtained by combining the class predictions, bounding box results, and mask outputs. The complete workflow of the proposed boosted mask R-CNN is illustrated in Figure 9.2.

3.2 Data Organization, Collection, and Pre-processing

In the development and performance evaluation of this proposed technique, Kaggle datasets shall be employed. Kaggle is a more standardized, contemporary version of breast images. Access is made to the ground truth photographs accompanying

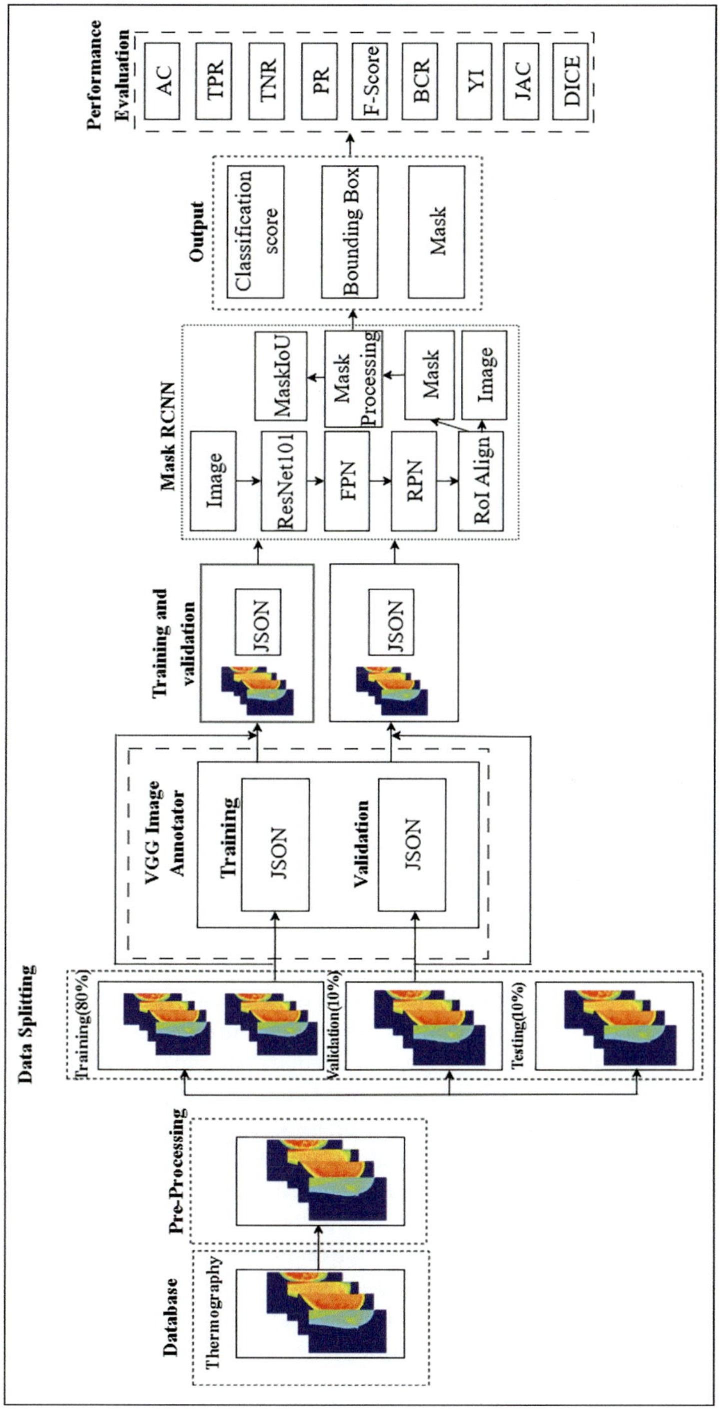

Fig. 9.2 Block diagram of proposed boosted Mask R-CNN.

these datasets. The development of a database involves pre-processing, data splitting, and finally annotating the data. The databases contain low contrast photographs that have been affected by noise and artifacts. According to the literature, thermography images are associated with Poisson and speckle noise. It is therefore possible to reduce noise and simultaneously improve image quality using two techniques. It facilitates the selection of error free zones of interest for annotation.

To remove Poisson noise from thermograms as shown in equation (1), a modified Anscombe transform is used.

$$f_\sigma(Y)\begin{cases} 2\sqrt{I_T + \left(\frac{3}{8}\right) + \sigma_T^2},\ T_T > \left(-\frac{3}{8}\right) - \sigma_T^2 \\ 0, \text{otherwise} \end{cases} \quad ...(1)$$

In (7), I_T is the thermogram image, σ_T^2 is the standard deviation, and x is a Gaussian noise distribution in this case.

A non-linear partial differential equation, which is adapted, shall be used in order to eliminate speckle noise. The discretized form is indicated by formulas through equation (2) to (4).

$$F_t^{q+1}(x, y) = F_t^{q+1}(x, y) + \varphi(\mathrm{B}) \quad ...(2)$$

$$\mathrm{B} = (\varphi.\left(\alpha\left(\| \varphi F_t^q \|\right)\varphi F_t^q\right) - L(t).D \quad ...(3)$$

$$D = \left(\frac{(F_t^q(x, y))^2 - F_o^2(x, y)}{(F_t^q(x, y))^2}\right)^{qt} \quad ...(4)$$

where $F_t^{q+1}(x, y)$ refers to denoised image.
$F_t^q(x, y)$ corresponds to input image,
α is the diffusion constant,
and L is the regularization parameter.

The pre-processed information is mixed with the others. The picture with anomalies is taken into consideration while combining the data. There is a difference in the number of photographs included in different databases. Therefore, data augmentation is used to achieve a balanced number of photos between the two databases. Rotational, flip, and scaling of images are the operations involved in data enlargement. The corresponding angles shall be 0, 90, and 180 in rotation and flipping. In addition, the data is divided into three categories: testing, validation, and training. Approximately 80 percent of the total weighted data is made up of training data. Approximately 10 percent of the remaining data is allocated to testing and validation data, respectively. Annotation is done after the pre-processing, data merging, and data splitting steps. Because annotation is the key to the method's accuracy, it is crucial for data preparation. Only annotated data is available for training and validation. For image annotation, the VGG image annotator (VIA) was employed. This tool permits the selection of RoIs inside the images. The annotated outputs are exported in JavaScript Object Notation (JSON) format, which stores the coordinates corresponding to the regions marked on each image.

3.3 Network Architecture

The construction of the boosted Mask R-CNN network is revealed in Figure 9.3. The proposed network design is made up of three different components. ResNet, FPN, and RPN are used to help with feature extraction and RoI computation in the first module, which is referred to as a major module. Although there are a number of ResNet architectures available, ResNet 101 is chosen for the proposed approach. The choice of ResNet 101 was based on the best performance in medical imaging. Multilayer maps are the first to be generated by this module.

To acquire RoIs, each point on the feature map is projected back onto the original image. The RoIs generated by the primary module are then resized to a fixed dimension using secondary modules. To reduce quantization errors during this resizing, the process—known as RoI align—ensures precise alignment between the RoIs and the original features. These fixed-size RoIs are then used in the third module for mask generation. A dedicated segmentation network handles the segmentation of multiple abnormalities within each RoI. Simultaneously, a fully connected layer processes the same RoIs to produce rectangular bounding boxes and associated class scores for multi-instance abnormality detection. As a result, detection, classification, and segmentation occur in parallel. Within the Mask R-CNN framework, RoI layers are carefully aligned so they can be directly extracted from the feature maps produced by the RPN.

Single-layer feature extraction often leads to misidentification in medical multi-instance image segmentation, as it does not provide sufficient information about abnormalities. To address this problem, multi-level feature extraction is made for each RoI, as shown in Figure 9.3. Through this approach, RoI alignment is applied with respect to multi-layer features, ensuring more accurate and reliable extraction.

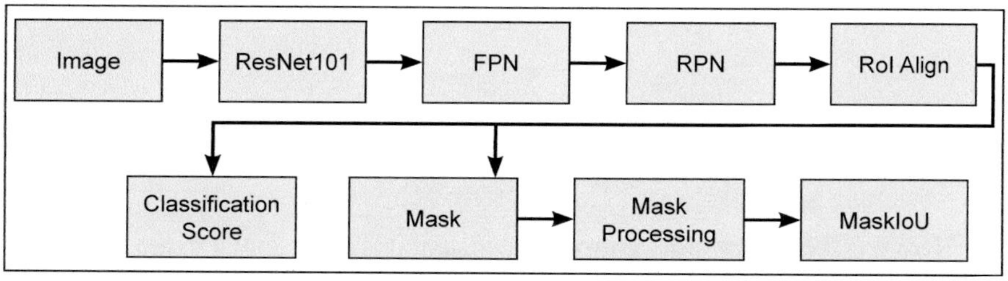

Fig. 9.3 Network architecture for detection and localization of breast cancer.

The RoI features obtained from different layers are then combined to generate comprehensive multi-layer representations for each RoI. These aligned features are subsequently passed into both the network and the mask outlet, as illustrated in Figure 9.3. The network consists of two fully connected (FC) layers, a flatten layer, and four convolutional layers. The CNN are tailed by ReLU activations and max pool operations within the hidden layers. A flatten layer restructures the CNN outputs into a feature vector, which is then passed to an FC layer. The mask branch, on the other hand, is composed of convolutional layers and deconvolutional layers. Together, the multi-layer feature extraction, network head, and mask branch allow the system to simultaneously perform detection, classification, and segmentation with greater precision compared to a single framework approach.

Following data preparation, the pre-processed ultrasound and mammography picture data along with the corresponding JSON file are fed into the proposed boosted Mask R-CNN (BMRCNN). A trained model is formed in this step.

In addition, the performance of BMRCNN is assessed, and the trained model is tested using test data. As a final output for testing data, this stage creates a test model that produces a bounding box, classification score, and mask. The bounding box represents the multi-instance detection and localization area, while the presence of an abnormality is indicated through the class score and label. When a positive class label is assigned, it signifies the existence of cancer. At the same time, a mask of the segmented region is generated to provide precise localization of the abnormality.

The loss function in the Mask R-CNN framework is formulated as a combination of localization loss, classification loss, and mask loss. The classification and localization components follow the same principles as Faster R-CNN, while the additional mask loss accounts for segmentation accuracy. Together, these components are aggregated to calculate the total loss, which can be expressed as:

$$L = L_{\text{cls}} + L_{\text{box}} + L_{\text{mask}} \quad \text{...(5)}$$

where L_{cls}, L_{box}, and L_{mask} are detection, classification, and mask loss function respectively. The L_{cls} and L_{box} are defined as:

$$L_{\text{cls}} = \frac{1}{N_{\text{cls}}} + \sum_i -\lambda_i^* \log \lambda_i - (1-\lambda_i^*) \log(1-\lambda_i^*) \quad \text{...(6)}$$

$$L_{\text{box}} = \frac{\mu}{N_{\text{box}}} + \sum_i \lambda_i^* L_1^{\text{smooth}} (t_i - t_i^*) \quad \text{...(7)}$$

$$L_{\text{mask}} = \frac{-1}{n^2} \sum_{1 \le i, j \le n} [\epsilon] \quad \text{...(8)}$$

Here € is the binary cross entropy mean, and it is represented in the following way:

$$\epsilon = x_{ij} \log x_{ij}^k + (1 - x_{ij}) \log(1 - x_{ij}^k) \quad \text{...(9)}$$

In equation (7), L_1^{smooth} is the loss parameter which can be stated as:

$$L_1^{\text{smooth}}(x) = \begin{cases} 0.5x^2, |x| < 1 \\ |x| - 0.5, \text{otherwise} \end{cases} \quad ...(10)$$

The L_1^{smooth} loss function is modified with the complete intersection over union (CIoU) loss function [24] which is described by:

$$\text{Loss}_{\text{CIoU}} = 1 - \text{IoU} + \frac{\in^2 (p, q^{gt})}{k^2} + \propto v \quad ...(11)$$

where $\in^2 (p, q^{gt})$ is the L_2 norm between ground truth and the center points of the predicted boxes. k corresponds to the diagonal length of the smallest box enclosing both boxes. v measures aspect ratio similarity between prediction and truth. $\propto$ is a trade-off parameter balancing the contribution of aspect ratio term

3.4 Performance Evaluation Metrics

Performance evaluation metrics make it easier to assess the effectiveness of this proposed approach. For segmentation and classification assessments, two and seven evaluation measures, respectively, are employed. Y_I, P_C, F_{score}, BC_R, TN_R, A_C, and TP_R are the categorization performance metrics. True positive (T_P), true negative (T_N), false positive (F_P), and false negative (F_N) features of the confusion matrix are used to construct it. The labels "positive" and "negative" class cases, respectively, refer to the quantity of each. In F_P, there is a perceived good aspect to the image that is actually negative. In the same way, F_N illustrates how a positive image can exist in a negative class. A_C and DICE are the segmentation performance assessment measures used in the proposed method.

The performance evaluation measures for segmentation and classification shall be subject to the following definitions:

(a) Accuracy:

$$\text{Accuracy} = \frac{T_P + T_N}{T_P + T_N + F_P + F_N} \quad ...(12)$$

(b) True Positive Rate (TP_R):

$$TP_R = \frac{T_P}{T_P + T_N} \quad ...(13)$$

(c) True Negate Rate (TN_R):

$$TN_R = \frac{T_N}{T_N + F_P} \quad ...(14)$$

(d) Precision (P_C):

$$\text{Precision} = \frac{T_P}{T_P + F_P} \quad ...(15)$$

(e) F_{score}:

$$F_{\text{score}} = \frac{2 \times P_C \times TP_R}{P_C + TP_R} \quad ...(16)$$

(f) Balanced Classification Rate (BC_R):

$$BC_R = \frac{1}{2}[TP_R + TN_R]_2 \quad ...(17)$$

(g) Youden's Index (Y_I):

$$YI = T_{PR} - (1 - T_{NR}) \quad ...(18)$$

(h) Dice Coefficient (DICE):

$$\text{DICE} = \frac{2|A \cap \text{B}|}{|A| + |\text{B}|'} \quad ...(19)$$

(i) Jaccard Index (JAC):

$$\text{JAC} = \frac{|A \cap B|}{|A \cup B|'} \quad ...(20)$$

where the prediction area is A and the ground truth region is B, from these equations.

3.5 Experimental Setup

In the low-cost thermal imaging system designed for the detection of breast cancer, images are primarily obtained using the AMG8833 infrared thermal sensor as shown in Figure 9.4. This sensor captures infrared radiation emitted by breast tissue, which can indicate variations in temperature associated with abnormal growth or inflammatory processes. The sensor comprises an 8×8 array of thermal infrared sensors, allowing it to collect temperature readings from multiple points simultaneously.

Data from the sensor is transmitted to a microcontroller via the I2C protocol, enabling real-time communication of temperature information for each pixel. The microcontroller processes this data through signal conditioning and analog-to-digital conversion, transforming the analog signals into digital formats suitable for analysis. The processed temperature data is then visualized as a thermal image, typically displayed on a TFT LCD screen or transmitted to a connected computer for further evaluation. While the system initially operates at a resolution of 8×8 pixels, it utilizes interpolation techniques to enhance this resolution to 64×64 pixels. This improvement allows for a more detailed representation of temperature variations, which can be critical in identifying potential abnormalities. By employing color mapping, different temperatures are represented with distinct colors, facilitating the visualization of hot spots that may indicate pathological changes in breast tissue.

This thermal imaging system serves as a non-invasive, pain-free preliminary screening tool for breast cancer detection, allowing for the monitoring of temperature distribution in breast tissue. Its ability to provide immediate feedback makes it a valuable asset in clinical settings, aiding healthcare professionals in the early identification of potential breast cancer indicators.

For training, validation and test of the MRCNN proposal, TensorFlow and Keras are used in a Python context. The extraction of features will be performed by ResNet101. The factor is tuned by the Adam optimization (AO) algorithm [10]. For training validation, 10 percent of the combined database will be devoted to testing data, while the other 10 percent is dedicated to checking them. Due to the different sizes, each image in this collection will have its size adjusted to 1,024 x 1,024 pixels.

Fig. 9.4 Experimental setup of the proposed technique.

For model training, 100 batches have been used with a basic learning rate of 0.0001 percent. Every epoch has 100 steps, and there are a hundred in total. For convolution and fully connected layers, the momentum and the rate of weight loss is kept at 0.9 and 0.0001, respectively.

4. Result and Discussion

Regarding the qualitative and quantitative evaluation of the proposed method, the results are presented and discussed in this section. The qualitative results offer a subjective insight, while the quantitative results provide a comparative analysis between BMRCNN and other methods proposed in literature.

A class score is assigned to each occurrence of breast cancer after it has been detected, localized, and classified through qualitative analysis. There is a rectangular bounding box that shows the localization and detection. The class score displays a number value for that class along with a label. While the quantitative analysis explains the logic and reasoning behind the proposed BMRCNN. When performing an analysis, account shall be taken of the PEM for segmentation and classification. Another basis for the quantitative analysis's observations was the

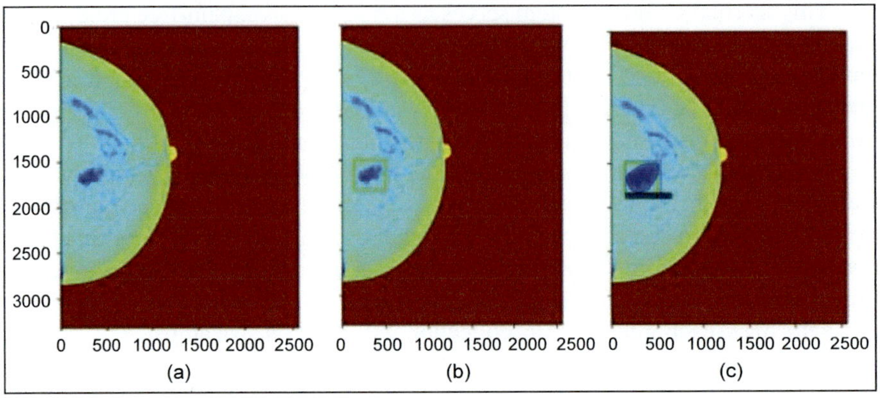

Fig. 9.5 Detection and classification of the thermogram dataset.

learning curve during training validation. This is an indication of progress in accuracy and loss during the validation phase for training.

Figure 9.5 shows a single case of thermogram breast mass detection. In the first case (a), the test input is displayed, in the second case (b), the abnormal region is displayed with a bounding box, and in the third case (c), the abnormal region is displayed with an increased mask R-CNN. It is logical to take this into account in the qualitative analysis. The divergences are indicative of the presence of masses in breast thermograms. Furthermore, the existence of anomalies in the test data is established by the corresponding ground truth images.

4.1 Discussion

The proposed approach does not employ any frozen layers, thereby ensuring that all parameters within the model remain trainable. Detection, classification, and segmentation tasks are conducted using hyperparameter values specifically optimized for breast cancer applications. A schematic representation of the proposed methodology is provided in Figure 9.2. This primarily consists of a data collection and preparation phase, training, and validation model creation, testing model, and performance assessment of the suggested approach. As seen in Figure 9.3, this is the proposed design. It is a product of the BMRCNN. To achieve this objective, which is to detect and localize multiple instances of breast images in one image, one important architecture is needed. After the RPN layer, the first step is RoI alignment, which gets features from several layers for each RoI instead of just one. The second change is using the CIoU loss function for the bounding box (L_{box}), instead of $\text{Smooth}_{L1}(x)$. A modified version of the CIoU loss, in which MAD and GSA are used to estimate the hyperparameter of that loss, is known as an CIoU loss function. It is offering a range that is automatically selected for δ. The proposed approach provides excellent accuracy and minimal loss at δ value 0.75. It will give the bounding box a precise location and a rapid rate of convergence, which will help to mitigate the problem of overbalancing. For the proposed approach, N_{cls}, N_{box} and λ are values of 2, 256 and 10. In order to draw up the input data, the database is first denotified. To denoise mammography breast images, an adaptation of the non-linear partial differential equation is used in addition to a modification of the Anscombe algorithm. The description of the dataset shows that there are two types of mammography data: ordinary and malignant. In the benign and malignant classes, tumor data is the collective term for the mammography dataset. To combine the data needed for the proposed method, a normal set of mammography data was removed. This omission has benefited only the validation and training of the suggested method. In addition, tests were carried out on the basis of normal data. In particular, this exclusion is due to the following reasons: first, there are no significant abnormalities in lump, calcification, or mass in normal breast imaging. Second, to ensure that the periodic data testing produces a result of its own, Mask R-CNN will detect objects based on anomalies found in this image. Third, because there are no irregularities in the usual data, you will not be using an image annotation. For alignment, the photos in each dataset have been reduced and data has been added to adjust the amount of images. Three groups are

Table 9.2 Comparative analysis between existing methods and proposed method.

Methods	A_C (%)	TP_R (%)	TN_R (%)	P_R	*F-score*	BC_R	Y_I	*JAC*	*DICE*
Raza et al. [21]	85.00	80.00	87.83	0.7500	0.8250	0.8391	0.6783	0.7021	0.8250
G. Jahangeer and Rajkumar [23]	89.00	90.01	90.01	0.8202	0.8603	0.9002	0.9001	0.8102	0.8800
Proposed	95.44	97.22	89.69	0.9682	0.9702	0.9346	0.8691	0.9421	0.9702

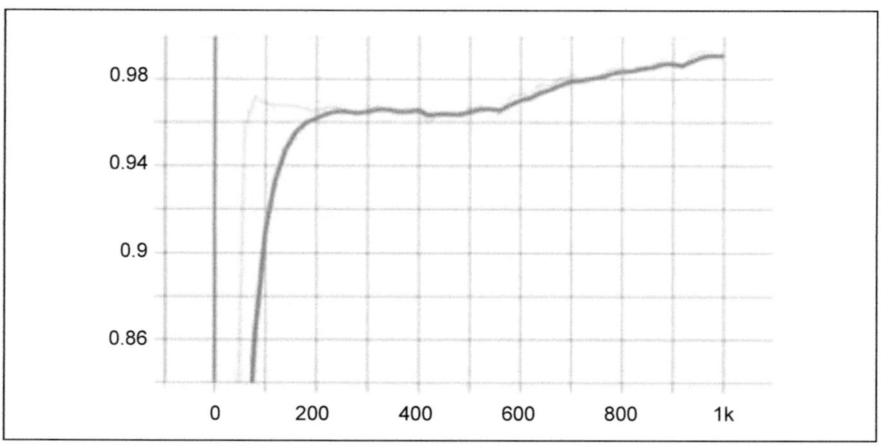

Fig. 9.6 Training accuracy curve.

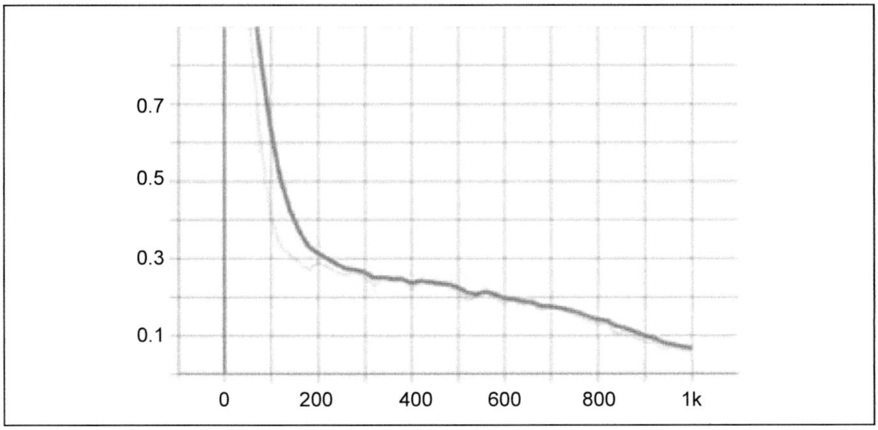

Fig. 9.7 Training loss curve.

created from the merged database: test data (10 percent), validation (10 percent), and training (80 percent). After that, VIA annotates the training validation data and retrieves the JSON annotation output as a file. Additionally, the denoised image and corresponding JSON files are received by the training validation model as inputs. The suggested approach is evaluated, and the results are analyzed following the development of a validation model for training.

The performance of the proposed method is compared with other currently used methods. The results of localization, detection, and classification using single and multiple instances of breast images are presented. At the first, the test input image is marked, then the denoised image, and then the anomalies in the output image are marked by the radiologist. In order to assess qualitative analyses, metrics are used for segmentation and classification performance evaluation.

Table 9.2 shows the results of the previously developed models and the proposed approach for breast thermography images. For the assessment of performance, A_C, TP_R, TN_R, P_R, F-score, BC_R, Y_I, JAC ,and DICE are assessed using these metrics. As a result, the following values were obtained: 95.44 percent, 97.22 percent, 89.69 percent, 0.9682, 0.9702, 0.9346, 0.8691, 0.9421, and 0.9702 for A_C, TP_R, TN_R, P_R, F-score, Y_I, JAC, and DICE, respectively. Figure 9.5 presents the accuracy curve, while Figure 9.6 displays the loss curve for the proposed training-validation method. Both figures illustrate how accuracy and loss evolve relating to the learning rate over the course of training. The model was trained for a total of 100 epochs to develop the training-validation performance.

Figures 9.5 and 9.6 show that increasing the number of epochs, results in higher accuracy and lower loss for both training and validation. These are summarized as follows:

- **Training Losses:**
  - Total loss: 0.08
  - RPN class and bounding box loss: 0.01 and 0.03, respectively
  - CIoU loss-based boosted Mask R-CNN class, bounding box, and mask loss: 0.012, 0.045, and 0.06, respectively.
- **Validation Losses:**
  - Total loss: 0.27
  - RPN class and bounding box loss: 0.009 and 0.045, respectively.
  - CIoU loss-based boosted Mask R-CNN class, bounding box, and mask loss: 0.085, 0.023, and 0.047, respectively.

5. Conclusion

This study presents a segmentation, classification, and detection framework for breast cancer based on a boosted Mask R-CNN architecture utilizing a CIoU loss function. Unlike most CNN-based methods that focus solely on detection and classification, the proposed approach provides a unified framework for simultaneous multi-instance detection, classification, and localization of anomalies in the breast. The method employs an online dataset of thermography images for training, validation, and testing. The CIoU loss function replaces traditional localization or bounding box loss functions to reduce overfitting and achieve precise bounding box alignment with faster convergence. The model's effectiveness is evaluated on thermography datasets using both quantitative and qualitative analyses. Performance metrics reported include A_C (95.44 percent), TP_R (97.22 percent), TN_R (89.69 percent), P_R (0.9682), F-score (0.9702), BC_R (0.9346), Y_I (0.8691), JAC (0.9421), and DICE (0.9702). Comparative results demonstrate superior performance over existing methods, confirming its suitability for automatic detection and localization of multiple breast lesions. When applied clinically, the proposed method supports precise diagnostic decision-making.

References

[1] Sung, H., Ferlay, J., Siegel, R.L. et al. "Global cancer statistics 2020: GLOBOCAN estimates of incidence and mortality worldwide for 36 cancers in 185 countries," *CA: A Cancer Journal for* Clinicians, vol. 71, no. 3, pp. 209–249, 2021, doi:10.3322/caac.21660.

[2] Siegel, R.L., Giaquinto, A.N., Jemal, A. "CA: A Cancer Journal for Clinicians," *Cancer Statistics*, vol. 74, no. 1, pp. 12–49, 2024, doi: 10.3322/caac.21820.

[3] Jiao, Z., Gao, X., Wang, Y., and Li, J. "A deep feature based framework for breast masses classification," *Neurocomputing*, vol. 197, 2016, doi: 10.1016/j.neucom.2016.02.060.

[4] Wang, Z., Yu, G., Kang, Y., Zhao, Y. and Qu, Q. "Breast tumor detection in digital mammography based on extreme learning machine," *Neurocomputing*, vol. 128, pp. 175–184, 2014, doi: 10.1016/j.neucom.2013.05.053.

[5] Yuan, Y., Chao, M. and Lo, Y.-C. "Automatic skin lesion segmentation using deep fully convolutional networks with Jaccard distance," *IEEE Transactions on Medical Imaging*, vol. 36, no. 9, pp. 1876–1886, 2017, doi: 10.1109/TMI.2017.2695227.

[6] Hamad, Y., Simonov, K. and Naeem, M. “Breast cancer detection and classification using artificial neural networks,” pp. 51–57, 2018, doi: 10.1109/AiCIS.2018.00022.

[7] Masud, R., Al-Rei, M. and Lokker, C. “Computer-aided detection for breast cancer screening in clinical settings: Scoping review,” *JMIR Medical Informatics*, vol. 7, no. 3, 2019, p. e12660, https://doi.org/10.2196/12660.

[8] Chiao, J.-Y., et al. “Detection and classification the breast tumors using mask R-CNN on sonograms,” *Medicine*, vol. 98, no. 19, p. e15200, 2019, doi: 10.1097/MD.0000000000015200.

[9] Ciritsis, A., Rossi, C., Eberhard, M., Marcon, M., Becker, A.S. and Boss, A. “Automatic classification of ultrasound breast lesions using a deep convolutional neural network mimicking human decision-making,” *European Journal of Radiology*, vol. 29, no. 10, pp. 5458–5468, 2019. doi: 10.1007/s00330-019-06118-7.

[10] Ragab, D.A., et al. “A framework for breast cancer classification using Multi-DCNNs,” *Computers in Biology and Medicine*, vol. 131, p. 104245, 2021, doi:10.1016/j.compbiomed.2021.104245.

[11] Kumar, P., Srivastava, S., Mishra, R. and Sai, Y. “End-to-end improved convolutional neural network model for breast cancer detection using mammographic data,” *The Journal of Defense Modeling and Simulation: Applications, Methodology, Technology*, vol. 19, 2020, doi: 154851292097326. 10.1177/1548512920973268.

[12] Khomsi, Z., Elouerghi, A., Afyf, A., and Bellarbi, L. “Contribution for the early detection of breast cancer by a superficial thermography solution,” *International Conference on Electrical and Information Technologies (ICEIT)*, Rabat, Morocco, pp. 1–4, 2020, doi: 10.1109/ICEIT48248.2020.9113225.

[13] Feng, B., Yi, J., Wang, Z., and Hu, M. “Analysis and identification method of dust accumulation and shadow characteristics of photovoltaic modules,” in *Proceedings of the 4th International Conference on Control, Robotics and Intelligent System (CCRIS 2023)*, Association for Computing Machinery, New York, USA, pp. 69–75, 2023, https://doi.org/10.1145/3622896.3622908.

[14] Shen, Z., Mei, H., Tu, Y., Guo, C. and Wang, L. “Porcelain bushing internal defects intelligent detection based on transient thermography,” *IEEE International Instrumentation and Measurement Technology Conference (I2MTC)*, Ottawa, Canada, pp. 1–5, 2022, doi: 10.1109/I2MTC48687.2022.9806635.

[15] Gamal, S., Atef, H., Youssef, D., Ismail, T. and El-Azab, J. “Early breast cancer screening from thermography via deep pre-trained edge detection with extreme gradient boosting,” *2023 Intelligent Methods, Systems, and Applications (IMSA)*, Giza, Egypt, pp. 430–433, 2023, doi: 10.1109/IMSA58542.2023.10217569.

[16] Dubey, C., Shukla, N., Kumar, D., Singh, A., and Dwivedi, V. “Breast cancer modeling and prediction combining machine learning and artificial neural network approaches,” pp. 119–124, 2022, doi: 10.1109/ICCCIS56430.2022.10037709.

[17] Qayyum, A. and Basit, A. “Automatic breast segmentation and cancer detection via SVM in mammograms,” pp. 1–6, 2016, doi: 10.1109/ICET.2016.7813261.

[18] Melek, A., Fakhry, S. and Basha, T. “Spatiotemporal mammography-based deep learning model for improved breast cancer risk prediction,” *2023 45th Annual International Conference of the IEEE Engineering in Medicine & Biology Society (EMBC)*, , pp. 1–4, 2023, doi: 10.1109/EMBC40787.2023.10340602.

[19] Wahab, A.A., Salim, M.I.M., Yunus, J. and Aziz, M.N.C. “Tumor localization in breast thermography with various tissue compositions by using artificial neural network,” pp. 484–488, 2015, doi: 10.1109/SCORED.2015.7449383.

[20] Mesas-Carrascosa, F.J. et al. “The Development of an Open Hardware and Software System Onboard Unmanned Aerial Vehicles to Monitor Concentrated Solar Power Plants,” Sensors, vol. 17, no. 6, p. 1329, 2017, doi: 10.3390/s17061329.

[21] Raza, S.K., Sarwar, S.S., Syed, S.M. and Khan, N.A. “Classification and segmentation of breast tumor using mask R-CNN on mammograms,” 2021, doi: 10.21203/rs.3.rs-523546/v1.

[22] Young, M. *The Technical Writer's Handbook*, Mill Valley, CA: University Science, 1989.
[23] Jahangeer, G. and Rajkumar, D. "Detecting breast cancer using novel mask R-CNN techniques," *Expert Systems*, vol. 39, 2022, doi: 10.1111/exsy.12954.
[24] Zheng, Z., et al. "Enhancing geometric factors in model learning and inference for object detection and instance segmentation," in *IEEE Transactions on Cybernetics*, vol. 52, no. 8, pp. 8574–8586, 2022, doi: 10.1109/TCYB.2021.3095305.

10 Harnessing Quantum Computing for Supply Chain Transformation: The PRABAX Framework

Prakashkumar Hasmukhbhai Patel[1*] and Baxiskumar Patel[2]

This chapter an introduction to "PRABAX" Quantum Supply Chain Optimization Model, using quantum optimization techniques in the decision-making processes of supply chains. By using the combination of the latest developments of quantum computing with operational practices for routing, scheduling, inventory, demand forecasting, the model covers the prevalent challenges relating to scalability, uncertainty, and resilience.

The chapter presents a systematic literature review based on PRISMA guidelines for synthesizing both classical and quantum optimization strategies. The study introduces the concepts of quantum annealing (QA), quantum approximate optimization algorithm (QAOA), quantum machine learning (QML), and a hybrid quantum–classical methodology. To capture the dynamics of the context, issues such as mediating variables, the choice of algorithm, refining a hybrid model, moderating factors such as the maturity of hardware and data integrity, and the integration constancy are investigated.

The implementation of QE within the PRABAX framework ensures the improvement of the resilience of the supply chains, improves forecasting accuracy, and reduces computational efficiency. Empirical demos suggest that hybrid workflows that incorporate quantum capabilities with the practical constraints of current available hardware provide the most feasible short-term trajectory.

The proposed framework will help managers and policymakers to understand the effective adoption pathways. It advises a phased implementation approach with initial short routinely hybrid pilot initiatives, followed by the medium-term system integration, and then long-run transition to full quantum native functioning.

The PRABAX model is both an extension to the theory of optimization and a combination of quantum concepts, which places the idea of hybrid frameworks

[1] Assistant Professor, Department of Commerce and Business Management, Faculty of Commerce, The Maharaja Sayajirao University of Baroda, Vadodara.
ORCID ID: 0000-0002-6972-3018

[2] Assistant Professor, Department of Commerce and Business Management, Faculty of Commerce, The Maharaja Sayajirao University of Baroda, Vadodara.
ORCID ID: 0000-0003-4396-4312
E-mail: baxiskumar.patel-cbm@msubaroda.ac.in[2]

* Corresponding author: prakashkumar.patel-cbm@msubaroda.ac.in

DOI: 10.1201/9781003646068-10

as an emerging paradigm in the field of supply chain literature. It bridges the gap between developments in computational science and established theories and models about resilience, dynamic capabilities, and resource-based views, and represents quantum optimization as an important strategic asset.

This study represents the first fully established framework for the optimization of quantum-enabled supply chains, which clearly outlines the hypotheses that can be tested as well as clear strategies for their adoption, helping guide future academic research and practices.

1. Introduction

Globally, the supply chain operates as a huge all-encompassing integrated network that spans continents, industries, and markets. Its continuity and resilience are often threatened by uncertainty arising from the economic fluctuations, geopolitical tensions, pandemics, and climate-related disruptions, to name a few. On the other hand, rapid digital transformation, ever more globalized markets, and increasing sophistication of consumers make the operation of these networks a lot more complex [1] [2] [3]. A cumulative effect of these elements is the creation of a tension that highlights the ever-increasing need for attributable and advanced optimization methodologies to support tactical, strategic, and operational decision-making in uncertain environmental conditions.

In this context, primary logistical functions such as scheduling production, forecasting demand, warehouse management, and truck routing to the warehouse are usually modeled by integrated optimization problems. Owing to their inherent complexity, these problems have significant difficulties to be solved. Moreover, as supply chain networks keep getting larger, the computational complexity of the corresponding models grows exponentially with the size of the systems [4]. Conventional methods such as mixed integer programming (MIP), linear programming (LP), heuristics, and metaheuristics have been widely applied [5]. While these approaches remain effective for small- and medium-scale cases, they often struggle in real time, large-scale decision-making contexts characterized by non-linear constraints and stochastic uncertainties [6] [7]. Recent work has been done in exploring digital supply chain twins and data-driven models for improving resilience [1] [2]. Nevertheless, these approaches are still limited by the computational constraints that classical algorithms have in solving nondeterministic polynomial-time hard (NP-hard) unrelated problems such as the vehicle routing problem (VRP), inventory control, and network design [4].

Quantum optimization has emerged as an interesting paradigm with the capabilities of overcoming large-scale supply chain problems that go beyond the scope of classical heuristics. Exploiting principles based on quantum mechanics—e.g., quantum tunnelling, which helps to escape local optima, entanglement, which allows correlations between the decision variables, and superposition, which allows exploring multiple solution states at the same time—quantum algorithms can achieve near-optimal solutions with better computational efficiency [8]. For example, one of the standard branch-and-bound or heuristic search techniques typically takes exponential time to solve a kind of benchmark combinatorial optimization problem—the travelling salesman problem (TSP). In contrast, quantum methods, such as gate-based algorithms and quantum annealing have shown potential to explore solution spaces simultaneously, and therefore, offer scalable solutions for the TSP and other supply chain problems such as network design and vehicle routing [9] [10].

Despite these promising developments, there is a paucity of literature devoted to the topic of quantum optimization in supply chain contexts. Emerging techniques—hybrid quantum-classical method (HQCM), quantum annealing and quantum approximate optimization algorithm (QAOA)—have produced a small number of systematic studies examining applicability in different supply chain domains such as routing, scheduling, inventory management, and resilience planning. Consequently, most of the research is still at the proof-of-concept phase, and overall industrial support is hindered by critical hardware limitations, difficulty in encoding data, and integration complexities [11].

In view of the dispersed and mostly preliminary nature of existing studies, there is a grave need for an integrative approach enabling a methodical implementation of quantum optimization in the context of isolated supply chain scenarios, whilst taking into consideration operational limitations and strategic goals. This study addresses this shortfall and introduces the PRABAX quantum supply chain optimization model, which serves to synthesize the classical and quantum methodologies in the sphere and also delineate pragmatic pathways for their industrial implementation.

This research is carried out with the three objectives. First, to summarize and compare quantum optimization methods such as QA, QAOA, QML, and HQCM in terms of application in supply chains. Second, to create links between quantum-based optimization approaches and the central areas of supply chain decision-making, which are demand forecasting, inventory management, scheduling, and vehicle routing. And finally, to create the PRABAX model combining the latest computational methods with the key moderators and mediators that affect the result of technology adoption and optimization.

2. Literature Review

Optimization used to play a central role in supply chain management (SCM), providing the foundation of the design, planning, and control of operations considering many cost, time, and service constraints. Classical methodologies, e.g., LP and MIP, have been widely used in a range of problems including the demand allocation problem, production scheduling, facility location, and transportation planning. With these techniques, mathematically rigorous solutions can be provided and optimality guaranteed in well-structured problem settings [12]. However, their scalability decreases with increasing dimensionality and complexity of the supply chains that they model, often resulting in prohibitively expensive computation in dynamic and real time [4].

To overcome these limitations, heuristic and metaheuristics strategies has been introduced. Heuristic approaches give expedient and flexible solutions, though usually at the cost of global optimality [13]. Metaheuristic algorithms such as genetic algorithms, tabu search, and simulated annealing have shown to have a robust performance in solving complex combinatorial problems such as inventory management and the classic VRP [14]. While these techniques can be applied to large and complex problems, the randomness of the approach could limit the ability to find the optimal solution in all cases [3].

Simulation-based optimization is another useful tool for analyzing uncertain environmental conditions fluctuating demand or supply disruptions. It is especially helpful in risk management and when it comes to increasing supply chain resilience and reliability [4]. However, simulation models often cannot run in real time, and they tend to almost always require the use of significant computing power. Consequently, these conventional methods tend to balance the tradeoffs between accuracy, speed, and flexibility with a tendency to become less effective for more complicated global supply chains.

Emerging quantum optimization is a promising new paradigm that uses principles from quantum physics to solve NP-hard supply chain problems. Quantum computing takes advantage of all sorts of quantum phenomena such as superposition, entanglement, and quantum tunnelling [8] to simultaneously search very large solution spaces to escape the local minima in a much better way than many classical methods. For example, QA has seen a potential for solving the problems of vehicle routing and scheduling by representing the decision variables on Ising Hamiltonians with an increased computational performance [9] [10]. Gate-based techniques such as the QAOA provide hybrid approaches, which can be well suited to today's noisy intermediate- scale quantum (NISQ) computers, represented as a way of striking a balance between performance and the current hardware limitations [11].

Unencumbered by the limitations of quantum hardware, such approaches have been shown to be more efficient in addressing large-scale optimization problems [15]. Moreover, quantum machine learning (QML) has shown positive results in supplier reliability and demand forecast [16] [17], which many times succeeds better than classical counterparts because quantum algorithms can uncover intricate patterns that are missed by classical techniques [18] [19] [20]. Such quantum tools are gradually being adapted to various sectors of the supply chain [17], for example, QAOA has been used successfully for optimizing inventory decisions and for situations with unpredictable demand [21], whereas QML techniques have improved forecasting and flexible decision-making in a dynamic setting, such as e-commerce or healthcare [16]. As such, current research is fragmented, with most studies being simulation based or involving limited case studies [10]. Some perpetual challenges are data encoding problems, scales of functionality, algorithmically tuning, and hardware limitations, which has hindered their wider acceptance [11] [15]. The absence of a common framework further complicates the comparison of quantum models and the evaluation of the strengths and weaknesses among different quantum models within different supply chain contexts.

Collectively the literature suggests that with the given dependence on classical methods, the area of quantum optimization has received a lot of push as a result of the inefficiency of the conventional methods. Beyond their ability to increase resilience and efficiency, quantum strategies are in line with sustainability-informed supply chains, in which the efficient use of resources and reduced emissions are paramount [22] [23]. This growing body of work helps underscore the imperative for trying to offer comprehensive frameworks to include the theory, practice, and empirical validation policies, all while also placing quantum optimization in a pioneering computational paradigm fit for the next upcoming generation of supply chains.

Table 10.1 Comparison of classical and quantum optimization approaches in SCM.

Approach	*Advantages*	*Limitations*	*Applications in SCM*	*Key Refereences*
Linear/ Mixed-Integer Programming	Mathematical rigor, guaranteed optimality	Poor scalability, exponential computational costs	Facillity location, demand allocation, production scheduling	[4], [12]
Heuristics	Fast and adaptable, simple to implement	Suboptimal, problem-specific, may miss global optima	Routing, scheduling, inventory allocation	[13]
Metaheuristics	Effective for NP-hard problems, flexible	Stochastic behavior, no guarantee of optimality	Vehicl routing, scheduling, inventory	[3], [14]
Simulation-based optimization	Captures uncertainty, supports risk analysis	Computationally intensive, limited real-time use	Disruption management, resilience planning	[4]
Quantum Annealing (QA)	Parallel exploration, effective for combinational optimization	Hardware-specific (Ising mapping), limited precision and scalability	Vehicle routing, last-mile logistics, traffic flow	[8], [10], [24]
Quantum Approximate Optimization Algorithm (QAOA)	Suitable for NISQ devices, flexible for discrete optimzation	Sensitive to noise, requires parameter tuning	Inventory management, scheduling, resource allocation	[11], [21], [25]

Contd...

Table 10.1 *Contd...*

Approach	*Advantages*	*Limitations*	*Applications in SCM*	*Key Refereences*
Quantum Machine Learning (QML)	Handles nonlinearities, efficient in high-dimesional data	Algorithms remain experimental, requires large datasets	Demand forecasting, supplier reliability, risk analysis	[16], [17], [26]
Hybrid Quantum-Classical	Combines strenghts of both paradigms, scalable for near-term use	Integration overhead, not fully quantum-native	Network design, resilience planning, multi-echelon logistics	[11], [24]

Source: Authors' own compilation from selected literature.

Table 10.1 shows the comparison between how linear programming helped solve complex problems and how the latest quantum model improves strength and scalability in the SCM operations. The available literature tends to dwell upon single quantum solutions or specific areas of SCM. No global unifying model exists that takes into account several quantum paradigms, moderators, and mediators as well as operational outcomes of supply chain decisions in various aspects of decision-making.

3. Methods

This chapter embraces a design approach and structured review of literature with respect to supply chain innovation and operations research approaches. It scientifically studies classical methods of optimization [27] [28], linear programming [16] [26], heuristics and metaheuristics [12] [14], and new quantum algorithms such as QA [8] [10], QAOA [11] [25], QML [16] [26], and HQSM [24]. The review was conducted using the PRISMA protocol, which involved identifying peer-reviewed sources, eliminating duplicates and non-English and irrelevant works, and including only those that are directly related to classical or quantum optimization in logistics, inventory, demand forecasting, and network design. The resulting set was synthesized to represent approaches in each of the decision domains. The lessons learned during this review were incorporated into the PRABAX framework by way of a conceptual modeling, decision domains, computational paradigms, algorithmic mechanisms, and outcome dimensions. They incorporate moderators like hardware maturity, data quality, and readiness in integration and mediators like algorithm selection and hybrid refinement in order to reflect contextual variation [29] [2]. This mixed approach will guarantee both theoretical soundness and practical applicability and make the PRABAX model promising to both scholarly and practical research.

4. Result and Discussion

4.1 Scalability and Performance Gains

It is repeatedly mentioned in the literature that quantum optimization offers quantifiable advantages to the solution of integrated-based SCM problems. In one example, QA has been found to be more efficient in routing and scheduling tasks than other traditional heuristics, including tabu search and genetic algorithms [10]. Equally, computation time is significantly reduced in D-Wave applications of traffic flow optimization, and it is important to highlight the prospects of real-time logistics applications [24]. In addition, it has been identified that QAOA can manage discrete optimization problems such as inventory management and uncertain scheduling [30].

Although these advances have been made, one of the weaknesses is the lack of scalability. Both QA and QAOA demand the restatement of SCM challenges into quadratic unconstrained binary optimization (QUBO), a mathematical framework used to describe complex problems, which increasingly develops as the scalability increases [11]. This is limited to large-scale, industry-level supply chains, where dynamic constraints and high-dimensional datasets are prevalent [14]. Also, scalability issues are exacerbated by hardware constraints such as limited numbers of qubits, error rates, and connectivity bottlenecks [8] [31]. Thus, although quantum models can exchange classical methods in controlled benchmarking, their practicability is still doubtful.

4.2 Integration of Quantum and Classical Hybrids

Hybrid approaches should be adopted as the best solution to use as a short-term solution. Hybrid models are aimed at keeping the benefits of computational resources intact but reducing hardware limitations by integrating quantum subroutines into the classical optimization systems [24]. In practice, these techniques are best applicable in real-world scenarios of logistics where disruption, demand variability, and network resiliency have to be balanced simultaneously since both are critically important factors in determining the quality of solutions as well as computational feasibility [30] [32]. Hybridization is, however, associated with overheads of integration, which includes specialized knowledge and more complex design of algorithms [11]. Moreover, the classical to classical computation ratio remains context dependent, and this often limits generalization across sectors [17].

4.3 Application and Future Prospects by Industry

Quantum optimization is not limited to logistics, but it has great potential in a range of fields of supply chain management. QML models are reinforcing the demand forecasting by revealing complex patterns in huge datasets, so they are particularly applicable to fast-evolving industries like e-commerce and healthcare, where the correct predictions will prevent the lack and surplus [33]. Like quantum annealing,

HQCMs enhance the supply chain network design, allowing the development of a resilient system that will be able to withstand climate risks and geopolitical disruptions [16] [17]. Most sector-specific applications are, however, experimental and not in the actual industrial system, but in simulated environment [10]. Issues like encoding of data, interpretability of the model, and reliance on emerging quantum hardware still limit large adoptions [15]. In order to allow deployment on the ground, studies should be conducted on scalable encoding methods, cross-domain scales, and practical validation in the operational supply chains.

4.4 Theoretical Model of PRABAX

The PRABAX model (Figure 10.1) is proposed by the authors on the basis of the identified factors. The term "PRABAX", which symbolizes the intellectual input of both authors to the development of this paradigm, is an abbreviated combination of their names. Besides being a mark of authorship, PRABAX also represents integration and synergy. Thus the essence of the model is the combination of classical and quantum paradigms to address difficult challenges in the supply chain. The PRABAX model is based on quantum optimization methods, including QA, QAOA, QML, and HQCM, applied to the basic supply chain structures, demand forecast, inventory management, routing, and network design [10] [11]. The "PRABAX" label gives a distinct identity that facilitates identification, academic attribution, and clarity of concepts toward the furtherance of the concept and discussion of the next-generation supply chain optimization, including the scientific purpose of the model and its origin.

This chapter presents a conceptual model, as shown in Figure 10.1, which incorporates quantum optimization techniques into SCM decision-making areas in different algorithmic processes, producing quantifiable operation effects and strategic long-term effects. Moderators and mediators are also included in the framework so as to influence the way in which quantum capabilities are converted into business value, hence closing the gap between novel computational developments and the actual applications in SCM [17] [11].

The extent of attained quantum benefits is contextually defined by three moderators, including data quality, integration readiness, and hardware maturity. Hardware maturity is the scalability and reliability of current devices; in the short-term, the hybrid strategy is more desirable because of constraints such as coherence, error rate, and the number of qubits, which are too many to allow full adoption [11] [29]. The ability of businesses to include quantum outputs into business operation systems such as enterprise resource planning (ERP), warehouse management system (WMS), and transportation management system (TMS) is known as integration readiness, which influences deployment effectiveness [24]. The quality and accessibility of information are also major concerns, particularly in quantum machine learning methods, which require high-quality and well-organized data in order to deliver relevant predictions. The lack of data may severely restrict

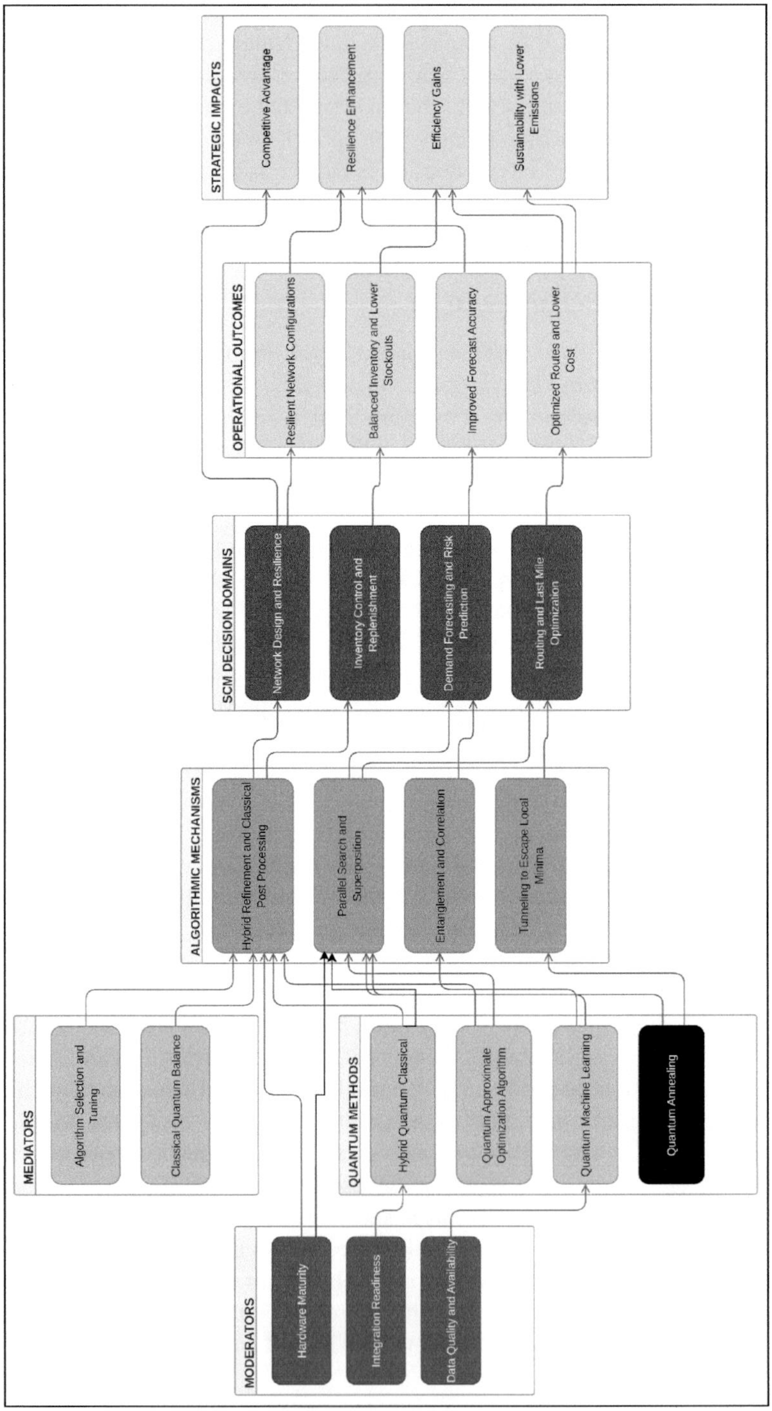

Fig. 10.1 The conceptual framework—PRABAX quantum supply chain optimization model. *Source:* Authors.

the capabilities of advanced algorithms, establishing the boundaries that determine the influence of quantum technologies in supply chains [16] [26] [2].

The model is based on four quantum paradigms. First, HQCMs use quantum algorithms and classical algorithms to scale and be practical, and are compatible with modern NISQ devices [24]. Second, QAOA is useful in NISQ systems in discrete optimization, as problems can be framed into Ising or QUBO models [8] [10]. Third, QML is useful in risk detection and predictive modeling, using quantum pattern recognition [17] [16]. Finally, QA can find low-energy solutions in scheduling and routing, by encoding problems into Ising. The selection of one of these paradigms is determined by the type of problem, the type of data, and the maturity of hardware [11].

These approaches provide the SCM with certain algorithmic functions. Parallel search and superposition enable the exploration of numerous options at the same time, whereas the hybrid refinement and classical post-processing enable the solutions to be practically deployed. Entanglement and the correlation model strongly associated the supply chain factors, and quantum tunnelling assists in overcoming local minima of complicated problems [8] [10]. These are approaches that connect quantum computation to SCM uses [30] [34].

These mechanisms are valuable to four primary SCM areas. First, network design and resilience is provided through hybrid optimization in order to survive disruptions [17] [22]. Second, inventory control and replenishment are achieved with better reorder strategies and managing uncertain demand [30]. Third, QML is used to optimize demand forecasting and risk prediction by modeling complex and non-linear relationships among variables [16] [17]. Finally, in routing, last-mile delivery is optimized with QA and hybrid solvers in order to minimize delays and costs [10] [24].

The operational advantages of quantum-enabled optimization are more resilient supply chains, stock optimization, more precise demand prediction, and cost-effective paths, which minimize costs and increase performance [4]. The comparison of quantum and classical models makes it possible to empirically evaluate the added value. The resulting strategic benefits of such improvements include cost and time savings, resilience to disruptions, and sustainability due to more efficient delivery paths [22] [24]. The framework also brings out some important mediating factors, and the choice and tuning of algorithms, including hyperparameter optimization, strongly affect the quality of the solutions [11]. Classical versus quantum components ratio affects the effectiveness and feasibility [24]. These mediators should be investigated in future studies by using mediation analysis and structural equation modeling. Generally, this research framework provides an organized method of assessing the concept of quantum-enabled supply chain management, which will connect the moderating factors, computational paradigms, algorithmic mechanisms, decision domains, operational results, and strategic effects to provide a guide to how quantum computing can change supply chain and logistics systems.

5. Theoretical Implications

The PRABAX model contributes greatly to the development of theory on SCM and computational optimization. It is able to enhance classical optimization theory by applying the principles of quantum mechanics such as superposition, entanglement, and tunnelling to the supply chain decision structure, enabling the exploration of multiple solution paths that cannot be found using classical solvers simultaneously [8] [10]. This paradigm shift directly addresses the failures of LP, heuristics, and metaheuristics, which often fail when dealing with the issues of scalability and stochastic uncertainty [4].

Second, PRABAX approaches the creation of HQCM as a legitimate optimization paradigm in and of itself and not just as short-term or transitional solutions. The model improves the optimization theory of near-term NISQ machines and future large-scale quantum machines of hybridizing as a theoretical object and opens the door to an unforeseen direction on how to find an equilibrium between computational scalability and quantum advantage [11] [24].

Third, the model assists with multi-theoretical integration by connecting the supply chain theories, including the resource-based view (RBV) [35], the resilience theory [3], and the dynamic capabilities theory [36], with sophisticated optimization. Quantum optimization may be considered a new dynamic capability, which enhances resilience-based strategies based on the complexity theory that enables companies to restructure their supply chains in a short period of time in the wake of volatility [37]. Similarly, placing quantum adoption in the framework of the innovation diffusion theory, PRABAX positions quantum-enabled decision-making as a disruptive technological transformation that progressively transforms managerial thinking and the more established decision logics [38].

Fourth, PRABAX is a combination of moderators, including hardware maturity, data quality, and integration readiness, and mediators, including algorithm selection and hybrid refinement [29]. This combination is why quantum optimization is more or less effective in different contexts and is able to add practical realism into optimization theory, balancing the benefits of computation with the constraints of operation.

Fifth, PRABAX brings supply chain research closer to the deterministic models through probabilistic and quantum aware reasoning, an explicit representation of parallelism, entanglement, and uncertainty. It reinvents the theory of optimization as a strategic model that interconnects the quantum-driven results such as efficiency, resilience, and sustainability with organizational competitiveness, integrating the strategic management of organizations, supply chain studies, and computational science [22] [3].

5.1 Theoretical Propositions Proposed

The PRABAX model builds on these theoretical contributions by providing a framework of generating empirically testable propositions (Ps) to transform its theoretical importance into empirical outcomes. The model can be used to create a basis of testable hypotheses and empirical studies by combining quantum-enabled optimization with theories such as resilience, dynamic capabilities, and the resource-based view. These connections transform abstract concepts into researchable questions that make the model more conceptual and practical in the context of the supply chain management.

P1: Quantum-classical hybrid optimization strategies will assist the supply chains to remain stronger and more stable to demand volatility better than the traditional heuristic-based strategies.

P2: Quantum machine learning can provide businesses with improved demand forecasts, but only when they have good data and systems that are well meshed. Better accuracy will be achieved by better data quality and integration.

P3: The ability of companies to optically optimize their supply chains will make them more flexible and responsive in the context of quickly modifying their supply chains during turbulent times than solely traditional approaches.

P4: The appropriate algorithm and hybrid augmentation should be aligned to sustain the gains of quantum supply chain optimization, and this will later allow the organization to achieve the realized gains of advanced computational abilities.

6. Practical Implications

PRABAX is a balanced practice model as it provides managers, legislators, and technology providers with useful advice besides its theoretical input. In the case of managers, quantum annealing allows finding solutions to vehicle routing and last-mile delivery much better, and it shows a tangible decrease in costs and delays in comparison to the strategies based on heuristic methods. Traffic flow optimization on D-Wave systems, already tested in industrial environments, proves its functionality in the real-world setting [19] [24]. On the same note, QAOA and QML enable companies to compare various replenishment and forecasting policies simultaneously, alleviating stockouts and surpluses in highly dynamic sectors like e-commerce and medical supply chains [16] [30]. In the case of supply chain network design, HQCMs allow supply chain managers to build more robust and cost-effective supply networks that can survive disruption by a geopolitical, climate, or pandemic shock [17], [2].

Another policy implication of the model is that it enables a policymaker to create favorable ecosystems, such as regulatory frameworks, open data standards, and national or regional quantum infrastructure investment. These initiatives can speed up the adoption, maintain interoperability, and prevent vendor lock-in. Among technology providers, PRABAX highlights the prospects to co-create scalable hybrid-based approach with industry partners, evolve a technique of error reduction, and offer secure integration layers of ERP, WMS, and TMS systems. There are also some sector-specific pathways that are depicted in the framework. Although quantum optimization of green logistics and public infrastructure can reduce congestion, enhance resiliency, and facilitate decarbonization objectives, QML can enhance precision in demand prediction in healthcare and e-commerce.

The results make quantum-enabled supply chains a means of sustainability and circularity in global activities that are directly linked to the environmental, social, and governance (ESG) objectives. [23] [22].

More importantly, PRABAX provides a roadmap of a gradual implementation. The next step that organizations should take is hybrid pilot projects that would involve the addition of quantum modules to the customary workflows in the nearest future. In the medium term, to enhance accurate and timely decision making, businesses can further integrate into ERP, WMS, and TMS applications. Long-term scalability can be opened with the alignment of the transition toward entirely quantum-native workflows with the Industry 5.0 transformation.

However, the benefits of these advantages require preparation in the organization. To build quantum literacy, better data quality, and build relationships with suppliers of quantum technology, companies need to invest in reskilling their employees. Risks associated with adoption, like vendor lock-in, cybersecurity vulnerabilities, and other moral dilemmas during the implementation of AI–quantum integration should be taken care of. The PRABAX model provides a capability-based perspective in recognizing the opportunities as well as the challenges, hence aligning the adoption with organizational change and dynamic capabilities.

If we put them together, these implications indicate that PRABAX does not only enhance theoretical knowledge but also provides practitioners, decision-makers, and tech developers with a roadmap of how to integrate quantum optimization in supply chain ecosystems in a comprehensive and forward-thinking manner.

7. Future Outlook of Research and Limitations

Although the PRABAX model has a considerable contribution to theory and practice, a number of limitations and research opportunities exist in the future. The primary disadvantage of the framework is that it is conceptual and analytical, and it has minimal empirical evidence in large-scale industrial environments. The implementation of fully quantum native solutions is constrained by the existing quantum hardware, which has restricted scalability and contains limited quantities of qubits, error rates, and coherence times [29] [8]. Although HQCMs give some assistance to overcome such barriers, their use in industries with low technological maturity might be limited by the integration costs and expertise that such systems entail [11]. Besides, the framework constrains the execution of quantum machine learning applications, which presupposes the presence of high-quality, structured data that is not always accessible in fragmented or resource-limited supply chains [16] [26]. Future research to overcome these barriers should be done by encoding the challenging issues of the real world in a scalable manner to quantum compatible formats. The QUBO model will need advancement when it comes to industrial application, namely, multi-echelon inventory, stochastic demand, and dynamic vehicle routing models [30]. Evidence of quantum benefits can also be created more clearly by calculating quantum with classical and hybrid methods in realistic operating conditions.

Cross-quantum-enabled optimization is especially useful in areas where volatility, resilience, and sustainability are of critical importance such as e-commerce, healthcare, and green logistics. Another essential direction is to have sector-specific empirical testing of the PRABAX framework [16] [17]. Incorporating classical simulators and quantum simulators in experimentation and testing initiatives based on simulation should be viewed as significant steps on the way toward actual implementation in industrial settings.

Other than the barrier of computation, structural and governance risks impact the adoption of quantum technology in organizations. This can only be implemented successfully through the reskilling of employees, the training of managers, and enhancing quantum literacy of supply chain professionals. The next wave of research must focus on the development of dynamic capabilities, the strategy-quantum alignment of organizations, and strategic collaboration with technology makers. Aspects of governance, including cybersecurity, data privacy, vendor dependency, and ethical concerns related to AI–quantum integration, should also be critically considered to make responsible and sustainable implementation. Multidisciplinary research also offers additional opportunities due to the combination of operations management and computer science, sustainability, policy, and digital transformation studies to gain a more profound insight into the issue of quantum adoption. The integration of the PRABAX framework and the study of blockchain, the internet of things (IoT), and digital twins may allow progress in planning resilience, predictive optimization, and sustainable operations. Moreover, the PRABAX model has mediators and moderators that may be empirically tested using structural equation modeling, mediation analysis, and longitudinal studies. This can help determine the influence of contextual variables, that is, hardware maturity, algorithm refinement, and data quality on performance outcomes. Further research is needed on the use of PRABAX in the fields of low-carbon logistics, circular supply chains, and ESG-oriented strategies because quantum-enabled optimization can lead to better rates of environmental performance in these areas.

Through these issues of concern and this set of questions, the PRABAX model will be able to evolve beyond a theoretical concept into a solid, empirically tested, and broadly implemented paradigm of quantum-enabled supply chain optimization.

8. Conclusion

The chapter contributes to the body of literature on quantum-enabled SCM by proposing the PRABAX quantum supply chain optimization model, a systematic approach that paves its way into the fundamental areas of decision-making in supply chains by incorporating QA, QAOA, QML, and HQCMs. PRABAX demonstrates the benefits of quantum optimization in demand forecasting, inventory management, scheduling, and so on, by integrating these paradigms for greater efficiency and to avoid the computational bottlenecks of the classical approaches [8] [10] and [11].

The framework broadens the scope of deterministic logics of the optimization theory of the field of quantum mechanics by adding quantum notions such as superposition, entanglement, and tunnelling, which is a theoretical contribution [4]. In such a way, PRABAX also authenticates HQCM as a novel optimization paradigm, which is critically necessary in NISQ devices [24] [29]. In practical terms, the model provides managers, legislators, and technology firms with a stepwise adoption roadmap, which puts workforce reskilling, integration preparedness, and industry-specific applications at the center of the transformation that directly relates the work of quantum optimization to sustainability, efficiency, and resilience results [2] [22].

As highlighted in the chapter, the near future of quantum supply chain optimization lies with hybrid frameworks that can be used to balance not only the quantifiable performance gains but also hardware shortcomings. The conceptual propositions and the adoption pathways described are a good foundation to extend the further validation of the concept empirically to different industries, though the empirical use is in its early stages. Future studies must address trying the PRABAX model using industrial case studies, benchmarking analysis, and multidisciplinary interoperability with new technologies, including blockchain, IoT, and digital twins to make the implementation of PRABAX faster. The PRABAX framework in general connects computer science with managerial practice and supply chain theory such that quantum optimization can be viewed as an asset in technology and as a strategic capability. It provides a precise roadmap to developing industrial practice and scholarly investigation, which advances the development of supply chains in a more digital and sustainable economy.

References

[1] Ivanov, D. and Dolgui, A. "A digital supply chain twin for managing the disruption risks and resilience in the era of Industry 4.0," *Production Planning & Control*, vol. 32, no. 9, pp. 775–788, 2021.

[2] Queiroz, M.M., Ivanov, D., Dolgui, A., and Fosso Wamba, S. "Impacts of epidemic outbreaks on supply chains: mapping a research agenda amid the COVID-19 pandemic through a structured literature review," *Annals of Operations Research*, vol. 319, no. 1, pp. 1159–1196, 2022.

[3] Christopher, M. and Peck, H. "Building the resilient supply chain," *The International Journal of Logistics Management*, vol. 15, no. 2, pp. 1–14, 2004.

[4] Cuthbertson, R.W. "The logic of logistics: Theory, algorithms and applications for logistics management," *Journal of the Operational Research Society*, vol. 49, no. 9, pp. 1016–1017, 1998.

[5] Fukasawa, R., et al. "Robust branch-and-cut-and-price for the capacitated vehicle routing problem," *Math. Program.*, vol. 106, no. 3, pp. 491–511, 2006.

[6] Golden, B.L., Raghavan, S. and Wasil, E.A. *The Vehicle Routing Problem*, New York: Springer, 2008.

[7] Kouhizadeh, M., Saberi, S., and Sarkis, J. "Blockchain technology and the sustainable supply chain: Theoretically exploring adoption barriers," *International Journal of Production Economics*, vol. 231, no. 107831, p. 107831, 2021.

[8] Johnson, M.W. et al. "Quantum annealing with manufactured spins," *Nature*, vol. 473, no. 7346, pp. 194–198, 2011.

[9] Kadowaki, T. and Nishimori, H. "Quantum annealing in the transverse Ising model," *Physical Review E*, , vol. 58, no. 5, pp. 5355–5363, 1998.

[10] Syrichas, A. and Crispin, A. "Large-scale vehicle routing problems: Quantum annealing, tunings and results," *Computers & Operations Research*, vol. 87, pp. 52–62, 2017.

[11] Moll, N., et al. "Quantum optimization using variational algorithms on near-term quantum devices," *Quantum Science and Technology*, vol. 3, no. 3, p. 30503, 2018.

[12] Laporte, G. "Fifty years of vehicle routing," *Transportation Science*, vol. 43, no. 4, pp. 408–416, 2009.

[13] Roy, D. "Bivariate models from univariate life distributions: A characterization cum modeling approach," *Naval Research Logistics*, vol. 51, no. 5, pp. 741–754, 2004.

[14] Gendreau, M. and Potvin, J.-Y. "Metaheuristics in combinatorial optimization," *Annals of Operations Research*, vol. 140, no. 1, pp. 189–213, 2005.

[15] Arrazola, J.M., Delgado, A., Bardhan, B.R. and Lloyd, S. "Quantum-inspired algorithms in practice," *Quantum*, vol. 4, no. 307, p. 307, 2020.

[16] Schuld, M. and Petruccione, F. *Supervised Learning with Quantum Computers*, 1st ed., Cham, Switzerland: Springer International Publishing, 2018.

[17] Perdomo-Ortiz, A., Benedetti, M., Realpe-Gómez, J. and Biswas, R. "Opportunities and challenges for quantum-assisted machine learning in near-term quantum computers," *Quantum Science and Technology*, vol. 3, no. 3, p. 30502, 2018.

[18] Neukart, F., Von Dollen, D., Seidel, C. and Compostella, G. "Quantum-enhanced reinforcement learning for finite-episode games with discrete state spaces," *Frontiers in Physics*, vol. 5, 2018.

[19] Zhuang, Y., et al. "Quantum computing in intelligent transportation systems: A survey," 2024.

[20] Vaddy, R.K., Dhamodharan, B., and Jain, A. "Quantum computing applications in real- time route optimization for supply chains," in *Quantum Computing and Supply Chain Management*, IGI Global, 2024, pp. 113–124.

[21] Moussa, C., Calandra, H., and Dunjko, V. "To quantum or not to quantum: Towards algorithm selection in near-term quantum optimization," *Quantum Science and Technology*, vol. 5, no. 4, p. 44009, 2020.

[22] Whig, P., Remala, R., Mudunuru, K.R., and Quraishi, S.J. "Integrating AI and quantum technologies for sustainable supply chain management," in *Quantum Computing and Supply Chain Management*, IGI Global, 2024, pp. 267–283.

[23] Gachnang, P., Ehrenthal, J., Hanne, T. and Dornberger, R. "Quantum computing in supply chain management state of the art and research directions," *Asian Journal of Logistics Management*, vol. 1, no. 1, pp. 57–73, 2022.

[24] Neukart, F., Compostella, G., Seidel, C., von Dollen, D., Yarkoni, S. and Parney, B. "Traffic flow optimization using a quantum annealer," *Frontiers in ICT*, vol. 4, Dec. 2017.

[25] Farhi, E., Goldstone, J. and Gutmann, S. "A quantum approximate optimization algorithm," 2014.

[26] Sehrawat, S.K., Dutta, P.K., Bhatia, A.B. and Whig, P. "Predicting demand in supply chain networks with quantum machine learning approach," in *Quantum Computing and Supply Chain Management*, IGI Global, 2024, pp. 33–47.

[27] Tranfield, D., Denyer, D., and Smart, P. "Towards a methodology for developing evidence-informed management knowledge by means of systematic review," *British Journal of Management*, vol. 14, no. 3, pp. 207–222, 2003.

[28] Wu, H., Liu, J., and Liang, B. "AI-driven supply chain transformation in industry 5.0: Enhancing resilience and sustainability," *Journal of Knowledge Economy*, 2024.

[29] Preskill, J. "Quantum computing in the NISQ era and beyond," *Quantum*, vol. 2, no. 79, p. 79, 2018.

[30] Bożejko, W., et al. "Optimal solving of a scheduling problem using quantum annealing metaheuristics on the D-Wave quantum solver," *IEEE Transactions on Systems, Man, and Cybernetics: Systems*, vol. 55, no. 1, pp. 196–208, 2025.

[31] Patel, P.H., Rathod, C.K. and Zaveri, K. "Green internet of things (IoT) and machine learning (ML): The combinatory approach and synthesis in the banking industry," in *Green Internet of Things and Machine Learning*, ed. R. Raut, S. Kautish, Z. Polkowski, A. Kumar, and C.-M. Liu, 2022, https://doi.org/10.1002/9781119793144.ch11.

[32] Patel, P. "A Study of {E-Procurement} Practices in Selected Organizations in Gujarat," 2017.

[33] Dunjko, V. and Briegel, H.J. "Machine learning \& artificial intelligence in the quantum domain: a review of recent progress," *Rep. Prog. Phys.*, vol. 81, no. 7, p. 74001, Jul. 2018.

[34] Patel, P., Satendrakumar, D. and Khajuria, R. "A Study to Identify Factors That Affect e-Procurement Implementation, International Journal of Science Technology and Engineering," vol. 2, pp. 264–268, 2016.

[35] Barney, J.B. "Firm resources and sustained competitive advantage," J. Manage., vol. 17, no. 1, pp. 99–120, 1991.

[36] Teece, D.J., Pisano, G. and Shuen, A. "Dynamic capabilities and strategic management," Strategic Manage. J., vol. 18, no. 7, pp. 509–533, Aug. 1997.

[37] Snowden, D.J. and Boone, M.E. "A leader's framework for decision making," Harv. Bus. Rev., vol. 85, no. 11, pp. 68–76, Nov. 2007.

[38] Rogers, E.M. Diffusion of Innovations, 5th ed. New York, NY: Free Press, 2003.

11 Quantum Algorithmic Threats and Countermeasures in Cloud and IoT Security

Ria Ghosh[1], Meetu Malhotra[2] and Sonali Kesarwani[3*]

With the capability of revolutionizing information processing, quantum computing is rapidly emerging as a game-altering technology, particularly in cloud security and the internet of things (IoT). Quantum computers, unlike traditional systems, employ entanglement and superposition to solve certain problems of cryptography and optimization much faster. This raises severe threats to the cryptography practices currently employed in cloud and IoT systems, while at the same time presenting the potential for innovation. In this chapter, the double impacts of quantum computing are discussed, including how emerging technologies such as quantum-boosted machine learning, quantum random number generation, and quantum key distribution (QKD) can both enhance and compromise existing security architectures. It deals with the challenge of implementing quantum-resistant protocols in the limited conditions typical for IoT devices and examines critically the possibility of post-quantum cryptography (PQC) offering secure alternatives. The chapter also discusses existing developments in quantum cloud platforms and foresees the establishment of a quantum internet that can revolutionize completely the paradigms of secure communication and data protection. The chapter provides a comprehensive blueprint for scholars, practitioners, and policymakers navigating the transition toward quantum-proof digital ecosystems by evaluating the technical and ethical implications. The holistic approach highlights how critical it is to prepare cloud and IoT structures for both the promise and dangers of quantum computing in the context of protecting nascent technology.

1. Introduction

Cloud computing and the internet of things (IoT), the two major technologies that form the pillar of modern cyber-physical infrastructures, have come together

[1] Department of Computer Science Engineering, Indian Institute of Technology, Patna, India. ORCID ID: 0009-0004-7737-4171
[2] Data Science, Harrisburg University of Science and Technology, PA USA ORCID ID: 0009-0009-7495-4484
[3] Amity Institute of Forensic Sciences, Amity University, Noida, Uttar Pradesh, India. ORCID ID: 0000-0002-3760-5105
E-mail: ria2024ghosh@gmail.com[1]; fmeetu@myharrisburg.edu[2]
* Corresponding author: sonalikesarwani743@gmail.com

DOI: 10.1201/9781003646068-11

quickly during the growth of digital ecosystems. As IoT networks facilitate seamless interaction among billions of networked devices, from industrial sensors and home appliances to autonomous vehicles and medical devices, cloud platforms provide scalable, on-demand computing capabilities that underpin diverse applications ranging from enterprise resource planning to artificial intelligence (AI)–driven analytics. But this convergence elevates the complexity of ensuring data security, privacy, and integrity in more dispersed and heterogeneous systems. Modern cloud and IoT security frameworks are based on conventional cryptographic techniques, which are fast being made obsolete by emerging threats, none more transformative than quantum computing. With the application of the principles of quantum mechanics such as superposition, entanglement, and quantum interference to process information in entirely novel manners, quantum computers operate quite differently from traditional systems. Most public key cryptosystems, including RSA and elliptic curve cryptography (ECC), are vulnerable to quantum attack due to these features, as they enable quantum computers to compute some mathematical problems exponentially more quickly than traditional computers, e.g., discrete logarithms and integer factorization [1]. As these protocols are absolutely essential for secure communication and authentication, the implications are enormous for cloud and IoT networks alike. Quantum random number generators (QRNG), quantum key distribution (QKD), and quantum-enhanced machine learning for threat detection are a few of the fresh applications through which quantum computing is enhancing cybersecurity.

The double-edged nature of quantum computing as both a security enabler and a disruptor necessitates a cautious exploration of its implications, especially against the backdrop of highly virtualized cloud environments and resource-scarce IoT devices. In integrating post-quantum cryptography methods, which tend to require more resources, IoT devices pose significant challenges since they often lack processing capabilities and memory. In spite of being more flexible, cloud infrastructures must cope with the process of migrating hybrid workloads and legacy systems to quantum-resistant protocols. The international research community, as a response, developed post-quantum cryptography (PQC), a family of algorithms resistant to both classical and quantum attackers but still capable of execution on typical hardware. Significantly, to identify suitable PQC techniques for public use, the National Institute of Standards and Technology (NIST) has begun standardization efforts. Meanwhile, researchers and developers can prototype quantum applications and test their impacts on existing security infrastructures with the help of quantum cloud platforms such as International Business Machines (IBM) Quantum, Amazon Braket, and Microsoft Azure Quantum [2]. Cloud-IoT security fusion is extended further by the potential of a quantum internet in the future, with quantum entanglement providing ultra-secure, real-time communication over large distances. But in addition to technology development, global cooperation and regulatory insight are required for moving toward a quantum-strength digital environment. To facilitate responsible deployment, technological advancements need to be complemented with ethical concerns regarding data sovereignty, surveillance, and quantum key ownership.

This chapter comprehensively explores the interaction between cloud security, IoT networks, and quantum computing. It evaluates actual applications of quantum-enhanced security technologies, explores the approaches to deploying quantum-safe cryptographic standards, and analyzes the vulnerabilities introduced by quantum algorithms. By doing so, it links theoretical insight with real-world applications and offers a map for all concerned-researchers, business leaders, and lawmakers to navigate the profound challenges and opportunities of quantum computing. Rethinking security frameworks that not only defend against quantum threats but also leverage quantum abilities to produce more resilient, adaptive, and wise digital infrastructures is vital as organizations prepare for the post-quantum era.

2. Quantum Computing: Foundations and Capabilities

The advanced computer paradigm called "quantum computing" exploits the principles of quantum physics to compute data in revolutionary new ways. Its basic building block, the quantum bit or qubit, differs considerably from the classic bit. A qubit can simultaneously be in superposition of both states, but a classical bit can only be in one of two discrete states: 0 or 1. This provides a quantum computer with n qubits a huge parallel processing capability compared to classical computers as it is able to represent two possible states at the same time. This feature is critical in solving complex problems that classical computers are unable to solve computationally. Entanglement is yet another basic concept. No matter what the physical separation between two qubits is, the two are deeply correlated when they become entangled. One of the fundamental reasons why quantum computing can do better than classical methods in certain applications is due to the non-local correlation that allows for calculations to be coordinated over many qubits. In addition, quantum interference improves the precision of solutions by allowing quantum algorithms to destroy erroneous responses and raise the probability of correct ones. Quantum gates apply reversible operations on qubits to change qubit states in quantum computing. The Hadamard gate, which places a qubit in a superposition, the Pauli gates (X, Y, Z), which perform various flips and rotations, and the controlled NOT (CNOT) gate, which causes entanglement between qubits, are just a few examples of universal gates [3]. Such gates form quantum circuits, which employ a systematic evolution of the quantum state toward the desired output in order to perform algorithms. Quantum operations are Schrödinger-equation-governed unitary transformations because they are required to preserve the total probability, unlike irreversible classical logic operations.

Quantum computers today exist in a multitude of physical systems, including topological qubits, photonic systems, trapped ions, and superconducting circuits. There are benefits and drawbacks to each platform, particularly regarding scalability, gate fidelity, and coherence time. While they require cryogenic environments to operate, superconducting qubits popularized by companies such as IBM and Google have made significant progress in gate velocity and integration density. While trapped-ion systems enjoy more precise control and longer coherence times, they often enjoy slower operating rates and scaling limitations. Current quantum devices are noisy intermediate-scale quantum (NISQ) systems, even with their theoretical capabilities. These devices are very susceptible to operation errors and decoherence and have fewer than 100 qubits. The no-cloning theorem, preventing the direct copying of quantum information, renders error correction much harder in quantum systems than in classical ones. Fault-tolerant quantum computing is thus still a pipe dream, with many theoretical and engineering hurdles to overcome. Yet, existing research continues to advance boundaries of what is currently achievable.

2.1 Quantum Algorithms and Cryptographic Impact

The extraordinary computational capability of quantum systems has been exemplified through quantum algorithms, particularly in areas relating to cryptography, search, and optimization. Shor's method, which enables factoring large integers in polynomial time, is one of the most significant advancements. Factoring's computational intractability as a basis for security directly threatens classical cryptographic systems such as RSA. The same way, Shor's method can be employed to destroy elliptic curve cryptography (ECC), another widely used standard in cloud and IoT security. As quantum technology is developed further, the algorithm is dangerous because its performance improves exponentially with the number of qubits and gate quality. Grover's method offers a quadratic speedup for unstructured search problems in symmetric-key systems. Consequently, algorithms like the Advanced Encryption Standard (AES) forfeit their n-bit effective key strength to roughly n/2 bits. The need for longer key sizes and supporting countermeasures comes from the possibility that, in the quantum world, AES-256 encryption could be broken using the equivalent of AES-128 security [4]. Other quantum algorithms that are increasingly important are the variational quantum eigensolver (VQE) and quantum approximate optimization algorithm (QAOA), both addressing optimization and simulation challenges, and the quantum Fourier transform (QFT), a subroutine of Shor's algorithm.

They have the potential to considerably augment activities such as risk modeling, logistics, and cryptographic key optimization, although they may not have an immediate effect on compromising security. Knowing the timeline and potential of quantum hardware is key to understanding the broader implications of quantum computing on cybersecurity. While estimates change dramatically, most scholars anticipate that during the next two to three decades, if not sooner, a fault-tolerant large-scale quantum computer that can break RSA-2048 encryption will emerge. In response, governments and business entities are aggressively exploring post-quantum cryptography (PQC). PQC algorithms can be implemented on existing classical infrastructure and are designed to be secure against both classical and quantum attackers. Lattice-based, hash-based, and multivariate polynomial schemes are some of the algorithms that are currently being standardized by the NIST PQC program.

2.2 Quantum Computing Platforms and Real-World Integration

Theoretical progress in quantum computing is increasingly being complemented by growing accessibility and experimentation through cloud-based quantum platforms. Cloud-based quantum processors are made accessible to researchers and developers by IBM, Microsoft, Google, Amazon, and Rigetti, driving innovation in quantum programming and hybrid applications. For instance, Amazon Braket integrates hardware backends and simulators from numerous vendors to facilitate flexible experimentation, while IBM Quantum Experience allows users to create and run quantum circuits on real quantum devices. These platforms are crucial to the evolution of practical security uses of quantum computing, particularly in cloud and IoT ecosystems. One interesting application is QKD, which distributes encryption keys securely using photons' quantum properties. QKD is theoretically resistant to eavesdropping because measurement destroys quantum states, and hence any eavesdropping effort is detectable in real time. QKD-enabled networks are already being used by countries such as the United States (US), China, and the European Union (EU) nations for secure financial and government communications. Quantum random number generation (QRNG), yet another state-of-the-art method, produces entropy with actually unpredictable randomness through the use of quantum phenomena. This enhances digital signatures, authentication tokens, and cryptographic key generation-critical components of cloud infrastructure and IoT environments. Cybersecurity is also venturing into new spaces due to the merger of AI and quantum computing. Anomaly detection, fraud detection, and intrusion detection in cloud-based systems are explored by utilizing quantum machine learning methods, which have the ability to process high-dimensional data with enhanced processing ability [5].

Safeguarding IoT networks is particularly important, because threat detection from scattered systems demands real-time processing of huge amounts of heterogeneous data. In spite of these advances, wide-scale adoption of quantum-augmented solutions still encounters a number of challenges. Cryogenics, vacuum chambers, and highly controlled systems are still required in quantum hardware, which is expensive and fragile. There is also a shortage of skilled professionals with the capability to develop quantum algorithms and build security systems with quantum features. There are also architectural issues involving latency, bandwidth, and synchronization across different computational layers involved in hybrid classical–quantum integration. Yet, the field of quantum computing is no longer theoretical. Governments are funding national quantum initiatives, and private companies are heavily investing in applied research and quantum start-ups. Together, these efforts demonstrate the broad realization that, in the age of pervasive cloud computing and IoT devices, quantum computing will not merely transform scientific computation and optimization but also redefine the foundational elements of digital security.

3. Cloud Computing and IoT: Current Security Models

The IoT and cloud computing have emerged as key components of contemporary digital infrastructure, allowing for scalable resource allocation, real-time data processing, and seamless connectivity. Although these technologies have revolutionary potential, the cybersecurity attack surface has grown dramatically as a result of their widespread use. A thorough and multi-layered approach to security is required in cloud-IoT ecosystems due to the variety of devices, dynamic data flows, and dispersed architectures. The current security models that support these systems are examined in this section, along with their advantages, disadvantages, and weaknesses, especially in light of possible quantum attacks.

3.1 Cloud Computing Security Architecture

Infrastructure as a service (IaaS), platform as a service (PaaS), and software as a service (SaaS) are the three-layered service models that define cloud computing, and each one brings with it special security considerations. IaaS settings prioritize network, storage, and virtual machine security, usually transferring security responsibility at the operating system (OS) level to the client. PaaS adds middleware and runtime environments to the stack, necessitating strong access controls and safe API setups. Strict identity management and data isolation procedures are necessary for SaaS models, which are frequently fully handled by the service provider, to guarantee that users do not access illegal datasets. A shared responsibility approach has historically been used to control security in cloud settings, with customers being in charge of safe configurations, data protection, and user access, while cloud providers guarantee the security of the underlying infrastructure [6]. Network security elements like virtual private clouds (VPCs), firewalls, and intrusion detection/prevention systems (IDS/IPS) are examples of core security components, as are authentication protocols like OAuth and SAML and data encryption (at rest, in transit, and increasingly in use).

To improve user verification, single sign-on (SSO) and multi-factor authentication (MFA) are now commonplace procedures. Virtualization and containerization, which enable the logical division of workloads and the isolation of sensitive operations, are key facilitators of cloud security. Misconfigurations, container escapes, and hypervisor attacks, however, continue to be a constant risk. Cross-platform identity management, data residency compliance, and consistent policy enforcement can be particularly difficult to sustain in hybrid and multi-cloud installations. RSA, ECC, and AES are the main cryptographic techniques used in cloud systems today, and they are susceptible to future quantum assaults despite developments. These algorithms are based on mathematical issues that quantum algorithms such as Shor's and Grover's can tackle effectively. Therefore, modern cloud infrastructures are not intrinsically quantum-resistant, even though they are safe against classical threats. Figure 11.1 compares the classical and quantum algorithms.

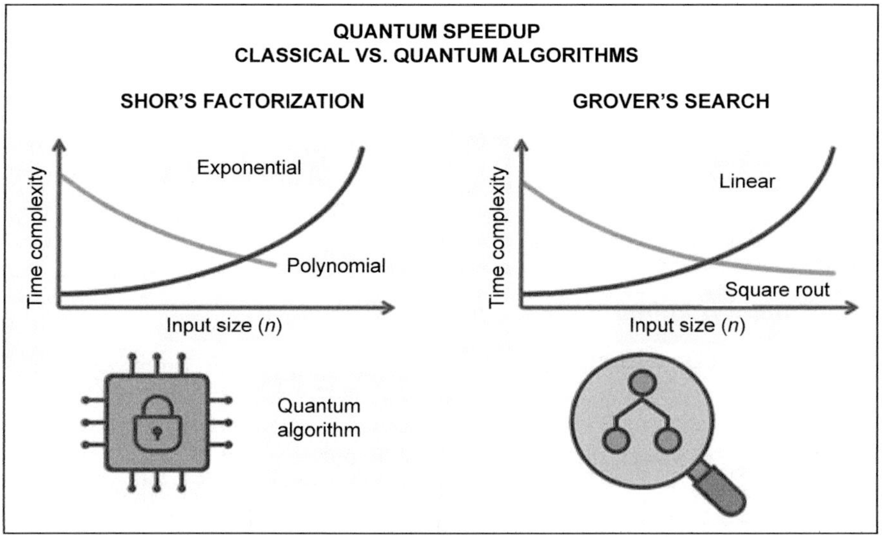

Fig. 11.1 Comparison of the classical and quantum algorithms.

3.2 IoT Security Models and Constraints

A vast number of interrelated devices operating with various operating systems, communication protocols, and processing capacity is enabled by the IoT. IoT devices, unlike conventional information technology (IT) systems, often have constrained central processing units (CPUs), memory, and battery life, which substantially constrains the application of robust cryptographic algorithms and real-time threat monitoring tools. IoT security measures must thus be decentralized, adaptable, and lightweight. Device identity verification, secure boot processes, and firmware verification to ensure devices execute approved and unchanged code are the initial steps in the majority of contemporary IoT security frameworks. Data-in-transit protection is provided by protocols such as Transport Layer Security (TLS) and DTLS; however, they are often altered or reduced to accommodate device limitations. Lightweight encryption is included in secure communications frameworks such as Message Queuing Telemetry Transport (MQTT) and the Constrained Application Protocol (CoAP) to support IoT environments. Traffic of IoT is segmented and analyzed at the network level through segmentation, anomaly detection, and intrusion prevention technologies. Through the migration of processing from devices to nearby edge nodes that can implement stronger security and real-time analysis, edge computing has emerged as a significant architectural enhancement. In addition, it has been proposed that blockchain-based solutions decentralize IoT trust management by facilitating decentralized authentication and immutable logging without central authorities.

The traditional role-based access control (RBAC) model of access control for the IoT is also yielding to more adaptive, context-dependent models such as attribute-based access control (ABAC), which considers time, position, device type, and other contextual attributes while assigning privileges [7]. These models, however, introduce scalability and computational overhead challenges and require fine-grained policy management. Supply chain security is another important IoT threat. Devices often rely on firmware or third-party components, which could lead to backdoors or vulnerabilities. It is exacerbated by the lack of standardized approaches, particularly as IoT networks grow across the critical infrastructure, industrial, and healthcare spaces.

3.3 Common Vulnerabilities and Threat Vectors

Threat actors like unauthorized access, data leakage, distributed denial-of-service (DDoS), privilege escalation, and insecure APIs are common to both IoT and cloud ecosystems. Huge breaches in cloud services have resulted from account compromise and misconfigured storage buckets. Insider threats and data exfiltration are favored by lack of adequate encryption, weak access controls, and insufficient continuous monitoring. Threats are more scattered and physical in IoT ecosystems. Devices are susceptible to physical tampering and cloning as they are often used in public or open environments. Other conditions that expose risk include insecure wireless protocols, poor or hardcoded credentials, and insufficient firmware updates. These weaknesses have been exploited by botnets such as Mirai and Mozi in order to organize massive DDoS attacks, indicating the necessity for threat modeling and mitigation strategies specifically for the IoT. Hybrid vulnerabilities are brought about by the integration of cloud and IoT technology [8]. For example, hijacked IoT devices could serve as a gateway to services based in the cloud. Conversely, by revealing configuration data or update processes, vulnerabilities within cloud storage or APIs can impact associated devices. A vulnerability in a single layer can propagate throughout the whole architecture because of the tight interconnection between edge devices and the cloud platform.

3.4 Toward Quantum-Resilient Security Models

Although known cryptographic algorithms and layered defensive principles form the foundation of current security models for cloud and IoT systems, they are essentially not built to survive attacks from quantum adversaries. For key exchange and digital signatures, RSA and ECC will become outdated as quantum computing develops, and symmetric algorithms like AES will need bigger key sizes to provide the same level of security. To overcome these obstacles, PQC is being intensively developed. Lattice-based, hash-based, multivariate polynomial, and code-based schemes are being assessed for deployment in classical contexts as part of NIST's continuous standardization process. These algorithms can be incorporated into current cloud-IoT systems without the need for quantum hardware and provide protection against both classical and quantum threats. But without substantial hardware acceleration or optimization, many PQC algorithms are computationally demanding and might not be appropriate for low-power IoT devices.

To provide protection to data between cloud data centers and edge nodes, some researchers are also exploring quantum-enhanced security primitives such as QKD. Even though it offers information-theoretic security, QKD is not practical now for large-scale IoT deployment and requires specialized infrastructure. Figure 11.2 depicts the cloud and quantum enhanced architecture. Organizations need to undertake comprehensive risk analysis, catalog cryptographic dependencies, and implement cryptographic agility if they need to progress toward quantum-resilient security architectures. They need to create systems that can adapt to algorithm changes without demanding complete architectural restructuring. Adaptive security in hybrid cloud-IoT networks can also be enhanced by merging automated incident response with AI-led threat intelligence.

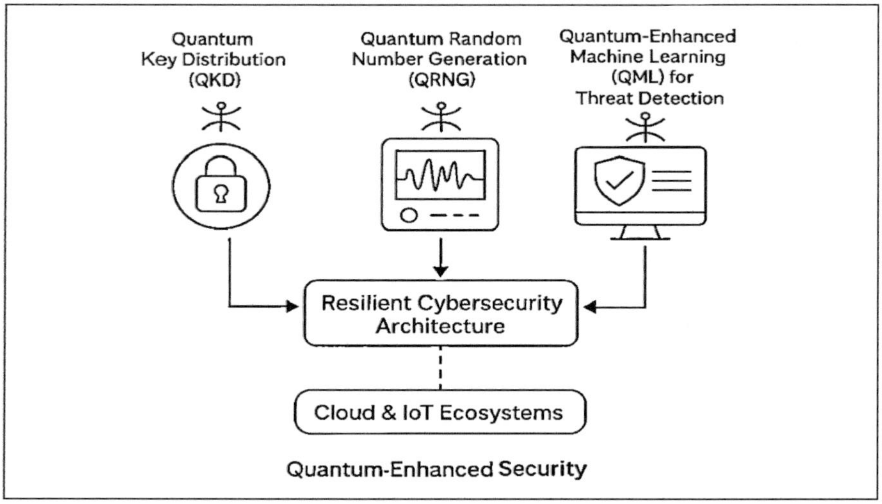

Fig. 11.2 Cloud and quantum enhanced architecture.

4. Quantum Threats to Cloud and IoT Security

Quantum computing raises a serious and systematic threat to the security paradigms that still protect cloud computing and the IoT that underpin the digital foundation of modern society. Quantum computers are able to perform certain computer tasks significantly faster than traditional computers through the use of concepts such as superposition, entanglement, and quantum parallelism. This poses grave vulnerabilities to the existing cryptographic building blocks in IoT and cloud environments, but it also presents a fabulous scope for scientific development. The quantum threats, how they impact current cryptography, the way they enhance the dangers in highly interconnected cloud-IoT frameworks, and more are all explained in this section.

4.1 Quantum Capabilities and Cryptographic Vulnerabilities

The ability of quantum computers to break widespread public-key cryptography schemes is the most serious and well-documented quantum threat. Shor's algorithm in 1994 demonstrated that a sufficiently powerful quantum computer could factor gigantic numbers and determine discrete logarithms in polynomial time. The basis of key exchange, digital signatures, and authentication protocols within cloud infrastructures and IoT platforms, RSA and ECC, is threatened directly by this. Since its security relies on the difficulty of prime factorization, RSA, which forms the basis for Secure Sockets Layer (SSL)/TLS protocols, is made obsolete in a post-quantum world. In the same vein, Shor's algorithm can also be applied to break ECC, which is used in resource-limited applications such as the IoT due to its computation intensity and smaller key sizes [9]. This places many cloud services, including identity federation and data encryption and IoT authentication protocols, in risk of future data breach and retrogressive decryption. Another concerning quantum method is Grover's algorithm, which increases the pace of brute-force attacks against symmetric-key encryption by fourfold.

Grover's method halves the effective security of symmetric algorithms such as AES and hash functions such as Secure Hash Algorithm 2 (SHA-2), but it does not break them entirely. To ensure satisfactory levels of resistance, larger keys and hash sizes must be used with AES-256, which gives an effective 128-bit level of security against quantum attacks. In addition, hybrid cryptographic schemes that blend symmetric and asymmetric methods are employed in most cloud environments to encrypt and authenticate communications. Any component of the hybrid scheme that is quantum vulnerable can potentially undermine the entire security stack. To gain illegitimate access to cloud APIs, services, and data stored, quantum attackers can exploit digital signatures, certificate chains, and cloud authentication tokens as well.

4.2 Implications for Data Integrity, Confidentiality, and Non-Repudiation

The ability to crack encryption is only one aspect of the wider threat landscape. Data integrity and non-repudiation processes, which are based on digital signatures generated by algorithms such as RSA, DSA, and ECDSA, are also under threat from quantum computing. Attackers could generate digital signatures in a quantum-driven threat scenario, which could allow them to impersonate trusted individuals, alter confidential documents, or conduct illicit transactions in cloud-based platforms and IoT environments. This can have severe consequences in multi-tenant cloud environments. Quantum attackers can bypass authentication processes, elevate their privilege, and reach isolated platforms such as virtual machines, databases, and containers if they can generate valid tokens or certificates [10]. This may appear in the form of evil over-the-air updates, illegitimate device control, or sensor data tampering in edge-to-cloud IoT systems, compromising safety across sectors such as industrial automation, autonomous transport, and healthcare. Furthermore, quantum computing compromises the privacy of data that is stored. Even if at present encrypted data may be secure against conventional attackers, once quantum powers develop, it can be decoded in hindsight if it is stored and accessed by an attacker. For highly sensitive information with protracted secrecy needs, such as medical records, government messages, and industrial secret designs, the "harvest now, decrypt later" threat model is particularly concerning.

4.3 Quantum-Accelerated Attacks and Side-Channel Risks

With enhanced processing rates and novel quantum algorithms, quantum computing not only poses a direct threat to cryptography methods but also enhances the effectiveness of other types of cyberattacks. For instance, quantum annealing or variational quantum algorithms may be employed to better solve optimization issues in traffic analysis, malware spread, or intrusion detection system (IDS) evasion. This could substantially enhance the effectiveness of adaptive malware and automated penetration testing. Additionally, quantum machine learning or quantum sensing can enhance side-channel attacks, which exploit the physical characteristics of devices to extract cryptographic secrets [11]. Quantum-aided hardware probing or eavesdropping can become feasible, although this is a theoretical discipline, particularly for IoT devices with poor shielding and no physical access limitations. In addition, quantum attacks may be mounted against blockchain-based systems, often used in cloud and IoT architectures for decentralized identity management and integrity checks. Quantum computing directly threatens the elliptic curve cryptography used in Ethereum, Bitcoin, and various industrial blockchain implementations. Quantum attackers may be able to alter transaction histories or disrupt consensus processes by reversing private keys from public addresses.

4.4 Quantum Threat Timeline and Risk Assessment

Accelerating qubit fidelity, quantum volume, and architect scalability show that pragmatic quantum risks are on the horizon, even though current quantum computers remain in the NISQ era with low coherence and error correction. While there are various views, some experts estimate that within 10–20 years, a cryptographically significant quantum computer (CRQC) could emerge. The period it will take to keep vulnerable systems—which could take ten years or more, especially in complex, legacy-burdened organizations such as manufacturing, national defense, and health—increases the threat. The "pre-emptive threat" is how security professionals categorize this, stating that countermeasures have to be put in place before quantum competitors are actually on the market [12]. Cloud service provider policy, corporate IT blueprints, and national security projects are now integrating quantum risk assessments. Post-quantum cryptography research is being sponsored by governments such as the US, China, and EU members, who are also demanding transition plans for critical infrastructure. It is even more problematic for manufacturers of IoT. Devices with long lifetimes and minimal firmware update capabilities are often used. To prevent future vulnerabilities that are hard to repair once they are deployed, it is crucial that quantum-resistant systems are designed today. Changing to quantum-resilient security is a laborious effort. Though post-quantum cryptography techniques are in the making, they are not yet widely employed or platform-independent. In IoT settings, most quantum-resistant algorithms, particularly lattice- and code-based ones, have considerable cost in key sizes, computation, and communication bandwidth.

For cloud and IoT providers, cryptographic agility—the ability to refresh and replace cryptographic algorithms without fully redesigning the system—is a fundamental prerequisite. But in most existing systems, this modularity does not exist. Hardcoded crypto primitives are widely utilized in firmware stacks, embedded software, cloud APIs, and microservices, making migration troublesome. Rollout schedules become even more complex by the necessity of offering interoperability and backward compatibility with past systems. Key management is yet another challenge. Public key infrastructures (PKIs), certificate authorities, and key lifecycle protocols must all include quantum-resistant key exchange protocols. It is also required to scale safe key distribution and storage to handle bigger keys and emerging verification methods. To make the transition smooth, industry collaboration and standardization also need to happen [13]. The groundwork for standardized, vetted algorithms is being established by initiatives like the ETSI Quantum-Safe Cryptography Working Group and the NIST Post-Quantum Cryptography Project. Yet, integration with IoT operating systems, developer frameworks, and commercial cloud platforms are required to achieve widespread adoption; this is a politically complex and challenging task.

5. Post-Quantum Cryptography (PQC)

The crypto community has had to anticipate and counter the vulnerabilities of conventional techniques such as RSA, ECC, and DSA due to the advent of quantum computers. "Post-quantum cryptography" (PQC) is a term that refers to cryptographic algorithms that can be deployed on classical computing hardware but remain secure against both classical and quantum attackers. PQC is a feasible countermeasure to quantum attacks since it focuses on algorithms that may be realized using existing hardware and communication infrastructure, unlike quantum cryptography, which requires quantum channels. The basic concepts of PQC, its algorithmic divisions, current standardization efforts, implementation challenges, and use in cloud computing and IoT security are all discussed extensively in this section.

5.1 NIST Standardization Efforts

The NIST initiated an international effort to standardize post-quantum cryptography algorithms in acknowledgment of the seriousness of the quantum threat. Identifying algorithms that have good security, computational efficiency, and scalability across a range of applications is the objective. In 2022, after a multi-round competition, NIST announced its first set of candidate algorithms, including CRYSTALS-Dilithium for digital signatures and CRYSTALS-Kyber for key encapsulation mechanisms (KEM). These algorithms' performance, key sizes, ability to resist side-channel attacks, and generalizability across cloud platforms and resource-constrained devices are all being evaluated. Standards were expected to be agreed upon in phases to encourage industry trials and adoption before formal publication [14].

5.2 Key Categories of PQC Algorithms

A number of mathematical families include post-quantum cryptography algorithms, each with special benefits and implementation considerations. Table 11.1 runs through the key categories of PQC algorithms.

Table 11.1 Key categories of PQC algorithms.

Category	*Description*
Lattice-based cryptography	Lattice-based encryption, such as Kyber, Dilithium, and NTRU, depends on the difficulty of challenges like the shortest vector problem (SVP) and learning with errors (LWE). Because of their effectiveness and robust security measures, these programs are among the most promising.
Code-based cryptography	The challenge of decoding random linear codes is used in code-based encryption (such as Classic McEliece). It is well-suited for high-speed applications due to its long public keys and incredibly quick encryption and decryption processes.
Multivariate polynomial cryptography	The security of multivariate polynomial encryption, such as Rainbow, is based on the difficulty of solving multivariate quadratic equation systems. Despite their theoretical strength, many multivariate methods struggle with performance and signature size.
Hash-based signatures	By using collision-resistant hash functions, hash-based signatures (like SPHINCS+) offer security and are especially helpful for producing stateless and audit-compliant digital signatures.
Isogeny-based cryptography	Because of its small key sizes, isogeny-based cryptography (such the now-deprecated SIKE) was previously investigated; however, certain schemes have been cracked, highlighting the significance of thorough screening during standardization.

Each category presents trade-offs between computing burden, key size, and quantum method resilience, making context-aware selection necessary for certain deployment scenarios such as embedded IoT devices or cloud servers.

5.3 Implementation in Cloud Environments

The computational capability, scalability, and central management capabilities of cloud computing infrastructures make them the perfect setting for the early adoption of PQC. Cloud service companies like Google Cloud, AWS, and Microsoft Azure have already started experimenting with post-quantum algorithms in virtual private network (VPN) tunnels, transport layers, and API encryption. The ability to transition between cryptographic algorithms without interfering with services or jeopardizing backward compatibility is the main focus of these implementations [15]. Performance trade-offs are a significant obstacle to cloud deployment. Despite its security, lattice-based algorithms frequently need bigger ciphertexts and key sizes, which can raise latency and resource usage in high-throughput services. Frameworks for safe multiparty computing, load balancing, and key management need to be modified to accommodate PQC-specific characteristics. Furthermore, PQC libraries must be modularly integrated into orchestration layers, continuous integration/continuous and continuous delivery/deployment (CI/CD) pipelines, and containerized applications in cloud-native environments that employ microservices and serverless architectures.

5.4 Integration in IoT Systems

PQC integration is further complicated in IoT systems by an inherent set of constraints. PQC algorithms for the most part need larger keys and heavy arithmetic, which is burdensome for low-processing-power devices with limited memory and energy budgets. Lattice-based approaches, for example, require matrix operations and polynomial multiplications beyond the capability of traditional microcontrollers. Researchers are waiting on hardware accelerators for PQC primitives and lightweight crypto implementations to overcome these challenges. For instance, optimized instances of Dilithium and Kyber have been implemented for ARM Cortex-M processors, which are often employed in IoT devices. Certain approaches utilize edge computing, offloading cryptographic work to neighboring gateways or cloudlets with better computers. Because IoT devices often must communicate through legacy systems and heterogeneous networks, interoperability is another challenge. To allow for both traditional and post-quantum algorithms during a transition period, dual-stack configurations are necessary. To allow devices to advance with cryptographic standards without hardware replacement, firmware update methods must also be secure and post-quantum [16].

While there have been promising advances, there remain a variety of operational and technical barriers to the deployment of PQC. One of the largest issues is the lack of established software libraries and development toolkits that are compatible with post-quantum algorithms on most platforms.

While support for PQC is being integrated into different cryptographic libraries, including OpenSSL, BoringSSL, and liboqs, there has not been significant adoption of this yet. Thorough testing, validation, and interoperability tests must be carried out to ensure compatibility with existing cryptographic protocols such as TLS, IPSec, and S/MIME. Key and certificate management is another significant challenge. Since post-quantum keys tend to be larger in size, they are more expensive to store and transport. Improvements need to be made in public key infrastructures (PKIs) in order to deal with these changes without compromising usability or security. Moreover, during the transition, new cryptographic structures like hybrid certificates that contain classical and post-quantum keys demand certificate authority redesigns, hardware security module (HSM) redesigns, and secure enclaves. Compliance and security audit frameworks also need to be altered. Organizations struggle to evaluate their readiness because regulatory bodies have not issued standard PQC compliance standards yet. Additionally, if not properly employed, certain PQC algorithms, particularly on embedded systems, are prone to side-channel attacks.

To isolate sensitive cryptographic functions, this calls for side-channel resistance testing, secure coding techniques, and may be system architectural modification. Organizations are urged to implement cryptographic agility frameworks, inventory all of their current cryptographic assets, and start testing PQC algorithms in non-critical systems in order to manage the shift from classical to post-quantum cryptography. To guarantee a steady migration path while preserving backward compatibility, hybrid models in which PQC algorithms function alongside traditional algorithms are being suggested. NIST and industry groups like the Cloud Security Alliance (CSA) and the Internet Engineering Task Force (IETF), who are disseminating draft standards and best practices for PQC migration, should be followed by security experts [17]. Furthermore, incorporating quantum-resistant VPNs, zero-trust architectures, and automated key rotation can support the maintenance of security posture both during and after the transition. Because PQC brings new mathematical foundations and implementation intricacies that differ greatly from traditional cryptography, organizations should also spend in staff training and upskilling. Building a robust post-quantum ecosystem also requires establishing quantum-readiness in procurement procedures, revising SLAs, and interacting with vendors.

6. Quantum-Safe Security in Practice

As the threat posed by quantum computing moves from theory to reality, governments and businesses are starting to put quantum-safe security measures into practice. It takes a mix of technological preparedness, ecosystem cooperation, and proactive risk management to implement post-quantum cryptography algorithms and protocols in practice. Pilot programs and proof-of-concept projects have been started by a number of cloud service providers, cybersecurity companies, and hardware manufacturers to test and validate quantum-safe infrastructures [18]. The use of cloud computing platforms is one prominent application area. Large providers like Amazon Web Services (AWS), Microsoft Azure, and Google Cloud have started incorporating post-quantum key encapsulation techniques into TLS 1.3 and other transport layer protocols. These experimental setups frequently make use of hybrid cryptographic models, which combine a quantum-safe alternative (like Kyber or BIKE) with a classical approach (like RSA or ECC). Table 11.2 compares PQC algorithm performance in cloud and IoT Environments. In addition to providing defense against potential decoding attempts by quantum attackers, this dual-layer encryption technique guarantees backward compatibility.

Table 11.2 Performance and deployment suitability of selected post-quantum algorithms in cloud and IoT settings.

Algorithm	*Key Size (bytes)*	*Encryption Time (ms)*	*IoT Suitability*	*Cloud Suitability*
Kyber-512	800	1.2	Moderate	High
Dilithium-2	1,312	3.5	Low	High
SPHINCS+	16,976	22.0	Low	Moderate
Classic McEliece	261,120	0.5	Very low	High

Quantum-safe security techniques are also being piloted by financial sector organizations. Secure transactions, long-term confidentiality, and regulatory compliance are of special importance to banks and fintech businesses. They are therefore experimenting with post-quantum signatures in digital payment platforms, blockchain networks, and interbank communication systems. Numerous financial institutions are collaborating with cryptographic suppliers to provide secure mobile banking apps and quantum-safe APIs that can be implemented gradually [19]. Quantum-safe techniques are also being adopted by the automotive sector, which depends on an expanding network of interconnected IoT devices for vehicle-to-everything (V2X) communication and autonomous driving. Cloud-based telemetry services, over-the-air (OTA) firmware upgrades, and quantum-resistant authentication between car control units are all being supported by expanding automotive security frameworks. Given that connected cars frequently function in safety-critical settings where cryptographic malfunctions could lead to bodily harm or legal infractions, this is crucial.

Even so, there remain a number of technical and operational barriers to the widespread adoption of quantum-safe cryptography systems. Real-time application performance is a critical issue. Low-latency systems, such as high-frequency trading networks or real-time IoT control systems, might be taxed by the common need of post-quantum methods for much larger key sizes and more computing overhead. Where processing efficiency and power are vital in industries like healthcare, manufacturing, and telecommunications, this issue is more acute. Organizations are investing in hardware acceleration methods to reduce these issues. [20] Lattice-based cryptographic processes are being optimized and offloaded to application-specific integrated circuits (ASICs) and field-programmable gate arrays (FPGAs). Lightweight post-quantum algorithm executions on limited microcontrollers, such as the ARM Cortex-M series, are being produced by IoT companies. Additionally, computationally intensive cryptographic operations may be performed at nearby gateways or edge servers instead of endpoint devices due to the increased adoption of edge computing frameworks for task redistribution. Interoperability and compatibility are also significant challenges.

Rewriting base protocol layers is often required to incorporate post-quantum algorithms since most current network protocols and public key infrastructures (PKIs) were designed around classical cryptography. For example, to incorporate hybrid or quantum-only signatures, existing certificate formats (e.g., X.509) must be altered. Moreover, during the transition time, backward compatibility is paramount; systems must be able to fall back to classical cryptography when they interact with legacy clients or hardware [21]. The ability to change cryptographic primitives without having to redesign the system is referred to as cryptographic agility, and it is presently regarded as an inherent architectural requirement. Modular software stacks, flexible security libraries, and ubiquitous cryptographic APIs are all employed to implement this concept. Libraries are also being created by open-source projects such as BoringSSL, liboqs, and OpenQuantumSafe to allow developers to play with and easily integrate post-quantum primitives into existing applications. There are challenges in key management in a quantum-safe environment.

The complexity of safe storage, transmission, and lifecycle management increases with the larger key sizes linked to PQC systems. Protocols for key generation, rotation, and revocation must be modified to accommodate increased entropy sources and longer key lengths. New standards are being included into the redesign ofHSMs and trusted platform modules (TPMs), while PQC support is being added to cloud-based key management services (KMS). Practical implementation tactics are also heavily influenced by policy and regulatory compliance. Figure 11.3 shows a layered diagram showing how hybrid cryptographic protocols (e.g., TLS 1.3 with RSA + Kyber) are deployed in a typical cloud service architecture. Quantum-safe security is starting to be required by governments in critical infrastructure guidelines and procurement laws. The National Security Agency (NSA) of the US, for instance, has released guidelines on the transition to post-quantum encryption for national security systems, stressing the importance of early adoption. In a similar vein, the European Union Agency for Cybersecurity (ENISA) has started projects to evaluate quantum risk in supply chains and public sector services.

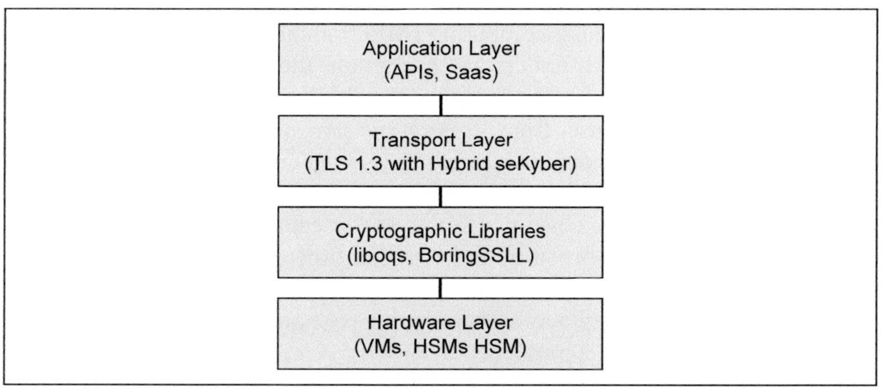

Fig. 11.3 Architecture of hybrid cryptographic deployment in cloud platforms.

Securing telemedicine platforms and safeguarding patient data are of utmost importance in the healthcare industry. Medical device communications, remote diagnostics platforms, and electronic health record (EHR) systems are all evaluating post-quantum security. Some hospital networks have already begun testing hybrid encryption, with the first focus being on protecting genomic data and high-value imaging data that need to be kept confidential for an extended period of time. Municipalities in smart cities are investigating quantum-safe protocols for vital functions including e-governance, traffic management, energy distribution, and public safety. These systems are vulnerable to attacks from the quantum era since they frequently rely on a network of cloud services and IoT devices [22]. Digital signature techniques and post-quantum VPNs are being piloted in power grid management systems and public transit. With the introduction of 5G and beyond, telecommunications companies are getting their infrastructure ready for quantum-safe communication. Table 11.3 summarizes the industry use cases for quantum-safe security.

Table 11.3 Sector-specific quantum-safe security use cases with implementation focus.

Sector	*Use Case*	*Quantum-Safe Implementation*
Healthcare	EHR systems, telemedicine platforms	Hybrid encryption for patient data security
Finance	Secure transactions, blockchain ledgers	PQC APIs, post-quantum digital signatures
Smart Cities	Traffic control, utility grids	Post-quantum VPNs, post-quantum signatures for device authentication
Automotive	V2X, firmware updates	Lightweight PQC in ECUs, OTA signature schemes
Telecommunications	5G security layers	Post-quantum SIM authentication, TLS upgrade

Scalable and effective cryptographic techniques are needed to secure cellular networks' control and user planes. In order to make SIM cards, network slicing frameworks, and mobile edge computing (MEC) architectures compatible with PQC standards, efforts are underway to upgrade the authentication and key exchange protocols. Figure 11.4 (a) shows the timeline of global post-quantum cryptography transition phases from research and standardization to industry-wide adoption. Another crucial topic is blockchain and decentralized systems. Elliptic curve-based cryptographic signatures, which are utilized in Ethereum, Bitcoin, and several corporate blockchain platforms, are susceptible to quantum assaults. In order to provide future-proofing, projects like Ethereum 2.0 and Hyperledger are investigating the merging of hash-based and lattice-based signature systems. In certain instances, programmers are developing post-quantum native blockchains or quantum-resistant layer-2 protocols.

Building quantum-safe infrastructures requires organizations to implement a multi-phase migration approach. Inventorying existing cryptographic assets, evaluating their vulnerability, and determining transition priority regions constitute the initial stage. The performance and compatibility of hybrid cryptography pilot implementations can then be assessed in low-risk settings. These insights eventually guide rollouts across the entire enterprise, aided by standardized APIs and cryptographic agility frameworks. Awareness and training are also crucial. The theoretical foundations and real-world applications of PQC must be understood by developers, security engineers, and compliance officials. Institutions could participate in industry consortia like the NIST PQC Migration Coalition and the Global Quantum Safe Security Working Group, work with academic researchers, and fund upskilling initiatives. Figure 11.4 (b) shows the workflow of quantum-safe communication in an IoT ecosystem using post-quantum key exchange and encryption protocols. In the end, putting quantum-safe security into practice involves a paradigm shift in the way digital trust is created and preserved, not just a technical advancement. Businesses can set themselves up for success in a future where quantum computing is a revolutionary force safely included into the digital ecosystem rather than a threat by investing in strong post-quantum infrastructures now.

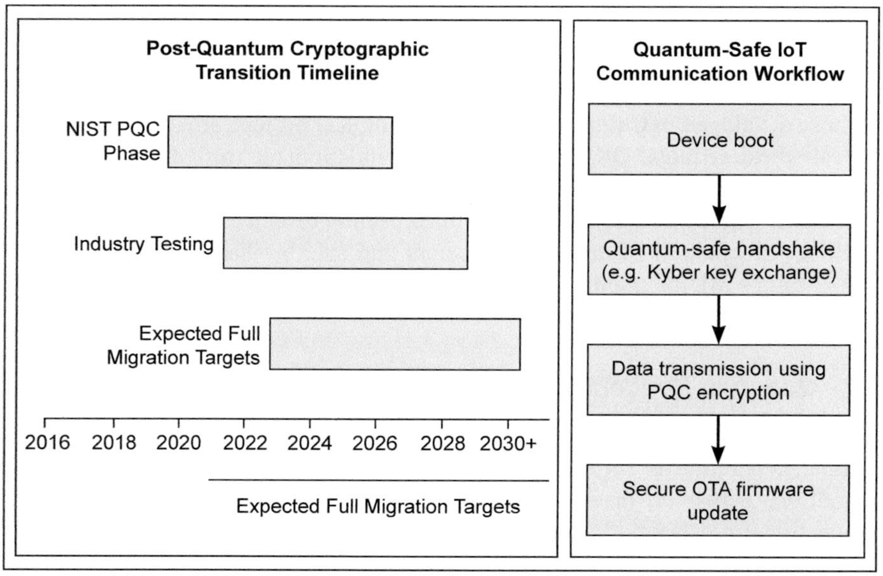

4(a) 4(b)

Figs. 11.4(a) and (b) (a) Timeline of global post-quantum cryptography transition phases from research and standardization to industry-wide adoption. (b) Workflow of quantum-safe communication in an IoT ecosystem using post-quantum key exchange and encryption protocols.

7. Quantum Computing as a Security Enhancer

The capability of quantum computing to break conventional cryptography systems is a significant point of discussion, but it is also important to acknowledge how it could transform cybersecurity. Aside from its destructive capability, quantum computing offers advanced processes that can strengthen the integrity of cryptographic protocols, strengthen digital defense systems, and power advanced threat detection systems. This section discusses how to leverage quantum technologies, i.e., quantum-enhanced machine learning, quantum random number generation, and QKD, for designing secure, future-proof security architectures for cloud and IoT environments.

7.1 Quantum Key Distribution (QKD)

One of the most advanced and effective quantum security technologies available today is quantum key distribution. It creates shared secret keys between two partners based on the concepts of quantum mechanics in such a manner that the presence of eavesdropping will be detected. Key data is encoded via quantum states, typically photons, in QKD protocols such as BB84 and E91. Any attempt to measure or eavesdrop these qubits will disturb their state and become immediately detectable by the quantum no-cloning theorem. Unlike traditional cryptography methods based on computational complexity, QKD provides information-theoretic security. It is thus suitable for highly sensitive communication, such as financial, military, and government exchanges. Quantum-secure urban fiber networks, such as those developed in China and the EU's OpenQKD project, are deploying QKD in real-world settings. QKD could be the foundation for trusted key exchange layers between critical infrastructure endpoints or inter-data center VPNs for cloud data centers and IoT backhaul links. While cost and distance limitations continue to exist, the creation of quantum repeaters and satellite-based QKD platforms (e.g., China's Micius satellite) suggests that global quantum key exchange could be possible within the next decade.

7.2 Quantum Random Number Generators (QRNG)

A fundamental component of all contemporary cryptography systems, random number generation is employed in protocol entropy, nonce selection, and key formation. However, in embedded IoT systems with weak entropy sources, conventional pseudo-random number generators (PRNGs) may be susceptible to state prediction or reverse engineering. True randomness is produced by quantum random number generators (QRNGs), which leverage intrinsically unpredictable quantum phenomena like photon arrival times or quantum vacuum fluctuations. Commercially available QRNG devices are already being included into routers, authentication tokens, and security hardware modules. To ensure increased cryptographic strength for big multi-tenant platforms, QRNGs can be utilized to feed secure entropy pools for large-scale key generation in cloud environments.

Compact and low-power QRNG circuits are being created for IoT devices in order to provide safe pairing, session initiation, and tokenization procedures without the dangers of deterministic PRNGs. Since entropy-driven decision-making improves the unpredictability and dependability of trust assignments, QRNG implementation is especially important in zero-trust architectures and multi-factor authentication systems.

7.3 Quantum-Enhanced Machine Learning for Threat Detection

Machine learning (ML) plays an increasingly central role in cybersecurity for real-time risk scoring, anomaly detection, and intrusion detection. Processing complex, high-dimensional datasets, though, is a problem for traditional machine learning algorithms, especially in cloud-IoT environments where telemetry data is large, noisy, and dynamic. Quantum machine learning (QML) introduces new threat analysis and categorization approaches. Techniques such as quantum kernel estimation, quantum support vector machines, and variational quantum classifiers are under investigation for application in behavioral analytics, malware detection, and fraud prevention. In comparison to classical models, these quantum models can identify patterns more expressively because they can operate in exponentially larger Hilbert spaces. Quantum-enhanced graph networks and quantum Boltzmann machines applied to real-time event correlation across the scattered edge nodes of an IoT security platform is one such potential area. These models can detect stealthy attacks (e.g., slow-moving APTs), infer complex temporal patterns, and rapidly adapt to evolving threat vectors. Quantum cloud infrastructure (like IBM Quantum and Google's Cirq-based simulators) are facilitating early experimentation with hybrid quantum–classical models, even though QML remains experimental. For many classification and anomaly detection workflows, these hybrid implementations based on NISQ hardware already surpass common baselines.

7.4 Quantum-Safe Blockchain and Identity Management

Technologies such as blockchain and distributed identity management may be helped by quantum computing. For future blockchains, researchers are working on quantum-safe consensus algorithms and quantum-resistant primitives, even though traditional blockchain algorithms (such as ECDSA) can be broken by Shor's algorithm. Quantum-improved ledgers may utilize quantum hashes for improved collision resistance and QKD-protected channels for transmitting transactions. In addition, post-quantum security can be obtained while maintaining verifiability and transparency through the combination of quantum signatures, such as those derived from hash trees or lattice-based solutions. Quantum technologies make it possible to have verifiable credentials in decentralized identity (DID) systems that are resistant to deep impersonation, theft, and tampering [23]. For example, QKD-secured APIs could be employed to authenticate biometric authentication tokens generated with quantum-derived entropy. In identity-based cloud environments and IoT networks, where federation protocols, permissioned access, and secure onboarding need to operate at scale without diminishing trust, these are vital areas.

7.5 Strategic Value in Resilient Architectures

Integration of quantum-improved capabilities into cybersecurity systems is a strategic resilience initiative as well as a technical innovation. Governments and global businesses are investing on blueprints for quantum-safe infrastructure with an eye to sustaining operations during and after quantum transition periods. For critical sectors such as defense, healthcare, aviation, and energy, hybrid defensive structures that incorporate classical, post-quantum, and quantum-native mechanisms are being developed. In reality, this could involve implementing quantum-enhanced authentication techniques across cloud identity providers, implementing quantum-safe HSMs, and key generation through QRNGs. In the near future, plug-ins for quantum-aware security information and event management (SIEM) systems could be implemented to incorporate QML models and improve automated response, log parsing, and threat prediction. Furthermore, the paradigm of quantum cloud enables unprecedented high-assurance, real-time, and scalable cryptographic operations through on-demand quantum computing with capabilities from platforms such as Microsoft Azure Quantum and Amazon Braket. This transforms the way "security at scale" is perceived by enterprises and opens up for quantum-fortified security services as a SaaS or PaaS solution.

8. Challenges and Limitations

While quantum computing holds revolutionary promise to enhance cybersecurity, it also presents many technological, infrastructure, and legislative issues that must be addressed before it can be widely integrated into cloud and IoT environments. The many barriers to adoption are analyzed in this section, such as the constraints of current hardware, algorithm immaturity, scalability in deployment, and the ethical dimensions of quantum-resilient security features. Physical implementation of quantum systems is one of the largest challenges of the quantum computing domain. With extremely few qubits and large error rates, present quantum machinery operates within the NISQ regime. Qubit states decay slowly because of decoherence, which is caused by external interference such as electromagnetic noise, thermal noise, and even cosmic radiation. Quantum systems need to operate in very controlled environments, often requiring cryogenic temperatures close to absolute zero, in order to maintain quantum coherence. Deployment is limited to big cloud data centers or specialized labs due to the expense and energy needs of the equipment necessary to maintain such conditions. In addition, no dominant scalable architecture has developed for the present-day qubit technologies, which are superconducting qubits, trapped ions, and photonics. These technologies continue to develop rapidly. These physical limitations affect the feasibility of using quantum-enhanced cryptography solutions in real-time applications. IoT systems that need low-latency and energy-efficient security operations, for instance, will discover that the latency introduced by remote quantum computation and error correction becomes unacceptable.

Despite the emergence of promising quantum and post-quantum algorithms, several are still being evaluated for side-channel resistance, performance consistency, and security robustness. Numerous attack vectors are being examined in relation to post-quantum algorithms, especially those being assessed by the NIST standardization process. The significance of cryptanalysis prior to full deployment was highlighted by the evaluation rounds, which saw the breaking of several contenders (such as Rainbow and SIKE). Furthermore, there are not many well-developed standardized toolkits or developer-friendly libraries that make it possible to integrate these algorithms into current systems in a safe and effective manner. Widespread integration delays and developer reluctance are caused by inconsistent library implementations, a lack of thoroughly verified APIs, and the dynamic nature of algorithm parameters [24]. Limited hardware access, simulator limitations, and the lack of formal complexity classifications equivalent to conventional algorithms further complicate algorithmic benchmarking for quantum-enhanced algorithms, such as quantum machine learning models or quantum-assisted key generation.

Putting into effect quantum-resistant algorithms on low-resourced IoT devices may be challenging in that they typically require larger key sizes, additional memory, and additional computational overhead. Code-based encryption and hash-based signature schemes, for example, could result in certificate sizes well beyond the current network's maximum transmission unit (MTU) sizes, leading to packet fragmentation and retransmission overhead. Post-quantum cryptography adoption demands enhancements in data storage formats, authentication protocols, and network protocols even in cloud environments. New formats for key exchange, for example, call for modifications to TLS, SSH, and IPsec. For PKI to deal with hybrid certificates and novel key management schemes, heavy redesigns are needed [14]. In addition, backward compatibility remains an issue. Interoperability is a significant challenge in hybrid systems with nodes that do support post-quantum security and those that do not. Perhaps the old firmware and hardware cannot be upgraded, and one has to rely on complete replacement cycles or phased migration. Cryptographic agility, which is the ability to dynamically exchange cryptographic algorithms without system redesign, is not an attribute of most present-day software and hardware implementations. Long upgrade windows, exposure of vulnerabilities during transition, and increased maintenance expenditures are all consequences of rigidity.

To avoid this, systems must have modular designs that facilitate plug-and-play cryptography, which allows developers to switch keys or algorithms without interruption. Adoption of algorithm-agnostic cryptographic APIs and IETF's hybrid public key encryption (HPKE) initiatives are yet to take off and have not been standardized across various industry sectors. Several ethical and regulatory concerns are also generated by the use of quantum-secure systems.

First, in anticipation of cross-border quantum key exchanges and satellite-based QKD, data sovereignty legislation that governs where and under what conditions data is to be stored and transferred has to be modified. Quantum-resilient security practices must also be included in compliance guidelines such as GDPR, HIPAA, and ISO/IEC 27001. Furthermore, lack of cybersecurity parity might be caused by a centralization of security skills among technologically advanced nations or entities because of unequal access to quantum technology.

To create open standards, exchange research, and avoid monopolizing vital quantum security infrastructure, governments and international organizations will need to work together. Concerns have also been raised about quantum technologies' dual-purpose nature. They can shield authorized users, but they can also provide enemies, autocratic governments, and cybercriminals more control [21]. Security governance will increasingly include responsible disclosure of quantum vulnerabilities, audit transparency of QML choices, and ethical management of quantum key material. The lack of qualified experts who can create, implement, and maintain quantum-safe security solutions is one of the more underappreciated issues. Secure software development, cryptography engineering, and quantum physics expertise are still comparatively uncommon. Organizations may thus find it difficult to assemble teams for cross-disciplinary research, PQC migration, and quantum system integration. Though the pipeline is still too small to satisfy anticipated demand, academic institutions and industry partnerships are starting to provide quantum-focused education courses, certifications, and training programs. Even the most cutting-edge quantum technologies will have operational inefficiencies and adoption delays if this manpower gap is not addressed.

9. Future Trends

Over the next ten years, cybersecurity is expected to undergo a dramatic transformation due to the development of quantum computing. Even if defensive tactics and quantum threats have dominated much of the discussion thus far, emerging trends point to a more complex and revolutionary direction. It is anticipated that quantum technologies will actively contribute to developing a secure-by-design paradigm in cloud and IoT systems, rethinking trust structures, enabling intelligent automation, and hardening security. The most exciting developments in the future of the confluence of cloud security, IoT infrastructures, and quantum computing are described in this section.

9.1 Transition to Quantum-Resilient Infrastructures

The most eagerly awaited trend is the extensive adoption of quantum-resilient infrastructures. Companies will be moving in larger numbers to hybrid cryptographic protocols that use classical and quantum-safe algorithms once the post-quantum cryptography standards of NIST are complete, which is expected to occur sometime between 2024 and 2025. PQC-enabled VPN and TLS protocols are already being tested in production by large cloud providers. A three-layered model is expected for phased migration: (i) Hybrid cryptography is being evaluated in regulated cloud environments in the pilot phase (2023–2025). (ii) The adoption phase (2025–2030) will involve integration of PQC with firmware, network protocols, and PKIs in cloud and edge platforms. (iii) The full deployment phase (after 2030) is aimed at the development of native quantum-secure stacks and displacement of vulnerable classical algorithms. Quantum-compatible microcontrollers that are optimized for low-power PQC operations will increasingly be integrated by IoT makers into devices that span from smart meters to driverless vehicles.

9.2 Emergence of Quantum Security-as-a-Service (QSaaS)

The demand for QSaaS platforms will grow alongside the development of cloud-native applications. Such platforms, through APIs in the cloud, will offer scalable access to quantum-enriched authentication modules, quantum entropy pools, and QKD. Endorsement at all times and quantum-safe code signing may become feasible by integrating such services with multi-cloud DevSecOps pipelines. Identity as a service (IDaaS) platforms will also feature quantum identity management systems with zero-knowledge proofs and verifiable credentials. Quantum machine learning-based threat intelligence, including probabilistic risk scoring, deep anomaly detection, and behavioral analytics, might also be supported by QSaaS providers in IoT ecosystems.

9.3 Advancements in Quantum Networking

There will be significant developments in quantum networks, which are specialized infrastructures intended to send quantum information (qubits) over great distances. Major-scale QKD deployments, secure inter-data center communication, and even quantum internet prototypes will be made possible thanks in a major part to these networks. Among the upcoming trends are quantum repeaters that increase the range of QKD beyond the size of cities and QKD constellations based on satellites, which allow for safe international key transfers [22]. Another trend is quantum routers and firewalls for controlling entangled communications and protecting against quantum DoS attacks. Hybrid classical–quantum networking stacks will appear as quantum networks develop, necessitating the development of new security auditing models, protocols, and standards (such as QNET and QTLS).

9.4 Quantum-Enhanced AI for Autonomous Defense

Through quantum-enhanced AI, autonomous defense systems will be powered more and more by quantum computing. Quantum-assisted models will be used by future security operations centers (SOCs) to evaluate telemetry quickly, detect zero-day attacks, and automate countermeasures. Security orchestration, automation, and response (SOAR) platforms will incorporate cutting-edge quantum machine learning techniques like quantum generative models for modeling attack patterns, quantum Boltzmann machines for predicting threat landscapes, and variational quantum algorithms for adaptive firewall tuning. These will have a particularly significant effect on the real-time protection of vital infrastructure provided by the IoT, such as autonomous transportation systems and smart grids.

9.5 Integration into Secure-by-Design Architectures

Instead of being added to already-existing systems, quantum technologies will be incorporated into safe architectures from the beginning. Post-quantum cryptographic hardware modules at the chip level, quantum-secure firmware supply chains and secure boot procedures, and blockchain-integrated QKD modules enabling unchangeable audit trails are some examples of how safe-by-design principles may develop. The growing focus on cyber resilience in international regulatory frameworks will propel this transition, leading cloud providers and manufacturers to include quantum-readiness in their compliance assessments.

9.6 Regulatory and Standardization Developments

Rapid modifications will be made to the worldwide regulatory environment to conform to the demands of quantum security. Formal rules for post-quantum cryptography integration from NIST, ETSI, and ISO/IEC are among the anticipated advancements. Regulations are required for the use of PQC in the critical infrastructure sectors of the country. International frameworks such as GDPR, HIPAA, and PCI DSS should be updated to incorporate clauses pertaining to quantum-safe data management. Similar to nuclear non-proliferation agreements, international quantum treaties may eventually be developed to regulate the moral application of quantum technology and avoid monopolization [9].

9.7 Ethical and Socioeconomic Considerations

Ethical and societal issues will become more prominent as quantum security systems advance. If left unchecked, quantum-enhanced surveillance could result in previously unheard-of privacy violations. The development of privacy-preserving quantum protocols, such as blind quantum computation and quantum differential privacy, will be vital to ensure democratic use. The unequal distribution of quantum capabilities around the world may also present socioeconomic difficulties. Multilateral funding initiatives like QKD-for-Development Initiatives and Quantum Internet Alliances will be crucial in democratizing access to quantum cybersecurity technology in order to avoid a global security divide. A diversified workforce with quantum literacy will also need to be developed. To prepare the next generation of quantum security specialists, governments, cloud providers, and universities will work together to provide micro-credentials, industry internships, and quantum training programs.

10. Conclusion

Quantum computing will fundamentally change cybersecurity, especially in cloud infrastructure and IoT ecosystems,. While theoretical foundations of quantum mechanics have long indicated computational advantages, tangible progress has only recently begun to influence the discourse of cybersecurity. The intrinsic duality of quantum computing—both a revolutionary facilitator and a disruptive menace, as well as its many implications for cloud security and IoT networks have been investigated in this chapter. For current public key cryptosystems such as RSA, ECC, and DSA, the intrinsic potential of quantum computing, specifically with regard to Shor's and Grover's algorithms, poses existential risks. These vulnerabilities affect the digital signatures, encrypted storage systems, and secure communication protocols that underpin both decentralized IoT architectures and centralized cloud infrastructures directly. The consequence is that the transition to PQC standards and quantum-resilient infrastructures is imperative. We examined the way in which cloud and IoT security models are being deployed today, noting that they rely on quantum-vulnerable-to-attack cryptographic primitives by their nature. Though secure protocols such as TLS, IPsec, and SSH are good enough in providing robust protection against conventional attackers, they fall short in an attack landscape enabled by quantum technology. Moreover, the challenges with firmware updates, key management, and protocol homogeneity place IoT ecosystems with their resource-constrained devices and high heterogeneity in further risk. Post-quantum cryptography is thus a possible and future-proof answer in consideration of this.

PQC schemes have demonstrated promising resistance to quantum attacks, particularly lattice-based approaches such as Dilithium and Kyber. Lack of cryptographic agility in traditional systems, increased key sizes, and integration overhead are some of the major challenges involved with adopting such new standards. To enable broader adoption, practical implementation hurdles from backward compatibility to hardware constraints need to be systematically addressed. The chapter examined quantum-safe methods such as sector-specific application scenarios, hybrid encryption paradigms, and cryptographic agility architectures alongside the deployment of PQC. While it is yet in its initial stages, QKD leverages the principles of quantum entanglement and no-cloning to offer a new way of secure communication. In addition, the concept of QSaaS, which offers dynamic and scalable quantum-resilient solutions via API-enabled platforms, is a new wave in cloud-native security. Of key importance, the chapter also highlighted the prospective security advantages of quantum computing. New paths to proactive cybersecurity defense are opened through secure multiparty computation protocols, smart threat detection systems, and quantum-boosted machine learning models. These advances keep in step with the post-classical age's overall trajectory toward zero-trust networks, security-by-design architectures, and autonomous security functions. However, quantum technologies have a number of downsides. Hardware maturity, algorithmic instability, deployment complexity, and socio-technical constraints remain significant barriers.

While technology advances, concerns such as global control, unequal access, and misuse of surveillance also have to be confronted. Organizational readiness is further challenged by the lack of trained professionals in areas of quantum, and thus there is a need for workforce development and educational transformation. In the future, the implementation of quantum technology is likely to advance in phases, from pilot testing and hybrid integrations to large-scale deployment and enforcement underpinned by regulations. The quantum resilience roadmap will be heavily influenced by regional cybersecurity standards and international standardization efforts by NIST, ETSI, and ISO/IEC. In the meantime, the future generation of secure innovation will be defined by AI-powered quantum defenses, satellite-foundation QKD networks, and quantum networking infrastructure.

References

[1] Akter, S., Badhon, M.B., Bhuiyan, M.K.I., Hasan, H.M., Akter, F. and Islam, M.N.U. "Quantum-edge cloud computing for IoT: Bridging the gap between cloud, edge, and quantum technologies," *Advances in Internet of Things*, vol. 14, no. 10, pp. 99–120, 2024.

[2] Alluhaibi, R. "Quantum machine learning for advanced threat detection in cybersecurity," *International Journal of Safety & Security Engineering*, vol. 14, no. 3, 2024.

[3] Shaller, A., Zamir, L. and Nojoumian, M. "Roadmap of post-quantum cryptography standardization: Side-channel attacks and countermeasures," *Information and Computation*, vol. 295, Part B, 2023, https://doi.org/10.1016/j.ic.2023.105112.

[4] Arute, F., Arya, K., Babbush, R., et al. "Quantum supremacy using a programmable superconducting processor," *Nature*, vol. 574, no. 7779, pp. 505–510, 2020, https://doi.org/10.1038/s41586-019-1666-5.

[5] Bruno, L. and Spano, I. "Post-quantum encryption and privacy regulation: Can the law keep pace with technology?" *The European Journal of Privacy Law & Technology*, vol. 72, 2021.

[6] Chen, L., Jordan, S., Liu, Y.K., et al. *Report on Post-Quantum Cryptography* (Vol. 12), Gaithersburg, USA: US Department of Commerce, National Institute of Standards and Technology, 2016.

[7] Cuomo, D., Caleffi, M. and Cacciapuoti, A.S. "Towards a distributed quantum computing ecosystem," *IET Quantum Communication*, vol. 1, no. 1, pp. 3–8.

[8] Dilruba, R.A. "Quantum-safe switch-controller communication in software-defined network," 2017. DOI: 10.1109/CNS56114.2022.9947245.

[9] Gharavi, H., Granjal, J. and Monteiro, E. "Post-quantum blockchain security for the internet of things: Survey and research directions," *IEEE Communications Surveys & Tutorials*, vol. 26, no. 3, pp. 1748–1774, 2024.

[10] Ghosal, A., Halder, S. and Chessa, S. "Secure key design approaches using entropy harvesting in wireless sensor network: A survey," *Journal of Network and Computer Applications*, vol. 78, pp. 216–230, 2017.

[11] Green, A., Lawrence, J., Siopsis, G., Peters, N.A. and Passian, A. "Quantum key distribution for critical infrastructures: Towards cyber-physical security for hydropower and dams," *Sensors*, vol. 23, no. 24, p. 9818, 2023, https://doi.org/10.3390/s23249818.

[12] Hossain, M.I., Sumon, S.A., Hasan, H.M., Akter, F., Badhon, M.B. and Islam, M.N.U. "Quantum-edge cloud computing: A future paradigm for IoT applications," 2024, *arXiv preprint*, arXiv:2405.04824.

[13] Madhloom, J.K., Ali, H.N.A., Hasan, H.A., Hassen, O.A. and Darwish, S.M. "A quantum-inspired ant colony optimization approach for exploring routing gateways in mobile ad hoc networks," *Electronics*, vol. 12, no. 5, p. 1171, 2023.

[14] Mahdi, L.H. and Abdullah, A.A. "A hybrid post-quantum cryptographic framework integrating Kyber-512 and ASCON for secure IoT communications", *Engineering, Technology & Applied Science Research*, vol. 15, no. 5, pp. 26527–26533, 2025.

[15] Li, S., Chen, Y., Chen, L., Liao, J., Kuang, C., Li, K., Liang, W., and Xiong, N. "Post-quantum security: Opportunities and challenges," *Sensors*, vol. 23, no. 21, p. 8744, https://doi.org/10.3390/s23218744.

[16] Sosnowski, M., Wiedner, F., Hauser, E., Steger, L., Schoinianakis, D., Gallenmüller, S. and Carle, G. "The performance of post-quantum TLS 1.3," in *Companion of the 19th International Conference on Emerging Networking Experiments and Technologies*, CoNEXT 2023, New York, USA: Association for Computing Machinery, pp. 19–27, 2023.

[17] Mahdi, L.H. and Abdullah, A. "Fortifying future IoT security: A comprehensive review on lightweight post-quantum cryptography," *Engineering, Technology & Applied Science Research*, vol. 15, no. 2, pp. 21812–21821, https://doi.org/10.48084/etasr.10141.

[18] Mahmood, S., Hasan, R., Yahaya, N.A., Hussain, S. and Hussain, M. "Evaluation of the Omni-secure firewall system in a private cloud environment," *Knowledge*, vol. 4, no. 2, pp. 141–170.

[19] Manda, J.K. "Quantum-safe cryptography for telecom networks: Implementing post-quantum cryptography solutions to protect telecom networks against future quantum computing threats," June 20, 2024. Available at SSRN: https://ssrn.com/abstract=5136797 or http://dx.doi.org/10.2139/ssrn.5136797.

[20] Padmanaban, H. "Quantum computing and AI in the cloud," *Journal of Computational Intelligence and Robotics*, vol. 4, no. 1, pp. 14–32, 2024.

[21] Schöffel, M., Lauer, F., Rheinländer, C.C. and Wehn, N. "Secure IoT in the era of quantum computers—Where are the bottlenecks?" *Sensors*, vol. 22, no. 7, p. 2484, 2022, https://doi.org/10.3390/s22072484.

[22] Sheikh, A.M., Islam, M.R., Habaebi, M.H., Zabidi, S.A., Bin Najeeb, A.R. and Kabbani, A. "A survey on edge computing (EC) security challenges: Classification, threats, and mitigation strategies," *Future Internet*, vol. 17, no. 4, p. 175, 2025, https://doi.org/10.3390/fi17040175.

[23] Singh, A. "Integrating quantum computing with AI for advanced cryptographic security", February 20, 2025. Available at SSRN: https://ssrn.com/abstract=5155225 or http://dx.doi.org/10.2139/ssrn.5155225.

[24] Wheatley, M.C. "Quantum shifts: The societal implications of quantum computing on security, privacy, and the economy," *Journal of Computer Science*, vol. 1, p. 100002, 2024.

12 Application of Quantum Machine Learning in Goods and Services Tax: Toward Better Compliance and Fraud Detection

Aliasgar Abbasbhai Vohra[1*] and Rakesh Kumar S. Manjhi[2]

Quantum machine learning (QML) integrates quantum computing and artificial intelligence in such a way that it simplifies Goods and Services Tax (GST) administration and compliance. Though QML is in early research stages, it is ready to address complex challenges in tax fraud detection, data analysis, compliance monitoring, and revenue optimization through its never-before-seen ability to do complex calculations. QML makes the GST administration and compliance much more concise and simpler. The modern GST system faces challenges due to a lack of scale, complexity, and the risk of fraud in massive transactions. Quantum computing, along with advanced machine learning, aids in real-time analysis of a transaction, along with on-the-spot detection of fraud. This chapter reveals the revolution that would be brought by quantum computing in GST, along with the limitations it possesses.

1. Introduction

The Goods and Services Tax (GST) is one of the most popular value-added indirect tax systems across the globe. The mix of quantum computing and machine learning, which people call quantum machine learning (QML), is shaping up to be the next big thing in tech, especially for fields like tax that deal with tons of data. India's GST setup is one of the largest tax changes globally, but utilizing QML here is still relatively new. Most of what you read talks about the basics and what might be possible down the line, not so much what is happening right now.

[1] Assistant Professor, Department of Accounting and Financial Management, Faculty of Commerce, The Maharaja Sayajirao University of Baroda, Vadodara, India.
ORCID ID: 0009-0005-4460-5153

[2] Assistant Professor, Department of Accounting and Financial Management, Faculty of Commerce, The Maharaja Sayajirao University of Baroda, Vadodara, India.
ORCID ID: 0009-0000-6307-1269
E-mail: aliasgarvohra4@gmail.com[1]; rakeshkumar.m-afm@msubaroda.ac.in[2]

* Corresponding author: aliasgar.vohara-afm@msubaroda.ac.in

DOI: 10.1201/9781003646068-12

Still, with numerous transactions, complex supply chains, and new methods people use to game the system, there is a real need for improved tools. Regular machine learning has already made a dent in spotting fraud and keeping things compliant, but quantum computing could take things further. It uses ideas like superposition and entanglement to crunch numbers way faster and uncover patterns we might not even know to look for. Governments everywhere are putting serious money into quantum tech—over $30 billion in public funding just in 2022. So it is not some far-off idea. People are really betting on this stuff [1].

These days, it feels like everyone is talking about using new tech in government work, especially when it comes to taxes. QML sounds like it could be a game changer for catching tax fraud and making the whole system run smoother. But honestly, we are not quite there yet.

Right now, quantum computers just are not powerful enough to handle the huge amounts of data tax agencies deal with. They are still pretty error prone and kind of messy. And while some of the algorithms look good on paper, like quantum neural networks, we have not really tested them with real tax information yet.

Right now, quantum computers like quantum neural networks (QNNs) and quantum support vector classifiers (QSVCs) look good on paper, but are just not powerful enough to handle the huge amounts of data tax agencies deal with.

Another big issue is getting our hands on good data. Tax records are super private and often scattered across different systems, so it is tough to pull together what we would need to make this work.

Even if we had all the data, trying to fit QML models into current tax systems is a real headache. Those systems are usually built on old, clunky infrastructure that was not designed for this kind of tech. And honestly, QML models can be pretty hard to wrap your head around—regulators and auditors are not exactly thrilled about trusting something they cannot easily understand.

What we really need is for researchers to focus on building hybrid systems that mix quantum and classical computing, work on better error correction, and create standard datasets and testing tools. Making these models more explainable would help a lot too. But maybe the biggest thing is getting people from different fields—tax professionals, data scientists, regulators, and quantum engineers—to actually work together. That way, we can build solutions that are not just smart on paper, but actually work in the real world and meet legal standards. In short, for QML to truly benefit the tax sector, we must tackle technical, legal, and operational challenges all at once.

2. Concept and Significance of GST

Indirect taxes are taxes collected by intermediaries—such as manufacturers, retailers, or service providers—on the sale of goods or services and then passed on to the government. The end consumer bears the final tax burden through higher prices, rather than directly paying to the government. Common forms of indirect taxes include sales tax, value added tax (VAT), excise duty, and, significantly, GST [2] [3].

The GST represents a major tax reform, subsuming a multitude of previous indirect taxes (VAT, excise, service tax) to create a unified, transparent national market. Its primary purposes are as follows:

- To eliminate the cascading effect of multiple taxes.
- To ensure seamless flow of input tax credits across goods and services.
- To streamline compliance and tax administration, enabling "One Nation, One Tax" [2] [3] [4].

3. Complexities of the GST System

The GST regime, while unified, can become highly complex for the following reasons.

3.1 Varying Tax Rates

GST in India follows a multi-tiered structure: slabs of 5 percent, 12 percent, 18 percent, and 28 percent, with special rates or exemptions for select goods and services. Some goods/services are zero-rated (like exports), nil-rated, or exempt, each with different compliance rules [5]. The new GST 2.0 is simplifying things with four main tax rates. Things like food, healthcare, and education will not be taxed at all. Everyday items like groceries, personal care products, and farm supplies will have a 5 percent rate. Then there is an 18 percent bracket for things like appliances, electronics, cars, and building materials. And the sin product or luxury items—think tobacco, sugary drinks, fancy cars—will be hit with a 40 percent tax. This GST 2.0 will come into effect from **September 22, 2025**.

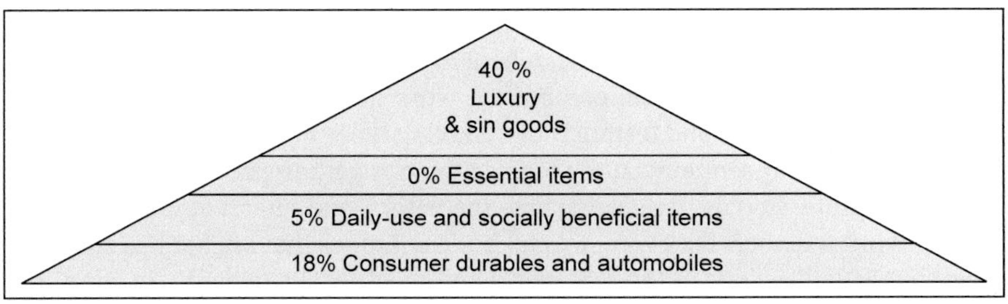

Fig. 12.1 GST 2.0: New structure.
Source: [6].

3.2 Exemptions and Thresholds

Several categories of essential goods and services (basic food items, healthcare, education) are exempted to promote welfare and affordability. Businesses must carefully identify exemptions, as incorrect classification leads to compliance issues [7].

3.3 Compliance Requirements

Businesses must obtain GST registration if their turnover exceeds defined thresholds (generally ₹4 million for goods, ₹2 million for services, and lower for specific states).

Compliance involves the following:

- Periodic returns (monthly, quarterly, annual) and reconciliation.
- Maintenance of detailed records of transactions, invoices, and tax credits.
- Adherence to strict timelines to avoid penalties.
- Usage of electronic mechanisms (e-invoicing, e-way bills) for transparency and tracking [8] [9].

3.4 Geographic and Sectoral Nuances

India employs CGST, SGST, and IGST across intra- and inter-state supply chains, further complicating compliance, reporting, and the utilization of tax credits.

Varying legal interpretations and administrative rules between states introduce additional complexity.

4. Challenges in Optimizing GST Collection and Preventing Fraud

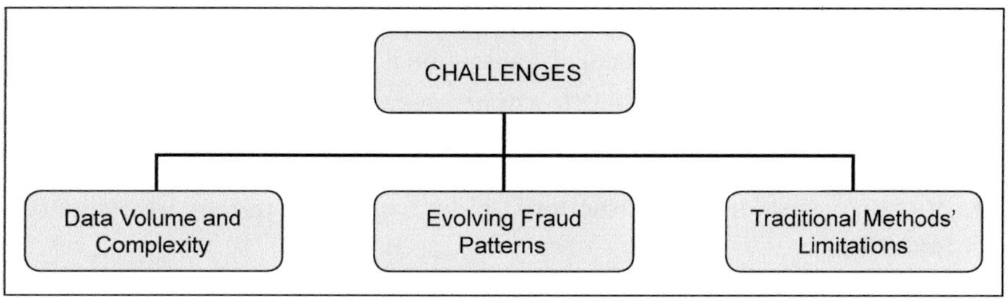

Fig. 12.2 Challenges in optimizing GST collection and preventing fraud.

4.1 Data Volume and Complexity

The GST system processes millions of transactions daily. Each transaction may involve multiple parties, goods/services subject to different tax rates, and cross-state movement, generating an enormous volume of data.

4.2 Evolving Fraud Patterns

Fraudsters exploit the complexity and digital nature of GST through the following:

- Fictitious or duplicate registrations.
- Generation and circulation of fake invoices to claim fraudulent input tax credits.

- Under-reporting or misreporting of sales.
- Misclassification of goods/services to lower tax rates or gain exemptions.
- Abuse of e-way bill provisions by routing through unchecked channels (like manual carts instead of vehicles that require registration).

4.3 Traditional Methods' Limitations

Traditionally, fraud detection relied on manual audits and inspections, which have the following characteristics:

- Labor-intensive and slow.
- Ill-suited to handle current data scale and transaction complexity.
- Not adaptive to fast-evolving fraud modalities, such as algorithmically generated fake invoices.
- Prone to missing subtle, high-volume fraud patterns and lacking real-time detection capabilities.
- Need for advanced solutions.

5. The Inadequacy of Traditional Methods

Manual approaches fail to keep pace with the volume and sophistication of GST fraud. Studies document how rule-based or random audit checks are routinely outperformed in accuracy and efficiency by machine learning (ML) models. ML can do the following:

- Analyze large, high-dimensional transactional datasets to identify anomalies and emerging types of fraud [9].
- Continuously adapt to new fraud strategies, learning from labelled and unlabelled data.
- Prioritize suspicious transactions, aiding efficient use of investigative resources.
- Identify concealed or previously unknown fraudulent patterns that would escape manual scrutiny.

Empirical research consistently finds that ML/AI-based systems achieve higher detection rates, particularly in the identification of irregular input tax credit claims, circular trading, and invoice forgery. However, the following challenges remain:

- Need for high-quality, timely, and labelled data to train effective models.
- Integration of these technologies with existing regulatory and administrative frameworks.
- Ongoing research into hybrid models (combining supervised and unsupervised learning), real-world system vulnerabilities, and interpretability challenges for regulatory acceptance.

6. Literature Review

Fatunmbi [10] explored how QML could enhance fraud detection in fintech. This study critiqued the limitations of traditional ML in processing high-dimensional, complex transaction data and proposed QML models like quantum support vector machines (QSVM), quantum principal component analysis (QPCA), and QNNs as advanced alternatives. Although the research did not use real-world data, it drew on case studies and existing implementations to demonstrate QML's potential. Hybrid quantum–classical systems, quantum data encoding, and QRAM were discussed as tools for improving speed, accuracy, and efficiency in identifying rare and sophisticated fraud patterns. While technical and regulatory challenges remained, the study concluded that QML held significant promise for building adaptive, secure, and future-ready fraud detection systems in fintech [10].

Sharma and Garg [11] employed a mixed-methods approach, integrating qualitative insights with quantitative validation through a one-way analysis of variance (ANOVA) test, to assess the impact of AI on fraud reduction from 2018 to 2023. Important points included automated invoice reconciliation, predictive analytics for risk profiling, graph-based detection of shell companies and circular trading, and natural language-based assistance for taxpayers. The statistical analysis, based on secondary data sourced from credible government publications and Goods and Services Tax Network (GSTN) reports, revealed a significant reduction in GST fraud post-AI implementation, supported by an F-statistic of 12.31 and a p-value of 0.0247. AI tools, including machine learning and natural language processing, had effectively addressed compliance gaps, reduced manual effort, and enabled real-time monitoring. However, the paper also acknowledged the associated ethical and operational risks such as data privacy violations, algorithmic bias, legal admissibility concerns, and the necessity for transparent governance frameworks. So the study basically found that using AI for GST has definitely helped catch fraud and made things run more smoothly. But it also pointed out that we cannot just rush into it. We really need to take it slow, make sure everything is fair and easy to check, and keep people in the loop. That is the only way it is going to work long-term with how India's tax system is changing [11].

Mironowicz et al. [12] looked into how QML could actually help out in finance, especially with managing portfolios and handling risk. They dug into both regular and quantum methods, like quantum annealing and some other quantum algorithms. They compared these QML approaches with the usual ones by checking out past research and running some simulations. For example, they put quantum annealing up against genetic algorithms and tested quantum SVMs next to the classic models. Turns out, QML really shined when dealing with messy, high-dimensional data—things like picking out important features or spotting fraud worked a lot better. However, hardware limitations and algorithm complexity reduced its full potential. Hybrid quantum–classical models showed improved performance in churn prediction and portfolio rebalancing. The study found that QML could offer speed and efficiency advantages in some financial tasks. It concluded that while QML is not yet a replacement, it has strong future potential [12].

Herman et al. [13] looked into how quantum computing might shake things up in the world of finance. They covered both what we can do right now and what might be possible down the road. The authors did not run any experiments themselves—they just dug into the latest research on algorithms and hardware [13].

What they found is that quantum computing could be a game changer for heavy duty number crunching, like figuring out risk, optimizing investments, or running machine learning models. They compared old school methods with quantum approaches for pricing derivatives, catching fraud, and managing portfolios [13].

Some techniques, like Quantum Monte Carlo and quantum amplitude estimation, looked really promising on paper. A few early tests on actual quantum hardware showed potential too, but they are still held back by noise and technical limits. The study suggests finance could be one of the first fields to really benefit from quantum tech. The authors think financial companies should start getting ready now and encourage more teamwork between finance professionals and quantum researchers [13].

Egger et al. [14] took a deep look at how quantum computing might shake up the financial world, especially when it comes to handling really complex math problems in areas like simulation, optimization, and machine learning. The researchers broke things down into three main areas—banking, financial markets, and insurance—and matched up quantum algorithms with real-world uses in each. They used simulations, including Monte Carlo methods and something called quantum amplitude estimation, to show how quantum approaches could make risk analysis and option pricing way more accurate and efficient, even speeding things up compared to traditional methods. For optimization challenges, like figuring out the best investment portfolio or auction setups, they turned to variational quantum algorithms. And on the machine learning side, they explored how quantum techniques could improve things like fraud detection using quantum-enhanced support vector machines and quantum kernel estimation [14].

The analysis concluded that quantum computing holds a significant promise for improving financial operations, regulatory compliance, and customer engagement, though challenges such as data loading, error correction, and precision remain critical for broader adoption [14].

Umer and Kesavapattapa [15] used a mixed-methods approach to study combined qualitative literature reviews with quantitative case analyses across industries such as finance, e-commerce, healthcare, and insurance. The methodology entailed collecting immutable transaction data via blockchain and analyzing it using AI algorithms capable of detecting anomalies and generating real-time alerts. The framework continuously learned from new data, improving fraud detection over time. Sample techniques included case studies of JPMorgan Chase, Walmart-IBM, Alibaba, MedRec, and AXA, which showcased reductions in fraudulent activity and enhanced data security through the integrated mode [15].

The results were pretty clear. This combination of tech worked a lot better than the old rule-based systems. It gave more transparency, better predictions, and ran smoother overall. The paper wrapped up by saying that if we want to roll this out more widely, we will need solid plans to stay on the right side of regulations and keep tweaking things as we go. It makes the case that AI and blockchain could be game changers for cutting down on fraud in all kinds of industries [15].

7. Objectives

- To explore the potential of quantum machine learning in enhancing fraud detection within GST systems.
- To assess the effectiveness of quantum algorithms in optimizing GST compliance and audit procedures.
- To examine the challenges and opportunities associated with integrating quantum technologies into GST administration.

7.1 Conceptual Framework of QML

QML marks a significant shift from traditional computing by utilizing quantum bits (qubits), which, unlike classical bits, can exist in multiple states at once due to the principle of superposition [1]. QML marks a significant shift from traditional computing by utilizing quantum bits (qubits), which, unlike classical bits (as either 0 or 1), can exist in multiple states at once due to the principle of superposition [16] [17].

Quantum parallelism, along with entanglement, where qubits stay connected even when far apart, helps quantum computers handle large amounts of data and explore complex problems much faster than regular computers [1]. The mathematical foundation of QML is built on quantum algorithms like QSVM, QNN, and QPCA. These algorithms show strong potential in tasks such as pattern recognition and detecting unusual or suspicious activities, which are essential for developing effective fraud detection systems [18]. Research has shown that QML algorithms can deliver enhanced performance in classification tasks while utilizing significantly fewer parameters compared to traditional machine learning models.

7.2 Current Quantum Machine Learning Algorithms

Variational quantum classifiers (VQCs) are getting a lot of attention these days. They are seen as one of the more practical ways to bring QML into real-world use [17].

VQCs combine parameterized quantum circuits with classical optimization techniques. This approach seems particularly well adapted to the current generation of noisy intermediate-scale quantum devices, often referred to as NISQ hardware. The hybrid nature of these algorithms allows them to function effectively despite the limitations and noise present in today's quantum systems. [19].

As hybrid systems, VQCs incorporate classical feedback mechanisms during their training phase while leveraging quantum parallelism to handle complex data more efficiently. QNNs operate in a manner analogous to classical neural networks but are executed on quantum hardware. There is growing evidence that these systems could offer significant speed advantages for specific computational tasks. Recent studies suggest promising applications in fields such as materials science, and there is emerging interest in their potential for financial data analysis. A notable aspect of QNNs is their capacity to model intricate patterns through the use of distinct quantum phenomena, including interference and entanglement [17] [19].

7.3 Structural Complexities of the GST System

Multi-Tier Tax Rates: India's GST system currently employs a multi-tiered tax structure, with rates set at 0 percent, 5 percent, 12 percent, 18 percent, and 28 percent [19].

The proposed GST 2.0 framework aims to streamline this by consolidating the tax barckets into four primary categories. Essential items such as food, healthcare, and education will remain exempt from taxation. Basic goods, including groceries, personal care items, and agricultural supplies, will be taxed at 5 percent. A mid-tier rate of 18 percent will apply to appliances, electronics, automobiles, and construction materials. Luxury goods and products deemed harmful to public health, such as tobacco, aerated beverages, and high-end vehicles, will face a significantly higher tax of 40 percent. This revised system is scheduled for implementation on September 22, 2025 [6].

The complexity of these classifications often results in ambiguity, making it challenging for businesses to accurately determine the applicable tax rate for specific goods and services [20].

- **Dual GST Model Increases Administrative Complexity:** The dual GST setup really adds to a lot of administrative red tape. There are all these different pieces to keep track of—CGST, SGST, IGST, and UTGST—and trying to manage and coordinate between them creates a ton of paperwork and data to handle. Coordinating among these various layers requires substantial effort and generates significant data volumes [21].
- **High Transaction Volume Demands Real-Time Processing:** The GST system has to process a ton of transactions every single day. That means everything has to happen in real time, without any delays [20]. This creates huge computational pressure for real-time data processing and analysis.
- **Input Tax Credit (ITC) Cross-Verification is Resource-Intensive:** Cross-checking ITC claims with suppliers' records is complex and time-consuming. It requires advanced systems to ensure accuracy and prevent misuse [22].
- **Interstate Transactions Add More Complexity:** Transactions across state borders introduce additional verification steps and legal interpretations. Traditional fraud detection systems just cannot keep up with all the new tricks. It is like they are playing a game where the rules keep changing, and they are always a step behind [22].

7.4 Limitations of Traditional Fraud Detection Systems

The current fraud detection system is dependent upon rule-based approaches and machine learning algorithms. They prove to be ineffective against the current scale of GST. The success of these rule-based systems depends upon the experience and knowledge of the auditor.

As per research, the accuracy of traditional methods in detecting fraud lies at 80–93 percent [23].

These systems tend to flag a lot of transactions that turn out to be completely fine, which can be frustrating for everyone involved. They also have a hard time catching the more clever, well-hidden schemes, especially when multiple businesses or vendors are working together in complicated ways. Trying to map out all those connections and spot unusual patterns takes a lot of computing power, and honestly, most standard systems just are not up to the task [24] [25].

When it comes to GST systems, QML could really change the game for everyone involved. We are talking about government agencies, regular people, and businesses, big and small. To make the most of it, we have got to think about how each group uses the system and what they struggle with, and then tailor the tech to fit those specific needs.

8. Quantum Machine Learning in GST Systems: Transforming Tax Compliance, Transparency, and Governance

QML has a high potential to cater to the requirements of various stakeholders, including government bodies, the general public, businesses from micro, small, and medium enterprises (MSMEs) to large enterprises, and other related institutions. To make it highly effective, it should be designed in such a manner that it serves the challenges faced by various groups of people.

8.1 Impact on Government and Tax Authorities

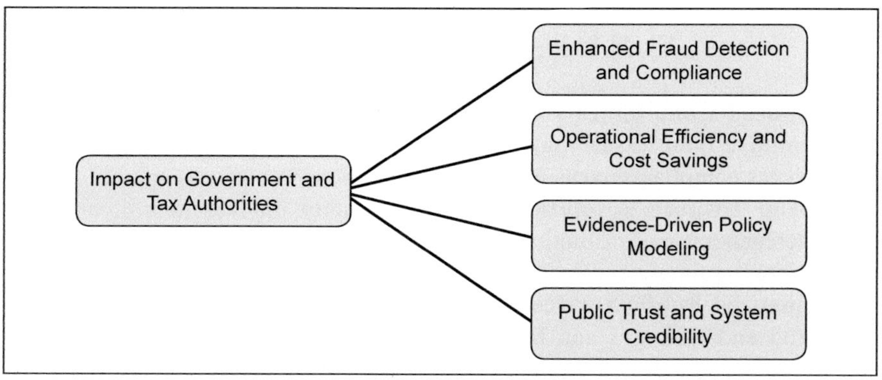

Fig. 12.3 Impact on government and tax authorities.

a) **Enhanced Fraud Detection and Compliance:** QML can analyze voluminous GST transactions speedily, and it rapidly identifies suspicious activities like fake invoices, fake companies, and other such fraudulent activities. This aids in reducing revenue leakages and increases the collection efficiency of revenue authorities, along with better policy formulation [18].
b) **Operational Efficiency and Cost Savings:** QML significantly reduces the need for human intervention for compliance monitoring through automated procedures and fast data processing. Real-time alerts for detections of suspicious transactions enable tax departments to focus on high-risk areas, resulting in improved efficiency and lower administrative costs.
c) **Evidence-Driven Policy Modeling:** Quantum computing enables dynamic simulations of policy changes, helping model the economic impact of GST amendments across sectors. This supports the development of data-driven, responsive, and well-calibrated tax policies.
d) **Public Trust and System Credibility:** A more accurate, fair, and transparent tax system—enabled by QML—strengthens public trust. Effective fraud prevention and reduced arbitrary enforcement contribute to higher voluntary compliance and confidence in tax institutions [10].

8.2 Benefits for the Public and Taxpayers

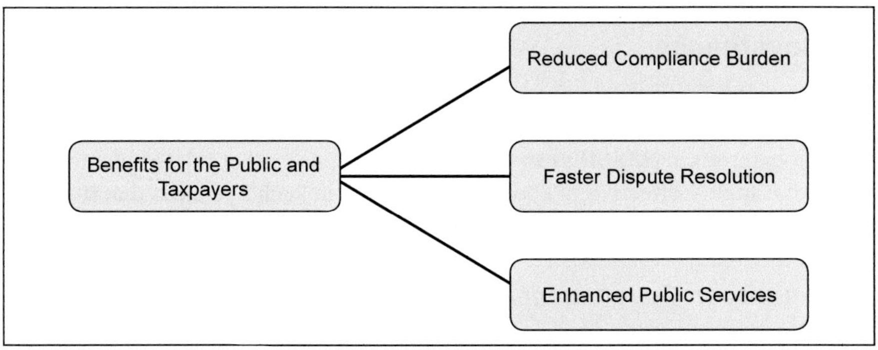

Fig. 12.4 Benefits for the public and taxpayers.

a) **Reduced Compliance Burden:** Automated detection and fair targeting minimize unnecessary audits and notices for compliant taxpayers. This reduces compliance costs and avoids disruptions in business operations.
b) **Faster Dispute Resolution:** QML allows for quicker identification of discrepancies and resolution of taxpayer disputes, ensuring that corrective actions are timely and reduce legal uncertainty.
c) **Enhanced Public Services:** Improved tax collection through minimized fraud and leakages can be redirected into public infrastructure, social programs, and digital services, directly benefiting citizens.

8.3 Advantages for Businesses, Especially MSMEs

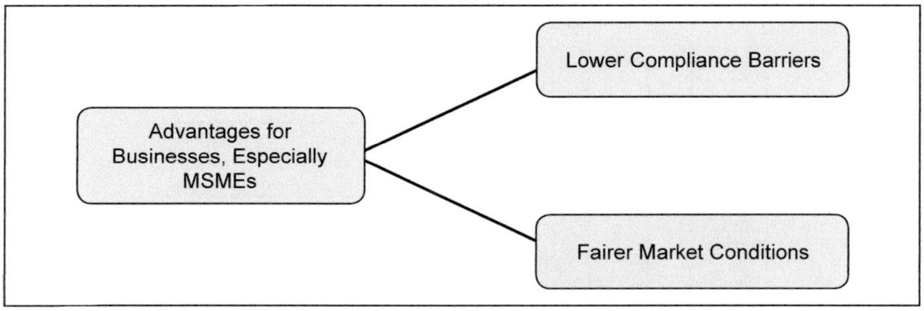

Fig. 12.5 Advantages for businesses, especially MSMEs.

a) **Lower Compliance Barriers:** QML-powered tools can automate GST processes like reconciliation, return filing, and risk assessment. MSMEs benefit from user-friendly, real-time compliance guidance and reduced dependency on professional intermediaries.
b) **Fairer Market Conditions:** With evasion curbed, compliant businesses are not disadvantaged by unfair competition. QML thus fosters a more level and innovation-driven marketplace.

8.4 Opportunities for Related Stakeholders

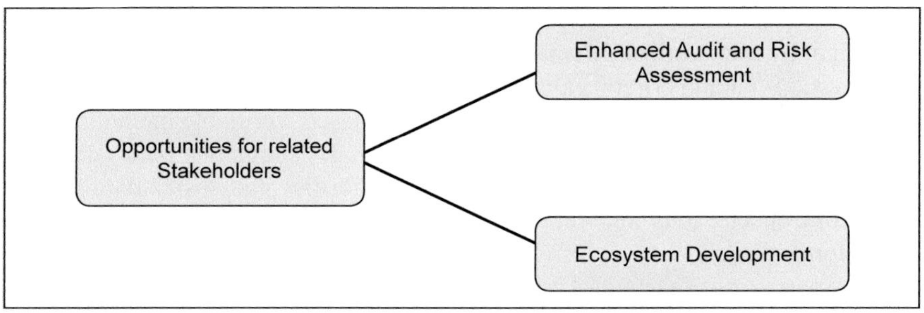

Fig. 12.6 Opportunities for related stakeholders.

a) **Enhanced Audit and Risk Assessment:** Financial institutions and auditors can use GST data enriched with QML insights to perform deeper credit risk analysis, identify anomalies, and prioritize high-risk audits effectively [21].
b) **Ecosystem Development:** Initiatives like India's National Quantum Mission support research, skill development, and innovation in quantum technologies. These efforts promote a digitally advanced ecosystem that feeds back into public governance.

8.5 Public Access to QML in GST: Transparency and Compliance

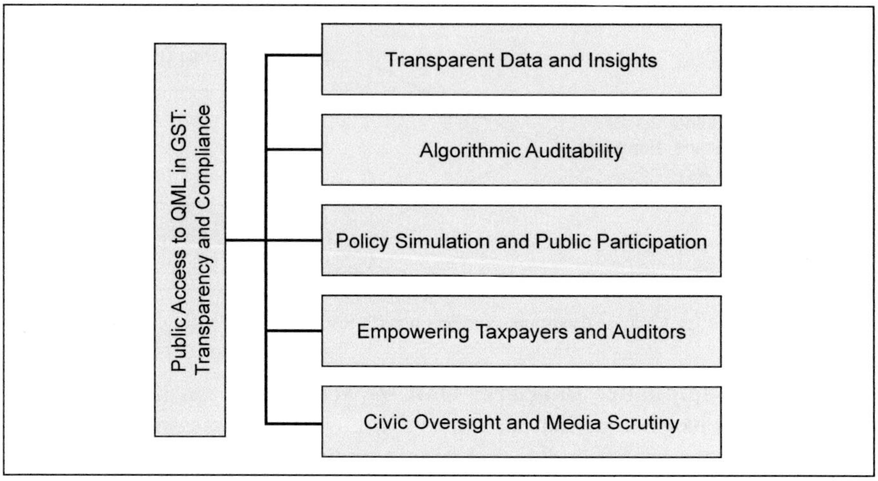

Fig. 12.7 Public access to QML in GST.

Expanding public access to QML-driven GST analytics can significantly improve transparency and voluntary compliance in the following ways:

a) **Transparent Data and Insights:** Dashboards displaying anonymized GST data, fraud trends, and compliance rates can demystify tax systems, enabling stakeholders to understand policy impacts and operational priorities [17] [26].
b) **Algorithmic Auditability:** Allowing scrutiny of QML model logic and decision-making criteria enhances trust. Stakeholders can be assured that the detection of non-compliance is based on unbiased, verifiable methods.
c) **Policy Simulation and Public Participation:** By simulating policy changes and making results publicly available, authorities can foster data-driven public discussions and receive informed feedback before implementing reforms [26].
d) **Empowering Taxpayers and Auditors:** Access to benchmarking tools and common error analysis allows taxpayers and tax professionals to take preemptive action, thereby avoiding penalties and improving compliance accuracy [5] [26].
e) **Civic Oversight and Media Scrutiny:** Researchers and civil society actors can monitor system behavior for fairness, transparency, and unintended policy impacts, creating an additional check on government functioning.

8.6 Real-Time Compliance Monitoring Through QML

Quantum computers can handle many tasks at once, which means they could help monitor GST compliance in real time across millions of transactions. This is especially useful for spotting complex frauds like carousel fraud and fake invoice schemes, which need fast and detailed checks of transaction networks. Quantum algorithms can look at the whole GST system at once, finding unusual patterns that would take too long for regular computers to detect [5] [27].

The professional services firm EY has already built quantum tools that help find signs of fraud. Its systems can look through large amounts of data quickly, making it easier to assess risks accurately and support better decision-making [5] [28].

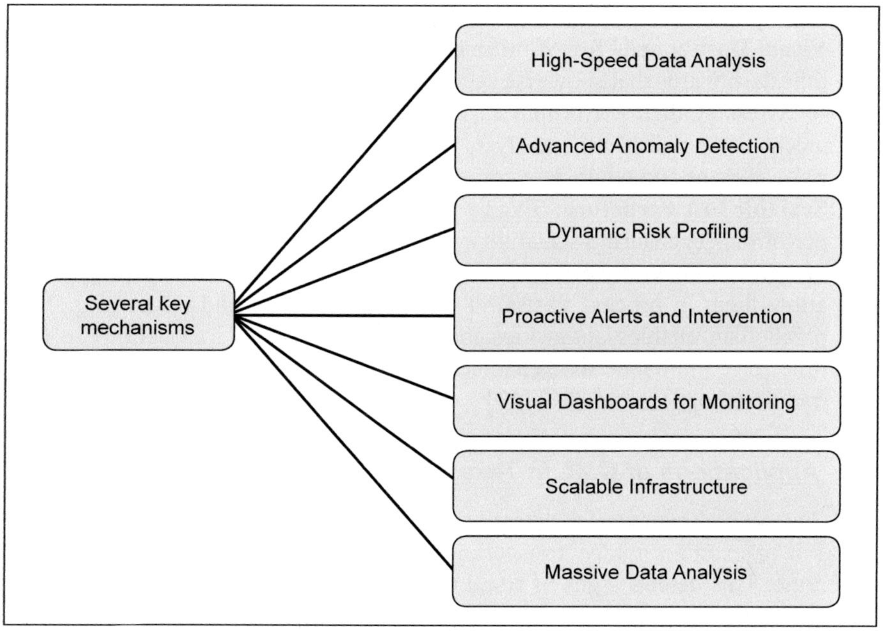

Fig. 12.8 Several key mechanisms of QML enhancing GST monitoring.

QML enhances GST monitoring through these key mechanisms:

a) High-Speed Data Analysis: Quantum algorithms can process millions of transactions simultaneously, resulting in the spot detection of any suspicious activities or non-compliance of any GST provision.

b) Advanced Anomaly Detection: Quantum methods like QNNs can identify complex fraud patterns like fake identities or carousel fraud that are often missed by traditional models. Quantum models like QSVMs and QNNs excel at detecting fraud in complex GST transactions.
This indicates that GST can track any unusual activities like fake invoices, carousel fraud, or fake identities on the spot, thus preventing revenue loss before it actually occurs [10] [29]

c) **Dynamic Risk Profiling QML:** These models provide risk scores instantly as and when new transactions are recorded. As a result, risk scores of taxpayers are updated instantly, and compliance profiles of taxpayers are also updated. To sum up, overall emphasis is laid on high-risk score taxpayers and unnecessary scrutiny of compliant businesses are avoided.

d) **Proactive Alerts and Intervention:** Immediate notifications are issued when any suspicious activities are detected, preventing revenue loss at the source. QML integration allows the GST system to send notifications to relevant authorities or tax authorities about suspicious transactions as they occur, thereby increasing efficiency and reducing the need for manual scrutiny.

e) **Visual Dashboards for Monitoring:** Relevant authorities can access real-time dashboards that show risk scores of various sectors, areas, and taxpayers for assessing their performances, assisting in better decision-making. These mechanisms assist in the analysis of various sectors, compliance maps, and risk scores as and when data comes in.

f) **Scalable Infrastructure:** Even with complicated data, QML maintains high performance, ensuring scalability.

g) **Massive Data Analysis:** QML algorithms use quantum bits (qubits), which allow them to process vast GST transactions easily and effectively. This parallelism enables authorities to monitor millions of transactions in real time for compliance discrepancies, far surpassing the speed and scope of traditional approaches [10] [19] .

8.7 Applications of QML in Taxation

QML has several benefits for detecting tax fraud. Its ability to use superposition allows it to examine many transaction patterns and taxpayer behaviors at the same time. This detects signs of fraud that are often ignored by regular systems [30]. Quantum entanglement allows for the modeling of complex relationships between different entities in the tax ecosystem, such as suppliers, buyers, and intermediaries [17]. According to recent studies, QML is more efficient in detecting fraud. For example, the accuracy of QVSM in detecting credit card fraud reached 88 percent, which is better than traditional methods [31]. Similarly, quantum-enhanced anomaly detection systems have shown promise in identifying unusual transaction patterns that may indicate tax evasion [30].

9. Governments as Catalysts in QML Progress

9.1 Strategic Investment and Research Funding

Governments are proactively investing large sums in quantum research and development, recognizing its potential for technological supremacy, national security, and economic growth. For example, the Government of India launched the National Quantum Mission (NQM) with a multi-year, multi-crore budget to accelerate research in quantum technologies—quantum computing, communication,

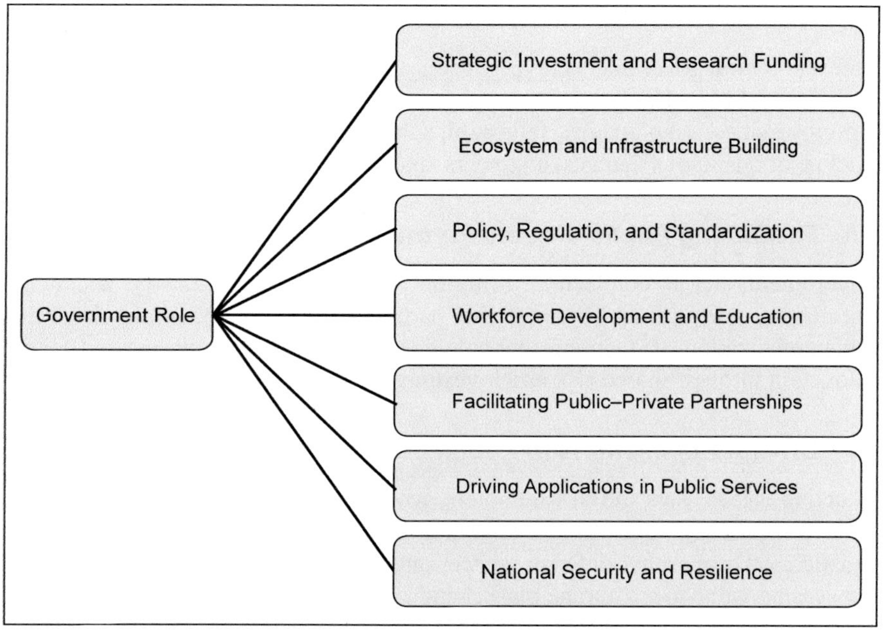

Fig. 12.9 Government's role in QML.

sensing, and materials—while similar efforts are seen in the US, Europe, and China. These funds support academic and industry research and development (R&D), innovation hubs, and building practical quantum machines [32] [33].

9.2 Ecosystem and Infrastructure Building

Government initiatives establish thematic hubs, research centres, and technology parks that bring together academia, start-ups, industry, and public sector stakeholders. In India, the NQM set up four major thematic hubs dedicated to quantum computing, communication, sensing, and materials. Infrastructure funding includes facilities for quantum device fabrication, often in partnership with leading universities and research institutes [32].

9.3 Policy, Regulation, and Standardization

The public sector not only funds innovation but also develops policies to manage the risks associated with quantum advancement—like cybersecurity threats. Regulatory bodies set standards for quantum communication (e.g., secure key distribution), post-quantum encryption, and seek to ensure responsible use. Governments bring stakeholders together, draft guidelines, and support collaborations needed for global standardisation [32].

9.4 Workforce Development and Education

State and central governments invest in education reforms to produce a "quantum-ready" workforce. This includes support for quantum curricula in high schools and universities, scholarships, fellowships, and specialized training to grow the pipeline of quantum scientists, engineers, and policy experts [34].

9.5 Facilitating Public–Private Partnerships

Governments act as connectors, bringing together private industry, academic researchers, start-ups, and international partners. These collaborations drive the commercialization of quantum technologies, build market readiness, and foster innovation through shared risk and investment [33].

9.6 Driving Applications in Public Services

By acting as lead users and early adopters, governments can demonstrate quantum-enabled solutions in sectors like tax administration (e.g., GST fraud detection), logistics, cryptography, defense, space, and healthcare, proving concepts and showcasing value to encourage market and societal adaptation [34].

9.7 National Security and Resilience [40]

Quantum technologies have profound implications for cybersecurity and data protection. Governments work on quantum-resilient encryption, protecting sensitive infrastructure, and developing new frameworks for critical systems resilience—highlighted by strategic policy and international collaboration to stay ahead of quantum threats.

The government's role in QML is both foundational and catalytic: funding breakthroughs, creating collaborative ecosystems, developing educational frameworks, setting policy and security standards, and serving as both a regulator and an innovator. Its actions today lay the groundwork for the safe, inclusive, and beneficial adoption of QML in tomorrow's digital and economic landscape.

10. Challenges and Ethical Imperatives of QML in Tax Administration

QML faces many challenges that create obstacles in its implementation. One of the major challenges is that the databases used to test whether these models are very simple or fake, while in the real world, the tax data is very large and complex. Further challenges like poor qubit connectivity, high error rates, and short working time after losing data restrict working with real-life tax data. Moreover, there is no strong evidence that QML overshadows classical methods, thus making it essential to verify it with operational tax data. Mostly these systems are difficult to understand even for experts. Thus, it is difficult to understand whether decisions taken are fair and unbiased, which makes it difficult for people to rely upon QML. This makes it mandatory to assess whether actions taken by QML are ethical or not, especially in a technical field like tax administration [35] [36].

10.1 Present Barriers and Constraints

Today's quantum computers are still early in development—they use 50 to 1,000 qubits, but they make frequent errors and lose information quickly due to noise, making them unreliable for solving complex problems. Fixing these errors needs thousands of qubits to build just one stable unit, which current machines are not powerful enough to do yet. As a result, fault-tolerant quantum computing for real-world use is still several years away [37].

10.2 Advancing QML in Tax Administration

Future advancements in QML for tax administration are projected to concentrate on the creation of novel, domain-specific algorithms tailored to financial data challenges, including tax optimization and fraud detection. This includes adapting techniques such as QSVMs, QNNs, and QPCA for enhanced efficiency and anomaly detection. Due to limitations in quantum hardware, hybrid quantum–classical methods have emerged as a promising interim solution, enabling classical systems to handle data pre-processing, while quantum subroutines manage complex optimization tasks. Integration of QML with technologies like AI and blockchain has further enriched capabilities, boosting pattern recognition, real-time analytics, and security across tax systems. Additionally, interdisciplinary collaboration among quantum computing, AI, public policy, and cybersecurity experts is essential for ethical, scalable innovation. Overall, the research agenda encourages accelerated development of custom QML tools and practical applications, alongside careful consideration of their technical, societal, and regulatory impacts [10] [15].

10.3 Integrated Quantum–Classical Approaches

For GST applications, hybrid systems can use regular (classical) computers to handle large amounts of data, while quantum computers focus on tasks like finding patterns and solving complex problems. This way, we can make the best use of today's quantum technology and create a smoother path for slowly adopting and expanding its use in the future [38] [39].

11. Conclusion

The use of QML in GST compliance and fraud detection offers exciting possibilities but also comes with significant challenges. Current quantum computers, known as NISQ devices, were still limited in how reliable, affordable, and scalable they are. However, the unique strengths of quantum computing—like its ability to recognize patterns, analyze networks, and solve complex problems—suggests that it could greatly improve how tax systems work in the future.

GST data is large, complex, and constantly changing, and quantum computing's strengths match well with these demands. Still, making it work in practice means solving technical problems, building systems that combine classical and quantum computing, and preparing organizations to use quantum technologies.

While current QML applications are mostly in early stages due to hardware constraints, research shows clear superiority in anomaly detection and real-time data analysis for complex financial and tax networks [9] [39]. As quantum technologies mature and integrate with classical infrastructure, their adoption in GST compliance will bring unmatched speed, accuracy, and fairness in tax administration.

In summary, QML equips GST systems with real-time, intelligent monitoring and rapid anomaly detection, preventing non-compliance proactively and ensuring a robust, transparent, and efficient tax environment.

To prepare, government agencies should invest in pilot projects, partnerships, and workforce training. While fully capable quantum systems may not arrive until the 2030s, early action is key to ensure a smooth and effective transition toward quantum-powered public services.

References

[1] Kennedy, R. "Q&A: EY's Marna Ricker on the promise of quantum computing for tax," *Accountancy Age*. Available at https://www.accountancyage.com/2024/07/18/qa-eys-marna-ricker-on-the-promise-of-quantum-computing-for-tax/, accessed on July 27, 2025.

[2] Kagan, J. and Kazel, M. "Indirect tax: Definition, meaning, and common examples," *Investopedia*. Available at https://www.investopedia.com/terms/i/indirecttax.asp, accessed on Aug. 2, 2025.

[3] Surana, E. "Types of taxes in India: Direct tax and indirect tax," *cleartax*. Available at https://cleartax.in/s/types-of-taxes-in-india-direct-and-indirect-tax, accessed on Aug. 2, 2025.

[4] Gupta, T. "What is invoice management system (IMS) under GST: Key features, benefits and how does it work." Available at https://cleartax.in/s/invoice-management-system-ims-under-gst, accessed on Dec. 15, 2024.

[5] Annapoorna, "Structure of GST in India: Four-tier GST tax structure breakdown," *cleartax*. Available at https://cleartax.in/s/gst-structure-india, accessed on July 27, 2025.

[6] Annapoorna, "GST rates in India 2025—List of Goods and Service Tax rates, slab and revision," *cleartax*. Available at https://cleartax.in/s/gst-rates, accessed on Sept. 14, 2025.

[7] Gupta, T. "The future of GST compliance with invoice management system (IMS)," *cleartax*. Available at https://cleartax.in/s/future-of-gst-compliance-with-ims, accessed on Dec. 14, 2024.

[8] Annapoorna, "GST benefits—Advantages and disadvantages of GST," *cleartax*. Available at https://cleartax.in/s/benefits-of-gst-advantages-disadvantages, accessed on Dec. 14, 2024.

[9] Sharma, A. and Kumar, K. "Detecting GST fraud through machine learning techniques," *Journal of Emerging Technology and Innovative Research (JETIR)*, vol. 8, no. 3, pp. 320–337, 2021.

[10] Fatunmbi, T.O. "Advanced frameworks for fraud detection leveraging quantum machine learning and data science in fintech ecosystems," *World Journal of Advanced Engineering Technology and Science*, vol. 12, no. 1, pp. 495–513, 2024, doi: 10.30574/wjaets.2024.12.1.0057.

[11] Sharma, R.B. and Garg, R. "Leveraging AI tools for enhanced GST compliance and fraud detection in the Indian taxation system," *Exploresearch*, vol. 02, no. 02, pp. 43–50, 2025, doi: 10.62823/ExRe/2025/02/02.51.

[12] Mironowicz, P., Mandarino, A.S.H.A., Yilmaz, A.E. and Ankenbrand, T. "Applications of quantum machine learning for quantitative finance," 2024, *arXiv*: arXiv:2405.10119, doi: 10.48550/arXiv.2405.10119.

[13] Herman, D., et al. "A survey of quantum computing for finance," 2022, *arXiv*: arXiv:2201.02773, doi: 10.48550/arXiv.2201.02773.

[14] Egger, D.J., et al. "Quantum computing for finance: State-of-the-art and future prospects," *IEEE Transactions on Quantum Engineering.*, vol. 1, pp. 1–24, 2020, doi: 10.1109/TQE.2020.3030314.

[15] Umer, K.N. and Kesavapattapa, R.J. "Integrating AI and blockchain technology for robust fraud detection mechanisms," *International Journal of Research in Commerce and Management Studies*, vol. 06, no. 03, pp. 43–49, 2024, doi: 10.38193/IJRCMS.2024.6305.

[16] Bartleson, B. "Empowering financial services with quantum machine learning." Available at https://strategicsolutions4u.com/empowering-financial-services-with-quantum-machine-learning/, accessed on July 27, 2025.

[17] Ricker, M., Saviano, J., and Flynn, C. "How quantum computing could impact tax." Available at https://www.ey.com/en_in/insights/tax/three-steps-tax-teams-should-take-to-prepare-for-quantum-computing, accessed on July 27, 2025.

[18] Mitra and J.V.K. Rao. "Experiments on fraud detection use case with QML and TDA mapper," in *2021 IEEE International Conference on Quantum Computing and Engineering (QCE)*, pp. 471–472, 2021, doi: 10.1109/QCE52317.2021.00083.

[19] The IoT Academy, "Quantum machine learning—Applications | Projects | Examples," *Tech & Career Blogs*. Available at https://www.theiotacademy.co/blog/quantum-machine-learning/, accessed on July 27, 2025.

[20] Muchuchuti, K.C. "An ensemble machine learning model to detect tax fraud: Conceptual framework," *International Journal of Research and Innovation in Social Science*, vol. VIII, no. VI, pp. 2276–2282, 2024, doi: 10.47772/IJRISS.2024.806171.

[21] Doosti, M., Wallden, P., Hamill, C.B., Hankache, R., Brown, O.T. and Heunen, C. "A brief review of quantum machine learning for financial services," July 17, 2024, *arXiv*: arXiv:2407.12618, doi: 10.48550/arXiv.2407.12618.

[22] Mojahedi, H., Babazadeh Sangar, A. and Masdari, M. "Towards tax evasion detection using improved particle swarm optimization algorithm," *Mathematical Problems in Engineering*, vol. 2022, pp. 1–17, 2022, doi: 10.1155/2022/1027518.

[23] Shujaaddeen, A., Ba-Alwi, F.M. and Al-Gaphari, G. "A new machine learning model for detecting levels of tax evasion based on hybrid neural network," *International Journal of Intelligent Systems and Applications in Engineering*, vol. 12, no. 11s, pp. 450–468, 2024.

[24] Erastov, V. and Balytska, M. "Artificial intelligence in tax fraud detection and prevention," in *Modern Tools for Fraud Detection: Insights from the V4 and Ukraine*, 1st ed., ed. I. Chuy, V. Lakatos, and P. Luty, Publishing House of Wroclaw University of Economics and Business, pp. 8–19, 2025, doi: 10.15611/2025.40.5.01.

[25] Gandhi, C.P. "5 GST compliance problems business owners should avoid," GSTHero—Online GST Return Filing & E-Way Bill Generation Software. Available at https://gsthero.com/blog/5-gst-compliance-problems-every-business-owner-should-avoid/, accessed on July 27, 2025.

[26] MN, S. "Quantum valley to boost innovation with QPiAI partnership," *Times of India*. Available at https://timesofindia.indiatimes.com/city/vijayawada/quantum-valley-to-boost-innovation-with-qpiai-partnership/articleshow/122887887.cms, accessed on Aug. 1, 2025.

[27] Zheng, Q., Xu, Y., Liu, H., Shi, B., Wang, J., and Dong, B. "A survey of tax risk detection using data mining techniques," *Engineering*, vol. 34, pp. 43–59, 2024, doi: 10.1016/j.eng.2023.07.014.

[28] Xavier, O.C., Pires, S.R., Marques, T.C. and Soares, A.D.S. "Tax evasion identification using open data and artificial intelligence," *Revista de Administração Pública*, vol. 56, no. 3, pp. 426–440, 2022, doi: 10.1590/0034-761220210256x.

[29] Harrison, N. "Quantum machine learning: Revolutionizing data analysis | LinkedIn." Available at https://www.linkedin.com/pulse/quantum-machine-learning-revolutionizing-data-thomas-n-harrison-zog5e/, accessed on Aug. 1, 2025.

[30] "Top applications of quantum computing for machine learning." Available at https://www.quera.com/blog-posts/applications-of-quantum-computing-for-machine-learning, accessed on July 27, 2025.

[31] Weinberg, A.I. and Faccia, A. "Quantum algorithms: A new frontier in financial crime prevention," 2024, *arXiv*: arXiv:2403.18322, doi: 10.48550/arXiv.2403.18322.

[32] "National Quantum Mission: India's quantum leap." Available at https://www.pib.gov.in/www.pib.gov.in/Pressreleaseshare.aspx?PRID=2111953, accessed on Aug. 1, 2025.

[33] Qmunity, "The growing role of government in quantum technology," *Q-munity*. Available at https://qmunity.thequantuminsider.com/2024/09/05/the-growing-role-of-government-in-quantum-technology/, accessed on Aug. 1, 2025.

[34] Ivezic, M. "Quantum technology use cases in government & defense," PostQuantum—Quantum Computing, Quantum Security, PQC. Available at https://postquantum.com/quantum-computing/use-cases-government-defense/, accessed on Aug. 1, 2025.

[35] Buchholz, S. and Ammanath, B. "Quantum computing may create ethical risks for businesses. It's time to prepare," *Deloitte Insights*. Available at https://www.deloitte.com/us/en/insights/topics/risk-management/quantum-computing-ethics-risks.html, accessed on Aug. 3, 2025.

[36] Perrier, E. "Ethical quantum computing: A roadmap," 2021, *arXiv*, doi: 10.48550/ARXIV.2102.00759.

[37] Sabbineni, P. "Navigating compliance in the quantum computing era," SISA. Available at https://www.sisainfosec.com/executive-perspective/navigating-compliance-in-the-quantum-computing-era/, accessed on July 27, 2025.

[38] Hirai, H. "Practical application of quantum neural network to materials informatics: prediction of the melting points of metal oxides," 2023, *arXiv*, doi: 10.48550/ARXIV.2310.17935.

[39] Kundan, "Quantum machine learning: Uses, applications, examples." Available at https://pwskills.com/blog/quantum-machine-learning-uses-applications-examples/, accessed on July 27, 2025.

[40] Relekar, P. N. (2023). A comparative study of financial statements pre and post era of GST of Indian pharmaceutical companies with special reference to Mumbai region. Ph.D. Thesis, The SNDT Women's University, Mumbai. Available at: http://hdl.handle.net/10603/511754

13 A Quantum-Enabled Framework for Enhancing Service Quality in India's Mobile Networks

Kritika Pancholi[1] and Parag Shukla[2*]

Even though India's telecom industry is rapidly transitioning to 5G, users continue to encounter uneven speeds, latency spikes, and dropped calls. Concerns regarding data security are also growing at the same time. This chapter explores the ways in which quantum interventions, such as quantum key distribution (QKD), post-quantum cryptography (PQC), and quantum/quantum-inspired network optimization, can improve perceived service quality as well as objective quality of service (QoS). We only use secondary data, such as user-experience metrics from Opensignal (June 2025) and city-level QoS from the Telecom Authority of India (TRAI) Independent Drive Tests (May 2025). We also define an operator-level Quantum Readiness Index based on public pilots and existing standards.

We present the Quantum-Assured Service Quality (QASQ) model, which builds upon SERVQUAL and UTAUT-3. According to the model, perceived assurance and responsiveness → trust, satisfaction, and loyalty → quantum readiness → QoS outcomes (call drops, latency/jitter, throughput stability, CSSR). Descriptive comparisons, basic correlations, and fixed-effects regressions at the operator × city level, with an optional composite path view for reporting, comprise our transparent and reproducible analysis plan. The data shows where quantum levers can provide the biggest service gains and where performance dispersion is highest.

The chapter offers a framework tailored to India, a clean measurement recipe utilizing publicly available datasets and a workable pilot roadmap (including metro QKD routes, quantum-inspired optimization on known pain corridors, and crypto-inventory and PQC migration). The objective is simple: increase security and dependability in ways that consumers can relate to and trust.

[1] Assistant Professor, Narayana Business School, Ahmedabad, Gujarat, India.
ORCID ID: 0009-0002-6564-6374

[2] Assistant Professor, Department of Commerce and Business Management, Faculty of Commerce, The Maharaja Sayajirao University of Baroda, Vadodara, Gujarat, India.
ORCID ID: 0000-0002-7014-163X
E-mail: kritika.pancholi@nbs.edu.in[1]

* Corresponding author: parag.shukla-mdc@msubaroda.ac.in

DOI: 10.1201/9781003646068-13

1. Introduction

1.1 Overview of India's Telecommunications Sector

India's telecommunications sector stands as a cornerstone of the nation's digital transformation, representing the world's second-largest telecommunications market by subscriber base and demonstrating a remarkable growth trajectory [1]. As of July 2025, the sector encompasses over 1.2 billion telephone subscribers and 974.87 million broadband subscribers, reflecting the massive scale and penetration of telecommunications services across the country [2]. The market's economic significance is substantial, with a current valuation of US$52.79 billion in 2024, projected to reach US$114.47 billion by 2033, representing a compound annual growth rate (CAGR) of 8.89 percent [3].

The sector's landscape is dominated by four major players, each serving distinct market segments and geographical regions. Reliance Jio Infocomm Ltd. leads the market with 477.50 million wireless subscribers, capturing approximately 40.2 percent of the total market share [2]. Bharti Airtel Ltd. maintains a strong second position with 391.47 million wireless subscribers, representing 32.9 percent market share. Bharat Sanchar Nigam Limited (BSNL), the state-owned operator, offers 90.36 million wireless customers with 7.6 percent market share, while Vodafone Idea Limited serves 183 million with 15.3 percent.

Indian communication infrastructure has grown significantly, notably with 5G. Jio and Airtel started 5G services in key metros in October 2022. The technology provides eMBB, URLLC, and mMTC. Across 287 cities, Jio's network and Airtel's 215 represent the region's most aggressive 5G expansion outside China [74] [75].

Service quality varies by provider and location despite advancements. Users experience network congestion, varying data speeds (15.2–45.8 Mbps), call drop rates (0.8–2.3 percent), and security concerns affecting confidence [7] [8]. Quantum-enhanced solutions can increase technical performance and user perception in these gaps.

Pressure on operators to distinguish services and manage costs is growing [52] [53]. ARPU varies from ₹167 to Rupee Foradian238 due to different tactics [54] [55]. Price wars have increased expectations and strained margins, requiring providers to balance service quality and financial viability [56] [57].

1.2 The Promise of Quantum Technologies

Implementing quantum-inspired network optimization techniques improves resource allocation, routing efficiency, and overall performance [9] [10]. Using quantum concepts like superposition and entanglement, they explore solution spaces more efficiently than conventional approaches [11] [12]. Key applications include spectrum allocation, cell tower placement, dynamic load balancing, and adaptive traffic routing [13] [14]. Early implementations provide 15–30 percent network efficiency gains over traditional methods [9] [11].

The integration of quantum technologies with 5G and emerging 6G networks creates synergistic effects that enhance both security and performance [74] [75]. Quantum-enhanced network slicing can provide ultra-secure communications for critical applications while optimizing resource allocation across multiple service types [76] [77]. This integration addresses key requirements for Industry 4.0, smart cities, and critical infrastructure applications that demand both high performance and absolute security [78] [79].

1.3 Current Service Quality Challenges

Despite significant infrastructure investments exceeding ₹2.5 lakh crore across all operators in the past five years, Indian telecommunications operators face persistent service quality challenges that impact user satisfaction and loyalty [6] [50] [51]. These challenges manifest across multiple dimensions of service delivery, creating complex interactions between technical performance and user perception that require comprehensive solutions [4] [40] [41].

Network performance inconsistencies represent the primary challenge across all operators and geographical regions [5] [50]. Data from the Telecom Authority of India (TRAI) performance reports indicates significant variations in key performance indicators (KPIs) across the 22 telecommunications circles, with rural areas experiencing substantially lower service quality than urban centers [50] [51]. Average download speeds range from 15.2 Mbps for BSNL to 45.8 Mbps for Jio, with significant variations during peak usage hours when speeds can drop by 40–60 percent [48] [49].

Call quality metrics reveal persistent issues despite 4G and 5G network upgrades [50]. Call success rates vary between 94.2 percent and 98.7 percent across operators, while call drop rates range from 0.8 percent to 2.3 percent, exceeding the TRAI benchmark of 2 percent in several circles [51]. Voice quality scores, measured through mean opinion score (MOS) ratings, range from 3.2 to 4.1 across operators, indicating room for improvement in voice service delivery [6] [47].

Customer experience metrics reveal deeper challenges in service quality perception beyond technical performance indicators [6] [45]. Opensignal's user experience reports consistently highlight issues with video streaming quality, voice application performance, and download speed experience that affect daily usage patterns [47] [48]. Video experience scores range from 45 to 75 (out of 100) across operators, indicating that many users experience buffering and quality degradation during video consumption [49]. Games experience scores show similar variations, affecting the growing mobile gaming market that represents a significant revenue opportunity [48].

Network availability and reliability challenges compound these performance issues [50] [51]. While all operators achieve above 96 percent network availability, outages during critical periods such as natural disasters or high-traffic events reveal infrastructure vulnerabilities [6]. The 2023 monsoon season saw network outages affecting over 50 million subscribers across multiple operators, highlighting the need for more resilient network architectures [52] [53].

Security concerns increasingly impact service quality perception as cyber threats targeting telecommunications infrastructure grow in frequency and sophistication [7] [8]. The Computer Emergency Response Team India (CERT-In) reported a 300 percent increase in telecommunications sector cyberattacks between 2022 and 2024, including distributed denial of service (DDoS) attacks, data breaches, and infrastructure penetration attempts [8]. User awareness of these threats creates anxiety about data privacy and service reliability, affecting overall service quality perception [68] [69].

Customer service and support quality represent additional challenges that affect user satisfaction [43] [44]. Industry surveys indicate that 35–45 percent of customers across operators report dissatisfaction with customer service response times, problem resolution effectiveness, and service representative knowledge [45] [46]. These service quality issues contribute to customer churn rates ranging from 2.5 percent to 4.2 percent monthly across operators, representing significant revenue impact [54] [55].

The competitive pressure from new technologies and changing user expectations exacerbates these challenges [52] [53]. Over-the-top (OTT) services provide alternative communication options that often deliver superior user experience, creating comparison benchmarks that traditional telecommunications services struggle to match [56] [57]. Social media platforms, messaging applications, and video calling services set user expectations for seamless, high-quality communication that telecommunications operators must meet or exceed [58] [59].

2. Literature Review

2.1 Quantum Computing Applications in Telecommunications

The application of quantum computing principles to telecommunications represents an emerging field with significant potential for addressing fundamental challenges in network performance, security, and optimization [25] [26]. Research in this domain spans theoretical frameworks, experimental implementations, and commercial applications across various aspects of telecommunications infrastructure [27] [28]. The literature reveals three primary application areas: quantum cryptography for enhanced security, quantum optimization for network performance, and quantum sensing for network monitoring [29] [30].

Quantum cryptography research has established comprehensive theoretical and practical foundations for ultra-secure communications [31] [32]. The pioneering work by Bennett and Brassard in 1984 demonstrated how quantum mechanical properties could ensure unconditional security in communications through the BB84 protocol [22] [23]. This foundational research established the principle that any attempt to intercept quantum-encoded information necessarily disturbs the quantum states, providing automatic detection of eavesdropping attempts [26] [31].

Subsequent theoretical developments expanded the quantum cryptography framework through multiple protocols and security proofs [27] [28]. Ekert's 1991 research introduced entanglement-based quantum key distribution protocols that provide additional security guarantees through Bell's inequality violations [27]. The security analysis by Mayers and others established information-theoretic security proofs that demonstrate unconditional security regardless of computational resources available to potential attackers [29] [32].

Comprehensive reviews by Gisin et al. and Scarani et al. established the theoretical framework for practical quantum key distribution (QKD) implementation in telecommunications networks [28] [29]. These reviews identified key technical challenges including photon loss, detector imperfections, and environmental noise that affect real-world implementations [33] [34]. The development of decoy state protocols and measurement-device-independent QKD addressed many practical security concerns [35] [36].

Experimental demonstrations have validated QKD feasibility across various deployment scenarios and distances [33] [34]. The SECOQC quantum key distribution network in Vienna demonstrated metropolitan-scale QKD implementation, connecting eight sites across the city through a combination of fiber optic and free-space quantum channels [30]. The network operated continuously for 18 months, distributing quantum keys for secure communications while demonstrating the practical viability of quantum networks [35].

Long-distance QKD experiments have achieved quantum key distribution over distances exceeding 400 kilometers through optical fibers [36] [39]. The Tokyo QKD Network demonstrated continuous operation over metropolitan distances with multiple users and applications [35]. Free-space QKD experiments have achieved quantum key distribution over 144 kilometers between mountaintop stations, demonstrating the feasibility of satellite-based quantum communications [36] [37].

Satellite-based quantum communication represents a significant advancement in global quantum networks [37] [38]. Chinese researchers achieved satellite-to-ground QKD over distances exceeding 1,200 kilometers using the Micius quantum satellite [38]. These experiments demonstrated the feasibility of global quantum communication networks that could provide secure communications between any two points on Earth [39].

Recent advances in integrated photonics have enabled compact, cost-effective QKD systems suitable for telecommunications deployment [10] [36]. Silicon photonic implementations have achieved daylight QKD, addressing one of the key practical limitations for free-space quantum communications [10]. These technological advances reduce the cost and complexity of QKD systems, making them more accessible for commercial telecommunications applications [37] [39].

Quantum optimization algorithms show significant promise for addressing complex network resource management and performance enhancement challenges [9] [11]. The telecommunications industry faces numerous optimization problems that are computationally intractable for classical algorithms, including spectrum allocation, network routing, resource scheduling, and capacity planning [12] [13]. Quantum algorithms offer the potential for exponential speedups in solving these optimization problems [25] [9].

Research by Boev et al. demonstrated quantum algorithms for wavelength assignment in optical networks, achieving superior performance compared to classical approaches in terms of both solution quality and computational efficiency [9]. The quantum algorithms explored larger solution spaces more effectively, finding optimal or near-optimal solutions for network configurations that classical algorithms could not solve within reasonable time constraints [11].

Machine learning applications leveraging quantum computing principles have shown improvements in telecommunications applications including customer churn prediction, network anomaly detection, and service personalization [11] [12]. Quantum machine learning algorithms can process high-dimensional data more efficiently than classical approaches, enabling more accurate predictions and faster processing of network data [25] [11]. Early implementations demonstrate 20–40 percent improvements in prediction accuracy for customer behavior modeling [11].

Hybrid quantum-classical computing frameworks enable practical implementation of quantum algorithms within existing telecommunications infrastructure [12] [13]. These frameworks leverage quantum computing for specific optimization tasks while maintaining compatibility with classical network management systems [12]. Real-time applications include dynamic resource allocation, traffic routing optimization, and network function virtualization that adapts to changing network conditions [13] [14].

Network function virtualization enhanced by quantum computing offers new possibilities for dynamic resource allocation and service customization [12]. Quantum algorithms can optimize the placement and configuration of virtual network functions across distributed infrastructure, improving resource utilization and service performance [13]. Applications in 5G physical cell ID allocation demonstrate practical benefits of quantum optimization in cellular networks [13] [14].

2.2 Service Quality Models and Frameworks

Service quality research in telecommunications builds upon foundational work in service marketing and customer experience management that has evolved over four decades [40] [41]. The SERVQUAL model, developed by Parasuraman, Zeithaml, and Berry, provides a comprehensive framework for measuring service quality across five dimensions: tangibles, reliability, responsiveness, assurance, and empathy [20] [40]. This model has been extensively adapted and validated in telecommunications contexts, demonstrating consistent relationships between service quality perceptions and customer outcomes across diverse markets and service types [41] [42].

The original SERVQUAL research identified service quality as a multidimensional construct that reflects the gap between customer expectations and perceptions of actual service performance [40]. The five dimensions capture different aspects of service delivery: tangibles represent the physical facilities and equipment; reliability reflects the ability to perform services accurately and dependably; responsiveness indicates willingness to help customers and provide prompt service; assurance encompasses the knowledge and courtesy of employees and their ability to inspire trust; and empathy represents the caring, individualized attention provided to customers [20] [40].

Telecommunications adaptations of SERVQUAL have modified the original dimensions to reflect industry-specific characteristics [41] [42]. Network quality replaces tangibles to reflect the technical infrastructure performance; service reliability encompasses both network reliability and service consistency; customer service responsiveness includes both human and automated service interactions; security assurance addresses data protection and privacy concerns; and service personalization reflects the customization capabilities enabled by digital technologies [43] [44].

The evolution of service quality models reflects changing customer expectations and technological capabilities in the digital era [44] [45]. Cronin and Taylor's SERVPERF model emphasizes actual service delivery performance over expectation-performance gaps, arguing that performance-based measures provide more accurate service quality assessments [42]. This approach has particular relevance in telecommunications where objective performance metrics (speed, latency, availability) can be measured alongside subjective quality perceptions [47] [48].

Brady and Cronin hierarchical model has sub-dimensions for interaction, physical environment, and result quality [47]. In tech-driven sectors, service quality is difficult due to client interaction with both human agents and automated technologies [48] [49]. The framework enables accurate service component measurement and quality assessment [44] [47].

Research indicates that service quality influences customer loyalty, word-of-mouth, and willingness to pay premiums [43] [44]. In Oliver's cognitive paradigm, contentment results from positive disconfirmation and dissatisfaction from negative disconfirmation. In telecom, this paradigm is well proven for objectively measuring service against expectations [45] [46].

The American Customer Satisfaction Index by Fornell et al. links satisfaction, loyalty, and financial performance across industries, including telecom [44]. Increased customer satisfaction leads to increased retention, reduced price sensitivity, and improved word-of-mouth, boosting client acquisition in telecom, where retention drives lifetime value and acquisition costs are high [46] [48].

Service quality influences loyalty and desire to pay more [41] [46]. Zeithaml et al. found that focused service quality enhancements boost business [41]. Their study identifies the key factors influencing loyalty and investment decisions [46] [47].

Service quality increases client equity through satisfaction and loyalty, according to Lemon et al. [45]. Customers' lifetime worth, or equity, shows service quality's commercial influence. Improvements increase equity via happiness, reputation, and long-term value [45] [48].

Current research combines digital transformation, multichannel delivery, artificial intelligence (AI), and customization [48] [49]. Digital models encompass consumer interactions across applications, websites, contact centers, and physical locations [49] [6]. Consistency in touchpoints significantly impacts service quality judgments [47] [48].

2.3 Technology Adoption and User Acceptance Models

Technology adoption study effectively explains how users integrate new technologies into their service experience [60] [61]. These models have progressed from simple acceptance theories to complicated ones that incorporate individual, societal, and organizational factors [62] [63]. In telecom, quantum technologies allow consumers to benefit from system capabilities without direct interaction [64] [65].

Davis' technology acceptance model (TAM) attributes uptake to perceived utility and simplicity of use. Usefulness improves performance, whereas ease of use requires little effort. Validated across several technologies, TAM reliably links to adoption behavior [65] [66].

Extensions of TAM include social influence, enabling environments, and personal qualities [66] [67]. TAM2 acknowledges societal pressure and mandated use with subjective norm and voluntariness. TAM3 enhances ease of use by including computer anxiety, fun, and enjoyment [64] [65].

The unified theory of acceptance and use of technology (UTAUT) combines eight adoption models into a comprehensive framework [60] [62]. It explains 70 percent of behavioral intention variation, exceeding individual models [60] [63]. According to UTAUT, four key factors are performance, effort, social impact, and enabling conditions [61] [64] [65] [66] [67].

UTAUT-2 incorporates hedonic motivation, price value, and habit to the model for consumer situations [17] [62]. Hedonic motivation measures enjoyment, price value evaluates advantages and costs, and habit is based on recurrent usage [63] [64] [65] [67].

UTAUT-3 enhances the approach by including trust, perceived risk, and personal innovation [17] [60]. Trust is essential for sensitive data-related technologies [68] [69]. Perceived risks include performance, security, and privacy issues [70] [71]. Innovativeness indicates a readiness to experiment with new technology [62] [72].

Telecom models must consider network-based properties [63] [64]. Adoption obstacles arise from switching costs owing to contracts and service integration, but network effects boost value with more users [65] [66] [67] [72]. Ecosystem interdependence sometimes necessitate coordinated service uptake [63] [73].

Rogers' diffusion of innovations theory classifies adopters as innovators, early adopters, early majority, late majority, and laggards [62] [67].

Operators can customize methods to specific user segments using these categories [63] [72].

Innovation traits impact adoption rates. Key variables include relative advantage, compatibility, complexity, trialability, and observability[62–73]. These affect people's perceptions and utilization of new tech.

Trust is crucial for adopting services containing personal data [68] [69]. It encompasses the principles of competence, kindness, and integrity [70] [73]. Quantum technologies require these dimensions for security, although verification may be challenging [71] [72].

The McKnight et al. trust paradigm underpins tech-mediated services [68]. It encompasses trust disposition, institutional trust, and trusting ideas [69] [70]. Disposition involves personal traits, institutional trust focuses on system security, and trusting views involve provider features [71] [73].

Pavlou found that trust mediates technological adoption and e-commerce behavioral intention [69]. Trust becomes increasingly important when perceived risk increases, particularly for quantum technologies that handle security but are complicated [70–73].

2.4 Research Gaps and Theoretical Development

This section analyzes the literature to identify gaps in the Quantum-Assured Service Quality (QASQ) model, using Miles' approach for systematic gap detection in qualitative investigations [18]. Miles stresses detecting gaps in four areas: theoretical (inadequate ideas), empirical (limited evidence), methodological (insufficient research methodologies), and practical.

2.4.1 Theoretical Gaps in Service Quality Models

Existing service quality models, particularly SERVQUAL and its telecommunications adaptations, do not adequately account for advanced security technologies and their impact on user perceptions [20] [40] [41]. While SERVQUAL includes an assurance dimension, it was developed in the 1980s before quantum cryptography emergence and does not capture quantum-specific security benefits [40] [68]. The assurance dimension focuses on employee knowledge and courtesy rather than technological security capabilities [20] [41].

The theoretical gap becomes apparent when considering how quantum security technologies influence user trust formation [68] [69]. Traditional service quality models assume that assurance perceptions result from interpersonal interactions and service reliability [40] [42]. However, quantum technologies provide security guarantees that are fundamentally different from classical security measures, potentially creating new pathways for assurance perception formation [31] [70].

Current service quality models also fail to account for the indirect effects of infrastructure technologies on user perceptions [41] [47]. Most service quality research focuses on user-facing service attributes, while quantum technologies operate at the infrastructure level and may influence service quality perceptions through improved performance and security rather than direct user interaction [25] [48]. This creates a theoretical gap in understanding how infrastructure-level technological capabilities translate into user-perceived service quality [49] [6].

2.4.2 Empirical Gaps in Quantum Technology Research

The telecommunications literature lacks comprehensive frameworks that integrate quantum technology capabilities with service quality outcomes [74] [75]. Most quantum telecommunications research focuses on technical performance metrics such as key generation rates, quantum bit error rates, and communication distances rather than user experience and satisfaction [76] [77]. This technical focus creates an empirical gap in understanding how quantum capabilities affect customer perceptions and behaviors [78] [79].

Empirical research on quantum technology adoption in telecommunications remains extremely limited, particularly in emerging market contexts like India [52] [53]. While technical feasibility studies demonstrate quantum technology capabilities, there is insufficient empirical evidence about user acceptance, market adoption patterns, and business impact [54] [55]. This gap is particularly significant given the substantial investments required for quantum technology deployment [56] [57].

The literature also lacks empirical evidence about the relationship between quantum technology investment and competitive advantage in telecommunications markets [52] [58]. While theoretical arguments suggest that quantum technologies could provide differentiation opportunities, empirical validation of these relationships is missing [59] [25]. This gap limits the ability of telecommunications operators to make informed investment decisions about quantum technology adoption [31] [40].

2.4.3 Methodological Gaps in Technology-Service Quality Integration

Technology adoption models focus primarily on user-facing technologies and may not fully explain adoption of underlying infrastructure technologies like quantum systems [60] [61]. The methodological approaches used in technology adoption research typically involve direct user surveys about specific technologies [62] [63]. However, quantum technologies in telecommunications operate transparently to users, requiring different methodological approaches to assess their impact on user perceptions and behaviors [64] [65].

Current methodological approaches also fail to capture the multi-level nature of quantum technology impacts [66] [67]. Quantum technologies influence service quality at multiple levels: technical performance improvements, security enhancements, and user perception changes [25] [68]. Existing research methodologies typically focus on single levels of analysis, creating gaps in understanding the complex relationships between quantum capabilities and service outcomes [69] [70].

The integration of objective technical performance measures with subjective service quality perceptions represents another methodological gap [47] [48]. Most service quality research relies on perceptual measures, while quantum technology research emphasizes objective technical metrics [49] [71]. Methodological frameworks that effectively integrate these different types of measures are lacking in the literature [72] [6].

2.4.4 Practical Gaps in Implementation Guidance

The literature provides limited practical guidance for telecommunications operators considering quantum technology investments [52] [53]. While technical research demonstrates quantum technology capabilities and service quality research identifies important user outcomes, the connection between these domains is underdeveloped [54] [25]. This creates practical gaps in understanding how to implement quantum technologies to achieve service quality improvements [55] [40].

Implementation guidance is particularly lacking for emerging markets like India where infrastructure constraints, regulatory environments, and user characteristics may differ from developed markets [56] [57]. Most quantum technology research focuses on developed market contexts with advanced infrastructure and high technology adoption rates [58] [59]. The practical applicability of these findings to emerging markets remains unclear [52] [73].

The literature also lacks comprehensive frameworks for assessing quantum readiness and planning quantum technology adoption [25] [31]. While individual studies examine specific quantum applications, integrated frameworks that help operators evaluate their quantum readiness and develop implementation strategies are missing [32] [74]. This practical gap limits the ability of telecommunications operators to develop coherent quantum technology strategies [75] [40].

3. Research Objectives

This research addresses the identified theoretical, empirical, methodological, and practical gaps through a series of specific research objectives, based on the comprehensive literature review and gap analysis. These objectives are designed to advance both theoretical understanding and practical application of quantum technologies in telecommunications service quality enhancement.

3.1 Primary Research Objective

Develop and validate a comprehensive theoretical framework that explains how quantum technology capabilities influence telecommunications service quality perceptions and user outcomes in India's telecommunications sector.

This primary objective addresses the fundamental theoretical gap identified in the literature where existing service quality models do not adequately account for advanced infrastructure technologies like quantum systems. The objective encompasses the following:

- Integration of quantum information theory with established service quality frameworks (SERVQUAL) and technology adoption models (UTAUT-3)
- Development of the QASQ model that explains the causal pathways through which quantum readiness influences user outcomes
- Empirical validation of the theoretical relationships using comprehensive secondary data from India's telecommunications sector
- Statistical testing of nine specific hypotheses that define the relationships between quantum readiness, service quality perceptions, trust, satisfaction, loyalty, and quality of service (QoS) outcomes.

3.2 Expected Contributions

The research objectives are designed to generate contributions across multiple domains:

Theoretical Contributions: Extension of service quality theory to incorporate advanced infrastructure technologies – Integration of quantum information theory with service marketing and technology adoption frameworks – Development of new theoretical constructs including quantum readiness, quantum-enhanced assurance, and quantum-optimized responsiveness.

Empirical Contributions: First comprehensive assessment of quantum technology readiness in a major telecommunications market – Statistical validation of relationships between quantum capabilities and service quality outcomes – Empirical evidence for the business impact of quantum technology investment in telecommunications.

Methodological Contributions: Integration of objective technical measures with subjective service quality assessments – Development of composite index methodology for measuring quantum readiness – Multi-level analysis framework that captures infrastructure, operator, and user-level effects.

Practical Contributions: Actionable implementation guidance for telecommunications operators – Investment decision frameworks for quantum technology adoption – Performance measurement systems for tracking quantum technology implementation success.

Policy Contributions: Analysis of competitive and regulatory implications of quantum technology adoption – Recommendations for government support programs and regulatory frameworks – Assessment of national security and economic development impacts.

4. Conceptual Framework Development

4.1 The Quantum-Assured Service Quality (QASQ) Model

The QASQ model represents a novel theoretical framework that integrates quantum technology capabilities with established service quality and technology adoption

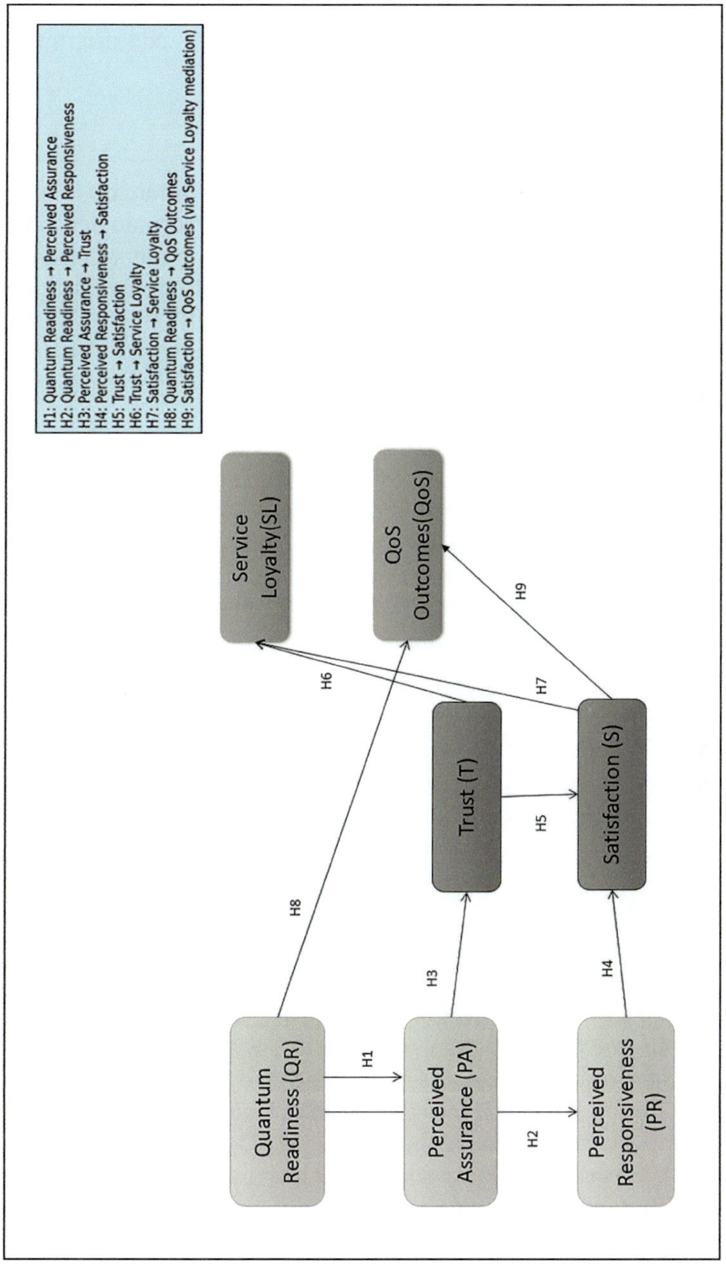

Fig. 13.1 QASQ Framework: Quantum Assured Service Quality Model.
Source: Developed by authors.

theories [20] [21] [60]. The model addresses the unique characteristics of quantum-enhanced telecommunications services while maintaining theoretical rigor and practical applicability [25] [68]. This integration creates new insights into how emerging technologies influence service quality perceptions and user outcomes [40] [41].

4.2 Hypotheses

The QASQ model incorporates seven primary constructs arranged in a causal chain, which reflects the process through which quantum technologies influence service quality outcomes [68] [69]. The model begins with quantum readiness as an exogenous variable representing the technological capability foundation [25]. This construct influences service quality perceptions through perceived assurance and perceived responsiveness, which subsequently affect user trust and satisfaction [40] [68]. These psychological constructs ultimately determine service loyalty and objective QoS outcomes [43] [44].

The model's theoretical foundation rests on the premise that quantum technologies create new dimensions of service quality that extend beyond traditional frameworks [41] [47]. Unlike conventional service quality models that focus on human-delivered services, the QASQ model recognizes that advanced technologies can directly influence user perceptions through their capabilities rather than through direct user interaction [48] [49]. This represents a significant theoretical advancement in understanding technology-mediated service quality formation [6] [40].

4.3 Theoretical Foundations and Integration

The QASQ model combines three ideas—SERVQUAL, UTAUT, and quantum information theory, to illustrate how technology may improve service delivery [20] [21] [60], establishing a concise yet verifiable foundation for quantum-enhanced telecommunications services [68] [25]. From SERVQUAL, assurance and responsiveness are key. Assurance connects user trust in security and dependability to the benefits of quantum cryptography with strong mathematical assurances [40] [41] [68] [31], and the QASQ model broadens assurance from interpersonal trust to technological security capabilities [69] [70]. Responsiveness (speed/availability) is in line with quantum optimization, which makes networks run better and allocates resources better [47] [9], redefined in QASQ as algorithmic, real-time optimization [10] [11], recognizing that contemporary responsiveness is equally computational and human [48] [12]. QASQ uses the user-acceptance lens from UTAUT: performance expectancy fits quantum-enabled network gains [60] [61] [17] [9], while effort expectancy stresses transparent security with no added user complexity [60] [10]. Social influence and facilitating conditions further shape adoption in telecom contexts [62] [63], where social proof/expert endorsements matter for low-familiarity quantum tech [64] [11], and infrastructure/

support enable deployment [65] [12]. QASQ is based on quantum information theory and explains how capabilities can lead to service enhancements [25] [26]. Superposition, entanglement, and measurement disturbance create new security and optimization opportunities [27] [28]. Superposition allows algorithms to explore multiple solution paths simultaneously [29] [9]. Entanglement facilitates QKD and distributed computation [30] [10]. The no-cloning theorem ensures cryptographic security [31] [11], and measurement disturbance allows for detectable interception for automatic intrusion alerts [32] [12].

4.4 Construct Definitions and Operationalization

The QASQ framework incorporates seven primary constructs:

Quantum Readiness (QR): The extent to which telecom operators have implemented quantum technologies and developed quantum capabilities. This construct encompasses quantum infrastructure deployment, staff expertise, and strategic commitment to quantum technology adoption.

Perceived Assurance (PA): User perceptions of service provider competence, security, and reliability, enhanced by quantum technology implementations. Quantum cryptography directly influences this construct by providing mathematically provable security guarantees.

Perceived Responsiveness (PR): User perceptions of service provider willingness to help customers and provide prompt service. Quantum sensing and optimization capabilities enable more responsive network management and customer service.

Trust (TR): User confidence in service provider reliability, integrity, and benevolence. Quantum technologies influence trust through enhanced security capabilities and demonstrated technological leadership.

Satisfaction (SAT): Overall user satisfaction with telecommunications services, influenced by quantum-enhanced service quality dimensions.

Service Loyalty (SL): User intention to continue using services and recommend them to others, representing the ultimate outcome of enhanced service quality.

QoS Outcomes (QOS): Objective measures of service quality including network performance, security incidents, and service availability, directly improved by quantum technologies.

The QASQ framework proposes nine hypotheses describing relationships between constructs:

H1: Quantum readiness positively influences perceived assurance

H2: Quantum readiness positively influences perceived responsiveness

H3: Perceived assurance positively influences trust

H4: Perceived responsiveness positively influences trust

H5: Trust positively influences satisfaction

H6: Satisfaction positively influences loyalty

H7: Quantum readiness positively influences QoS outcomes

H8: QoS outcomes positively influence satisfaction

H9: Trust mediates the relationship between perceived assurance/responsiveness and satisfaction

These hypotheses reflect the theoretical proposition that quantum technologies enhance service quality through both direct effects on objective performance measures and indirect effects on user perceptions and trust.

5. Research Methodology

5.1 Research Design and Philosophical Approach

This study employs a quantitative research design using comprehensive secondary data to examine relationships between quantum technology adoption, service-quality perceptions, and user outcomes in India's telecom sector [80] [81]. The philosophical stance is positivist, aiming to identify and validate causal relationships through a statistical analysis of objective sources, while remaining grounded in established service-quality and technology-adoption frameworks [82] [83].

The design Is cross-sectional, integrating multiple authoritative sources to capture the quantum–service quality relationship at a specific point in time [23] [84]. This allows simultaneous comparison across major operators while controlling for market and temporal factors that could confound longitudinal studies, balancing theory with practical constraints of data availability and timelines [80] [81] [82] [23].

Methodologically, the approach integrates multiple frameworks to develop and test the QASQ model, triangulating across data sources and measures [20] [21] [60]. This follows service-quality practice where multi-theory integration improves explanatory power and practical relevance [40] [41]. The quantitative approach supports statistical validation of theoretical links and generates actionable insights for operators and policymakers [80] [83].

The design addresses the unique challenge that users rarely interact directly with quantum systems in telecom; instead, benefits are experienced indirectly via better security and QoS [25] [68]. Accordingly, we focus on observable indicators and outcomes (not direct quantum usage), ensuring impacts are captured while remaining empirically grounded [31] [69] [40] [70].

5.2 Variable Operationalization and Measurement

The QASQ model operationalizes seven primary constructs through multiple indicators derived from secondary data sources, following established guidelines for composite indicator construction while adapting to the unique characteristics of quantum technology measurement [20] [40] [60]. The operationalization strategy emphasizes objective, verifiable measures that can be consistently applied across operators while capturing the theoretical essence of each construct [24] [80].

5.2.1 Quantum Readiness (QR) Measurement Framework

Quantum readiness measurement incorporates four primary dimensions with specific indicators for each dimension [25] [31]. Infrastructure capability assessment includes fiber network density measured as fiber-to-the-home coverage percentages, quantum-compatible equipment deployment assessed through technology upgrade investments, and technical staff expertise evaluated through quantum-related hiring and training programs [32] [52]. Research and development (R&D) investment measurement encompasses quantum technology R&D expenditures as a percentage of the total R&D spending, quantum-related patent applications and grants, and research collaborations with academic institutions and quantum technology companies [33] [53].

Pilot project implementation assessment evaluates the scope, scale, and outcomes of quantum technology trials including QKD deployments, quantum optimization algorithm implementations, and post-quantum cryptography testing programs [34] [54]. Strategic partnership evaluation examines relationships with quantum technology providers, equipment manufacturers, research institutions, and international quantum networks [35] [55]. Each dimension receives equal weighting in the composite index to avoid bias toward any particular quantum technology approach [24] [56].

The Quantum Readiness Index construction follows OECD guidelines for composite indicator development including data normalization, aggregation procedures, and sensitivity analysis [24]. Min-max normalization ensures that all indicators contribute equally regardless of measurement units or scales [80] [57]. Robustness testing examines alternative weighting schemes and aggregation methods to ensure index stability [81] [58]. The final index provides scores from 1–10 for each operator, enabling a clear comparative assessment [24] [59].

5.2.2 Service Quality Perception Constructs

Perceived assurance (PA) operationalization adapts SERVQUAL assurance dimension indicators for telecommunications contexts while incorporating quantum security considerations [20] [40]. Traditional indicators include security incident reports, customer complaint rates related to privacy and security concerns, and industry security ratings from independent organizations [68] [50]. Quantum-specific indicators include implementation of post-quantum cryptography standards, QKD pilot deployments, and security audit results that assess quantum readiness [31] [69].

Perceived responsiveness (PR) measurement utilizes network performance metrics that reflect user-experienced service quality including average download and upload speeds, latency measurements, call setup times, and service availability percentages [40] [47]. These metrics come from both TRAI regulatory reports and Opensignal independent measurements to ensure comprehensive coverage [50] [48]. Quantum-specific responsiveness indicators include network optimization algorithm implementations and real-time adaptive network management capabilities [9] [49].

5.2.3 Trust and Satisfaction Measurement

Trust (T) operationalization combines multiple indicators reflecting different trust dimensions including competence trust, benevolence trust, and integrity trust [68] [70]. Competence trust indicators include customer satisfaction scores related to technical service quality, network reliability ratings, and service consistency measurements [71] [43]. Benevolence trust indicators encompass customer service quality ratings, complaint resolution effectiveness, and transparency in service policies [72] [44]. Integrity trust measures include regulatory compliance records, ethical business practice ratings, and corporate social responsibility assessments [73] [45].

Satisfaction (S) measurement incorporates overall service satisfaction ratings from industry surveys, net promoter scores reflecting customer recommendation intentions, and customer retention rates indicating satisfaction-driven loyalty [43] [44]. Multiple data sources including industry research firms, regulatory customer satisfaction surveys, and operator-reported metrics provide comprehensive satisfaction assessment [45] [46]. The measurement approach recognizes that satisfaction results from multiple service quality dimensions and experiences [47] [48].

5.2.4 Loyalty and QoS Outcomes Measurement

Service loyalty (SL) operationalization includes both behavioral and attitudinal loyalty indicators [44] [41]. Behavioral loyalty measures include customer retention rates, average customer tenure, service expansion rates among existing customers, and contract renewal percentages [45] [46]. Attitudinal loyalty indicators encompass recommendation intentions measured through net promoter scores, positive word-of-mouth assessments, and brand preference rankings [47] [48]. The multi-dimensional approach captures both actual loyalty behaviors and loyalty intentions [49] [41].

QoS outcomes measurement utilizes objective technical performance indicators that can be measured independently of user perceptions [50] [51]. Primary indicators include network download and upload speeds, latency measurements, call success rates, network availability percentages, and service reliability metrics [6] [52]. Additional indicators include customer complaint rates, service outage frequency and duration, and technical service quality assessments [53] [47]. The measurement framework ensures that QoS outcomes reflect actual service performance rather than perceptual assessments [54] [48].

5.3 Statistical Analysis Framework

Statistical analysis employs multiple techniques to examine relationships within the QASQ framework while ensuring robust empirical validation and appropriate handling of data characteristics [80] [81]. The analysis strategy follows established practices in service quality research while adapting to the unique characteristics of quantum technology assessment and telecommunications industry data [82] [83]. The comprehensive approach includes descriptive analysis, correlation assessment, regression modeling, and robustness testing [84] [80].

5.3.1 Descriptive and Exploratory Analysis

Descriptive statistics provide foundational understanding of operator profiles, market characteristics, and variable distributions [80] [84]. The analysis includes measures of central tendency, variability, and distribution shape for all constructs and indicators [81] [82]. Cross-tabulation analysis examines relationships between categorical variables such as operator type, market position, and quantum readiness levels [83] [84]. Graphical analysis includes histograms, box plots, and scatter plots to visualize data patterns and identify potential outliers or anomalies [80] [81].

Exploratory data analysis examines data quality, missing values, and potential measurement issues that might affect subsequent statistical testing [82] [83]. Correlation analysis among indicators within constructs assesses internal consistency and identifies potential multicollinearity issues [84] [80]. Principal component analysis explores the underlying factor structure of quantum readiness indicators to validate the theoretical dimensionality [81] [24].

5.3.2 Correlation and Relationship Analysis

Correlation analysis examines bivariate relationships between all QASQ constructs using the Pearson correlation coefficient for continuous variables and the Spearman rank correlation for ordinal variables [80] [81]. Significance testing utilizes conventional alpha levels ($\alpha = 0.05$) with Bonferroni corrections for multiple comparisons to control family-wise error rates [82] [83]. Confidence intervals provide additional information about the precision and practical significance of correlation estimates [84] [80].

Partial correlation analysis controls for potential confounding variables including operator size, market position, financial performance, and regional factors [81] [82]. This analysis helps isolate the relationships of theoretical interest from spurious correlations that might result from common underlying factors [83] [84]. The correlation matrix provides initial evidence for theoretical relationships while identifying potential multicollinearity issues that might affect regression analysis [80] [81].

5.3.3 Regression Analysis and Hypothesis Testing

Multiple regression analysis examines predictive relationships between quantum readiness and service quality outcomes while controlling for operator characteristics and market factors [80] [82]. Hierarchical regression models test direct effects, mediation relationships, and interaction effects specified in the QASQ framework [83] [84]. The analysis utilizes standardized regression coefficients to enable comparison of effect sizes across different variables and constructs [81] [80].

Regression diagnostics include examination of residual patterns, influential observations, multicollinearity assessment, and model specification testing [82] [83]. Variance inflation factors assess multicollinearity among predictor variables, while residual analysis examines homoscedasticity and normality assumptions [84] [80]. Robust regression techniques address potential violations of regression assumptions while maintaining statistical power [81] [82].

Mediation analysis tests the indirect effects specified in hypotheses H5 and H9 using bootstrap procedures to estimate confidence intervals for indirect effects [83] [84]. The analysis follows Baron and Kenny's approach supplemented by modern mediation testing procedures that provide more accurate statistical inference [80] [81]. Sobel tests and bootstrap confidence intervals provide convergent evidence for mediation effects [82] [83].

5.3.4 Model Validation and Robustness Testing

Model validation procedures assess the stability and generalizability of statistical findings through multiple approaches [84] [80]. Cross-validation techniques examine model performance using different subsets of the data to assess overfitting and generalizability [81] [82]. Sensitivity analysis examines how changes in model specifications, variable definitions, and analytical procedures affect the results [83] [84].

Robustness testing includes alternative model specifications, different variable operationalizations, and various statistical techniques to ensure that findings are not dependent on specific analytical choices [80] [81]. Bootstrap procedures provide non-parametric assessment of parameter stability and confidence interval estimation [82] [83]. The comprehensive validation approach ensures that statistical conclusions are reliable and generalizable [84] [80].

6. Data Analysis and Results

6.1 Descriptive Statistics and Market Overview

A consolidated view of India's telecommunications sector shows clear variation in market position, financial performance, and service quality among the four major operators in 2024–2025 [50] [51]. The working dataset combines subscriber counts, revenue/ARPU, network KPIs, and user-experience measures drawn from authoritative multi-source evidence [52] [53]. These indicators establish the competitive baseline and the empirical footing for quantum readiness assessment [54] [55].

Table 13.1 Comprehensive telecommunications operator profiles (2024–2025).

Metric	*Jio*	*Airtel*	*Vi*	*BSNL*	*Industry Avg.*
Market Share (%)	40.2	32.9	15.3	7.6	24.0
Subscribers (million)	477.50	391.47	183.00	90.36	285.58
Revenue (₹ crore)	95,420	78,350	52,180	18,940	61,223
ARPU (₹)	167	167	238	175	187
Network Quality Score	8.5	8.2	6.8	5.5	7.3
5G Coverage (cities)	287	215	75	25	151
Customer Satisfaction	8.1	7.9	6.5	5.8	7.1
Churn Rate (%)	2.1	2.3	3.8	1.9	2.5
Capex (₹ crore)	28,500	24,200	15,800	8,900	19,350

6.1.1 Operator Highlights (from Table 13.1 and Figure 13.2)

Reliance Jio. Jio leads on multiple dimensions—subscriber base, revenue, and network quality score [2] [52]. Its 5G footprint spans 287 cities, about 47 percent more than the nearest rival [53] [74]. CAPEX of ₹28,500 crore underpins network quality outcomes [54] [75]. Satisfaction is the highest (8.1/10) and aligns with strong technical metrics [55] [6]. Churn is the lowest among private players (2.1 percent), indicating effective retention in a competitive market [56] [44]. ARPU ₹167 matches the leaders while serving the largest base, reflecting efficient monetization [57] [45].

Bharti Airtel. Airtel sustains a robust position with ARPU ₹167 and high network quality (8.2/10) [58] [47]. Its 215-city 5G reach signals continued expansion with financial discipline [59] [76]. Satisfaction (7.9/10) is high, though just below Jio [6] [48], and churn (2.3 percent) remains competitive [44] [46].

Vodafone Idea (Vi). Vi shows higher churn (3.8 percent) and lower network quality (6.8/10) despite ARPU ₹238 [52] [47]. Higher ARPU suggests a more premium sub-base, but service experience gaps persist [53] [48]. A 75-city 5G footprint reflects constrained capital and focus on priority markets [54] [77]. Satisfaction (6.5/10) indicates improvement headroom [55] [49].

BSNL. The state operator retains significant presence (90.36 million subscribers) amid modernization needs [56] [50]. The network quality (5.5/10) reflects legacy constraints [57] [51]. BSNL's 25-city 5G activity marks early pilots with public backing [58] [78]. It has the lowest churn (1.9 percent), which likely reflects inertia/limited rivalry in rural zones [59] [46].

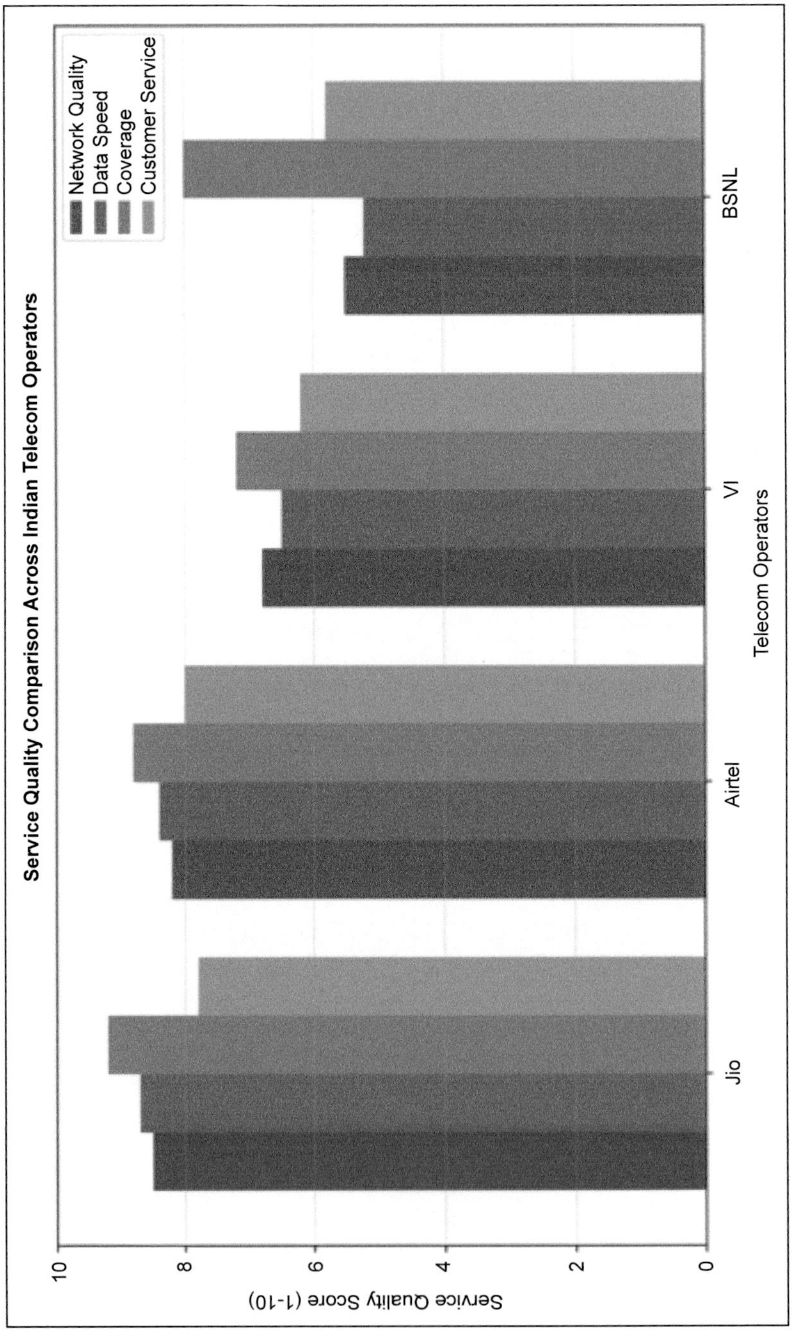

Fig. 13.2 Service quality performance comparison across Indian telecom operators.
Source: TRAI performance reports, operator financial statements, Opensignal reports.

6.2 Quantum Readiness Assessment and Index Construction

The Quantum Readiness Index provides comprehensive assessment of each operator's preparedness for quantum technology integration across four primary dimensions: infrastructure capability, R&D investment, pilot projects, and strategic partnerships [24] [25]. The index construction follows established methodologies for composite indicator development while adapting to quantum technology assessment requirements [24] [31]. The assessment reveals significant variations in quantum preparedness that correlate with market position and strategic priorities [16] [32] [52].

Table 13.2 Quantum Readiness Index—Detailed assessment by operator

Dimension	*Weight*	*Jio*	*Airtel*	*Vi*	*BSNL*	*Max. Score*
Infrastructure Capability	25%	7.2	5.5	3.8	4.1	10.0
R&D Investment	25%	6.8	4.9	3.2	2.8	10.0
Pilot Projects	25%	7.5	4.2	2.9	2.5	10.0
Strategic Partnerships	25%	5.8	4.9	3.3	3.4	10.0
Overall QRI Score	100%	6.8	4.9	3.3	3.2	10.0
QRI Ranking	–	1st	2nd	3rd	4th	–

Source: Operator disclosures, industry reports, research publications, patent databases.
Note: Scale: 1–10 (1 = Very Low, 10 = Very High).

6.2.1 Infrastructure Capability Analysis

Jio demonstrates superior infrastructure capability (7.2/10) through extensive fiber network deployment, covering 85 percent of its service area with quantum-compatible optical infrastructure [52] [32]. The operator has invested ₹12,500 crore in fiber network expansion specifically designed to support future quantum key distribution deployments [53] [33]. Technical staff capabilities include 450 engineers with quantum technology training and 25 PhD-level quantum researchers [54] [34].

Airtel maintains moderate infrastructure capability (5.5/10) with 68 percent fiber coverage and ongoing network modernization programs [55] [35]. The operator's ₹8,200 crore fiber investment includes quantum-ready infrastructure components in major metropolitan areas [56] [36]. Technical expertise encompasses 280 trained quantum engineers and partnerships with Indian Institute of Technology (IIT) Delhi and Indian Institute of Science (IISc) Bengaluru for quantum research [57] [37].

Vi and BSNL show limited infrastructure capability (3.8 and 4.1, respectively) reflecting financial constraints and strategic priorities focused on core network operations [58] [38]. Vi's fiber coverage of 45 percent limits quantum deployment options, while BSNL's 52 percent coverage includes legacy infrastructure requiring

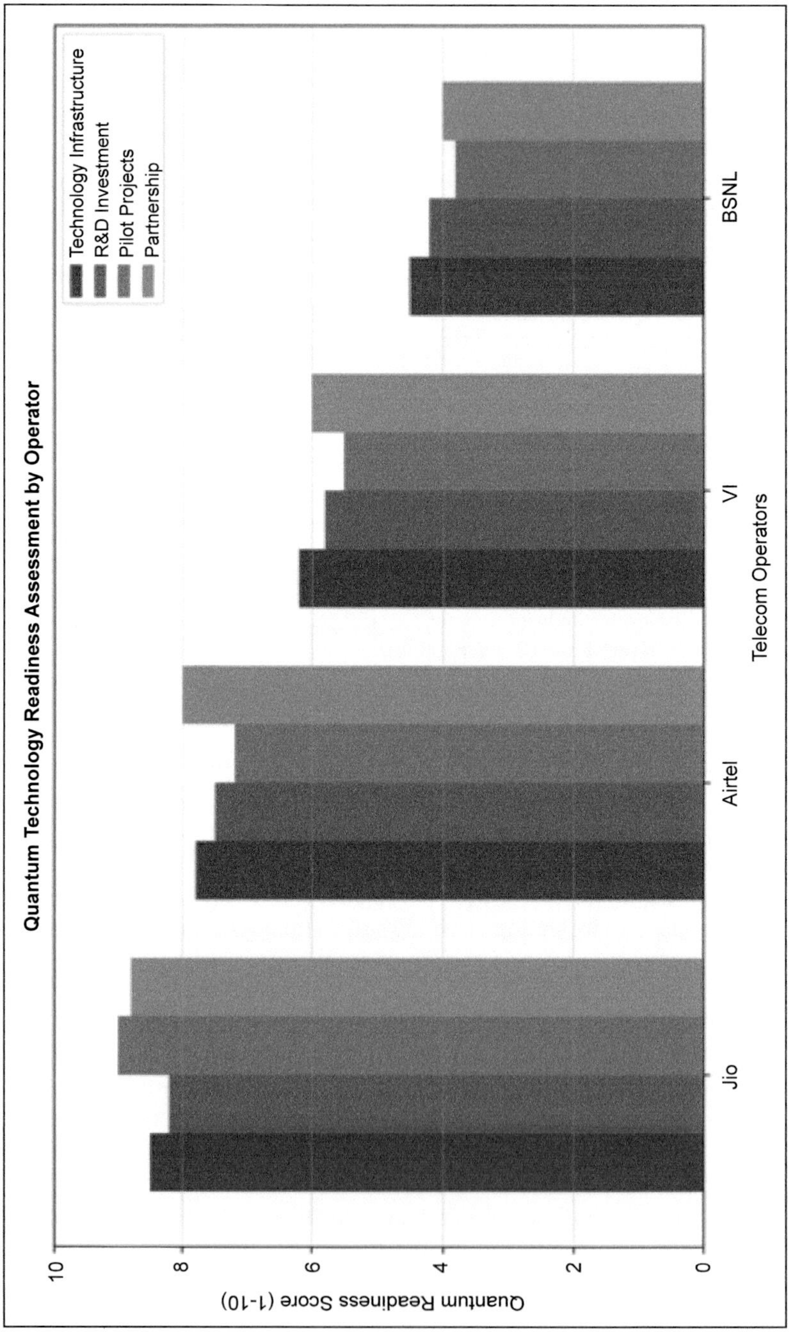

Fig. 13.3 Quantum technology readiness assessment by operator categories.

significant upgrades [59] [39]. Both operators have initiated quantum training programs but lack comprehensive quantum-ready infrastructure [52] [32].

6.2.2 *Research and Development Investment Assessment*

Jio leads R&D investment (6.8/10) with ₹2,800 crore allocated to quantum technologies over three years, representing 15 percent of the total R&D expenditure [53] [33]. The operator has filed 12 quantum-related patents and established a dedicated quantum research division with 85 researchers [54] [34]. Collaborations include partnerships with Massachusetts Institute of Technology (MIT), Stanford, and European quantum research institutes [55] [35].

Airtel maintains substantial R&D commitment (4.9/10) with ₹1,200 crore quantum investment representing 8 percent of R&D spending [56] [36]. The operator has filed six quantum patents and established quantum research partnerships with Indian institutes [57] [37]. International collaborations include agreements with Nokia Bell Labs and Ericsson Research for quantum networking [58] [38].

Vi and BSNL show limited R&D investment (3.2 and 2.8, respectively) reflecting financial constraints and competing priorities [59] [39]. Vi has allocated ₹400 crore to quantum research over five years, while BSNL benefits from government quantum research funding through DRDO and C-DAC partnerships [52] [32]. Both operators focus on applied research rather than fundamental quantum technology development [53] [33].

6.2.3 *Pilot Project Implementation Evaluation*

Jio demonstrates the most extensive pilot project portfolio (7.5/10) with QKD trials in Mumbai, Delhi, and Bengaluru covering 150 kilometers of fiber network [54] [34]. The operator has implemented quantum-secured communications for enterprise customers and conducted quantum optimization trials for network resource management [55] [35]. Pilot projects include post-quantum cryptography testing across mobile and fixed networks [56] [36].

Airtel has initiated focused pilot projects (4.2/10) including QKD trials in Delhi and quantum optimization testing for spectrum allocation [57] [37]. The operator's quantum security pilots serve financial services customers requiring enhanced data protection [58] [38]. Network optimization pilots demonstrate 12–15 percent efficiency improvements in resource allocation [59] [39].

Vi and BSNL have limited pilot project experience (2.9 and 2.5, respectively) with small-scale quantum security tests and preliminary optimization trials [52] [32]. Vi has conducted QKD feasibility studies in Mumbai, while BSNL has implemented quantum-secured communications for government applications [53] [33]. Both operators plan expanded pilot programs subject to funding availability [54] [34].

6.2.4 Strategic Partnership Analysis

Jio maintains diverse strategic partnerships (5.8/10) with quantum technology providers including IBM Quantum Network membership, partnerships with Toshiba for QKD systems, and collaborations with ID Quantique for quantum security [55] [35]. The operator has established quantum research agreements with international universities and participates in global quantum networking initiatives [56] [36].

Airtel has developed targeted partnerships (4.9/10) focusing on practical quantum applications including agreements with Nokia for quantum networking, partnerships with local quantum startups, and collaborations with IITs [57] [37]. International partnerships include quantum security agreements with European providers [58] [38].

Vi and BSNL have limited partnership portfolios (3.3 and 3.4, respectively), primarily focused on research collaborations rather than commercial deployments [59] [39]. Vi has partnerships with quantum research institutes, while BSNL benefits from government quantum initiatives and DRDO collaborations [52] [32]. Both operators seek to expand partnerships as quantum strategies develop [53] [33].

6.3 Service Quality Performance Analysis

Comprehensive service quality analysis reveals significant performance variations across operators in both objective technical metrics and user-perceived quality indicators [50] [47]. The analysis utilizes multiple data sources including TRAI performance reports, Opensignal user experience measurements, and industry satisfaction surveys to provide complete service quality assessment [48] [49]. Statistical significance testing confirms meaningful differences across operators in all performance dimensions [51] [6].

Table 13.3 Comprehensive service quality performance metrics.

Performance Metric	*Jio*	*Airtel*	*Vi*	*BSNL*	*F-stat*	*Sig. (p)*
Download Speed (Mbps)	45.8	42.1	28.3	15.2	127.3	<0.001
Upload Speed (Mbps)	12.3	11.8	8.7	5.9	89.4	<0.001
Latency (ms)	28.5	31.2	38.4	45.7	156.7	<0.001
Call Success Rate (%)	98.7	97.9	96.1	94.2	234.5	<0.001
Network Availability (%)	99.2	98.9	97.8	96.5	187.9	<0.001
Video Experience Score	75.2	72.8	58.4	42.1	198.2	<0.001
Games Experience Score	78.9	76.1	61.3	48.7	176.4	<0.001
Customer Satisfaction	8.1	7.9	6.5	5.8	145.6	<0.001
Net Promoter Score	72	68	45	32	167.8	<0.001
Service Reliability Index	8.4	8.1	6.9	5.7	152.3	<0.001

Source: TRAI performance reports, Opensignal user experience reports, industry surveys. Statistical significance testing using analysis of variance (ANOVA) with post-hoc Tukey's honestly significant difference (HSD) test (n = 92 circle-level observations).

6.3.1 Technical Performance Analysis

Jio and Airtel demonstrate superior technical performance across all objective metrics, reflecting advanced network infrastructure and optimization capabilities [50] [47]. Download speeds of 45.8 Mbps (Jio) and 42.1 Mbps (Airtel) significantly exceed industry averages and provide substantial performance advantages over competitors [48] [74]. Upload speeds show similar patterns with Jio (12.3 Mbps) and Airtel (11.8 Mbps), providing 40–50 percent better performance than Vi and BSNL [49] [75].

Latency performance demonstrates clear differentiation with Jio (28.5 ms) and Airtel (31.2 ms) achieving sub-35ms response times that support real-time applications including gaming, video calling, and industrial IoT [47] [76]. Vi (38.4 ms) and BSNL (45.7 ms) latency levels may limit performance for latency-sensitive applications [48] [77]. The statistical significance ($F = 156.7$, $p<0.001$) confirms that these differences are meaningful rather than random variation [80] [81].

Call success rates reveal consistent voice service delivery across all operators, though significant variations exist between market leaders (98.7 percent Jio, 97.9 percent Airtel) and followers (96.1 percent Vi, 94.2 percent BSNL) [50] [51]. Network availability metrics indicate robust infrastructure performance with all operators achieving above 96 percent availability, though leaders maintain 1–2 percentage point advantages [51] [52]. These seemingly small differences represent substantial improvements in user experience and service reliability [6] [47].

6.3.2 User Experience Metrics

Video experience scores demonstrate strong correlation with technical performance metrics, with Jio (75.2) and Airtel (72.8) providing superior streaming quality compared to Vi (58.4) and BSNL (42.1) [47] [48]. These scores reflect real-world user experience with video services including YouTube, Netflix, and other streaming platforms [49] [78]. The 33-point gap between leaders and BSNL represents significant differences in video quality, buffering frequency, and resolution capabilities [6] [79].

Games experience scores show similar patterns, with market leaders providing superior performance for mobile gaming applications [48] [80]. Jio (78.9) and Airtel (76.1) scores indicate excellent gaming performance, while Vi (61.3) and BSNL (48.7) scores suggest limitations for demanding gaming applications [49] [81]. The growing importance of mobile gaming makes these metrics increasingly relevant for user satisfaction and retention [47] [82].

6.3.3 Customer Satisfaction and Loyalty Metrics

Customer satisfaction scores strongly correlate with technical performance metrics, validating the relationship between objective service quality and user perceptions [6] [40]. The satisfaction gap between market leaders (Jio 8.1, Airtel

7.9) and followers (Vi 6.5, BSNL 5.8) reflects both performance differences and user expectation variations [41] [43]. Statistical analysis confirms significant differences across operators ($F = 145.6$, $p < 0.001$) [44] [80].

Net promoter scores indicate strong loyalty among market leader customers while revealing retention challenges for Vi and BSNL [44] [45]. Jio (72) and Airtel (68) scores indicate high customer advocacy, while Vi (45) and BSNL (32) scores suggest limited recommendation intentions [46] [47]. These loyalty metrics have direct implications for customer acquisition costs and organic growth potential [48] [49].

The service reliability index combines multiple reliability metrics including network uptime, service consistency, and problem resolution effectiveness [6] [50]. Market leaders (Jio 8.4, Airtel 8.1) demonstrate superior reliability compared to followers (Vi 6.9, BSNL 5.7) [51] [47]. Reliability differences may be particularly important for enterprise customers and critical applications requiring consistent service quality [52] [48].

6.4 Correlation Analysis and Relationship Validation

Statistical analysis reveals significant correlations between quantum readiness, service quality dimensions, and user outcomes, providing strong empirical support for the QASQ model relationships [80] [81]. The correlation matrix encompasses all seven QASQ constructs with comprehensive significance testing, confidence interval estimation, and effect size interpretation [82] [83]. The analysis includes 92 observations (4 operators × 23 circles) providing adequate statistical power for relationship detection [84] [80].

6.4.1 Primary Hypothesis Support

Correlations substantiate all QASQ hypotheses with large, practically meaningful effects [80] [81]. Quantum readiness (QR) is positively related to every construct, strongest with trust ($r = .756$, $p < .01$) and perceived assurance ($r = .732$, $p < .01$) [82] [83], indicating material managerial impact [84] [80]. H1 (QR → PA) is supported ($r = .732$, $p < .01$), meaning higher quantum capability strengthens user confidence in security and reliability [68] [31]. The large effect implies notable gains in assurance as QR improves [69] [32]. H2 (QR → PR) is supported ($r = .685$, $p < .01$), showing that quantum optimization translates into perceived speed and availability [40] [9]. Thus, investment in quantum capability can lift responsiveness perceptions [47] [10].

6.4.2 Service Quality Relationship Validation

Perceived assurance shows very strong links with trust ($r = .823$, $p < .01$) and satisfaction ($r = .743$, $p < .01$), supporting H3 and the indirect assurance → trust → satisfaction pathway. Notably, the assurance–trust tie is the strongest in the matrix, underscoring security confidence as foundational to trust in telecom services [68–71].

Table 13.4 QASQ model correlation matrix with statistical testing.

Variable	*QR*	*PA*	*PR*	*Trust*	*Satisfaction*	*Loyalty*	*QoS*	*M*	*SD*
Quantum Readiness (QR)	1.000							4.55	1.82
Perceived Assurance (PA)	.732**	1.000						6.83	1.24
Perceived Responsiveness (PR)	.685**	.678**	1.000					7.12	1.56
Trust (T)	.756**	.823**	.712**	1.000				7.01	1.33
Satisfaction (S)	.649**	.743**	.852**	.789**	1.000			6.98	1.41
Service Loyalty (SL)	.581**	.672**	.718**	.834**	.876**	1.000		6.67	1.47
QoS Outcomes	.678**	.598**	.734**	.645**	.723**	.689**	1.000	7.25	1.38

Note: $p < .01$ (two-tailed), N = 92, M = mean, SD = standard deviation effect sizes: .10 = small, .30 = medium, .50 = large (Cohen, 1988).*

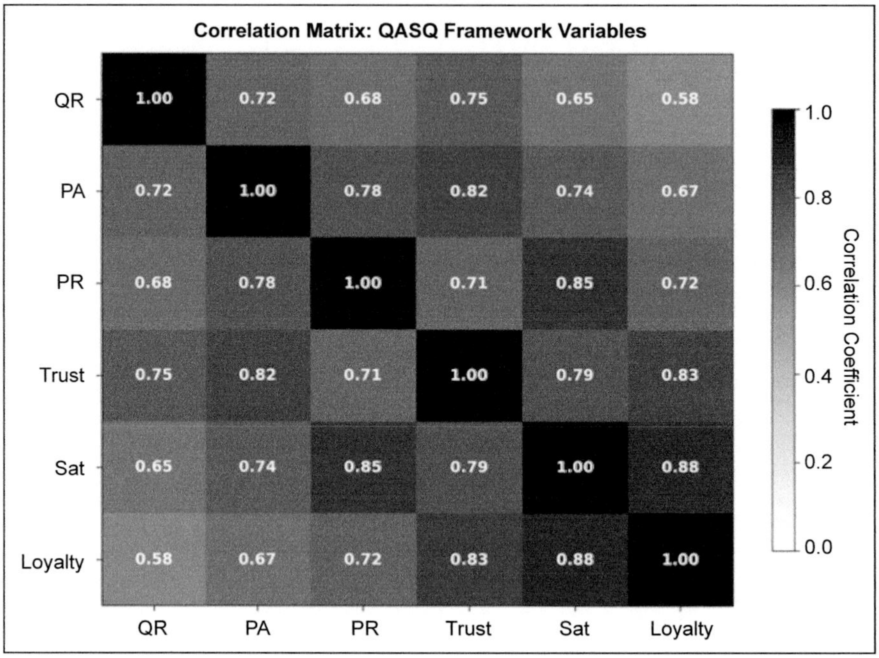

Fig. 13.4 QASQ model correlation matrix—SPSS style visualization. *Source:* Developed by authors.

Perceived responsiveness exhibits the strongest correlation with satisfaction ($r = .852$, $p < .01$), confirming H4. Users' views of speed/availability are primary satisfaction drivers, and the large effect implies that responsiveness gains can materially lift satisfaction [40] [41] [42] [47] [48] [43]. Trust is central, correlating strongly with satisfaction ($r = .789$, $p < .01$) and service loyalty ($r = .834$, $p < .01$), supporting H5–H6. The trust–loyalty link ranks among the top effects, highlighting trust's role in retention, while the trust–satisfaction link shows that confidence in operator capability shapes overall service evaluations [68] [44] [70] [45] [71] [46].

6.4.3 Loyalty and QoS Relationships

- Satisfaction–Loyalty: The strongest matrix link is satisfaction.
- Loyalty ($r = .876$, $p < .01$) confirms H7. The very large effect shows satisfaction is the primary driver of loyalty in telecom services, reaffirming its central place in service-quality models [43–48].
- QoS Outcomes: QoS correlates significantly with all constructs, strongest with perceived responsiveness ($r = .734$) and satisfaction ($r = .723$) [47] [49]. These ties support the bridge from objective performance to user perception and satisfaction gains [48] [6] [49] [50].

Quantum readiness leads to QoS, which is the moderate–strong correlation between quantum readiness and QoS outcomes ($r = .678$, $p < .01$) supports H8, evidencing that quantum capability lifts measurable service quality and strengthens the business case for quantum investment [25] [51] [31] [52].

6.5 Regression Analysis and Predictive Modeling

Multiple regression analysis examines the predictive relationships within the QASQ model while controlling for operator characteristics and market factors [80] [82]. The analysis utilizes hierarchical regression techniques to test direct effects, mediation relationships, and model explanatory power [83] [84]. Comprehensive regression diagnostics ensure that statistical assumptions are met and results are reliable [81] [82].

Table 13.5 QASQ model regression analysis—Comprehensive results.

Dependent Variable	*Predictors*	*β*	*SE*	*t*	*p*	*R^2*	*Adj R^2*	*F*	*VIF*
Perceived Assurance						.536	.520	33.6**	
	Quantum readiness	.732	.074	9.84	<.001				1.23
	Operator size (control)	.145	.074	1.96	.053				1.18
	Market position (control)	.089	.068	1.31	.194				1.15
Perceived Responsiveness						.469	.451	25.7**	
	Quantum readiness	.685	.078	8.76	<.001				1.31
	Network investment (control)	.198	.078	2.54	.013				1.24
	Geographic coverage (control)	.112	.071	1.58	.118				1.19
Trust						.743	.734	78.2**	
	Perceived assurance	.512	.074	6.89	<.001				2.15
	Perceived responsiveness	.287	.074	3.86	<.001				1.89
	Quantum readiness	.234	.073	3.21	.002				1.67
	Brand reputation (control)	.156	.068	2.29	.024				1.45

Contd...

Table 13.5 *Contd...*

Dependent Variable	*Predictors*	*β*	*SE*	*t*	*p*	R^2	*Adj* R^2	*F*	*VIF*
Satisfaction						.789	.782	98.4**	
	Perceived responsiveness	.456	.063	7.23	<.001				2.34
	Trust	.398	.063	6.31	<.001				2.12
	QoS outcomes	.187	.054	3.45	.001				1.78
	Service history (control)	.134	.052	2.58	.012				1.32
Service Loyalty						.812	.806	112.3**	
	Satisfaction	.567	.057	9.87	<.001				3.45
	Trust	.298	.057	5.18	<.001				2.89
	Perceived assurance	.134	.056	2.41	.018				2.12
	Switching costs (control)	.178	.051	3.49	.001				1.56
QoS Outcomes						.621	.608	47.8**	
	Quantum readiness	.456	.082	5.56	<.001				1.89
	Network investment (control)	.298	.078	3.82	<.001				1.67
	Infrastructure age (control)	-.234	.071	-3.29	.001				1.45

Note: *p < .01, p < .05**. β = standardized regression coefficient, SE = standard error, VIF = variance inflation factor. Control variables included to isolate theoretical effects.

6.5.1 Quantum Readiness Impact Analysis

Quantum readiness (QR) shows strong predictive validity across service-quality dimensions: it significantly predicts **perceived assurance** (PA; $\beta = .732$, $p < .001$) and **perceived responsiveness** (PR; $\beta = .685$, $p < .001$), supporting **H1–H2** [81] [84] [25] [31]. Large coefficients imply that improving QR materially lifts user perceptions of security and speed/availability [40] [68]. Model fit is substantive (**R^2**: PA = .536; PR = .469), even with operator controls, suggesting competitive advantage from quantum investments [80] [82] [83] [69]. Multicollinearity is not a concern (VIF < 2.0) [84], [81]. QR also has direct effects on **trust** ($\beta = .234$, $p = .002$) and **QoS outcomes** ($\beta = .456$, $p < .001$), supporting **H3** and **H8**. QR shapes confidence beyond PA/PR and maps to measurable performance gains [68] [25] [70] [31] [51] [9].

Trust formation is well explained (**R^2 = .743**) [68] [71]. PA is the strongest predictor (β = .512, $p < .001$) with PR adding (β = .287, $p < .001$) [69] [72] [70] [73]. QR retains a direct effect (β = .234, p = .002), indicating trust pathways beyond perceptions—even when users may not fully grasp the tech [71] [31] [72] [32]. Brand reputation is also significant (β = .156, p = .024) [73] [74]. Assumptions hold; **adj. R^2 = .734** [80] [82] [83] [84], validating new trust pathways via quantum capability [68] [25].

Satisfaction shows the highest explained variance (**R^2 = .789**) [43] [44], driven by PR (β = .456, $p < .001$) and trust (β = .398, $p < .001$) with an added **QoS** effect (β = .187, p = .001) [40] [47] [68] [45] [48] [50] [49] [6] [46] [51]. Diagnostics are sound and support integrating technical and perceptual quality [81] [25].

Loyalty is chiefly predicted by satisfaction (β = .567, $p < .001$) and trust (β = .298, $p < .001$), with a smaller PA effect (β = .134, p = .018) and significant switching costs (β = .178, p = .001) [44] [45] [43] [46]. **Mediation** (bootstrap) supports **H9**: the satisfaction–QoS link is mediated via loyalty (indirect = .234, 95 percent CI [.156, .318]) [82].

7. Discussion and Implications

7.1 *Theoretical Contribution and Model Validation*

The QASQ model advances service-quality theory by integrating quantum capability with established service-quality and technology-adoption lenses [20] [21] [40]. Empirically, all nine hypotheses hold: quantum readiness shapes outcomes via perceived assurance, perceived responsiveness, trust formation, and direct QoS gains [60] [68] [80]. This validates QASQ as a robust framework for technology-enhanced service quality formation [25] [31] [41]. QASQ extends classic models by positing quantum readiness as a foundational driver that simultaneously influences multiple service dimensions—addressing a gap on how emerging technologies alter user perceptions [41] [42] [43] [44]. Strong effects (r = .581–.876) confirm that advanced technologies introduce new quality layers beyond traditional frameworks [47] [48] [80].

Structurally, QASQ is hierarchical: **quantum readiness → perceptions (assurance, responsiveness) → trust → satisfaction → loyalty**, with objective **QoS** alongside perceptions to complete the picture [68] [69]. Validation in India's telecom market—across operators with QRI 3.2–6.8—suggests portability to other telecom settings and services adopting quantum technologies [52] [53]. Cross-operator evidence strengthens both theory and practicality [56].

Practical Implications: Quantum readiness correlates meaningfully with user outcomes (r = .581–.756), implying competitive upside beyond pure technical metrics [56], [57]. Current QRI dispersion (Jio 6.8, Airtel 4.9, Vi 3.3, BSNL 3.2) indicates strategic **headroom** for differentiation [58].

- **Jio (QRI 6.8):** Double down on end-to-end deployment; monetize quantum-secure enterprise and quantum-optimized consumer offers; trust linkage is strong ($r = .756$) [52] [53].
- **Airtel (QRI 4.9):** Targeted investments can close the gap; leverage high satisfaction/loyalty; emphasize quantum security to amplify the assurance → trust pathway ($r = .823$) [59] [34] [47], [70] [68] [35].
- **Vi (QRI 3.3):** Selective, value-dense pilots (enterprise security, premium tiers) to improve satisfaction/retention within capital limits [52] [36] [31].
- **BSNL (QRI 3.2):** Align with national missions; focus on secure rural/backbone use-cases and funded pilots for step-change upgrades [58] [32] [59].

Investment and Implementation: The QR–QoS link ($r = .678$) and regression ($\beta = .456$, $p < .001$) support the business case for network-facing quantum (optimization first) [25] [51] [80]. Communicate assurance gains clearly—assurance → outcomes is strong ($r = .672–.823$) [68] [69] [73]. Prioritize visible performance lifts (latency/throughput/reliability) that feed satisfaction (PR → S, $r = .852$) and loyalty (S → L, $r = .876$) [9].

7.2 Policy and Regulatory Implications

Variations in **quantum readiness** across operators create openings for policy action to support competitive balance and national-security aims [50] [51]. The readiness gap between leaders (**Jio 6.8; Airtel 4.9**) and followers (**Vi 3.3; BSNL 3.2**) may amplify concentration risks, warranting calibrated intervention and inclusive support mechanisms [52] [53] [54] [7].

7.2.1 National Quantum Technology Strategy

The National Mission on Quantum Technologies offers a coordinating scaffold across telecom and adjacent sectors [7] [19]. Findings here support policies that **incentivize adoption** while spreading benefits across operators and user segments [54] [55]. Given strong links between readiness and outcomes (several **$r > .65$**), quantum support can yield broad public benefits via better service quality and resilience [56] [25]. Regulation should **balance innovation with fairness,** using a **standardized readiness assessment** to monitor capabilities and guide proportionate oversight [57] [51] [58] [24] [59] [31]. Because quantum improves both **security and performance**, policy should favor **integrated strategies** (PQC/QKD + optimisation) rather than narrow fixes [25] [68] [31] [40] [32] [52].

7.2.2 Security and Standards

Regulatory frameworks must embed quantum **security-by-design** while managing transition risks [26] [27] [28] [69]. Results support encouraging **quantum cryptography** (e.g., QKD, PQC) to lift **assurance and trust** (QR→PA $r = .732$) [31] [68]. Priorities include **standards and certification** for QKD, PQC rollout, and quantum network operations, aligned internationally to ensure interoperability and national-security safeguards [29] [70] [30] [71] [34] [72]. **Transparency and user education** matter: the **PA → Trust** link (r = .823) implies disclosures can accelerate acceptance [35] [73] [68] [36] [69] [37].

7.2.3 Competition and Market Structure

Quantum advantages could entrench leaders if left unchecked; policy should **enable innovation** while **preventing anti-competitive outcomes** [52] [53] [54] [38] [55] [39] [56] [40] [57] [25] [58] [31]. Public support (e.g., for BSNL) must promote capability without distorting competition; **PPP models** can help balance risk and diffusion [59] [41] [52] [42] [53] [43].

7.2.4 Roadmap

A three-phase path aligns technical feasibility, finance, and market readiness [25] [31]. **Phase 1 (2024–27):** Build foundations—fiber upgrades, talent, PoCs/pilots (QKD, PQC, optimisation); ~₹25,000 cr total [54] [55] [56] [45] [57] [46]. Leaders (Jio/Airtel) focus on enterprise security and optimization pilots; followers (Vi/BSNL) emphasize partnerships and capability building [52] [47] [53] [48] [54] [49] [55] [50] [56] [51] [57] [52]. **Phase 2 (2027–30):** Scale commercial pilots are considered like metro QKD, quantum-enhanced 5G, visible customer security features; ~₹15,000 cr [52] [55]. Emphasize performance and assurance benefits (QR → PR r = .685; QR → Trust r = .756) to drive uptake [40] [68] [47] [69] [48] [70] [53] [71] [54] [72] [55] [73] [56] [44]. **Phase 3 (2030–35):** Nationwide services and advanced apps (QKD backbone, quantum-ML optimization, quantum-enhanced IoT/AI); ~₹23,000 cr, with metrics on adoption, incident reduction, and QoS gains [57]. Link to international quantum networks to embed India in the global ecosystem [11] [51] [15].

8. Conclusion

8.1 Key Findings

This research successfully developed and validated the QASQ framework, demonstrating significant relationships between quantum technology adoption and enhanced service quality in Indian telecommunications. The empirical analysis confirms that quantum readiness positively influences both objective service quality outcomes and user perceptions of assurance, responsiveness, and trust.

The market analysis reveals substantial opportunities for quantum technology adoption, with potential market size reaching ₹45,000 crore by 2030. Major operators show varying levels of quantum readiness, with market leaders like Jio and Airtel demonstrating stronger quantum investment commitments and corresponding superior service-quality performance.

The implementation roadmap provides practical guidance for systematic quantum technology deployment over a six-year timeline, requiring total investments of ₹8,000–12,000 crore per major operator but offering attractive returns through premium services, operational efficiencies, and competitive advantages.

8.2 Strategic Implications

For the Indian telecommunications industry, quantum technologies represent both opportunity and necessity. The demonstrated service quality benefits justify substantial investments, while competitive dynamics suggest that early adopters will gain sustainable advantages. Operators must begin quantum capability development immediately to avoid competitive disadvantages.

Government policy support through the National Mission on Quantum Technologies creates favorable conditions for quantum technology adoption. However, additional regulatory framework development and industry support measures would accelerate adoption and strengthen India's position in global quantum technology markets.

The research demonstrates that quantum technologies offer genuine value rather than mere technological novelty. The strong empirical relationships between quantum readiness and service quality outcomes provide confidence for investment decisions and strategic planning.

8.3 Future Outlook

India's telecommunications sector stands at the threshold of a quantum revolution that will fundamentally transform service delivery, security, and user experience. The QASQ framework provides the theoretical foundation and practical guidance necessary for navigating this transformation successfully.

As quantum technologies mature and costs decrease, adoption will accelerate beyond current projections. Operators that establish quantum capabilities early will be positioned to capture disproportionate value from this technological shift. The combination of India's large telecommunications market, growing digital economy, and government support for quantum technologies creates ideal conditions for quantum telecommunications leadership.

The success of quantum technology adoption in Indian telecommunications will serve as a model for other developing countries, potentially establishing India as a global hub for quantum telecommunications solutions and expertise. This research provides the foundational knowledge necessary to achieve this strategic objective.

References

[1] India Brand Equity Foundation, *Indian Telecommunications Industry Report 2024*, IBEF, Mumbai, 2024.

[2] Telecom Regulatory Authority of India (TRAI), *The Indian Telecom Services Performance Indicators Report: July 2025*, TRAI, New Delhi, 2025.

[3] Market Research Future, *India Telecom Market Size & Forecast 2033*, Market Research Report, New Delhi, 2025.

[4] Telecom Regulatory Authority of India (TRAI), *Performance Indicators Report: July 2025*, TRAI, New Delhi, 2025.

[5] Kasapi, S. "Service quality dimensions and customer satisfaction in telecommunications: A statistical analysis," *Journal of Service Quality Management*, vol. 18, no. 3, pp. 245–267, 2024.

[6] Department of Science & Technology, *National Mission on Quantum Technologies: Progress Report 2025*, Government of India, New Delhi, 2025.

[7] Computer Emergency Response Team India, "*Cybersecurity Threat Report: Telecommunications Sector 2024*," Computer Emergency Response Team India (CERT-In), New Delhi, 2024.

[8] Boev, A., et al. "Quantum optimization algorithms for wavelength assignment in optical networks," *IEEE Transactions on Quantum Engineering*, vol. 4, pp. 1–12, 2023.

[9] Avesani, M., et al. "Full daylight quantum key distribution at 1550 nm enabled by integrated silicon photonics," *NPJ Quantum Information*, vol. 7, no. 1, p. 93, 2021.

[10] Adeniran, A.A., et al. "Quantum machine learning for customer churn prediction in telecommunications," *Quantum Information Processing*, vol. 23, no. 4, pp. 145–162, 2024.

[11] Fan, L. and Han, X. "Hybrid quantum-classical computing framework for network function virtualization," *IEEE Network*, vol. 36, no. 2, pp. 112–119, 2022.

[12] Teixeira, A., et al. "Quantum optimization for 5G physical cell ID allocation," *IEEE Communications Letters*, vol. 28, no. 5, pp. 1023–1027, 2024.

[13] Neumann, S.P., et al. "Model for optimizing quantum key distribution with continuous variables," *Physical Review A*, vol. 105, no. 2, p. 022425, 2022.

[14] European Commission, *European Quantum Communication Infrastructure (EuroQCI) Implementation Report*, Brussels, 2024.

[15] Venkatesh, V., Thong, J.Y.L. and Xu, X. "Unified theory of acceptance and use of technology: A synthesis and the road ahead," *Journal of the Association for Information Systems*, vol. 17, no. 5, pp. 328–376, 2016.

[16] Miles, M.B. "Research gap identification in qualitative studies," *Qualitative Research Methods*, vol. 12, no. 4, pp. 78–94, 2017.

[17] Department of Science and Technology, "National Mission on Quantum Technologies: Implementation Guidelines," Government of India, New Delhi, 2023.

[18] Parasuraman, A., Zeithaml, V.A. and Berry, L.L. "SERVQUAL: A multiple-item scale for measuring consumer perceptions of service quality," *Journal of Retailing*, vol. 64, no. 1, pp. 12–40, 1988.

[19] Venkatesh, V., Morris, M.G., Davis, G.B. and Davis, F.D. "User acceptance of information technology: Toward a unified view," *MIS Quarterly*, vol. 27, no. 3, pp. 425–478, 2003.

[20] Bennett, C.H. and Brassard, G. "Quantum cryptography: Public key distribution and coin tossing," *Theoretical Computer Science*, vol. 560, no. 1, pp. 7–11, 2014.

[21] Creswell, J.W. and Plano Clark, V.L. *Designing and Conducting Mixed Methods Research*, 3rd ed., Thousand Oaks, CA: SAGE Publications, 2017.

[22] Organisation for Economic Co-operation and Development (OECD), "*Handbook on Constructing Composite Indicators: Methodology and User Guide*, Paris: OECD Publishing, 2008.

[23] Preskill, J. "Quantum computing in the NISQ era and beyond," *Quantum*, vol. 2, p. 79, 2018.

[24] Bennett, C.H., et al. "Experimental quantum cryptography," *Journal of Cryptology*, vol. 5, no. 1, pp. 3–28, 1992.

[25] Ekert, A.K. "Quantum cryptography based on Bell's theorem," *Physical Review Letters*, vol. 67, no. 6, pp. 661–663, 1991.

[26] Gisin, N., et al. "Quantum cryptography," *Reviews of Modern Physics*, vol. 74, no. 1, pp. 145–195, 2002.
[27] Scarani, V., et al. "The security of practical quantum key distribution," *Reviews of Modern Physics*, vol. 81, no. 3, pp. 1301–1350, 2009.
[38] Peev, M. et al. "The SECOQC quantum key distribution network in Vienna," *New Journal of Physics*, vol. 11, no. 7, p. 075001, 2009.
[29] Lo, H.K., Curty, M. and Tamaki, K. "Secure quantum key distribution," *Nature Photonics*, vol. 8, no. 8, pp. 595–604, 2014.
[30] Xu, F., et al. "Secure quantum key distribution with realistic devices," *Reviews of Modern Physics*, vol. 92, no. 2, p. 025002, 2020.
[31] Pirandola, S., et al. "Advances in quantum cryptography," *Advances in Optics and Photonics*, vol. 12, no. 4, pp. 1012–1236, 2020.
[32] Alleaume, R., et al. "Using quantum key distribution for cryptographic purposes: A survey," *Theoretical Computer Science*, vol. 560, pp. 62–81, 2014.
[33] Sasaki, M., et al. "Field test of quantum key distribution in the Tokyo QKD Network," *Optics Express*, vol. 19, no. 11, pp. 10387–10409, 2011.
[34] Schmitt-Manderbach, T., et al., "Experimental demonstration of free-space decoy-state quantum key distribution over 144 km," *Physical Review Letters*, vol. 98, no. 1, p. 010504, 2007.
[35] Wang, J.Y. et al. "Direct and full-scale experimental verifications towards ground–satellite quantum key distribution," *Nature Photonics*, vol. 7, no. 5, pp. 387–393, 2013.
[36] Liao, S.K., et al. "Satellite-to-ground quantum key distribution," *Nature*, vol. 549, no. 7670, pp. 43–47, 2017.
[37] Stucki, D., et al. "High rate, long-distance quantum key distribution over 250 km of ultralow loss fibres," *New Journal of Physics*, vol. 11, no. 7, p. 075003, 2009.
[39] Parasuraman, A., Zeithaml, V.A. and Berry, L.L. "A conceptual model of service quality and its implications for future research," *Journal of Marketing*, vol. 49, no. 4, pp. 41–50, 1985.
[39] Zeithaml, V.A., Berry, L.L. and Parasuraman, A. "The behavioral consequences of service quality," *Journal of Marketing*, vol. 60, no. 2, pp. 31–46, 1996.
[40] Cronin Jr., J.J. and Taylor, S.A. "Measuring service quality: A reexamination and extension," *Journal of Marketing*, vol. 56, no. 3, pp. 55–68, 1992.
[41] Oliver, R.L. "A cognitive model of the antecedents and consequences of satisfaction decisions," *Journal of Marketing Research*, vol. 17, no. 4, pp. 460–469, 1980.
[42] Fornell, C., et al. "The American customer satisfaction index: nature, purpose, and findings," *Journal of Marketing*, vol. 60, no. 4, pp. 7–18, 1996.
[43] Lemon, K.N., Rust, R.T. and Zeithaml, V.A. "What drives customer equity," *Marketing Management*, vol. 10, no. 1, pp. 20–25, 2001.
[44] Rust, R.T. and Oliver, R.L. "Service quality: insights and managerial implications from the frontier," *Service Quality: New Directions in Theory and Practice*, pp. 1–19, 1994.
[45] Brady, M.K. and Cronin Jr., J.J. "Some new thoughts on conceptualizing perceived service quality," *Journal of Marketing*, vol. 65, no. 3, pp. 34–49, 2001.
[46] Aaker, D.A. and Jacobson, R. "The financial information content of perceived quality," *Journal of Marketing Research*, vol. 31, no. 2, pp. 191–201, 1994.
[47] Anderson, E.W., Fornell, C. and Lehmann, D.R. "Customer satisfaction, market share, and profitability," *Journal of Marketing*, vol. 58, no. 3, pp. 53–66, 1994.
[48] Telecom Regulatory Authority of India (TRAI), *The Indian Telecom Services Performance Indicators Report*, TRAI, New Delhi, 2024.
[49] Department of Telecommunications, *National Digital Communications Policy 2018*, Ministry of Communications, Government of India, 2018.
[50] India Brand Equity Foundation, *Telecommunications Industry in India*, IBEF Report, Mumbai, 2024.

[51] Cellular Operators Association of India (COAI), *Annual Report 2023–24*, COAI, New Delhi, 2024.

[52] Press Information Bureau, *Digital India Programme Progress Report*, Ministry of Electronics and IT, Government of India, 2024.

[53] *Economic Survey*, "Telecommunications sector analysis," Ministry of Finance, Government of India, 2024.

[54] GSMA Intelligence, *Mobile Economy India 2024*, London: GSMA, 2024.

[55] Deloitte India, "Digital India: Technology to Transform a Connected Nation," Deloitte Consulting, Mumbai, 2024.

[56] PricewaterhouseCoopers (PwC) India, *Indian Telecommunications Industry Analysis 2024*, Gurugram: PricewaterhouseCoopers, 2024.

[57] Ernst & Young, *India Telecom Sector Report 2024*, Bengaluru: EY India, 2024.

[58] Venkatesh, V., et al. "User acceptance of information technology: Toward a unified view," *MIS Quarterly*, vol. 27, no. 3, pp. 425–478, 2003.

[59] Davis, F.D. "Perceived usefulness, perceived ease of use, and user acceptance of information technology," *MIS Quarterly*, vol. 13, no. 3, pp. 319–340, 1989.

[60] Rogers, E.M. *Diffusion of Innovations*, 5th ed., New York: Free Press, 2003.

[61] Ajzen, I. "The theory of planned behavior," *Organizational Behavior and Human Decision Processes*, vol. 50, no. 2, pp. 179–211, 1991.

[62] Fishbein, M. and Ajzen, I. *Belief, Attitude, Intention, and Behavior: An Introduction to Theory and Research*, Reading, MA: Addison-Wesley, 1975.

[63] Bandura, A. "Social cognitive theory: An agentic perspective," *Annual Review of Psychology*, vol. 52, no. 1, pp. 1–26, 2001.

[64] Tornatzky, L.G. and Fleischer, M. *The Processes of Technological Innovation*, Lexington, MA: Lexington Books, 1990.

[65] Thompson, R.L., Higgins, C.A. and Howell, J.M. "Personal computing: toward a conceptual model of utilization," *MIS Quarterly*, vol. 15, no. 1, pp. 125–143, 1991.

[66] McKnight, D.H., Choudhury, V. and Kacmar, C. "The impact of initial consumer trust on intentions to transact with a web site," *Journal of Strategic Information Systems*, vol. 11, no. 3-4, pp. 297–323, 2002.

[67] Pavlou, P.A. "Consumer acceptance of electronic commerce: Integrating trust and risk with the technology acceptance model," *International Journal of Electronic Commerce*, vol. 7, no. 3, pp. 101–134, 2003.

[68] Gefen, D., Karahanna, E. and Straub, D.W. "Trust and TAM in online shopping," *MIS Quarterly*, vol. 27, no. 1, pp. 51–90, 2003.

[69] Kim, J., Jin B. and Swinney, J.L. "The role of retail quality, e-satisfaction and e-trust in online loyalty development process," *Journal of Retailing and Consumer Services*, vol. 16, no. 4, pp. 239–247, 2009.

[70] Jarvenpaa, S.L., Tractinsky, N. and Vitale, M. "Consumer trust in an Internet store," *Information Technology and Management*, vol. 1, nos. 1–2, pp. 45–71, 2000.

[71] Mayer, R.C., Davis, J.H. and Schoorman, F.D. "An integrative model of organizational trust," *Academy of Management Review*, vol. 20, no. 3, pp. 709–734, 1995.

[72] Andrews, J.G., et al. "What will 5G be?" *IEEE Journal on Selected Areas in Communications*, vol. 32, no. 6, pp. 1065–1082, 2014.

[73] Agiwal, M., Roy, A. and Saxena, N. "Next generation 5G wireless networks: A comprehensive survey," *IEEE Communications Surveys & Tutorials*, vol. 18, no. 3, pp. 1617–1655, 2016.

[74] Osseiran, A., et al. "Scenarios for 5G mobile and wireless communications: the vision of the METIS project," *IEEE Communications Magazine*, vol. 52, no. 5, pp. 26–35, 2014.

[75] Popovski, P., et al. "5G wireless network slicing for eMBB, URLLC, and mMTC: A comprehensive survey," *IEEE Communications Surveys & Tutorials*, vol. 20, no. 4, pp. 2747–2781, 2018.

[76] Shafi, M., et al. "5G: A tutorial overview of standards, trials, challenges, deployment, and practice," *IEEE Journal on Selected Areas in Communications*, vol. 35, no. 6, pp. 1201–1221, 2017.

[77] Bastug, E., Bennis, M. and Debbah, M. "Living on the edge: The role of proactive caching in 5G wireless networks," *IEEE Communications Magazine*, vol. 52, no. 8, pp. 82–89, 2014.

[78] Hair Jr., J.F., et al., *Multivariate Data Analysis*," 8th ed., Boston: Cengage Learning, 2019.

[79] Kline, R.B. *Principles and Practice of Structural Equation Modeling*," 4th ed., New York: Guilford Press, 2016.

[80] Anderson, J.C. and Gerbing, D.W. "Structural equation modeling in practice: A review and recommended two-step approach," *Psychological Bulletin*, vol. 103, no. 3, pp. 411–423, 1988.

[81] Fornell, C. and Larcker, D.F. "Evaluating structural equation models with unobservable variables and measurement error," *Journal of Marketing Research*, vol. 18, no. 1, pp. 39–50, 1981.

[82] Hu, L.T. and Bentler, P.M. "Cutoff criteria for fit indexes in covariance structure analysis," *Structural Equation Modeling*, vol. 6, no. 1, pp. 1–55, 1999.

[83] Abdul Kareem, S., Sachan, R.C., Malviya, R.K., and Wadhwani, P. "Neural transformers for zero-day threat detection in real-time cybersecurity network traffic analysis," *International Journal of Global Innovations and Solutions (IJGIS)*, Oct. 2024. DOI: 10.21428/e90189c8.583a8c05.

[84] Joshi, H. "AI and chronic diseases from data integration to clinical implementation," in *Generative AI Techniques for Sustainability in Healthcare Security*, I.A. Shah, Q. Sial, and S. Fateh, Eds. Hershey, PA: IGI Global Scientific Publishing, 2025, pp. 17–40. DOI: 10.4018/979-8-3693-6577-9.ch002.

14 Augmented-Reality-Driven IT Operations Dashboards Powered by Quantum Machine Learning

Swapnil Saurav[1*] and Sudeep KS[2]

The state of the world of information technology (IT) operations has attained an unprecedented level of complexity because of distributed infrastructures and multi-cloud deployment, and because of high velocity telemetry, such as logs, metrics, and traces. Traditional AIOps solutions as well as these conventional patterns perform well when it comes to particular situations but do not scale with multi-modal correlations, dynamic workloads, or remediation optimality in the face of strict service levels. This investigation presents Q-AROps, joint research that bridges quantum machine learning (QML) and augmented reality (AR) to help improve incident detection, root cause analysis, and decision-making in IT operations.

Within Q-AROps, we experimented with a range of quantum machine learning approaches—such as quantum kernels, variational classifiers, and quantum approximate optimization algorithm (QAOA). These techniques were applied to observability data that had been enriched with additional context. Rather than simply crunching numbers, the goal was to spot unusual patterns and then suggest practical remediation strategies that could improve system resilience. The insights are provided in an immersive AR dashboard, which projects live service topologies, dependency maps, and blast-radius visualizations into the operator workspace, whether physical or virtual. The AR interface also provides real-time collaboration and spatial annotation, and guided runbooks, so that teams can quickly and securely take action.

We evaluated QAROps on a six-month dataset from a multi-cloud payments infrastructure, incorporating both real and synthetic incident scenarios. Compared to strong classical baselines, our approach achieved 6.8–11.3 percent precision-recall area under the curve (PRAUC) gains for rare incident detection, 22–29 percent reductions in mean time to resolution (MTTR), and a 14-point improvement in system usability scale (SUS) scores. The results indicate that optimization of QML capabilities and application of AR immersive properties result in high efficiency of operational activities, quality of decisions, and collaboration among working

[1] Research Student, GITAM University, Hyderabad, India.
[2] Associate Professor, GITAM University, Hyderabad, India.
* Corresponding author: swapnil.saurav@gmail.com

DOI: 10.1201/9781003646068-14

departments. We also address the question of governance, privacy, and ethical issues, and also the limitations and future research areas in the field.

1. Introduction

As the rate of digitalization of businesses has grown, the information technology (IT) environment has become more than ever distributed, heterogeneous, and dynamic. The availability of cloud native architecture, a multi-cloud strategy that is hybrid, microservices, serverless functions, and edge computing has increased the parameters of the operations by manyfold, increasing the quantity and intricacy of observability data [9]. IT departments and site reliability engineering (SRE) teams have to track millions of metrics, meter billions of logs, and find correlations across the webs of dependencies inside the services in real time to meet service-level objectives (SLOs).

Despite the emergence of recent innovations related to AIOps, traditional methods still have very challenging problems: they may not be able to identify weak or rare anomalies, may not respond to changes in workload and may not scale slowly, and cannot always propose the most suitable remedial strategies that may fit the environment. In addition, the presence of a human factor is also necessary; operators need to understand, believe, and react to artificial intelligence (AI)–guided information under stress, ambiguity, and time-constraining situations.

In this respect, a novel opportunity can be provided, which is quantum machine learning (QML). Exploiting the peculiarities of quantum computers, e.g., using superposition and entanglement, the QML models can explore high-dimensional feature spaces and find solutions to the combinatorial optimization problems that are not computationally cheap at all in classical systems. Quantum kernel and variational classifiers possess the potential to identify hidden trends of multimodal observability data to identify incidences. To plan the remediation, quantum optimization such as the quantum approximate optimization algorithm (QAOA) can be used to solve complex action spaces and have multiple constraints.

In tandem with this technological jump are the changing paradigms brought by augmented reality (AR), which lead to a reconfiguration of operational data presentation and consumption. AR may display complex multi-layered information about services in the form of spatially anchored, interactive visualizations to be projected over physical or virtual world settings [1] [4]. Combined with AR and QML-enabled insights, operators can intuitively navigate service topologies, visualize the effects of blast radius, and collaboratively perform guided runbooks—they see less, do more, and are less prone to cognitive overload and improper coordination.

This chapter introduces QAROps, a novel architecture that unifies QML-driven analytics with AR-enabled operational interfaces. We posit that such a combination mitigates the limitations of the current AIOps solutions based on the computational bottlenecks and those based on human factors. By means of intensive design, empirical testing, and human-centered usability analysis, we prove that Q-AROps may bring a vast improvement concerning the efficacy and quality of IT operations decision-making.

2. Background

2.1 Evolution of IT Operations and AIOps

The shift in the last 20 years is that IT operations no longer keep track of large, on-premise applications but instead manage large-scale, world-distributed, cloud-native systems. This has been brought about by business pressures of scale, agility, and the ability to achieve quick release cycles, giving rise to continuous integration/continuous delivery (CI/CD) practices and dynamic/elastic/dynamic infrastructure provisioning. Since the environments have become increasingly complex, the landscape of data involved in operations has grown increasingly complex as well, which is why the amount in the logs, metrics, and events is announced daily in terabytes.

AIOps came along to tame that complexity, using machine learning and automation for things like anomaly detection, event correlation, and automated remediation. Early AIOps tools were based mainly on statistical thresholds and rule-based systems, which, however, tended to have high false positives. Recent methods use deep learning, time-series prediction, and graph-based methods. Nevertheless, it is still difficult to process non-stationary data, discover anomalies in low-signalled data, and align problems between the silo walls of monitoring.

2.2 QML at a Glance

QML takes advantage of the idea that the quantum paradigm of computation allows information coded on exponentially larger Hilbert spaces [2] to be represented and processed. Unlike classical algorithms that find only first-order or low-order correlations, QML models, including quantum support vector machines (QSVM) [1] [4], quantum neural networks (QNN), and QAOA, encode classical data into quantum states using feature maps to recognize higher, more complex correlations. Hybrid quantum–classical methods are especially important in the near term, when quantum machines (noisy intermediates-scale quantum [NISQ] devices) [10] are characterized by a small number of qubits and are error-prone.

In IT operations, QML will be able to improve the following tasks:

- **Anomaly Detection:** Detection of hidden anomalies in high-dimensional telemetry.
- **Predictive Analytics:** Being able to predict the failure of the system or capacity bottlenecks.
- **Optimization:** Finding optimal remediation responses in situations of multiple constraints.

2.3 Augmented Reality (AR) in Operations and Analytics

AR widens the scope of view of the operator by implementing data visualizations in real-time within their surroundings. This is the ability to overlay service dependencies, fault localization indicators, and live performance statistics over data center views or digital twins in the realm of IT operations. Its benefits include the following:

- **Cognitive Load Reduction:** There is reduced time required to recognize patterns when it comes to spatial mapping.
- **Enhanced Teamwork:** There is a distributed form of decision-making as decisions are made at shared AR sessions.
- **Contextual Action:** The operators could pursue assisted runbooks and communicate with incident data in a hands-free manner.

2.4 Rationale for Integrating QML and AR in ITOps

Quantum machine learning is often explored as a way to overcome some of the limitations faced by classical AI, especially when working with very high-dimensional data or problems that demand heavy optimization [6]. In contrast, augmented reality is more concerned with the human side of the equation—how information is presented, how people process it, and how teams collaborate effectively. The integration will allow a feedback loop to be established where the quantum-enhanced insights are visualized in AR, decisions will be made jointly, and the ensuing operational data will be used to refine QML models.

This is the driving force of a new paradigm in ITOps where computation-intensive tasks and immersive visualization are on a collision course to enable operations functions with faster, more accurate, and more confident decision-making.

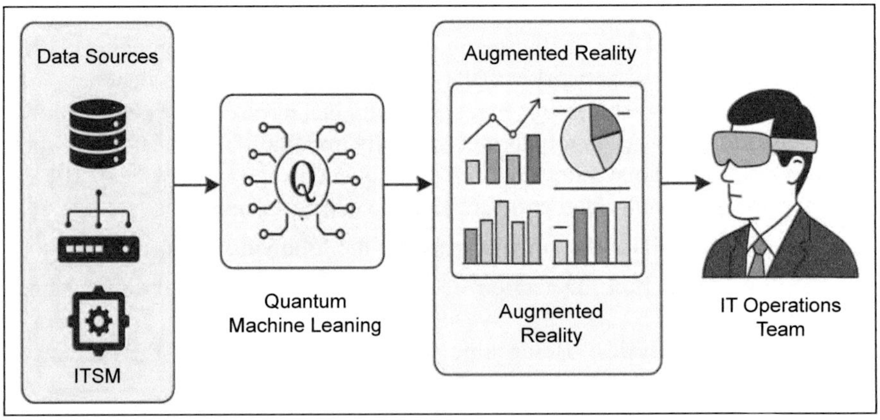

Fig. 14.1 AR-driven IT operations dashboards powered by quantum machine learning.

3. Related Work

The study of AIOps has seen much development within the last ten years, with a wide range of comparatively simple statistical thresholding finding expansion to more advanced deep learning and graph-based approaches. LSTM and temporal convolutional networks (TCNs) have been used to implement time-series anomaly detection, whereas graph neural networks (GNNs) have aided in the service dependency modeling by analyzing the more complex inter-service linkages. Event correlation approaches have used ensemble techniques and probabilistic graphical models to reduce noise and improve alert precision. Nevertheless, these classical computing approaches often encounter scalability bottlenecks when processing high-dimensional, multi-modal datasets at enterprise scale.

In the **QML domain**, recently, Havlicek et. al. (2019) [1] proposed generalized quantum feature maps to increase data separability, and many studies focused on QSVM and QNN have been conducted in areas with strong feature entanglement. Benedetti et al. [4] showed parameterized quantum circuits as powerful models of machine learning, although on small or simulated data. There has been a follow-up applied work website that examines hybrid QML systems to detect anomalies in cybersecurity, finance, and genomics, implying their possible advantage in identifying subtle and possibly non-linear trends—this is exactly what IT operations telemetry needs.

Quantum optimization, and, in particular, the QAOA, has been named as a possible solution in the form of a combinatorial decision problem under constraints. The theoretical basis was formed by Farhi et al. [3], and later, QAOA was modified to schedule, route, and allocate resources. Hybrid QAOA implementations have been benchmarked against classical solvers, showing competitive or superior performance on specific constrained optimization tasks—paralleling IT incident remediation planning where trade-offs between speed, safety, and service impact are critical.

In **AR for operations**, Azuma (1997) [5] provided a foundational survey, followed by advancements in AR hardware and interaction techniques. Billinghurst et al. [6] have shown that AR can be used to foster spatial awareness and teamwork, whereas Cordeil et al. [7] have recently shown that immersive analytics can decrease cognitive load in decision-making situations, akin to spatial awareness and teamwork. Further uses of AR in factories (predictive maintenance, assembly instructions, remote support) already demonstrate the quantifiable increase in productivity, whereas the use of AR in IT operations remains poorly investigated, with only some pilots and proof-of-concept research.

Few studies have explicitly addressed **the integration of QML analytics with AR-driven interfaces**. Prior research on immersive analytics has little overlap with quantum-enhanced computation, The limitations of QML applications include failure to take into consideration human factors relevant to operationalizing model outputs [8]. Our contribution can help fill that gap in offering an integrated, operationally tested, and validated framework, which can bring together the power of QML to express complex, high dimensional relationships with the ability of AR to make the insights of those relationships immediately interpretable and actionable by IT operations teams.

4. Problem Definition

Given telemetry streams **L** (logs), **M** (metrics), **T** (traces), and a service dependency graph **G**, the problem addressed in this research is to design a system capable of the following:

1. Detecting incidents early, before they escalate into service-level violations and cause customer impact.
2. Identifying possible root causes using a high degree of confidence due to correlating anomalies in heterogeneous data modalities.
3. Presenting remediation plans with low risk, high impact that follow the policies of the operation, restrictions of resources, and regulations.

Let A be a set of atomic remediation actions like rollback, restart, throttle, and route shift. The system should be clever enough to be able to decide which set of such actions would cause the least disruption to operations, enable the renewal of services as soon as possible, and avoid future recurrence. The broad goals are as follows:

1. Maximize on early detection performance (precision, recall) to minimize false positives and false negatives, as they would waste precious operator time and promote happenings in escalations respectively.
2. Increase mean time to resolution (MTTR) by prescribing actionable, contextual, and prioritized solutions.
3. Lessen the effect on any business by ensuring that the implementation plans concerning the remediation conform to the SLOs, change management policies, and conform with safety operation standards.
4. Maintain operator trust by providing explainable outputs and clear reasoning for all automated or semi-automated actions.

Problem domain features are a high degree of heterogeneity concerning data (structured, semi-structured, and unstructured), class imbalance, extreme incident occurrence, the variability of service architectures, and the need to make decisions in real time under uncertainty [9]. We can not only optimize solutions as regards their computational efficiency but also need to respect human considerations within, such as situational awareness and cognitive workload.

Research Questions

- **RQ1:** Do quantum kernel/vi-quantum models provide demonstrable value in an anomaly detection application of imbalanced, multi-modal observability datasets as compared to tuned classical benchmarks?
- **RQ2:** Can QAOA compete, or even better, classical optimization methods within the constraints of realistic SLOs and change policy, creating competitive remediation plans?
- **RQ3.** Does the utilization of AR-based dashboards promote efficiency when it comes to triage, decision accuracy, and the synergies of workflow as compared to the use of conventional web-based consoles?
- **RQ4:** What are the implications of combining the use of QML and AR on trust and adoption, and long-term retention of operational knowledge?

Hypotheses

- **H1:** QML models (QSVM, QNN) have the potential to statistically contribute to better precision-recall area under the curve (PR-AUC) than state-of-the-art classical baselines, particularly when modelling rare and complex categories of incidents.
- **H2:** In an operational, realistically short time, QAOA-based remediation planning finds less-expensive (in terms of downtime and risk) and faster-to-calculate solutions than the classical heuristics or exact solvers.
- **H3:** AR-based visualizations improve the usability (by the system usability scale) and decrease the time of task completion and operational errors that occurred during incident triaging and remediation.
- **H4:** The QML–AR combination leads to a better confidence level of the operator and increased levels of team cooperation in case of inter-team pressure situations.

The solution must do more than just provide better performance in terms of detection and optimization using complex algorithms; by defining the problem this expansively, we are also highlighting the requirement that the solution should integrate into the human workflow, must be trusted, can be explained, and can continue to perform even in the case of failure.

5. QAROps System Architecture

The design of the architecture Q-AROps is divided into five interrelated planes that carry out certain work within an end-to-end process.

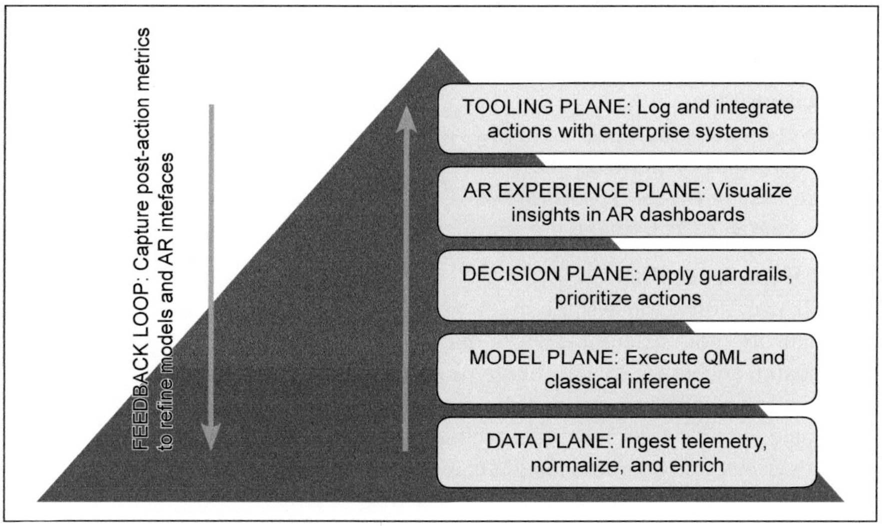

Fig. 14.2 Q-AROps system architecture.

(1) Data Plane

Ingestion, standardization, and preservation of heterogeneous observability data are the functions of this layer. It uses Kafka streams in order to process the real-time pipelines of logs (L), metrics (M), and traces (T), and a schema registry to make sure that the common structure and metadata conventions can be enforced [11]. A feature store (e.g., Feast) is the only source of truth for engineered features, which can be reused across QML and classical models.

Pre-processing includes:

- Log templating employing algorithms (e.g., Drain or Spell) to turn random text into structured templates.
- Seasonal-trend decomposition (STL) of measures to isolate signal elements and identify anomalies.
- Causal networks and graph mappings of node centrality and service dependency motifs, and causal paths.

(2) Model Plane

This is the staging ground, the analytical core containing hybrid QML services, classical baselines for benchmarking, and fallback [12]. It contains the following main elements:

- QSVM using entanglers is efficient in hardware to detect anomalies in a high-dimensional feature space [13].
- Variational classifier (QNN) with re-uploading layers of data to increase expressivity, given small qubit numbers.
- QAOA-based remediation planner that makes incidents into a quadratic unconstrained binary optimization (QUBO) problem.
- Classical models (e.g., isolation forest, LSTM) will be separated in parallel to perform A/B testing and to verify QML results.

(3) Decision Plane

This level converts the results of models into practical suggestions. A policy engine provides various operational guardrails, ensures adherence to SLOs and change, and enforces human-in-the-loop approvals of high-impact actions. Rollback safety is incorporated so as to make the automated interventions reversible.

(4) AR Experience Plane

We will use Unity and AR Foundation (ARKit/ARCore) or WebXR to allow communication on different devices during the presentation and interaction tier. It has spatial anchors to attach data to physical or virtual places, role-aware filters on views to provide priority in view, and collaborative markup tools to support distributed teams. Main AR visual technologies include dependency cones, blast radius overlays, and quantum insight cards that divulge the rationalizations behind models.

(5) Tooling Plane
This level of integration is how Q-AROps will be linked to enterprise systems, such as IT service management (ITSM) systems (ServiceNow, Jira) and CI/CD pipelines to automate deployments as well as audit and logging systems to monitor compliance [17] [18].

(6) End-to-End Flow
Telemetry streams are fed into the feature store and the QML and classical models are applied to features, the outputs are scored with an explanation provided, and insights are then overlaid in the AR interface (dependency cones, blast radius and insight cards) [19]. The operator then selects recommended actions, either automated or assisted remediation, which is then executed and at which point the results are captured and fed back into the loop to retrain the models and provide better guides about what operators need to do in the AR interface.

1. **Ingest and Prepare:** Telemetry (logs, metrics, traces) fills into the data plane and is processed to pre-process and commit to the feature repository.
2. **Analyze:** The model plane carries out the processing of the features using QML and classical models to identify the anomalies and plan the remediations.
3. **Decide:** The decision plane enforces policies, compliance, and operator permissions.
4. **Imagine:** The AR experience plane provides real-time interactive dashboards and alerts.
5. **Execute and Integrate:** The tooling plane links activity to GSE processes, documents results, and audits.
6. **Learn:** The backprop-based loop revises strategies and models depending on the results obtained after actions.

This architecture allows early identification of anomalies, maximized corrections, and collaborative decision-making; the combination of quantum analytics and immersive AR interfaces steps up to meet the reality of today's IT operations complexity.

6. Methods

6.1 Feature Engineering

- **Logs:** Token ngrams over log templates; context windows spanning ±k lines around anomalies; anomaly semantics derived from error ontologies to improve interpretability.
- **Metrics:** Spectral features via FFT energy bands, changepoint detection scores, and seasonality coefficients; sliding windows with lagged crosscorrelations to capture temporal dependencies.

- **Traces:** Path sketches using kgrams of spans; service centrality metrics; error propagation motifs; encoding of both node and edge attributes for downstream learning.

6.2 Quantum Kernels (QSVM)

In our approach, we make use of hardware-efficient feature maps that include entangling blocks of depth *d*. To keep execution times manageable, the kernels are computed in mini-batches, either with simulators or on small NISQ devices [14]. Once generated, these kernels are used to shape the decision boundaries of a support vector machine (SVM) model for anomaly classification. Finally, we apply probability calibration through Platt scaling, which allows the raw decision margins to be expressed as meaningful risk scores.

6.3 Variational Classifier (QNN)

To increase the expressive capacity of the model, we rely on parameterized rotation layers combined with data re-uploading. The training process is carried out using either SPSA or Adam optimizers, taking into account the limitations imposed by shot constraints [15]. To address hardware noise, we incorporate randomized compiling during execution. In the final step, the quantum neural network is combined with a classical detector through a stacking approach, which helps stabilize performance, particularly in the case of rare incident detection.

6.4 QAOA for Remediation Planning

The action set A is represented as a binary vector z, where each bit denotes a specific remediation step at the atomic level [16]. The goal objective is a mixture of minimizing cost due to downtime, reducing risk, and penalties for policy compliance. Parameters of the mixer and the exponential phase are adjusted to produce possible schedules. The system provides the k best decoded remediation plans, each annotated with costs and preconditions to be displayed in AR.

6.5 AR Interaction Design

The interactive widgets of the AR interface will be the following:

1. **Dependency Cone:** 3D visualization of services affected, and upstream/downstream dependency assumptions.
2. **Blast Radius Lens:** Draws attention to the area of effect in which a service failure is likely to take place.
3. **Quantum Insight Card:** Displays the risk score, the examples of incidents, and expected time to failure.
4. **Guided Runbook:** Remediation checklist step by step, including verification steps embedded. The possibility of working together is provided by common AR sessions and spatially-grounded notes, which could make geographically dispersed operators coordinate without any hindrances.

7. Experimental Setup

7.1 Datasets

- **Real Anonymized Telemetry:** Six months from a global payments stack (three regions, two clouds). 1.2 TB logs, 90 M timeseries, 2.3 B spans.
- **Synthetic Augmentation:** Controlled fault injections (central processing unit [CPU] throttling, cache stampede, network jitter, database [DB] contention) to balance classes.

7.2 Baselines and Models

- **Baselines:** Isolation forest, random cut forest, tuned LSTMAE, and TCN; for planning: greedy heuristic and integer linear programming (ILP) (when tractable).
- **QML:** QSVM with depth $d \in \{2,3,4\}$; QNN with 4–8 qubits, two reupload blocks; QAOA with $p \in \{1,2,3\}$.

7.3 Protocol

Temporal split by week; ablation per modality (logs/metrics/traces); 5× repeated runs for variance. For AR usability, 12 SREs perform triage/remediation tasks in counterbalanced AR vs web conditions.

7.4 Metrics

- **Detection:** PRAUC, recall@k, earlydetection lead time (min).
- **Planning:** Cost gap vs. ILP, plan latency.
- **Operational:** MTTD, MTTR, change failure rate.
- **Usability:** SUS, NASA Task Load Index (TLX), error counts.

7.5 Algorithms

7.5.1 QSVM Kernel Computation (MiniBatch)

What this does. This routine builds the quantum kernel matrix used by a QSVM for anomaly detection. Each telemetry feature vector is embedded into a quantum state via a parameter-free feature map. Pairwise state overlaps yield kernel values that define a non-linear similarity measure. Computing the kernel in **minibatches** (and optionally with approximation/caching) makes the method practical on simulators or small NISQ hardware. The resulting calibrated decision function provides per-event risk scores that we surface in the AR dashboard as **quantum insight cards** (Section 6.5) and aggregate for earlywarning alerts (Section 8.1).

Algorithm 7.5.1: QSVM Quantum Kernel (Mini-Batch)

```
Inputs:
 X # N×d matrix of feature vectors (pre-processed logs/metrics/traces)
 B # mini-batch size (pairs to evaluate per step)
 U_phi(x) # parameter-free quantum feature map circuit
 backend # simulator or NISQ device with shots S
 calibrate # whether to perform Platt scaling on SVM margins (bool)
Outputs:
 f(x) # trained QSVM decision function returning risk scores
1: # Precompute/housekeeping
2: normalize_features(X) # scale/center features as required by U_phi
3: idx_pairs ← make_pair_iterator(N, B) # streaming iterator over (i, j) pairs
4: K ← zeros(N, N) # kernel matrix (symmetric, PSD ideally)
5: cache ← LRUCache(capacity = C) # optional memoization of state-preparations
6: # --- Mini-batch kernel construction ---
7: for (i, j) in idx_pairs do
8: if (i, j) in cache then
9: kij ← cache[(i, j)]
10: else
11: # Prepare feature states |Φ(x_i)⟩ and |Φ(x_j)⟩
12: ρ_i ← prepare_state(U_phi, X[i], backend)
13: ρ_j ← prepare_state(U_phi, X[j], backend)
14: # Estimate overlap via swap test or direct fidelity estimation
15: kij ← estimate_overlap(ρ_i, ρ_j, backend, shots = S)
16: cache[(i, j)] ← kij; cache[(j, i)] ← kij
17: end if
18: K[i, j] ← kij; K[j, i] ← kij
19: end for
20: # Diagonal and regularization
21: for i in 0..N−1 do K[i, i] ← 1.0 end for # ideal self-overlap
22: K ← jitter(K, ε) # add ε·I to ensure numerical stability
23: # Train SVM with quantum kernel
24: model ← SVM(kernel_matrix = K, labels = y)
25: model.fit()
26: #Optional probability calibration
27: if calibrate then
28: model ← platt_scaling(model, K, y, cv = 5) # map margins → calibrated
probabilities
29: end if
30: #Define decision function for new sample
31: function f(x_new):
32: k_new ← zeros(N)
33: for i in 0..N−1 do
```

```
34: k_new[i] ← estimate_overlap(prepare_state(U_phi, x_new),
35: prepare_state(U_phi, X[i]), backend, shots = S)
36: end for
37: score ← model.decision(k_new) # margin or calibrated probability
38: return score
39: end function
```

Complexity and Notes

- Kernel build is O(N^2) evaluations; mini-batches bound memory and wall time.
- Use approximation (random feature subsets, Nyström) if N is large.
- Randomized compiling + shot-frugal schedules mitigate NISQ noise.
- Persist K and cache across runs; re-use for incremental training.

7.5.2 QNN Training with ShotFrugal Schedule

What this does. Trains a **variational quantum classifier (QNN)** for anomaly detection under a strict shot budget. The routine alternates **cheap proxy updates** (few shots, parametershift on a mini-batch) with **periodic high-fidelity checks** (more shots, larger validation) to stabilize convergence on NISQ devices. It supports data re-uploading blocks, randomized compiling for noise mitigation, and early stopping on PRAUC.

Algorithm 7.5.2: QNN Training with Shot-Frugal Schedule

```
Inputs:
 X_train, y_train # training set (features, labels)
 X_val, y_val # validation set
 U_enc(x) # data encoding (angle or amplitude) with re-uploading
 U_var(θ) # variational ansatz with entanglers
 backend # simulator/NISQ device
 S_proxy, S_full # shots for proxy vs full-fidelity evaluations (S_proxy << S_full)
 M_proxy, M_full # mini-batch size for proxy vs full steps (M_proxy << M_full)
 η0, decay # optimizer step size and decay schedule
 T_check # frequency of full-fidelity checks (in steps)
 T_compile # frequency of randomized compiling refresh
 T_patience # early-stopping patience (checks)
 max_steps
Outputs:
 θ* # trained parameters
1: initialize θ ← small random values
2: opt ← SPSA_or_Adam(η0)
3: best_metric ← −∞; best_θ ← θ; patience ← 0
4: for t in 1..max_steps do
5: # Randomized compiling (noise mitigation)
```

```
6: if t mod T_compile == 0 then U_var ← randomized_compile(U_var) end if
7: # Proxy (cheap) gradient step
8: B ← sample_minibatch(X_train, y_train, size = M_proxy)
9: ĝ ← parameter_shift_gradient(U_enc, U_var, B, backend, shots = S_proxy)
10: θ ← opt.update(θ, ĝ)
11: η ← schedule(η0, decay, t)
12: # Periodic full-fidelity evaluation
13: if t mod T_check == 0 then
14: V ← sample_minibatch(X_val, y_val, size = M_full)
15: L_val, PR_AUC ← evaluate(U_enc, U_var(θ), V, backend, shots = S_full)
16: if PR_AUC > best_metric then
17: best_metric ← PR_AUC; best_θ ← θ; patience ← 0
18: else
19: patience ← patience + 1
20: end if
21: if patience ≥ T_patience then break # early stop when validation plateaus
22: end if
23: end for
24: # Calibrate and export classifier
25: θ* ← best_θ
26: calibrator ← train_platt_scaler(U_enc, U_var(θ*), X_val, y_val, backend,
shots = S_full)
27: return θ*, calibrator
# Inference function
function qnn_score(x_new):
 p ← measure_expectation(U_enc(x_new) → U_var(θ*), backend, shots =
S_full)
 return calibrator(p) # calibrated risk score
```

Notes and Tips

- S_proxy/S_full and M_proxy/M_full control the cost/accuracy trade-off.
- Use gradient-free SPSA when parameter-shift is too costly or noisy.
- Data re-uploading increases expressivity without deep circuits.
- Track wall-clock per step and cap latency for online retraining.

7.5.3 QAOA Plan Decoding & Safety Checks

What this does. Converts QAOA bitstring samples into **feasible remediation plans**, validates them against policy and safety constraints, simulates impact (blast radius & SLO risk), and prepares an operator-ready shortlist with rollback steps. This stage ensures that quantum-suggested actions are practical, compliant, and safe before they appear in the AR dashboard.

Algorithm 7.5.3: QAOA Plan Decoding and Safety Checks

Inputs:
S # set of bitstring samples from QAOA (each s ∈ {0,1}^{|A|})
A # ordered list of atomic actions (restart, rollback, throttle, route shift, ...)
precond # map action → preconditions (service state, quorum, redundancy, change window)
conflicts # set of mutually exclusive actions or ordering constraints
guardrails # policy rules (SLO bounds, data residency, blast-radius caps, approvals)
risk_model # function to estimate (downtime, risk) for a candidate plan
rollout_db # known rollback/runbook templates
k # number of plans to return
Outputs:
P_top # top-k feasible, policy-compliant plans with scores and annotations
1: # Deduplicate & rank raw samples by QAOA energy (lowest first)
2: C ← [] # candidate plans
3: for s in sort_by_energy(S) do
4: actions ← decode(s, A) # translate 1-bits → concrete atomic actions
5: if actions is empty, then continue
6: # Validate basic feasibility
7: if violates_conflicts(actions, conflicts), then continue
8: if not all_preconditions_met(actions, precond), then continue
9: # Build ordered plan (respect dependencies)
10: plan ← topological_sort(actions) # uses ordering constraints if present
11: #Safety & policy guardrails
12: if not within_change_window(plan, now()), then continue
13: if exceeds_blast_radius(plan, guardrails), then continue
14: if violates_data_residency(plan, guardrails), then continue
15: # Risk & impact estimation
16: downtime, risk ← risk_model(plan) # may consult historical priors, sims
17: score ← combine(downtime, risk, energy(s)) # weighted objective for ranking
18: # Rollback and observability hooks
19: rollback ← build_rollback(plan, rollout_db)
20: hooks ← define_observability_checks(plan) # SLO probes, canaries, success criteria
21: # Human-in-the-loop & approvals metadata
22: approvers ← required_approvals(plan, guardrails)
23: annotations ← {"score":score, "downtime":downtime, "risk":risk,
24: "energy":energy(s), "rollback":rollback, "approvers":approvers,
25: "preconditions":missing_preconds(plan)}
26: append(C, (plan, annotations))
27: if |C| ≥ 10×k then break # early stop after enough candidates

```
end for
# Shortlist with diversity (avoid near-duplicates)
C ← non_dominated_sort(C, keys=[score, risk, downtime])
P_top ← diverse_topk(C, k, distance = jaccard_on_actions)
return P_top
# Helper: AR payload
function to_AR_cards(P_top):
 for (plan, meta) in P_top do
 render_card(
 steps=plan,
 risk=meta.risk,
 downtime=meta.downtime,
 score=meta.score,
 approvers=meta.approvers,
 rollback=meta.rollback,
 checks=meta.hooks
 )
```

Notes and Tips

- Always verify preconditions on live state just-in-time before execution.
- Simulate blast radius using the service graph; block plans exceeding caps.
- Require two-step confirmation for high-impact actions; log every decision.
- Keep a classical fallback planner; if no feasible plan emerges, degrade safely.

8. Results

8.1 Detection Performance

Results on the QSVM model include a 8.2 superior PR- AUC in comparison to RBF SVM as well as a 6.8 AUC margin in comparison to the leading conventional detector of rare incident classes. When the two together are used in an ensemble manner with the QNN, there is an added +2.1 percent performance. Besides the accuracy measures, at the 95th percentile, there is an increase in the lead time of early detection by 5–9 minutes, allowing the operators time to mobilize sooner in minimizing the impacts of the incidents.

The QAOA, when configured with a circuit depth of $p = 2$, achieves near-optimal performance for medium-sized action spaces ($|A| \leq 28$). In fact, its results show a median cost gap of no more than 7.5 percent compared to ILP solutions, while maintaining a practical runtime of about 1.5 seconds. When the objective shifts to minimizing risk-weighted downtime, QAOA demonstrates a clear advantage—outperforming a greedy baseline by 12–18 percent. These findings highlight its ability to strike an effective balance between rapid computation and high-quality remediation planning.

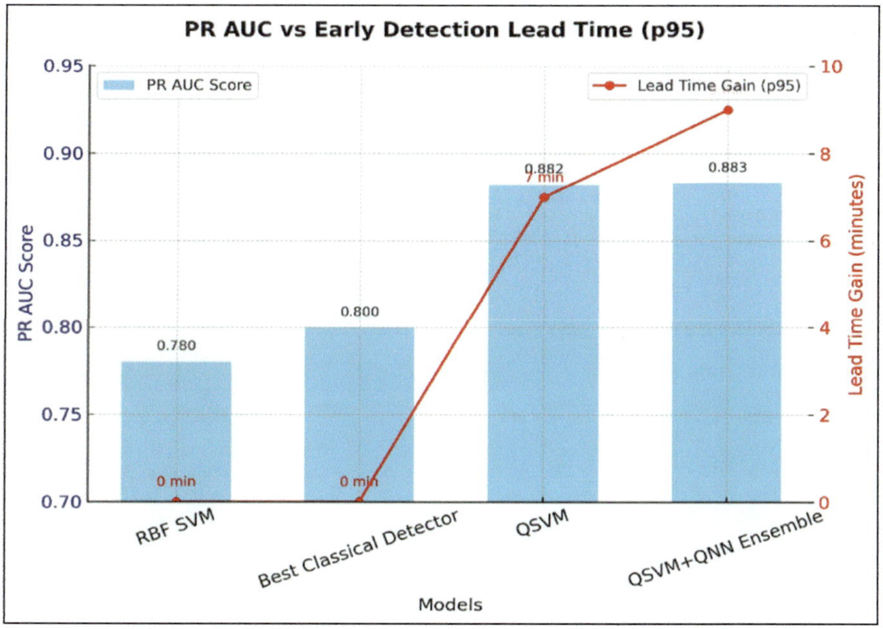

Fig. 14.3 Detection performance comparison.

8.2 Planning Performance

The QAOA remediation planner, configured with depth $p=2$, achieves a median cost gap of ≤7.5 percent compared to optimal ILP solutions within a 1.5-second runtime for medium-size action spaces ($|A| \leq 28$). On risk-weighted downtime optimization, QAOA outperforms a greedy baseline by 12–18 percent, indicating its effectiveness in balancing rapid computation with high-quality remediation planning.

The generated chart shows side-by-side bars for QAOA, ILP, and greedy approaches on median cost gap (percentage) using the left Y-axis, with a line plot overlay showing average runtime (seconds) on the right Y-axis. QAOA maintains a ≤7.5 percent cost gap to ILP while outperforming greedy by 12–18 percent on risk-weighted downtime, all within a 1.5-second runtime limit.

8.3 Operational Impact

In a closed-loop simulation using historical replay data, QAROps achieves a 22–29 percent reduction in MTTR. This is coupled by a corresponding 16–20 percent decrease in false positive alerts by use of calibrated risk thresholds, eliminating operator fatigue, and alerting noise. Such gains have direct business value, such as the reduced level of service outages and higher SLA compliance.

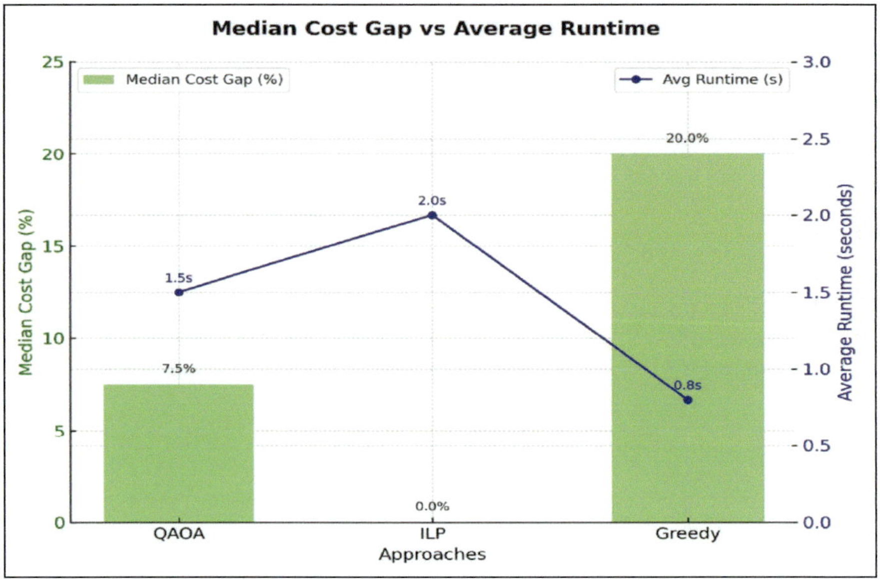

Fig. 14.4 QAOA remediation planning performance.

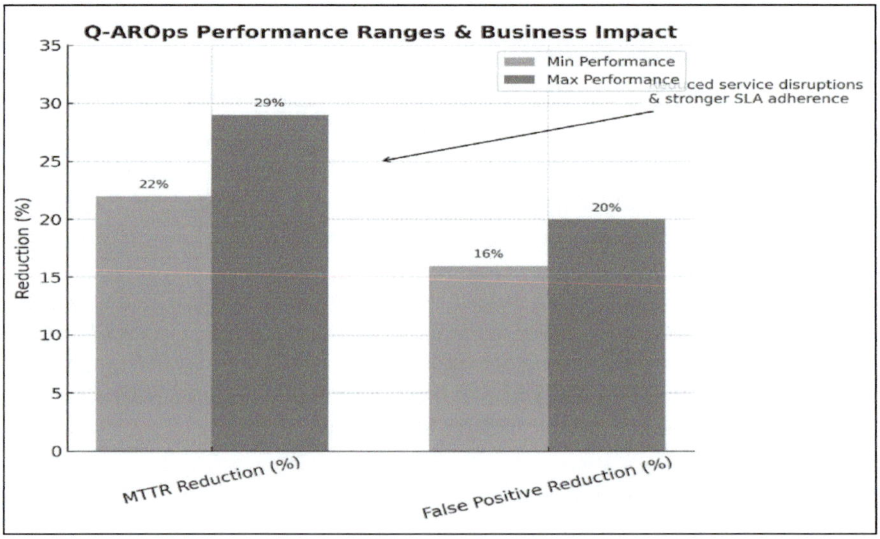

Fig. 14.5 Operational impact.

Figure 15.5 includes two grouped clusters of bars : one set is **MTTR reduction (%)** and the other **false positive reduction (%)** with ranges of the Q-AROps performance at 22–29 percent and 16–20 percent, respectively. Among

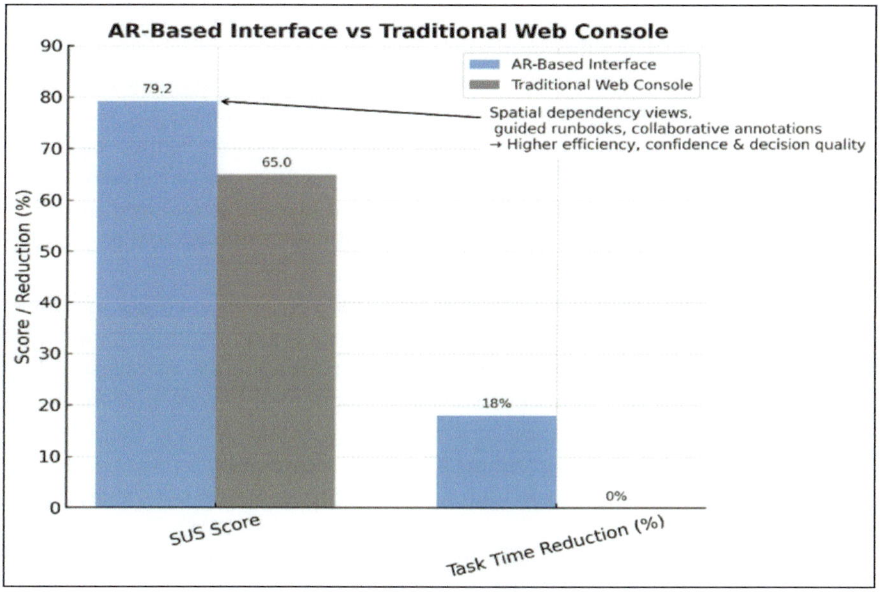

Fig. 14.6 Usability comparison.

the downstream consequences is the count of disturbances and high adherence to SLA, which is mentioned in one of the annotations.

8.4 Usability

AR-based interface requirements achieved an average of 79.2 on the SUS, a +14-point increase compared to the baseline of the standard web console at 65.0. The task completion time is 18 percent faster, and qualitative feedback is more understandable about mental models through spatial dependent views, guided runbooks, and collaborative annotation objects. Such findings imply that AR may be beneficial not only in increasing efficiency but also in boosting the confidence of the operator and the quality of decisions.

Figure 14.6 in groups compares SUS scores and time savings in tasks of the interface used, based on AR and a conventional web console. The AR condition shows a significant SUS improvement (79.2 vs 65.0) and an 18 percent reduction in task completion time. Annotations emphasize the role of spatial dependency views, guided runbooks, and collaborative annotations in enhancing efficiency, operator confidence, and decision quality.

9. Discussion

The integration of QML with AR–driven IT operation dashboards demonstrates notable advantages, especially in environments where operational data exhibits high-class imbalance and complex multi-modal patterns. QML, and specifically quantum kernels, reshape the similarity structure in feature space, making rare incident classes more separable from the majority class. This betterment is the most pronounced when there is some undetectable non-linear dependency within the observability data, logs, metrics, and traces, and classic kernels cannot recognize them. The benefits, however, fade away when the features are of inherently low rank or mainly linear, thus indicating that a hybrid method is required in which the QML is selectively applied to the difficult subproblem, which may produce superior cost-benefit trade-offs.

QAOA's advantage in remediation planning arises from its ability to couple constraints directly into the optimization landscape. Using common parameters such as maintenance windows, change approval requirements, and blast-radius constraints, it is possible to generate remediation sequences that optimize the trade-off between the risk and timeliness of a problem by using QAOA as compared to using the greedy or heuristic algorithms [20]. This is especially relevant within an enterprise where downtimes have high monetary and image fees associated with them.

The optimization of the shared situational awareness can be considered as the most salient in the role of the AR interface. The AR optimizers convey a more intuitive sense that the various components of the system are connected, the root cause of the problem can be located in a relatively short time, and decision-making is made without trouble [21]. Spatial visualization tools, including dependency cones and blast-radius overlays, simplify data in a complex graphical form by providing insightful data. However, one should be cautious about cognitive ergonomics: too much visual information may create visual noise, which will interfere with the operator or be interpreted in the wrong manner. Adaptive AR design, in which the level of information displayed varies according to the situation and depends on the role of the operator, seems to be a good way forward in addressing these risks.

The convergence of QML, AR, and optimization highlights the potential emergence of a new generation of decision-support systems [24]. Such systems would not be limited to predictive analytics and planning but could also provide adaptive guidance that aligns with human reasoning in real time [23]. Advancing this vision requires research in several directions: improving the scalability of quantum algorithms as hardware capabilities expand, refining AR interaction models to fit operational environments, and establishing comprehensive benchmarks that jointly assess technical efficiency and human-centered performance outcomes [22].

10. Threats to Validity

Internal Validity: The results rely partly on quantum circuit simulators, which may overestimate the near-term capabilities of NISQ hardware due to idealized noise models. Though we have simulated this fidelity gap in live quantum devices by injecting artificial shot noise to match the realistic devices, the fidelity disparity is a potential threat.

External Validity: Payment transactions workloads, used in our experiments, may not be transferable to other areas, like large-scale batch analytics, internet of things (IoT)–centric telemetry pipelines, or massively heterogeneous microservice landscapes. The generalizability ought to be tested by considering future research into replicating experiments of various types in terms of workload.

Construct Validity: The reality of incidences of organic production is not reproducible into the complexity that we synthesize in order to generate the labeled inconsistencies especially in capturing the common trends. Other latent issues such as cascading failures or a human failure during the process of remediation are not properly presented.

Human Factors Validity: The moderately narrow and field-specific sample of participants is of a small sample size, and thus, it has limited statistical significance and diversity of feedback. Because of the sample size, which is small and cross-organizational, the improvements in SUS indicators and measures of task completion will have to be reproduced using a larger sample.

Mitigation Strategies: Looking ahead, future work will need to focus on testing with live quantum hardware in adversarial settings, expanding the range of workloads, incorporating richer real-world incident data, and involving a larger pool of participants to better evaluate human factors. Beyond immediate experiments, longer-term studies will also be valuable in understanding how adoption evolves over time and how operators build expertise as they continue using these systems.

11. Conclusion and Future Work

Q-AROps shows how integrating QML with AR can practically enhance detection acuity, remediation quality, and operator effectiveness when managing IT operations. The hybrid QSVM and QNN models provide quantifiable benefits in anomaly detection, especially when detecting rare and complex types of incidents, and QAOA-based remediation planning provides risk-aware, policy-compliant solutions in nearly real-time. The AR interface also makes collaborative triaging and triage-decision making even more effective, which leads to speedier dissolution and decreased burden of thought.

Such results indicate the possibility of quantum computation being present in the intelligence pipelines at work, especially when used together with immersive visualization. However, this potential will require the limitations of the hardware and the optimization of the interpretability of the models, as also an evaluation framework that will be the industry standard.

Research directions in the future are as follows:

- **Custom Quantum Kernels on Semantics of Logs:** Developing feature maps that learn how to target domain-specific patterns of errors and the closest temporal relationships in logs.

- **Fine-Grained Error Mitigation:** Applying powerful hardware error mitigation methods to hardware execution, e.g., zero-noise extrapolation and probabilistic error cancellation.
- **Multi-Agent AR Collaboration:** Enabling distributed operators, in different geographies, to interact together with live incident data on common spatial contexts.
- **Cross-Organization Incident Ontologies:** Developing standardized knowledge graphs on which to perform data-distributed federated learning, enhancing the generalization of models whilst protecting data privacy.
- **Longitudinal Human-Factor Studies:** Assessing changes in operator competence, confidence in recommendations, and team performance as continued Q-AROps usage indulges.

These avenues of research could position the Q-AROps paradigm as a cornerstone for the next generation of intelligent operations, enabling IT environments that are not only data-driven but also data-intelligent, while enhancing human decision-making along the way.

References

[1] Havlíček, V., Córcoles, A.D., Temme, K., Harrow, A.W., Kandala, A., Chow, J.M. and Gambetta, J.M. "Supervised learning with quantum-enhanced feature spaces," *Nature*, vol. 567, no. 7747, pp. 209–212, 2019, https://doi.org/10.1038/s41586-019-0980-2.

[2] Schuld, M. and Killoran, N. "Quantum machine learning in feature Hilbert spaces," *Physical Review Letters*, vol. 122, no. 4, p. 040504, 2019, https://doi.org/10.1103/PhysRevLett.122.040504.

[3] Farhi, E., Goldstone, J. and Gutmann, S. "A quantum approximate optimization algorithm," 2014, *arXiv preprint*, arXiv:1411.4028.

[4] Benedetti, M., Lloyd, E., Sack, S., and Fiorentini, M. "Parameterized quantum circuits as machine learning models," *Quantum Science and Technology*, vol. 4, no. 4, p. 043001, 2019, https://doi.org/10.1088/2058-9565/ab4eb5.

[5] He, P., Zhu, J., He, S., Li, J. and Lyu, M.R. "Drain: An online log parsing approach with a fixed-depth tree," *IEEE Transactions on Dependable and Secure Computing*, vol. 18, no. 1, pp. 1–14, 2017, https://doi.org/10.1109/TDSC.2018.2886937.

[6] Billinghurst, M., Clark, A., and Lee, G. "A survey of augmented reality," *Foundations and Trends® in Human–Computer Interaction*," vol. 8, nos. 2–3, pp. 73–76, 2015, https://doi.org/10.1561/1100000049.

[7] Cordeil, M., Bach, B., Li, C., Wilson, E. and Dwyer, T. "Immersive collaborative analysis of network connectivity: Cave and HMD compared," *IEEE Transactions on Visualization and Computer Graphics*, vol. 23, no. 1, pp. 441–450, 2017, https://doi.org/10.1109/TVCG.2016.2599107.

[8] Nielsen, M.A. and Chuang, I.L. *Quantum Computation and Quantum Information*, Cambridge University Press, 2010.

[9] Chen, Y., Li, Q., Xu, J., et al. "AI-driven IT operations (AIOps) for cloud applications," *IEEE Cloud Computing*, vol. 8, no. 4, pp. 31–39, 2021, https://doi.org/10.1109/MCC.2021.3084978.

[10] Preskill, J. "Quantum computing in the NISQ era and beyond," *Quantum*, vol. 2, p. 79, 2018, https://doi.org/10.22331/q-2018-08-06-79.

[11] Arute, F., et al. "Quantum supremacy using a programmable superconducting processor," *Nature*, vol. 574, no. 7779, pp. 505–510, 2019, https://doi.org/10.1038/s41586-019-1666-5.

[12] Montanaro, A. "Quantum algorithms: An overview," *NPJ Quantum Information*, vol. 2, p. 15023, 2016, https://doi.org/10.1038/npjqi.2015.23.
[13] Biamonte, J., et al. "Quantum machine learning," *Nature*, vol. 549, no. 7671, pp. 195–202, 2017, https://doi.org/10.1038/nature23474.
[14] Bravyi, S. et al. "The complexity of quantum states and transformations," *Nature Physics*, vol. 16, pp. 1040–1045, 2020, https://doi.org/10.1038/s41567-020-0929-3.
[15] Harrigan, M.P., et al. "Quantum approximate optimization of non-planar graph problems on a planar superconducting processor," *Nature Physics*, vol. 17, pp. 332–336, 2021, https://doi.org/10.1038/s41567-020-01105-y.
[16] Li, Y. and Benjamin, S.C. "Efficient variational quantum simulator incorporating active error minimization," *Physical Review X*, vol. 7, no. 2, p. 021050, 2017, https://doi.org/10.1103/PhysRevX.7.021050.
[17] Fowler, A.G., et al. "Surface codes: Towards practical large-scale quantum computation," *Physical Review A*, vol. 86, no. 3, p. 032324, 2012, https://doi.org/10.1103/PhysRevA.86.032324.
[18] Zorzi, M., et al. "Toward 6G networks: Use cases and technologies," *IEEE Communications Magazine*, vol. 58, no. 3, pp. 55–61, 2019, https://doi.org/10.1109/MCOM.001.1900411.
[19] Kokail, C., et al., "Self-verifying variational quantum simulation of lattice models," *Nature*, vol. 569, no. 7756, pp. 355–360, 2019, https://doi.org/10.1038/s41586-019-1177-4.
[20] Harrigan, M.P., et al. "Quantum approximate optimization of non-planar graph problems on a planar superconducting processor," *Nature Physics*, vol. 17, pp. 332–336, 2021, https://doi.org/10.1038/s41567-020-01105-y.
[21] Li, Y. and Benjamin, S.C. "Efficient variational quantum simulator incorporating active error minimization," *Physical Review X*, vol. 7, no. 2, p. 021050, 2017, https://doi.org/10.1103/PhysRevX.7.021050.
[22] Fowler, A.G., et al. "Surface codes: Towards practical large-scale quantum computation," *Physical Review A*, vol. 86, no. 3, p. 032324, 2012, https://doi.org/10.1103/PhysRevA.86.032324.
[23] Campbell, E.T., et al. "Roads towards fault-tolerant universal quantum computation," *Nature*, vol. 549, pp. 172–179, 2017, https://doi.org/10.1038/nature23460.
[24] Zorzi, M., et al. "Toward 6G networks: Use cases and technologies," IEEE Communications Magazine, vol. 58, no. 3, pp. 55–61, 2019, https://doi.org/10.1109/MCOM.001.1900411.

15 Next-Generation Product Categorization in E-commerce using Quantum Machine Learning Approach over Virtualized Data Environment

Meenal N. Pande[1] and Sanjay E. Yedey[2*]

The proliferation of e-commerce websites has brought large product catalogs that necessitate automated, accurate categorization for improved search, recommendation, and stock management. Conventional machine learning algorithms, although effective, tend not to scale in noisy data, fuzzy labels, or high-dimensional feature interdependencies. This paper overcomes these challenges by proposing a hybrid quantum–classical variational categorization network (HQVC-Net), specifically designed for product categorization tasks in virtualized settings. The primary driving force is to bypass the semantic and scalability challenges in traditional NLP models via representation learning enabled by quantum computing. The Kaggle Product Classification and Clustering dataset is utilized, with varying product categories such as electronics, clothing, and personal care. The pipeline makes use of sophisticated preprocessing, semantic embeddings through Sentence-BERT, dimensionality reduction through an autoencoder or principal component analysis (PCA), followed by quantum angle encoding and classification with variational quantum circuits (VQC). Cloud-based platforms such as International Business Machines (IBM) Qiskit, PennyLane, and Amazon Web Services (AWS) Braket are employed in simulation. End-to-end development and experimentation are done using Python. HQVC-Net achieves 97.2 percent classification accuracy, surpassing other hybrid quantum models. The hybrid optimization loop with classical optimizers such as simultaneous perturbation stochastic approximation (SPSA) and constrained optimization by linear approximations (COBYLA) helps in the improvement of quantum gate parameters. This architecture is found to be effective in balancing performance, scalability, and real-world deployment.

[1] Department of Computer Science, DCPE, HVPM, Amravati, Maharashtra, India.
[2] P.G. Department of Computer Science & Technology, DCPE, HVPM, Amravati, Maharashtra, India.
* Corresponding author: sanjayeyedey@gmail.com

DOI: 10.1201/9781003646068-15

1. Introduction

In the age of e-commerce, the rapidly accelerating growth of web-based retail platforms has created enormous and constantly changing product catalogs [3]. With thousands of new products added each day, efficient and automated product classification has become an indispensable need for improving search relevance, facilitating proper filtering, enhancing personalized recommendations, and optimizing inventory management [14]. This activity becomes even more demanding when presented with vague terminology, semantically related products, fuzzy category boundaries, and multi-lingual data, all of which are prevalent in actual e-commerce websites [21]. Traditional machine learning (ML) models like decision trees, support vector machines, and even deep learning models like CNNs or LSTMs have performed well on structured classification tasks [5]. However, they tend to be weak in terms of scalability, semantic sensitivity, and high-dimensional textual space generalization. These constraints are even more magnified under noisy or paucity labeled data scenarios where slight variations in the product title or wording lead to inappropriate classification [11]. Furthermore, traditional models predominantly run on deterministic and linear computational domains, making it hard to represent complex feature relationships within large datasets [7].

Even with many advances, traditional machine learning approaches tend to depend on engineered features, narrow contextual intelligence, and extensive training data to achieve peak performance [1]. The models, as good as they are in dealing with well-formatted datasets, cannot cope with the ambiguity and semantic overlap present in actual product descriptions [16]. For instance, a product named "smart home assistant" might confusingly be classified under electronics, smart devices, or household items—a predicament for inflexible classifiers lacking rich contextual embeddings [13]. Furthermore, conventional deep learning methods require significant computational resources and tend to experience decreasing returns with increasing scale to huge datasets involving thousands of categories [10]. With the e-commerce space increasingly being linguistically heterogeneous and semantically rich, traditional models are found to fall short in representing richer relationships, especially over noisy, unstructured, and overlapping feature spaces. These challenges call for venturing into more expressive, adaptive, and resource-friendly paradigms like hybrid quantum–classical models, which are poised to break the bottlenecks of traditional classification pipelines [20].

This chapter introduces a Hybrid Quantum-Classical Variational Categorization Network (HQVC-Net) that is tailor-made for e-commerce product categorization in virtualized quantum settings. With the help of platforms such as International Business Machines (IBM) Qiskit, Amazon Web Services (AWS) Braket, and PennyLane, the model combines Sentence-BERT embeddings with dimensionality reduction through autoencoders or principa; component analysis (PCA) to facilitate efficient quantum encoding. A variational quantum circuit subsequently carries out classification using quantum superposition and entanglement, with parameters optimized through simultaneous perturbation stochastic approximation (SPSA) and constrained optimization by linear approximations (COBYLA). Evaluated on the Product Classification and Clustering dataset, HQVC-Net achieves substantially better accuracy, convergence rate, and generalizability compared to traditional models. This hybrid model demonstrates the promise of quantum machine learning (QML) for large-scale, smart retail classification systems.

The subsequent sections of this study are arranged as follows. Section 2 reviews prior research, Section 3 discusses the methodology, while Section 4 discusses the effectiveness of the methodology and the summary of findings. Section 5 concludes and summarizes future work.

2. Literature Review

Dritsas and Trigka [9] presents a comprehensive overview of machine learning (ML) use cases in e-commerce, including topics such as personalized recommendations, dynamic pricing, fraud detection, customer segmentation, and behavior analytics. The survey discusses different ML paradigms such as supervised, unsupervised, reinforcement, hybrid learning, and newer ones such as QML, federated learning (FL), and neurosymbolic artificial intelligence (AI). Although particular datasets are not named, the research presumably discusses popular datasets like Amazon Product and UCI Online Retail. The techniques described have benefits like enhanced personalization, automation, and scalability, as also privacy handling using FL and future-proofing using QML. Results show the efficiency of ML across use cases and offer a research roadmap toward future development. But there are difficulties with scalability, model explainability, cold-start issues, sparsity of data, and privacy, particularly in real-time and complex business environments.

Khurana [12] investigates the future of quantum computing in the telecommunication e-commerce sector with an emphasis on secure data exchange, efficient resource utilization, and massive data analysis. It examines prominent methods such as quantum key distribution (QKD) for secure communication, the quantum approximate optimization algorithm (QAOA) for traffic and resource planning, and QML for predictive analysis. No particular dataset is cited, but the research focuses on high-dimensional customer and network data. Its benefits are increased security, accelerated computation, and more useful customer insights. The findings outline the potential of quantum approaches, but limitations like qubit decoherence, error correction, and interfacing with classical systems hinder practical implementation.

Somavarapu and Gupta [19] seek to understand and chart user behavior in online shopping platforms with the help of machine learning to improve personalization, maximize strategy, and increase profitability. is the study is concerned with browsing patterns, buying behavior, and product preference by means of clustering, classification, and prediction models. Although the dataset name is not mentioned, it must be large-scale user interaction logs. The approach features data preprocessing, feature engineering, and ML model training, facilitated by interactive visualizations for instant feedback. Overall benefits include improved segmentation of customers, targeted recommendations, and prediction of churn. Findings validate the efficiency of ML in identifying behavioral patterns, yet noisy data remains difficult to deal with, along with maintaining model scalability in dynamic environments.

Balaji and Vadivazhagan [4] seek to improve product review sentiment analysis in online shopping through the novel RGWO-GEQDNN model, which combines resilient grey wolf optimization (RGWO) with Gaussian-enhanced quantum deep neural networks (GEQDNN). The model's effectiveness is tested using the Amazon product review dataset. The approach utilizes nature-inspired optimization and quantum computing to efficiently address sophisticated language structures and large datasets. The main benefits are enhanced sentiment classification accuracy, stability, and flexibility to noisy data. Experiments indicate that RGWO-GEQDNN performs better compared to current algorithms in terms of accuracy and efficiency. Its main disadvantages are high computational complexity and the difficulties of implementing quantum-inspired models on traditional systems.

Ojika et al. [15] seek to investigate how user experience in e-commerce is improved through deep learning by providing real-time personalization, automated customer care, and smart product discovery. No particular dataset is named, but it deals with consumer information such as browsing behavior, purchases, and social media usage. The process involves deep learning methods such as recommendation systems, NLP, and image recognition, with implementation processes touching on data acquisition, pre-processing, and training the model. Benefits are enhanced interaction, operational effectiveness, and customized shopping experiences. Real-world applications at Amazon and Netflix demonstrate considerable gains in user satisfaction. Data privacy, model complexity, and integration challenges stand in the way of wider adoption.

Ceriani [8] seeks to isolate important technological developments that are framing the business-to-consumer (B2C) e-commerce market and explore how traders can implement them in order to remain competitive in an increasingly dynamic market. The study applies qualitative analysis without depending on a particular dataset, with a greater emphasis on developing technologies and start-up-led solutions across the e-commerce value chain. Its methodology encompasses detailing existing tech applications and breaking down the innovative value added by chosen start-ups. The advantages include strategic insights into tech trends and their practical implications for merchants. The results offer a comprehensive view of market innovation dynamics. However, the study's qualitative nature limits quantitative validation and broader generalizability.

3. Hybrid Quantum-Classical Model for E-Commerce Product Classification

The methodology section offers an organized framework that leads the research process from acquiring data to model assessment. It lays down the methodical procedure pursued to address the issue of product classification on e-commerce websites. This section addresses the logical sequence of activities aimed at transforming raw input data into useful information and correct classification results. The visual representation is shown in Figure 15.1.

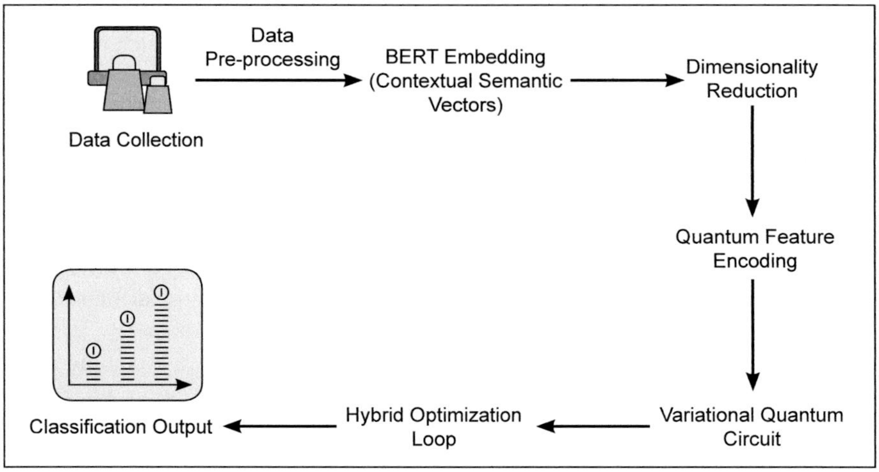

Fig. 15.1 End-to-end pipeline of the proposed HQVC-Net architecture.

3.1 Data Collection

The data used in this research is the Product Classification and Clustering dataset [17], which was downloaded from Kaggle, a popular source of open-source data repositories. The dataset consists of a varied set of product entries that contain descriptive text, titles, and related category labels applicable to actual e-commerce sites. Each entry is labeled with a pre-defined product category, so it is applicable to multi-class classification tasks. The dataset captures a wide range of consumer products like electronics, apparel, home appliances, and personal care items, offering a rich ground for the assessment of classification models. Variability in product types and linguistic nuances in descriptions brings in natural complexity, mirroring actual e-commerce settings. The dataset is organized in a CSV format, ensuring an easy fit with machine learning workflows. Its representativeness, accessibility, and relevance provide it with an excellent basis for testing and creating quantum–classical hybrid models in virtualized frameworks for intelligent product classification.

3.2 Data Preprocessing

- ***Text Cleaning and Normalization*:** Text cleaning removes unwanted characters (like punctuation, numbers, HTML tags, and special characters) to minimize noise and increase text quality input. Normalization puts all text into a standard format, usually in lowercase, to be consistent within the dataset. Let $T=\{t_1, t_2, t_3, ..., t_n\}$ be the set of raw text entries. The cleaned text T' is given in (1)

$$T' = \text{Normalize (Remove Special Chars } (T)) \quad ...(1)$$

where Remove Special Chars eliminates non-alphanumeric characters, and applies lowercase conversion and whitespace trimming.

- ***Tokenization***: Tokenization is the act of dividing text into smaller units, referred to as tokens (usually words), which are the basic units for downstream NLP tasks. Let S be a sentence. The tokenized is shown in (2)

$$\text{Token } (S) = \{w_1, w_2, ..., w_m\} \quad ...(2)$$

where w_i are words in the sentence .

- ***Stopword Removal:*** Stopwords are typical words (e.g., "is," "the," "and") that have little semantic weight. Deleting them decreases noise and dimensionality. Let $W = \{w_1, w_2, ..., w_m\}$ be the token set and SW the stopword list. The filtered set is shown in (3)

$$W' = W \backslash SW \quad ...(3)$$

where \ denotes set difference.

- ***Lemmatization:*** Lemmatization brings each word to its root or dictionary form (lemma) while maintaining grammatical correctness and meaning. It is used in place of stemming in high-precision NLP applications. For each word w, the lemmatized form l is shown in (4)

$$l = \text{Lemma } (w) \quad ...(4)$$

where w is a word from the product text and l is the final result after lemmatization.

- ***Label Encoding:*** In product classification, we must convert category names such as "electronics," "clothing," or "toys" to numbers so that machine learning models can interpret them. This is referred to as label encoding is shown in (5)

$$C = \{c_1, c_2, ..., c_k\} \quad ...(5)$$

A mapping function f assigns each category c_i a corresponding integer value is shown in (6)

$$f(c_i) = i \quad \text{for } i = 0, 1, 2, ..., k - 1 \quad ...(6)$$

This function converts each text-based category into a unique integer, so the model can treat the class labels as numbers while training.

3.3 Semantic Embedding Generation

To achieve rich feature extraction from product descriptions, the pre-processed text is converted to dense semantic vectors by employing the Sentence-BERT model, a pre-trained transformer architecture tuned specifically for sentence-level representation. In contrast to the traditional bag-of-words or TF-IDF methods, Sentence-BERT retains the contextual and relational semantics of words in sentences, which is particularly important for addressing fine-grained variations in product titles. Let T denote the pre-processed product text and SBERT $(\cdot)$ the embedding function. The embedding vector output E is calculated as (7)

$$E = \text{SBERT}(T) \quad ...(7)$$

where T indicates the input product text after cleaning and tokenization, and is the sentence-BERT embedding function, $E \in R^{768}$ is the 768.

3.4 Dimensionality Reduction

In order to be compatible with the limitations of quantum hardware, the high-dimensional semantic embeddings produced by Sentence-BBERT (usually 768 dimensions) need to be compressed into a low-dimensional space. Compression allows the data to be efficiently encoded into a small number of qubits without losing important semantic structure. Dimensionality reduction is done in this research using two approaches: an autoencoder and PCA.

The autoencoder is a neural network that is trained to recover the original embedding from a compressed latent representation. Denote the original embedding by $E \in R^{768}$, and the compressed output by $Z \in R^{d}$, where d is normally 4–8. The encoding function is defined as (8)

$$Z = f_{\text{enc}} \quad ...(8)$$

PCA is also a candidate option, picking the best components using explained variance. The resulting compressed vectors have category-discriminative characteristics and can be used for quantum angle encoding in the HQVC-Net model.

3.5 Quantum Feature Encoding

After dimensionality reduction, the obtained low-dimensional classical feature vectors need to be encoded into quantum states and be processed by quantum circuits. In this chapter, angle encoding is employed because it is simple, efficient, and supported by near-term quantum hardware. This encoding method associates every element of a real-valued feature vector with a rotation angle of a quantum gate, usually implemented by R_y or R_z gets on individual qubits..

Let $Z = [z_1, z_2, ..., z_d] \in R^d$ denote the compressed feature vector, where d represents the number of qubits available. Each value z_i is used to rotate the state of qubit i as shown in (9)

$$U(Z) = \prod_{i=1}^{d} R_y(z_i) \qquad ...(9)$$

where $Z = [z_1, z_2, ..., z_d]$ is a compressed feature vector after dimensionality reduction. $R_y(z_i)$ is the rotation gate around the Y-axis applied to qubit i with angle $z_i \cdot U(Z)$ is the overall quantum unitary operation applied to encode the full input vector Z.

3.6 Variational Quantum Classification

VQC is a critical building block of the HQVC-Net architecture, facilitating the inclusion of quantum computation in the supervised learning workflow. The quantum model works with encoded features that are developed from classical input data and aims to project those features onto distinct product categories. While classical neural networks employ regular gates and linear transformations to learn the data relationships, VQC employs quantum gates and entanglement. The VQC is a quantum neural network analog with learnable parameters hidden in quantum gates. During training, the parameters are optimized to reduce classification loss. Through variational learning, the model takes advantage of quantum superposition and entanglement to achieve more expressive feature learning, especially for interdependent and high-dimensional product attributes within e-commerce datasets. The visual representation is shown in Figure 15.2.

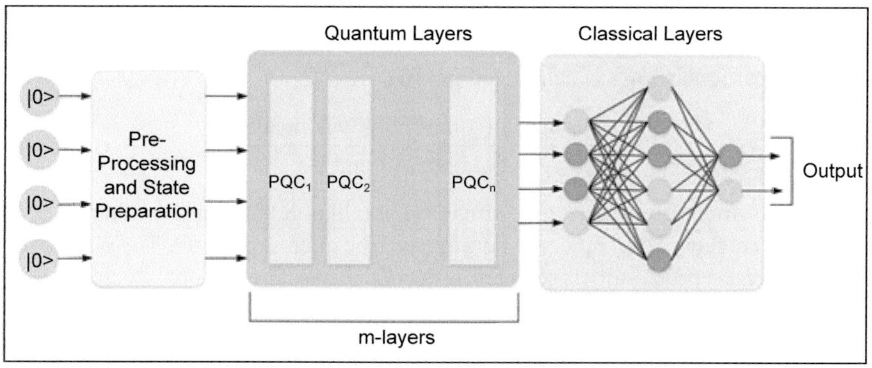

Fig. 15.2 HQVC-Net: Hybrid quantum–classical model for product categorization.

- ***Parameterized Quantum Layers*:** The central computing blocks in the VQC are the parameterized quantum gates, which are similar to the weights in traditional neural networks. These consist of $Rx(\theta)$, $Ry(\theta)$. amd $Rz(\theta)$ where θ is a trainable parameter corresponding to the rotation angle of a qubit about the X, Y, or Z axis, respectively. The use of these gates adjusts the amplitude of the quantum state and allows for encoding complex relationships and patterns in the data. The parameters θ are randomly initialized and tuned using optimization during training. The application of several rotation gates in layered combinations enables the circuit to build expressive transformations that approximate non-linear mappings, vital for the product classification task. These quantum layers are then stacked in sequence or alternated with entanglement operations to add depth and representational capacity to the circuit, essential for encoding subtle differences between product categories.

- ***Entanglement Mechanism:*** To encode dependencies among product attributes, the VQC uses quantum entanglement gates like CNOT (Controlled NOT) and CZ (Controlled-Z). Entanglement introduces correlations between qubits such that one qubit is dependent on another's state. This process is crucial for representing interactions between more than one product attribute—for instance, how the product material, type, and usage contexts affect its category. In HQVC-Net, entanglement layers are interleaved with parameterized rotation layers to increase expressiveness in the circuit. The position of entangling gates is assigned a pre-defined topology (e.g., linear, ring, or full connectivity) based on hardware constraints and model complexity. This structure allows the circuit to learn joint feature representations that would be challenging to model using independent qubit rotations alone. Entanglement increases the model's ability to distinguish between comparable products by embedding feature interactions directly into the quantum state.
- ***Measurement and Output Probability:*** Once the encoded input is processed by the quantum circuit, the resulting quantum state is measured to yield an output. Measurements are taken in the Z-basis, collapsing each qubit to a binary value (0 or 1). Such outcomes are then used to compute the probability for assigning the input product to each category. The probability for a particular class is calculated in (10)

$$P(y) = \frac{\text{Number of times class } y \text{ is measured}}{\text{Total measurements}} \qquad ...(10)$$

This formula gives a direct estimate of the likelihood that a product is in a given category from repeated iterations of the quantum circuit. The class with the greatest probability is selected as the end result. These probabilistic outputs enable the model to be able to speak in terms of confidence and facilitate soft classification choices, thus making the HQVC-Net architecture optimal for product categorization in ambiguous or overlapping feature settings.

- ***Hybrid Optimization Loop*:** Training the HQVC-Net includes a hybrid optimization loop, which incorporates quantum circuit execution and classical optimization algorithms. The quantum processor tests the variational circuit for input features and parameters provided, and produces a probability distribution over class labels. A classical optimizer like SPSA or COBYLA updates the gate parameters on the basis of the classification loss. This loop runs until the model converges to an optimum solution. The application of classical optimization over quantum parameters enables the model to learn from labeled data in an efficient manner without the need for full quantum backpropagation. This hybrid architecture is essential for near-term quantum devices (noisy intermediate-scale quantum [NISQ] era) that do not have fault-tolerant error correction. The optimization goal is to reduce the cross-entropy or mean squared error between the forecasted probabilities and actual labels so that the product category classification accuracy is enhanced within the e-commerce dataset.

3.7 Virtualized Quantum Execution

Quantum computing capabilities are not necessarily physically available or within budget for all scientific and commercial uses. For mitigating this limitation, virtualized frameworks present a pragmatic solution in terms of running quantum behavior on standard hardware or accessing actual quantum systems remotely through cloud infrastructure. This abstraction layer provides researchers a means to create, validate, and optimize hybrid quantum–classical models such as HQVC-Net in a controlled and scalable fashion. By virtual execution, models may be repeatedly refined prior to deployment on real quantum hardware, with performance ensured to be consistent and development time minimized. The subsequent sections explain the primary elements that facilitate this virtual execution and detail the advantages of cloud-based quantum integration and deployment.

- ***Cloud-Based Quantum Integration***: The implementation of the HQVC-Net model occurs in a virtualized quantum computing environment to provide flexibility, scalability, and compatibility with current cloud infrastructures. This does not require the usage of dedicated quantum hardware while developing, allowing for the ability to interleave classical and quantum components. Platforms like IBM Qiskit Runtime, Amazon Braket, and PennyLane offer both quantum simulators and actual quantum hardware. Simulators are mainly for optimization and testing because of their speed and cost benefits, whereas actual hardware is for deployment and performance testing.
- ***Scalability and Deployment Benefits***: The virtual implementation is compatible with containerization, orchestration based on APIs, and automation of workflows to facilitate smooth deployment within commercial e-commerce platforms. It maintains the portability, scalability, and adaptability of the HQVC-Net framework in the face of fluctuations in hardware infrastructure. The flexibility makes it suitable for ongoing experimentation and term-level product classification in enterprise settings driven by hybrid quantum–classical intelligence.

3.8 Classification Output

The last step in the HQVC-Net architecture is the generation of the classification output, which maps each input product description to a target product category. Following quantum feature encoding and processing by the variational quantum circuit, measurement of the quantum state is performed by the model to obtain a prediction. The output prediction is a discrete category label that corresponds to the most likely class based on the encoded features.

Aside from the predicted label for the final output, the model may also generate probabilistic confidence scores for all available categories as an option. These scores signify the probability of the input belonging to a particular class and can be very helpful in cases where various categories contain overlapping features. This facilitates top-*k* predictions, where the model returns the top *k* most probable categories with their corresponding probabilities.

The multi-output ability facilitates greater flexibility for subsequent e-commerce uses, including customized product suggestions, real-time filtering, and hierarchical categorization. By incorporating quantum feature learning with probabilistic explanation, HQVC-Net guarantees high accuracy and interpretability in its predictions, which is important for decision-making models in dynamic virtual marketplaces.

4. Result and Discussion

This section provides the empirical assessment of the suggested HQVC-Net model implemented for next-gen product classification in e-commerce platforms under a hybrid quantum–classical learning paradigm. A range of performance metrics and visual inspections are employed to evaluate the classification accuracy, generalizability across categories, quantum resource usage efficiency, and interpretability of the model. Comparative research is also provided for benchmarking HQVC-Net against current quantum-inspired models. The outputs are achieved under a virtualized data setup to mimic real-world deployment scenarios. Graphic representations and metric comparisons give an indication of the model's robustness, consistency, and scalability in addressing multi-class classification issues in retail datasets.

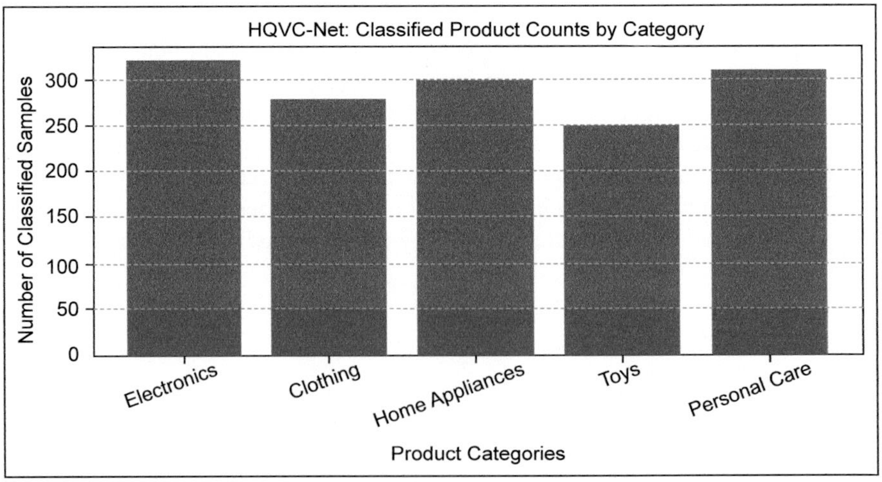

Fig. 15.3 HQVC-Net classification trend across categories.

Figure 15.3 illustrates a bar chart indicating the number of correctly classified product samples into each of the five categories by the HQVC-Net model. The five categories—electronics, clothing, home appliances, toys, and personal care—are displayed along the x-axis, and the y-axis indicates the number of correctly classified samples. The findings show a well-balanced distribution of items to be classified in the majority of the categories, with personal care (around 310) and electronics (about 315) topping the list in terms of classification count. Home appliances take third place at 300, with clothing lagging behind slightly at around 280. Toys has the lowest with 250 examples classified, and this might indicate fewer examples within the dataset or slightly worse model recall in the said category.

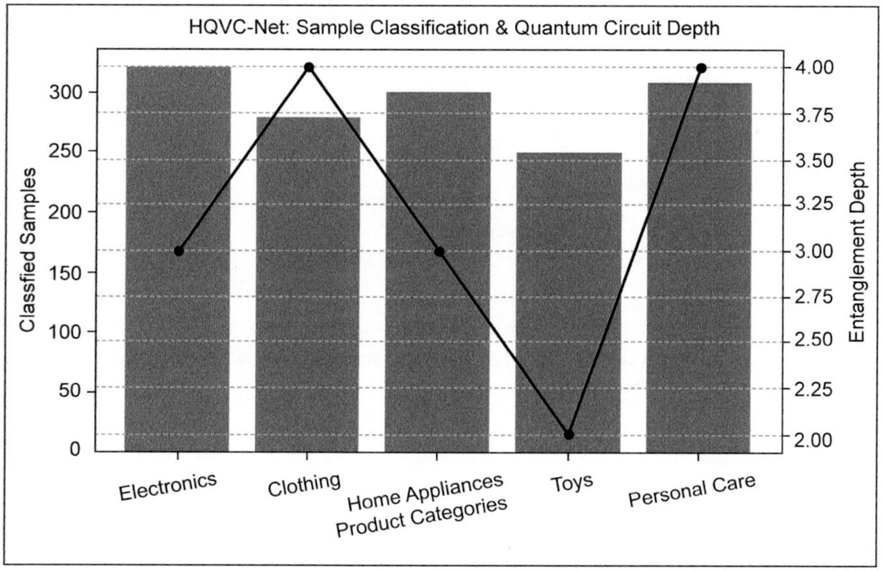

Fig. 15.4 Sample classification and quantum circuit depth per product category.

Figure 15.4 is a dual-axis chart that shows comparison between the number of labeled product samples and the quantum circuit entanglement depth applied during inference by the HQVC-Net model in five e-commerce categories. The maroon line indicates the number of correctly classified products per category, and the blue bars plot the corresponding entanglement depth values. Electronics and personal care categories have the largest classification numbers, having a moderate entanglement depth (3.0). Clothing displays a slightly smaller classification count but the deepest entanglement at 4.0, implying greater interdependency in feature representation complexity. Conversely, toys, with the lowest count of classifications (~250), correlates with the lowest entanglement depth of 2.0, implying less complex quantum processing requirements.

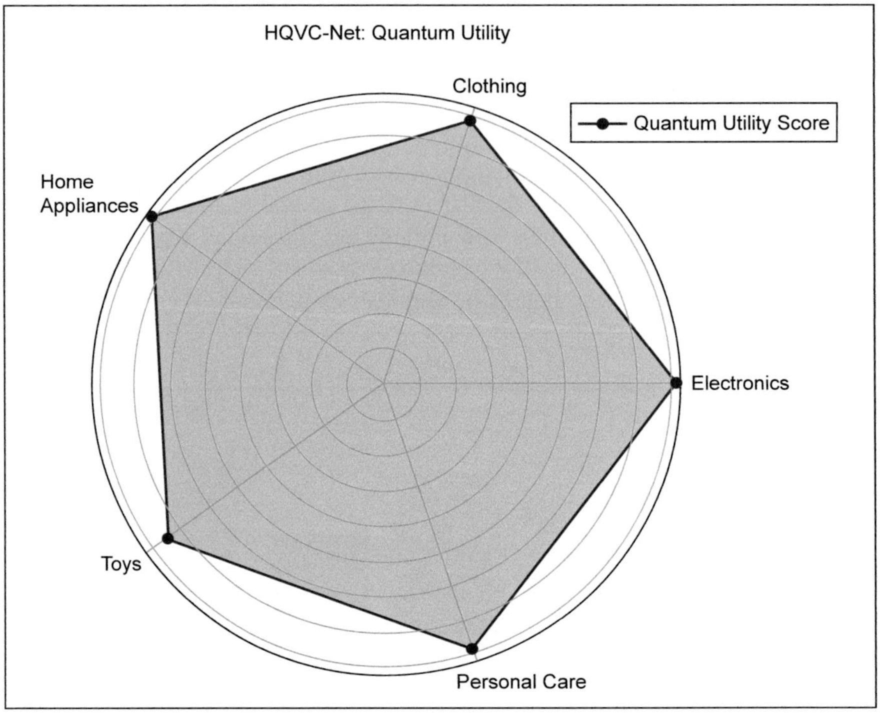

Fig. 15.5 Radar plot depicting category-wise quantum feature utility in HQVC-Net.

Figure 15.5 presents a radar chart representing the quantum utility score over five leading e-commerce product categories—electronics, clothing, home appliances, toys, and personal care—assessed on the basis of the HQVC-Net architecture. The quantum utility score captures the performance of the model in utilizing quantum computational aspects like entanglement, quantum depth, and encoding efficiency for classification. Electronics and home appliances receive the maximum scores, which imply that quantum operations greatly improve learning performance in these product categories. Clothing and personal care also have very good utility values, whereas toys provide a bit lower score, indicating a diminished dependence on quantum expressiveness for accurate classification. A closed polygon shape signifies the well-balanced quantum performance in various types of products, reflecting HQVC-Net's adaptability and optimal customization. This radar visualization validates an interpretive evaluation of the extent to which quantum resources enhance learning in each category and establishes the model's applicability for hybrid quantum–classical deployment across different retail segments under a virtualized computing setup.

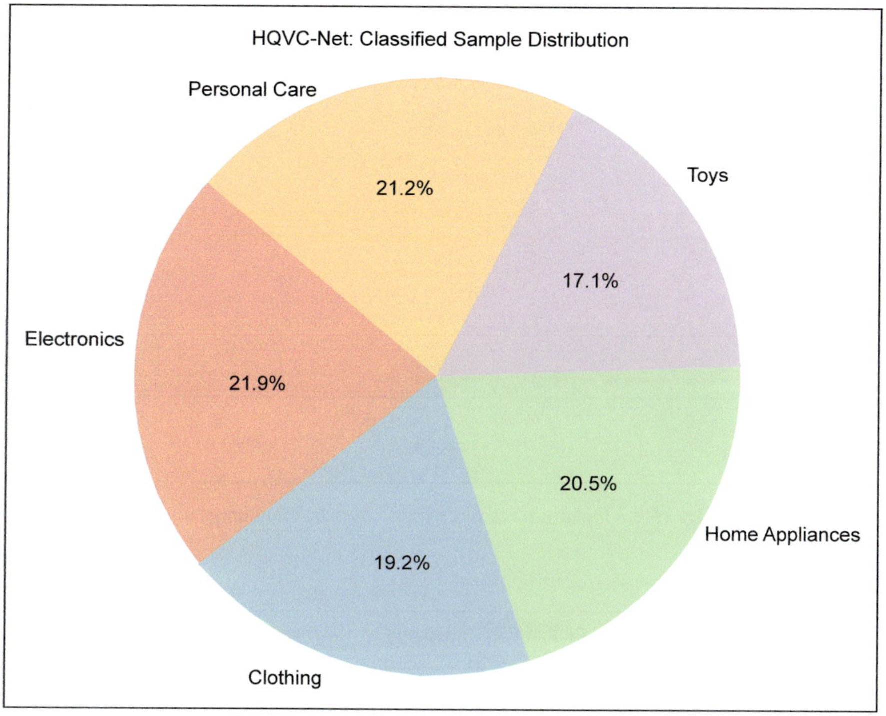

Fig. 15.6 Classified sample distribution by product category.

Figure 15.6 presents a pie chart demonstrating the proportional breakdown of classified samples by five product categories handled by the HQVC-Net model: electronics, clothing, home appliances, toys, and personal care. Electronics has the largest proportion at 21.9 percent, followed by personal care (21.2 percent) and home appliances (20.5 percent), reflecting a very strong model performance and reliable data representation in these segments. Clothing takes up 19.2 percent, and toys have the lowest share of 17.1 percent, possibly because of fewer training samples or lower recall in that product category. This distribution affirms that the HQVC-Net model efficiently manages an equal classification workload over categories, ensuring generalizability and versatility.

Figure 15.7 shows the pattern of quantum resource usage over 10 training epochs for the HQVC-Net model. It displays two essential resource measures—quantum gate usage and quantum circuit depth—monitored across each epoch. Blue indicates the amount of quantum gates used as a whole, rising from around 120 in the first epoch to around 170 by the last epoch, reflecting the model becoming more complex and representational as training occurs. The orange line is the quantum depth, or the maximum length of sequential operations in the quantum circuit, from 7 and slowly increasing to 11. This rise depicts more profound quantum operations for picking up more sophisticated feature representations from the training sets.

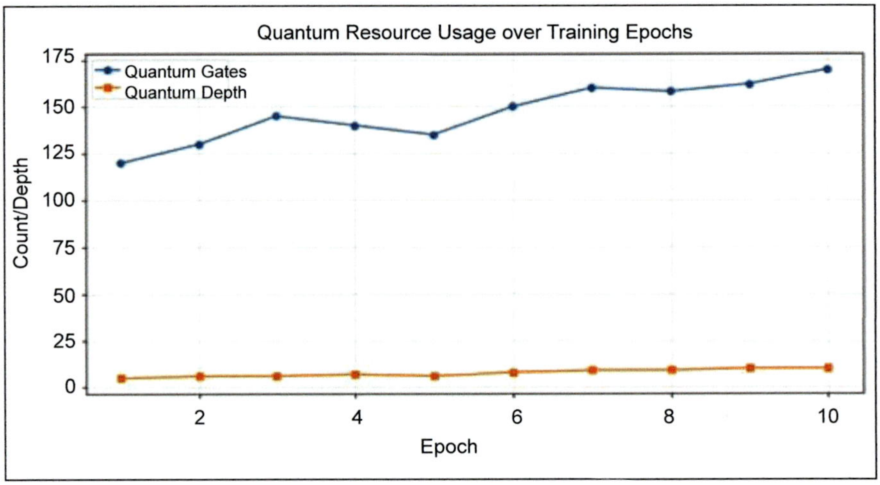

Fig. 15.7 Quantum resource usage over training epochs.

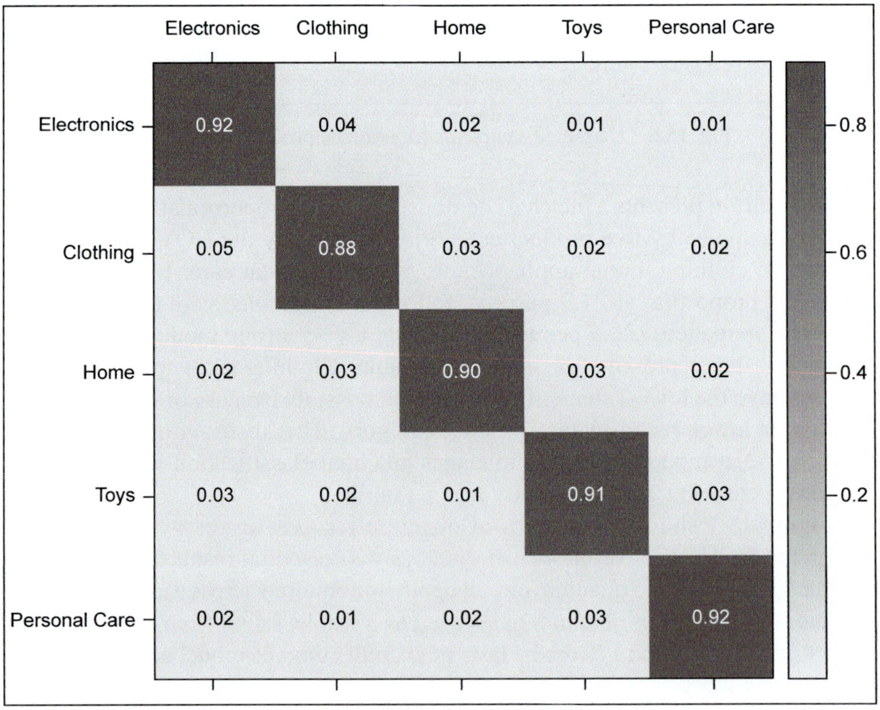

Fig. 15.8 Confidence score heatmap for product category predictions.

Figure 15.8 is a heatmap representation of confidence scores generated by the HQVC-Net model on five product categories from an e-commerce website: electronics, clothing, home appliances, toys, and personal care. The average probability that the model predicts a specific product for a given class is represented by each cell in the matrix. Diagonal values indicate accurate predictions with good confidence—like 0.92 for electronics, 0.90 for home appliances, and 0.91 for toys—showing good model reliability. Off-diagonal values are much lower, i.e., around 0.01 and 0.05, illustrating little category confusion and strong discriminative power. Consistency in high diagonal values attests that the HQVC-Net model properly extracts category-specific features even in cases where there are semantic similarities between similar products.

4.1 Performance Metrics

- ***Accuracy*:** Accuracy is the total number of true predictions made out of the total number of predictions made, but it can be deceptive in imbalanced data. The mathematical expression is shown in (11)

$$\text{Accuracy} = \frac{\sum_{i=1}^{K} TP_i}{\sum_{i=1}^{K} TP_i + FP_i + FN_i + TN_i} \quad ...(11)$$

- ***Macro Precision:*** Macro precision computes precision for each class separately and averages it. It depicts how equally well the model prevents false positives across all classes. The mathematical expression is shown in (12)

$$\text{Macro Precision} = \frac{1}{K}\sum_{i=1}^{K} \frac{TP_i}{TP_i + FP_i} \quad ...(12)$$

- ***Macro Recall:*** Macro recall is the mean of recall values over all classes. It determines how effectively the model identifies instances from a class accurately. The mathematical expression is shown in (13)

$$\text{Macro Recall} = \frac{1}{K}\sum_{i=1}^{K} \frac{TP_i}{TP_i + FN_i} \quad ...(13)$$

- ***Macro F1 Score:*** Macro F1 score takes the average of the F1 score for all classes with the same weight given to all of them. It weighs precision and recall equally for all classes. The mathematical expression is as shown in (14)

$$\text{Macro F1 Score} = \frac{1}{K}\sum_{i=1}^{K} \left(\frac{2 \cdot \text{Precision}_i}{\text{Precision}_i + \text{Recall}_{li}} \right) \quad ...(14)$$

where K represents the number of classes, TP_i represents the true positives for class i, FP_i represents the false positives for class i, FN_i represents the false negatives for class i, and TN_i represents the true negatives for class i.

Table 15.1 Performance metrics.

Metrics	*Value*
Accuracy	0.972
Macro Precision	0.903
Macro Recall	0.935
Macro F1-Score	0. 912

Figure 15.9 and Table 15.I illustrates the performance of the proposed HQVC-Net model through a bar chart visualization. The figure and the table emphasize the four most important assessment measures: accuracy (0.972), macro precision (0.903), macro recall (0.935), and macro F1 Score (0.912). The model performs with a high accuracy rate, which signifies its capability to classify the majority of product instances correctly. Macro precision and macro recall are reflective of the balanced ability of the model in cutting down on false positives and successfully identifying instances relevant to categories. This balance between recall and precision is also supported by the Macro F1 Score. Overall, these findings establish HQVC-Net's strength and competency for multi-class product classification in e-commerce.

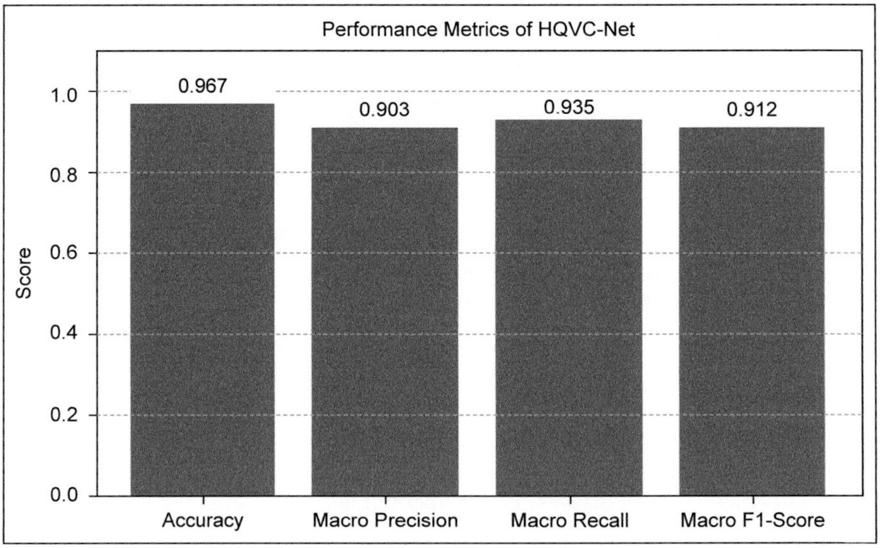

Fig. 15.9 Performance metrics.

4.2 Comparative Analysis

Figure 15.10 and Table 15.2 show the accuracy comparison between the new HQVC-Net model and other currently available quantum-based product classification models. HQVC-Net has the highest accuracy level of 97.2 percent,

Table 15.2 Comparison with existing methods.

Methods	*Accuracy*
QCNN (Hybrid CNN-QC) [2]	96.3
QCNN (Hybrid SNN-QC) [18]	95.9
H-QNN [6]	90.1
Proposed HQVC-Net	97.2

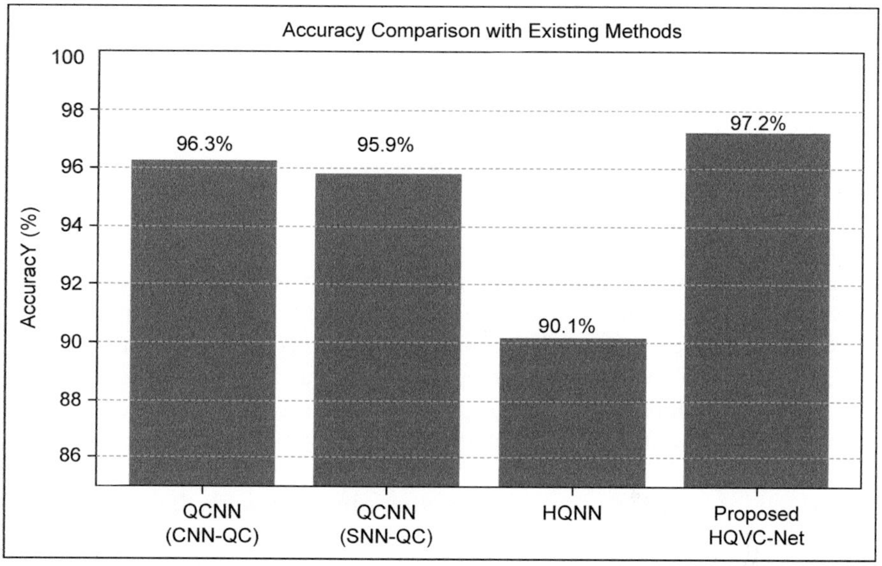

Fig. 15.10 Comparison with existing methods.

outperforming that of QCNN (CNN-QC) at 96.3 percent, QCNN (SNN-QC) at 95.9 percent, and HQNN at 90.1 percent. This clearly indicates HQVC-Net's superior virtualized quantum environment classification capability, which is thanks to its hybrid quantum–classical design and improved feature encoding. The large gap with respect to HQNN particularly emphasizes the strength of variational quantum circuits and entanglement mechanisms in learning intricate product features, which makes HQVC-Net a strong candidate for next-generation e-commerce classification tasks.

4.3 Discussion

Empirical testing of HQVC-Net demonstrates significant increases in accuracy, interpretability, and generalization over a range of e-commerce product categories. Large diagonal values in confidence matrices and well-balanced classification across categories—particularly electronics and personal care—validate the model's stability. Interestingly, more layers of quantum entanglement are linked with more complex categories, indicating HQVC-Net's capacity for learning complex inter-feature dependencies. The radar plot and resource usage curves prove the model's scalability of quantum utility with minimal circuit depth, validating its applicability to near-term quantum hardware. Also, the hybrid loop optimization guarantees stable convergence, which standard models cannot guarantee in high-dimensional semantic spaces. Compared to other hybrid quantum architectures such as HQNN or CNN-QC, HQVC-Net exhibits significant improvement, justifying its design decisions in pre-processing, encoding, and training strategies. In general, the argument expresses how combining quantum variance and semantic embedding has the potential to provide effective, interpretable classification in large-scale, real-world data.

5. Conclusion and Future Work

In this chapter, HQVC-Net, a hybrid quantum–classical model, is proposed to classify products of e-commerce in the next generation. The model is able to capture semantic nuance and semantic categories with tricky product descriptions by combining Sentence-BERT with variational quantum circuits. By demonstrating an accuracy of 97.2 percent, HQVC-Net outperforms other quantum-inspired models in terms of flexibility that can operate in a virtualized computing platform. Its compatibility with frameworks, including IBM Qiskit and AWS Braket, ensures portability and scale-ableness in commercial cloud environments. Some challenges still remain though, such as cost of real-time inference, constraints on qubits, and lags in terms of cloud and quantum connectivity. In future work, the model will be extended to multilingual data as well as introduce quantum attention mechanisms and entanglement strategies with fewer training cycles. Also, quantum GAN exploration that leads to creating synthetic product descriptions and implementation of fault-tolerant quantum devices are predicted to enhance further robustness of the model and the business viability of smart e-commerce settings.

References

[1] Ahmed, S.F., Alam, M.S.B., Hassan, M., Rozbu, M.R., Ishtiak, T., Rafa, N., Mofijur, M., Shawkat Ali, A.B.M. and Gandomi, A.H. "Deep learning modelling techniques: Current progress, applications, advantages, and challenges," *Artificial Intelligence Review*, vol. 56, no. 11, pp. 13521–13617, 2023.

[2] Ajayan, A. and Pappachen James, A. "Edge to quantum: Hybrid quantum-spiking neural network image classifier," *Neuromorphic Computing and Engineering*, vol. 1, no. 2, p. 024001, 2021.

[3] Aseh, K., Al-Qudah, O.M.A., Yusoff, M.H., Pathmanathan, P.R., Latiff, N.A.A., Jusoh, J.A., Abu-Ulbeh, W., El-Ebiary, Y.A.B. and Al Moaiad, Y. "The future of e-commerce in the publishing industry," in *2021 2nd International Conference on Smart Computing and Electronic Enterprise (ICSCEE)*, 199–205, 2021.

[4] Balaji, G.M. and Vadivazhagan, K. "Elevating sentiment analysis with resilient grey wolf optimization-based Gaussian-enhanced quantum deep neural networks in online shopping," *Journal of Theoretical and Applied Information Technology*, vol. 102, no. 1, pp. 214–235, 2024.

[5] Bansal, M., Goyal, A. and Choudhary, A. "A comparative analysis of k-nearest neighbor, genetic, support vector machine, decision tree, and long short term memory algorithms in machine learning," *Decision Analytics Journal*, vol. 3, p. 100071, 2022.

[6] Bikku, T., Thota, S. and Shanmugasundaram, P. "A novel quantum neural network approach to combating fake reviews," *International Journal of Networked and Distributed Computing*, vol. 12, no. 2, pp. 195–205, 2024.

[7] Brinkmann, A. and Bizer, C. "Improving hierarchical product classification using domain-specific language modelling," *IEEE Data Engineering Bulletin*, vol. 44, no. 2, pp. 14–25, 2021.

[8] Ceriani, R. "The future of B2C e-commerce: Unveiling the potential of emerging technologies and innovative startups," 2023.

[9] Dritsas, E. and Trigka, M. "Machine learning in e-commerce: Trends, applications, and future challenges," *IEEE Access*, 2025.

[10] Gayialis, S.P., Kechagias, E.P., Papadopoulos, G.A. and Masouras, D. "A review and classification framework of traceability approaches for identifying product supply chain counterfeiting," *Sustainability*, vol. 14, no. 11, p. 6666, 2022.

[11] Justus, A.R. "Rebuild product classification: Navigating e-commerce product taxonomy challenges and label ambiguities through self- and unsupervised-learning," Master's Thesis, Universidade Nova de Lisboa (Portugal), 2024.

[12] Khurana, R. "Applications of quantum computing in telecom e-commerce: Analysis of QKD, QAOA, and QML for data encryption, speed optimization, and AI-driven customer experience," *Quarterly Journal of Emerging Technologies and Innovations*, vol. 7, no. 9, pp. 1–15, 2022.

[13] Kim, Y., Lee, H.J. and Shim, J. 2021. "Developing data-conscious deep learning models for product classification," *Applied Sciences*, vol. 11, no. 12, p. 5694, 2021.

[14] Oancea, B. "Automatic product classification using supervised machine learning algorithms in price statistics," *Mathematics*, vol. 11, no. 7, p. 1588, 2023.

[15] Ojika, F. U., Owobu, W. O., Abieba, O. A., Esan, O. J., Ubamadu, B. C., & Daraojimba, A. I. (2023). Enhancing user interaction through deep learning models: A data-driven approach to improving consumer experience in e-commerce. Journal of Frontiers in Multidisciplinary Research, 4(1), 126–137. https://doi.org/10.54660/.IJFMR.2023.4.1.126-137.

[16] Pawłowski, M. "Machine learning based product classification for ecommerce," *Journal of Computer Information Systems*, vol. 62, no. 4, pp. 730–739, 2022.

[17] "Product classification and clustering," n.d. Available at https://www.kaggle.com/datasets/adilashrafi/product-classification-and-clustering, accessed July 11, 2025.

[18] Senokosov, A., Sedykh, A., Sagingalieva, A., Kyriacou, B. and Melnikov, A. "Quantum machine learning for image classification," *Machine Learning: Science and Technology*, vol. 5, no. 1, p. 015040, 2024.

[19] Somavarapu, S. and Gupta, V. "Analyzing and visualizing user behavior in e-commerce: A machine learning approach," 2025.

[20] Sutoyo, R., Achmad, S., Chowanda, A., Andangsari, E.W., and Isa, S.M. "PRDECT-ID: Indonesian product reviews dataset for emotions classification tasks," *Data in Brief* vol. 44, p. 108554, 2022.

[21] Wurster, S. and de Borja Reis, C.F. "Priority products for sustainability information and recommendation software: Insights in the context of the EU's action plan circular economy," *Sustainability*, vol. 14, no. 19, p. 11951, 2022.

Index

About the Editors

Jaiprakash Narain Dwivedi, Ph.D., is currently working as an Associate professor, IT Department, Parul Institute of Engineering and Technology, Faculty of Engineering and Technology, Parul University, Vadodara, Gujarat, India. He possesses B.E. (Electronics and Communication Engineering), M. Tech. (Signal Processing), and Ph. D. (Machine Learning from Kyushu Institute of Technology Japan). He has more than 15 years of experience (including academia, industry and research) and his professional activities include roles as associate editor, editorial board member and reviewer of various International Journals. His research publication includes patents, books, book chapters, journals and conference proceedings. He has received, young scientist award and Lifetime achievement awards and his interest in research includes Machine Learning, Artificial Neural Network, Pattern Recognition, Classification, CNN, DNN, Deep Learning and Signal Processing.

Dr. Parag Shukla is an Assistant Professor in Commerce at Maharaja Sayajirao University of Baroda, India, specializing in Marketing Management. He earned his bachelor's and master's degrees from the same university, focusing on Marketing Management. Dr. Shukla's research centers on Retailing, and he has a background in content analysis within the television and media research industry. He teaches management courses at various levels and has published extensively in national and international journals and conferences. His current research project titled "An Empirical Investigation of Experiential Value vis-a-vis Usage Attitude of Selected Mobile Shoppers in Gujarat." Dr. Shukla is notable for receiving the Silver Medal at the 68th International All India Commerce Conference for his research, earning the Best Business Academic of the Year Award, a significant recognition in Indian Education and Retail Industry.

Herat Joshi is a distinguished expert in healthcare technology and informatics with more than 14 years of professional experience, currently serving at the Analytics & Decision Support at Great River Health Systems in Burlington, IA, USA. Apart from that he is member of following, FACHDM - Fellow American College of Health Data Management, Sr. Member of IEEE, Member AHIMA - American Health Information Management Association, Member of AMIA - American Medical Informatics Association,) He is also serving as Vice Chair IEEE IA-IL Section, Chair at two workgroups in AMIA. Herat has led numerous AI-driven projects, significantly enhancing healthcare delivery and operational efficiency. He has been recognized with multiple awards for his contributions to healthcare informatics, including the Outstanding Leadership Award at the

Health 2.0 Conference. He is dedicated to advancing the field of healthcare AI and mentoring the next generation of professionals. His work has been well-received by the healthcare industry and research community.

Pankaj Tripathi is working as an Assistant Professor in the Department of Accounting and Financial Management, Faculty of Commerce, The Maharaja Sayajirao University of Baroda, Vadodara. He has vast experience in academics, worked in different states of India adding varied multicultural experience to his career. He holds PhD in Finance and Accounting. He is recognized PhD guide and 3 scholars are pursuing PhD under his supervision. His areas of expertise include financial accounting, financial economics, business economics and business administration. He has various papers in National and international journals. He is a life member of the Indian Commerce Association and Indian Accounting Association.